Leading Continuous Improvement in Schools

This volume provides a set of principles and systematic methods for improvement to help district and school leaders achieve the continuous improvement goals embedded in the Professional Standards for Educational Leadership (PSEL) and the National Educational Leadership Program (NELP) standards. Bringing the PSEL Standard 10 to life, this book tackles the why, how, and what of continuous improvement through an equity lens.

In the first section, *Leading Continuous Improvement in Schools* provides an overall introduction to and rationale for continuous improvement, situating current approaches to continuous improvement in education within broader historical and sectoral contexts. The second section highlights how the tenets of improvement science – such as making iterative, incremental, evidence-based advancements; utilizing practical measurements; and acknowledging variability – position school and system leaders to adaptively integrate systematic and evidence-based approaches to change as part of ongoing organizational processes. The book concludes with a section that invites readers to consider leadership approaches that forward improvement work, how leaders can build internal capacity to engage in improvement, and how policy can support efforts to build and sustain the capacity for continuous improvement. Special features include beginning-of-chapter highlights, end-of-chapter connections to standards, and action inventories throughout each chapter. Overall, the volume provides a focus on the continuous improvement aspects of the NELP and PSEL standards that serve as a bridge, supporting students preparing to become educational leaders in their journey from learning about continuous improvement to learning how to lead continuous, equity-oriented improvement work in their own contexts.

Erin Anderson is Associate Professor of Educational Leadership and Policy Studies at the University of Denver, USA.

Kathleen M. W. Cunningham is Assistant Professor of Educational Leadership and Policies at the University of South Carolina, USA.

David H. Eddy-Spicer is Professor of Education in the Department of Leadership, Foundations, and Social Policy at the University of Virginia, USA.

PSEL/NELP LEADERSHIP PREPARATION SERIES

Series Editors: Michelle Young, Margaret Terry Orr

The New Instructional Leadership
ISLLC Standard Two
Edited by Rose Ylimaki

Political Contexts of Educational Leadership
ISLLC Standard Six
Edited by Jane Clark Lindle

Developing Ethical Principles for School Leadership
PSEL Standard Two
Edited by Lisa Bass, William Frick, and Michelle Young

Leading Continuous Improvement in Schools
Enacting Leadership Standards to Advance Educational Quality and Equity
By Erin Anderson, Kathleen M. W. Cunningham, and David H. Eddy-Spicer

For more information about this series, please visit: www.routledge.com/PSELNELP-Leadership-Preparation/book-series/PSEL

Leading Continuous Improvement in Schools

Enacting Leadership Standards to Advance Educational Quality and Equity

Erin Anderson, Kathleen M. W. Cunningham, and David H. Eddy-Spicer

NEW YORK AND LONDON

First published 2024
by Routledge
605 Third Avenue, New York, NY 10158

and by Routledge
4 Park Square, Milton Park, Abingdon, Oxon, OX14 4RN

Routledge is an imprint of the Taylor & Francis Group, an informa business

ISBN: 978-1-032-48479-2 (hbk)
ISBN: 978-1-032-46185-4 (pbk)
ISBN: 978-1-003-38927-9 (ebk)

DOI: 10.4324/9781003389279

Typeset in Aldus and Helvetica Neue
by Apex CoVantage, LLC

Access the Support Material: www.routledge.com/9781032461854

Contents

Foreword

Over the past few decades, educational research has highlighted the crucial role of principal leadership in school improvement and has advanced our understanding of specific leadership practices that make a difference. Studies have identified common leadership domains in which principals spend their time, including administration, instructional leadership, internal and external relations, and teachers' professional development (Lee, 2021).

In November 2015, the Professional Standards for Educational Leaders (PSEL), previously known as the Interstate School Leaders Licensure Consortium (ISLLC) standards, were approved by the National Policy Board for Educational Administration (NPBEA). Grounded in current research and leadership experience, these standards outline the knowledge and skills expected of educational leaders (Canole & Young, 2013; CCSSO, 1996; CCSSO, 2008). The 2015 PSEL standards place a strong emphasis on students and student learning, outlining foundational principles of leadership to ensure that each child receives a high-quality education and is prepared for the 21st century (CCSSO, 2015, p. 2). These standards are student-centric, guiding educational leaders in their practice to improve student learning outcomes and promote equity (CCSSO, 2015, p. 1). The 2015 PSEL standards encompass various leadership domains, including Mission, Vision, and Improvement; Ethics and Professional Norms; Equity and Cultural Responsiveness; Curriculum, Instruction, and Assessment; Community of Care and Support for Students; Professional Capacity of School Personnel; Professional Community for Teachers and Staff; Meaningful Engagement of Families and Community; Operations and Management; and School Improvement.

As a companion to the PSEL standards, the NELP standards were developed to guide leadership preparation programs in designing curriculum, pedagogy, and clinical experiences that prepare aspiring leaders to effectively assume their roles (NPBEA, 2018). Educational leadership preparation programs play a critical role in equipping leaders with the necessary tools and competencies to excel in their roles. This book series, aligned with both the NELP and PSEL standards, serves as a valuable resource for educational leadership preparation faculty and students, connecting the standards to research and practice. The series highlights the specific knowledge and skills essential for effective leadership, such as working collaboratively with others, using multiple sources of data, and making informed decisions, and it provides guidance on how to work effectively with others, use multiple sources of data, and make sound decisions, among other critical functions.

Throughout the books in this series, authors provide opportunities for aspiring leaders to engage in practical work and consider diverse perspectives on authentic problems of practice, including those of students, teachers, parents, administrators, and community members. Through real-world scenarios, case studies, and problem-based learning, aspiring leaders can develop their abilities in understanding and addressing complex challenges with various stakeholders. As Anderson, Cunningham, and Eddy-Spicer assert, this book and others in this series support readers in their journey from learning about the work described in the standards to learning how to undertake and lead such work in their own schools.

This particular volume focuses on the continuous improvement aspects of the NELP and PSEL standards. Drawing from concrete improvement science examples, the book offers principles and systematic methods for school and system leaders to achieve continuous improvement goals as outlined in the PSEL and the NELP standards. The book is divided into three sections that explore the *why, how,* and *what* of continuous improvement through an equity lens. The first section provides an introduction and rationale for continuous improvement, situating current approaches within broader historical and sectoral contexts. The second section highlights *how* improvement science principles enable school and system leaders to effectively integrate evidence-based approaches for ongoing organizational processes. The final section focuses on the *what* of continuous improvement through an equity lens.

Anderson, Cunningham, and Eddy-Spicer have designed an extraordinary resource. The book is intentionally designed to support powerful learning and exceptional leadership. The authors backward map from what we want leaders to know and be able to do to inform a powerful learning journey about continuous improvement.

Michelle D. Young, Ph.D.
University of California, Berkeley

Rose M. Ylimaki, Ph.D.
University of Northern Arizona

BIBLIOGRAPHY

Canole, M., & Young, M. D. (2013). *Standards for educational leaders: An analysis.* Council of Chief State School Officers.

Council of Chief State School Officers (CCSSO). (1996). *The interstate school leaders licensure consortium: Standards for school leaders.* Author.

Council of Chief State School Officers (CCSSO). (2008). *Educational leadership policy standards: ISLLC 2008.* Author.

Council of Chief State School Officers (CCSSO). (2015). *Professional Standards for Educational Leaders (PSEL).* Author.

Lee, M. (2021). Principals' time use as a research area: Notes on theoretical perspectives, leadership domains, and future directions. In *How School Principals Use Their Time* (pp. 9-21). Routledge.

NPBEA. (2018). *National Educational Leadership Preparation (NELP) program recognition standards building level.* www.npbea.org

Preface

You are reading this book because you are an educator who cares deeply about students, families, and your colleagues. You hope to find guidance on how to be part of positive change in school systems. It is possible you have become frustrated with the slow pace of improvement in the complex system of schools and districts. You may also want to understand how to uphold the educational values of equity, social justice, and liberation. You may be new to the profession or considering a career in education and want to explore the messy world of school improvement. You may be a seasoned educator looking for a way to make sense of your professional experiences. Regardless of what brought you here, this book will be a useful addition to your repertoire of resources for leading continuous change in schools and school systems. This book adds an important missing element to the current research – how to *lead* equity-oriented, continuous improvement.

THE NEED FOR IMPROVEMENT

Despite a century of research on school effectiveness, school improvement, and school reform (or regeneration or renewal or turnaround), initiating and sustaining desired change in schools and school systems remains a pressing concern (Bryk, 2015) across domestic and international contexts (e.g., Datnow et al., 2022). Educational leaders are positioned at the nexus of decision-making, influencing the expectations and demands of the educational system. W. Edwards Deming, a founding figure in current approaches to continuous improvement across sectors, characterized education as a field with "miracle goals and no methods" (Deming, 1992). This book stresses methods over externally determined goals. A continuous improvement approach provides systematic methods for school and school system improvement. The need for this approach is apparent regarding the social justice mission of schools and school leadership to provide opportunities for all students to learn and realize their potential, especially students from communities that have been historically marginalized due to factors such as race, gender, primary language, religion, and socioeconomic status. This volume offers an approach to fulfill the "miracle goal" of redressing inequities through continuous improvement.

This volume of the PSEL/NELP Leadership Preparation Series responds to a shift to prioritizing continuous improvement (CI), enacted through a body of systematic and evidence-based approaches to organizational change in schools and school systems, as leadership. The 2015 Professional Standards for Educational Leaders (PSEL) and 2018 National Educational Leadership Preparation standards (NELP) historically reference uses of evidence or data for reflection and organizational improvement. However, in the most recent revision to the national PSEL standards, continuous improvement received its own standard, Standard 10 (See Appendix C); namely, continuous improvement as a separate standard foregrounds continuous improvement as a distinctive approach to change in schools and school systems and a priority lever for school and system leaders. This volume offers a much-needed complement to the standards by providing conceptual and practical elaboration while drawing out implications for continuous improvement tackling multilayered and multidimensional issues involved in organizational change with an emphasis on redressing systemic inequities.

The direct purpose of this volume is to bring PSEL Standard 10 and related standards to life by serving as guide rails to initiating and sustaining cycles of continuous improvement for district and school leaders and teachers; furthermore, it is a resource for scholars and students of educational leadership. The book highlights how the tenets of continuous improvement crystallized in improvement science – making iterative, incremental, evidence-based advancements; utilizing practical measurement; and acknowledging variability – enable school and system leaders to adaptively integrate systematic and evidence-based approaches to change as part of ongoing organizational processes.

Recent books in this field cover the theoretical and practical aspects of "how to do" improvement science. By coupling conceptual understanding of continuous improvement principles that form the foundation of NELP and PSEL standards with clear explanations and examples of how to enact those standards in practice, this volume explicitly addresses "how to lead" continuous improvement. This book is not Bryk's and colleagues' (2015) *Learning to Improve*, the foundational book on improvement science in education. We do not seek to retread that theoretical ground. This book is not Hinnant-Crawford's (2020), *Improvement Science in Education: A Primer*, the foremost practical guide to implementing equity-oriented improvement science in schools and districts. We do not seek a better explanation of the process and tools than she has provided. Adding to these sources, we offer a third text for leaders and leadership programs focused on equity-oriented leadership for improvement. We consider how leaders enact improvement practices for continuous improvement, establishing how continuous improvement can engage leadership practices that support effective schools.

THE STANDARDS

Throughout this volume, we refer not only to the standards for improvement (e.g., PSEL 10), but also many other PSEL and NELP standards focused on professional norms, equity, community with students and families, teaching and learning, and managing the day-to-day operations of a school or school system. The standards are written for building and district leaders, and we share excerpts from and connections to building standards throughout this book, including a *NELP and PSEL Connection Box for Educational Leadership Faculty* at the end of Chapters 2 through 10. Table 0.1 is an overview of the standards with chapter bibliography entries.

Table 0.1 Crosswalk of NELP, PSEL, and Volume Chapters

NELP Building Level	*PSEL*	*Chapters*
Standard 1: Mission, Vision, and Improvement	Standard 1: Mission, Vision, and Core Values Standard 10: School Improvement	**All Chapters** • Focus of Chapter 2 – Continuous Improvement • Focus of Chapter 3 – Leadership • Focus of Chapter 7 – Spread and Scale
Standard 2: Ethics and Professional Norms	Standard 2: Ethics and Professional Norms Standard 3: Equity and Cultural Responsiveness Standard 5: Community of Care and Support for Students	**All Chapters** • Focus of Chapter 4 – Equity
Standard 3: Equity, Inclusiveness, and Cultural Responsiveness		• Focus of Chapter 4 – Equity
Standard 4: Learning and Instruction	Standard 4: Curriculum, Instruction, and Assessment	Chapter 5 – Problem Formation Chapter 6 – Disciplined Data Chapter 9 – Organizational Capacity
Standard 7: Building Professional Capacity	Standard 6: Professional Capacity of School Personnel Standard 7: Professional Community for Teachers and Staff	Chapter 8 – Leadership Toolbox Chapter 9 – Organizational Capacity
Standard 5: Community and External Leadership	Standard 8: Meaningful Engagement of Families and Community	Chapter 8 – Leadership Toolbox Chapter 9 – Organizational Capacity
Standard 6: Operations and Management	Standard 9: Operations and Management	Chapter 9 – Organizational Capacity

ENACTING IMPROVEMENT

Enacting improvement holds the potential to develop an improvement mindset that nurtures and sustains collective and organizational learning. This volume provides overarching principles and systematic methods for leading school organizations to achieve goals embodied in the PSEL and NELP standards, which identify the conditions and outputs for improvement but do not provide guidance on using evidence as a source of reflection and continuous school improvement to create those conditions. This volume focuses on conceptual foundations coupled with practical knowledge from current improvement initiatives that have implications for leadership practice, particularly within diverse contexts.

Figure 0.1 illustrates three areas that facilitate the improvement work for which the standards call. The arrows moving from left to right capture the forward progression of continuous improvement. The arrow that links each labeled arrow to the other accompanying arrows reinforces the double-loop learning progression that occurs across the three areas.

Throughout this book, we will discuss improvement mindsets, enacting improvement, organizational learning, and their interconnectedness.

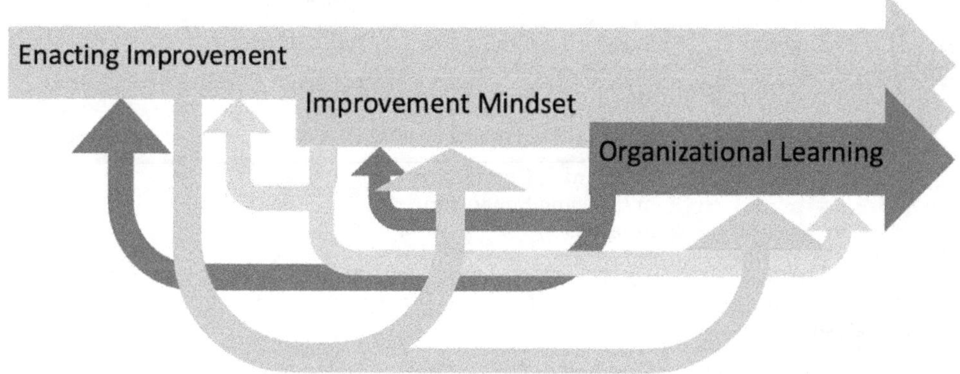

Figure 0.1 Relationship Across Enacting Improvement, Improvement Mindsets, and Organizational Learning.

Source: Created by the author.

CONTINUOUS IMPROVEMENT AS IMPROVEMENT SCIENCE

Various forms of continuous improvement align to the PSEL and NELP standards: design thinking, liberatory design, lesson study, solidarity-driven decision-making, design-based improvement research, Data Wise, and more. Each continuous improvement methodology presents slightly different approaches and priorities of improvement – from community involvement and liberatory justice to a focus on efficiency and scalable ideas. For this book, we focus on improvement science as a form of continuous improvement. We select improvement science to illustrate enacting improvement and leadership for several reasons:

1) The core principles underlying the process are broadly applicable across various models of continuous improvement.
2) We see promise for equity, justice, and liberation in the model of improvement, particularly as defined by Brandi Hinnant-Crawford (2020).
3) In our work as educators, we align our thinking with improvement science as a foundation to lead, teach, and learn improvement in our own work. The authors of this book each have five to ten years of experience leading or supporting leaders using improvement science in K–12 schools and institutions of higher education. Each author has taught classes on improvement science to aspiring leaders at the certificate, masters, and EdD level. Each has also published research on the use of improvement science in educational settings, contributing to the field of improvement-focused research.

OVERVIEW OF IMPROVEMENT SCIENCE PROCESS AND CORE PRINCIPLES

The improvement science methodology is a nonlinear inquiry cycle (Bryk et al., 2015); however, it can be divided into four phases that allow for the progression from problem identification to scaling measurable solutions. It is a disciplined approach to educational innovation that supports teachers, leaders, and researchers in collaborating to solve specific problems of practice:

1) **Phase One**: Understanding a problem and the system that produces it through user-centered design, causal and systems analysis, and the existing knowledge base.
2) **Phase Two**: Focusing collective efforts on analysis, defining a theory of improvement with a clear and specific aim and identified drivers, and the development of solutions or change ideas to test.
3) **Phase Three**: Testing and building evidence through measurement of processes and outcomes and short cycles of inquiry known as plan-do-study-act (PDSA) cycles.
4) **Phase Four**: Spreading and scaling solutions, or bundles of solutions, found to be successful through iterations of PDSA cycles but also willingly abandoning ideas that have failed. For teachers, school leaders, and system leaders, improvement science is an approach to design-based, evidence-driven continuous improvement to increase the effectiveness of educational practice.

The first two phases are undergirded by three core principles – (a) being user-centered and problem-focused, (b) seeing the system, and (c) attending to variation. The next two phases focus on the other three core principles of (d) disciplined inquiry, (e) embracing measurement, and (f) accelerating learning through networks. That said, all the core principles (Bryk et al., 2015) are pertinent to each phase.

HOW ARE WE DEFINING LEADERS?

This book is about enacting leadership through improvement and highlights leadership practices defined by the national standards for practicing leaders (PSEL) and leadership preparation programs and aspiring leaders (NELP). Leadership is often defined by formal leadership positions, such as a principal. The definition of leadership in the standards is focused on school and district leaders. Other leaders, such as assistant principals, are typically prepared in school leadership programs based on the same set of standards. However, in many schools, teacher leader roles such as deans, instructional coaches, team leads, and department chairs, are commonplace. Those leaders may not have been formally trained in leadership, but they are asked to lead in important ways. A lot of leadership is done by people not holding official leadership positions.

The examples discussed in this book, including the case presented in Chapter 1, center the principal as the leader. This is done for clarity. However, the standards for leadership and improvement brought to life in this book are important foundations for any educational leader, whether formal or informal, licensed or unlicensed, school-based or district-based. If you are not a principal, this book is still for you. Leadership and leadership practices should be shared throughout the school to harness the collaborative spirit and collective will be necessary for improvement.

We write about continuous improvement, in general, and improvement science, in particular, as team activities. Throughout the illustrative case in Chapter 1 and the rest of the volume, we talk about improvement teams and improvement design teams, stressing the team collaborative aspects of the process. Improvement in teams is the ideal way to engage with continuous improvement (e.g., Boudett et al., 2013). To make the systemic changes necessary to transform schools into more equitable, just, supportive, inclusive, and joyful places, you need the power of the collective. However, if you are the only one in your school or district that is interested in this topic, you can still start the work of improving and leading impactfully in your organization. We refer to anyone in the school community engaged in continuous improvement as improvers, a term you will see throughout the book. Improvers without an improvement team can lead the work from their place within the organization. The ideas in this book can be applied at the classroom level, where teaching is a form of leadership, to the superintendency level, where leadership expectations loom large, and in other non-K–12 organizations like schools and colleges of education.

GENERAL PLAN AND TABLE OF CONTENTS

This book is organized to help readers grasp the *why, how,* and *what* of continuous improvement, with a particular focus on improvement science. In Part I, we provide an overall introduction to and rationale for continuous improvement, establishing connections with relevant leadership standards, as well as situating current approaches to continuous improvement in education within broader historical and sectoral contexts and improvement movements (e.g., Bhuiyan & Baghel, 2005) Deming, 1986; Singh & Singh, 2015; Smylie, 2009). The landscape view of continuous improvement in the initial section is distilled to focus on professional practice, drawing on lessons learned and examples of improvement science. Chapters 1, 2, 3, and 4 provide orientation for *why* the work of continuous improvement is essential in schools today.

To ground the main points in this volume, Chapter 1, "Ava's Story of Equity-Oriented Improvement," introduces a case featuring a school leader who is simultaneously leading a school through improvement while learning about improvement science in her graduate class. Chapter 1 introduces you to Ava Jackson, a middle school principal in a suburban neighborhood. She is also a graduate student, pursuing an Educational Doctorate (EdD). Throughout the case, we illustrate what equity-oriented improvement science looks like through learning and leading the process. Ava is in a networked improvement community (NIC) made up of her EdD inquiry group. At the same time, she works with her school-based team to lead improvement science in her building. She learns and works with her inquiry group to develop the skills to facilitate the process and develop the personal and group habits, dispositions, and organizational capacity for making significant positive change in each respective school; she learns alongside her improvement team. The case shows that solving a problem can be a multi-year process, while teams move through the drivers toward a change bundle or package that addresses the problem. It also demonstrates how Ava applies improvement science, which she learned in graduate school, as a leader in a school. The case ends with Dr. Ava Jackson, a newly-hooded graduate, continuing the work in her building by tackling a new problem of practice.

Chapter 2, "What Is (and Isn't) Continuous Improvement in Education?," defines continuous improvement using three dimensions that will be used to conclude the chapters throughout the book: instrumental methods, social relations, and moral values. Chapter 3, "Enacting Leadership through Continuous Improvement," foregrounds the standards, describing agreed upon leadership practices reflected in the ten PSEL and eight NELP standards. Summarizing the standards into four areas – setting direction for learning, securing equity for learning, developing people and relationships for learning, and securing accountability for learning – this chapter argues implementing improvement science enacts the key leadership practices identified in the standards and leadership research. Chapter 4, "Equity-Oriented Continuous Improvement," explains equity-oriented improvement science, exploring strong versus weak equity and how equity is part of the lens, process, and outcomes of improvement. At the end of Part I, you should have a foundational knowledge of improvement, leadership, and equity.

Part II of the book – Chapters 5, 6, and 7 – transitions into *how* to lead and facilitate improvement work at the school and systems level. These chapters support leaders and scholars to understand and, in turn, implement the process more deeply. This section uses improvement science as the jumping off point for enabling leaders to carry out improvement work in their schools and school systems.

Chapter 5, "Problem Identification and Framing," provides guidance on how to identify, define, and formulate a problem of practice for disciplined inquiry. Chapter 6, "Data for Improvement and Disciplined Inquiry," explores data for improvement and explains practical measures that help track progress toward improvement. Chapter 7, "Spread and Scale: The Promise (and Perils) of Networks and Systems Change," describes what happens when you find an idea or ideas that addresses your problem to then spread and scale that learning to others. This section should give you an overview of the process.

Part III – Chapters 8, 9, and 10 – articulates *what* factors need to be considered to lead improvement effectively. These final chapters also offer insight into *what* the next version of leadership standards might need to address to fulfill the demands of policy and practice. This section invites readers to consider how leaders prepare themselves for improvement work, how leaders build organizational capacity to engage in improvement, and how policy can support these efforts. Part III extends the theory to practice bridge where readers will move from learning about continuous improvement to learning how to lead continuous improvement work in their own contexts.

Chapter 8, "Building a Toolbox for Leading Continuous Improvement," provides the leadership dispositions and tools of improvement that guide leaders' work, a toolbox for leadership informed by equity-oriented improvement science. Chapter 9, "Building Organizational Capacity for Continuous Improvement," shows how to use that toolbox to build organizational capacity for continuous improvement throughout their school and community. Chapter 10, "Policy Considerations for Continuous Improvement," navigates the local, state, and federal policy environment for continuous improvement.

A final note about the structure of the book. Each chapter is written so that it can stand alone. Although it ties to learning in the other chapters, there is typically a short definition of improvement science and reference to the core principles. Also, key concepts that will be summarized in the conclusion to this book thread throughout chapters.

PRACTICAL APPLICATIONS

Action inventories are embedded within the chapters to help you actualize the learning. The inventories are markers that provide direction to the reader and can be adopted or adapted. Faculty could use the inventories as teaching activities for class. Aspiring and practicing leaders could use the inventories for leading equity-oriented improvement in their schools.

Stories or cases of improvement are embedded in the chapters. The fictional Ava, her improvement team, and her NIC are weaved throughout the book to illustrate key concepts. In addition to Ava's story, practical applications of real-life improvement based on the authors' facilitation of improvement science and accompanying research are used to bring the ideas to life.

CONCLUSION

Continuous improvement, by its very nature, is evolving. This book captures our collective thinking at a moment in time based on our contemporaneous understanding of leadership, equity, and improvement. As the world evolves, so will the ideas presented in this volume and so will your perception and implementation of the concepts.

BIBLIOGRAPHY

Bhuiyan, N., & Baghel, A. (2005). An overview of continuous improvement: From the past to the present. *Management Decision, 43*(5), 761–771. https://doi.org/10.1108/00251740510597761

Boudett, K. P., City, E. A., & Murnane, R. J. (Eds.). (2013). *Data wise: A step-by-step guide to using assessment results to improve teaching and learning.* Harvard Education Press.

Bryk, A. S., Gomez, L. M., Grunow, A., & Lemahieu, P. G. (2015). *Learning to improve: How America's schools can get better at getting better.* Harvard Education Press.

Datnow, A., Park, V., Peurach, D. J., & Spillane, J. P. (2022). *Transforming education for holistic student development: Learning from education system (re) building around the world.* Center for Universal Education at The Brookings Institution. https://www.brookings.edu/articles/transforming-education-for-holistic-student-development/

Deming, W. E. (1986). *Out of the crisis.* MIT Press.

Deming, W. E. (1992). Shaping America's Future III. *Proceedings of the National Forum on Transforming Our System of Educating Youth with W. Edwards Deming.* National Educational Service. https://eric.ed.gov/?q=ED358230&id=ED358230

Hinnant-Crawford, B. N. (2020). *Improvement science in education: A primer.* Myers Education Press.

National Educational Service. (1992). *Shaping America's future III: A national forum on transforming our system of educating youth, with W. Edwards deming.* Transcript of the forum.

National Policy Board for Educational Administration. (2015). *Professional standards for educational leaders 2015.* Author. www.npbea.org/psel/

National Policy Board for Educational Administration. (2018). *National Educational Leadership Preparation (NELP) program standards: Building level.* www.npbea.org

Singh, J., & Singh, H. (2015). Continuous improvement philosophy: Literature review and directions. *Benchmarking: An International Journal, 22*(1), 75–119. https://doi.org/10.1108/bij-06-2012-0038

Smylie, M. A. (2009). *Continuous school improvement.* Corwin Press.

Acknowledgements

We would like to thank the following people for their support with this book. First, we would like to thank Michelle Young and Rose Ylimaki for inviting us to submit a proposal for this series and for their continued assistance throughout the writing process. We would also like to thank the graduate assistants who helped prepare a draft of this book – James Ringer at the University of Denver and David Osworth and the University of South Carolina. We would like to thank Aaron Ullrey for his outstanding revisions of drafts of the manuscript. Without his input, there would be far too many prepositions and articles in these chapters.

We would like to thank the improvement colleagues, collaborators, and school and district teams and improvers we've worked with on continuous improvement throughout the years. Also, we would like to thank Brandi Hinnant-Crawford and David Osworth for their thought partnership on two book chapters that built off existing projects.

Finally, we would like to thank our families, including our furry friends, for their encouragement during the process of writing this the book.

Action Inventories

CHAPTER 2

CHAPTER 3

CHAPTER 4

CHAPTER 5

CHAPTER 6

CHAPTER 7

CHAPTER 8

CHAPTER 9

CHAPTER 10

PART I

Why Continuous Improvement?

CHAPTER 1

Ava's Story of Equity-Oriented Improvement

Ava Jackson is thrilled to pursue an Educational Doctorate (EdD). She is in her third year as principal of Moose Hill Middle School (MHMS). Before becoming the principal, she spent two years as the assistant principal (AP); this was her seventh year at MHMS and her twelfth year in education. Before that, she was a science teacher at two different schools in the district, including two years at MHMS where she served as the department head and an instructional coach. Ava is a 35-year-old white woman (she/her) who majored in biology as an under graduate and her education administration degree and then received a master's degree in secondary science education from a large public university in a different part of the state.

AVA'S SCHOOL

MHMS is in a large suburb outside a small city. The district is mid-sized, enrolling about 15,000 students in 15 elementary schools, five middle schools, and three high schools. MHMS has a diverse student body of about 650 students, grades six through eight. The demographic makeup of the school is 40% white, 30% Latine, 20% Black, and 10% Asian American Pacific Islander (AAPI). The student body includes 49% female and 48% male students (including cisgender and transgender) students, and there are several students who identify as nonbinary (1%). Ava's school and all the middle and high schools in the district have an active Gay Student Alliance (GSA) comprised of mostly eighth graders. According to self-reported survey data, about 5% of the student body identify as lesbian, gay, bisexual, transgender, or queer (LGBTQ+). The student body has a range of socioeconomic statuses; the school has a high number of students who qualify for free or reduced lunch (75%) and a few wealthy families. The school population also has multilingual education (MLE) programming for students with

DOI: 10.4324/9781003389279-2

emerging English language skills (EL), including English as a Second Language (ESL) classes. Thirteen percent of the student body is enrolled in MLE programming at some point during their time at MHMS. The school serves students with individualized education plans (IEPs) who are enrolled in special education programming, and in total, 25% of students are in special education.

AVA'S EDD PROGRAM

Now that Ava has her footing as a principal and has built relationships with her staff, she wants to focus on how to lead improvement in the building. She recognizes differing outcomes for marginalized student groups, and she wants to increase her competency as a culturally responsive and inclusive leader and systems change leader. Ava was ready to pursue her EdD and enrolled in a highly reputable, NELP-aligned, accredited EdD program at a nearby university. She selected this program because improvement science is the signature pedagogy, and the program is known throughout the state for its focus on diversity, equity, inclusion, accessibility, and social justice (DEIAJ). This graduate program felt perfect for her professional needs and career goals, and one year into her degree, she is happy with her decision. Ava is in a cohort of 20 students who are in leadership positions at their schools. Across her coursework, she regularly works in an inquiry group of middle school leaders from districts located within a few hours driving distance of the university.

Ava's program is designed to take three years to complete. The school is on a quarter system, allowing her cohort to take a full-time schedule of two, five-credit classes per quarter in the fall, winter, and spring. Her coursework is designed to introduce concepts, practice those concepts in an inquiry group, and then apply that learning to a dissertation in practice (DiP), which involves leading her school-based team through the improvement science process to solve a persistent organizational problem. In addition to her coursework on research methods and the improvement science methodology, she also takes courses in transformational and instructional leadership practices, transformative leadership, adaptive leadership, systems change leadership, social justice leadership, culturally responsive leadership, shared or distributed leadership, and community leadership as well as courses exploring equity and social justice in education and facilitating change in organizations. Her schedule is in Table 1.1.

In the first year, the cohort takes a sequence of classes that provide an introductory understanding of inquiry-based practices. As part of the research strand, the students learn about research design and how to critique existing research with a critical lens. They also take a sequence of leadership classes to get an understanding of leadership for equity and continuous improvement as well as the transformational and transformative leadership practices included in the PSEL. In the second year, the cohort takes additional classes about leadership dispositions, leadership for organizational capacity building, and leadership for complex systems.

Table 1.1 Ava's Improvement Science EdD Schedule

Year and Course	*Fall*	*Winter*	*Spring*
Year 1: Leadership	Leadership Practices for Learning	Leading for Equity and Social Justice	Leading for Continuous Improvement
Year 1: Research	Foundations of Research	Critical Inquiry	Advanced Research Methods
Year 2: Leadership	Leadership Toolbox: Dispositions for Learner Stances	Leading Organizational Capacity Building	Leading Complex Systems
Year 2: Research	Problem Formulation	Theory of Improvement and System of Measures	Testing, Iterating, Spreading, and Scaling
Year 3: Dissertation in Practice (DiP)	Apply Improvement Science to School-wide Problem: Defend Proposal	Conduct Cycles of Improvement	Summarize Learning: Defend DiP

The research strand for the second year includes a series of three aligned courses in which Ava and her classmates investigate and explore a problem through in-depth analysis using empathy interviews with the school community, process and systems mapping, research and practice expertise, and local data, including data from an equity audit of the practices and policies in her building. After collecting these data, the inquiry group learns how to conduct root cause analysis using affinity mapping, five whys, and a fishbone diagram.

In the next quarter, the group learns how to design a theory of improvement, including writing an aim statement, determining primary and secondary drivers, and brainstorming change ideas that would impact those drivers and the aim. The cohort also learns about the system of measures that will help them understand their improvement journey and gain an understanding of how to write and track an aim statement through outcome measures, how to measure and track progress toward the primary drivers, how to determine the improvement work is actually happening through process measures, and how to pay attention to a school's system by determining balancing measures or other areas of focus within the school that may inadvertently be impacted by the improvement effort.

In the last quarter, the cohort learns about developing prototypes of change ideas and testing them through small tests of change or PDSA cycles that are iterated and scaled up based on their success. The students seek to identify bundles of change ideas that when implemented at the classroom, team, or school level address their problem of practice, as determined through the system of measures. They also learn to structure and lead NICs to spread and scale successful change ideas.

AVA'S INQUIRY GROUP

Ava thinks an effective program feature is that the students are placed in small, inquiry groups based on each student's school's demographic factors. The inquiry group works together throughout their classes like a NIC. Her inquiry group includes three classmates, Luis Díaz, who is a 40-year-old Latino (he/his/él) and the principal of a diverse, rural middle school; Jamie Hewitt, who is a 32-year-old mixed-race woman (she/her) who identifies as Black and is an assistant principal at an urban middle school with similar demographics to MHMS; and Emma Patrizia, a 43-year-old white woman (she/her) who identifies as LGBTQ+ and is deeply connected to her Italian familial roots and who works as an instructional coach at another middle school in Ava's district.

AVA'S LEADERSHIP TEAM

Ava also works closely with her leadership team at the MHMS, both in her role as the school leader and as a burgeoning improvement scientist. Her team at school includes a number of members:

- Marcus Johnson, a 30-year-old Black man (he/him), was the unanimous choice for Assistant Principal (AP) when Ava became principal. He became an AP when he was only 27, after less than 5 years in the classroom, and he is a talented instructional leader, who also has deep roots in the community since MHMS is his alma mater. He attended a Historically Black College or University (HBCU), and upon graduating from a 5-year program for teaching, he earned his bachelor's and his master's degrees in secondary mathematics education. Marcus taught high school math for two years in Washington, DC, public schools. When he returned to the district, he began teaching middle school algebra; he enrolled in a certificate program for educational leadership and became licensed to be a principal. After only a year at MHMS, he was promoted to AP.
- Randy Weinberg is a 45-year-old white, nonbinary (they/them) social studies teacher, department chair, and faculty sponsor of the GSA. They have been in the district for nearly 15 years and have taught sixth, seventh, and eighth grades at MHMS. Currently, Randy is teaching sixth grade because they love helping the kids with the transition to middle school. They graduated from the university where Ava is getting her doctorate and are proud of their alma mater. Randy is excited for Ava to be in the program so they can also learn about improvement and equity through working with her.
- Isabella Ramírez is a 42-year-old, Latina (she/her/ella) who serves as the dean of students. In her seven years as dean, she enjoys the connection with students and families. In her role as dean, she supports Ava and Marcus with instruction but is also responsible for organizing and administering the school's behavioral responses to student discipline. She is a proponent of

restorative practices and has been instrumental in helping the school rethink its punitive approaches to discipline. She began this restorative work when Ava became principal and has a lot of experience with leading change at MHMS. She is well-respected by the students, families, and teachers. Her child just began sixth grade and is in Randy's class.

- Chris Butler is a 27-year-old white woman (she/her) and the newest member of the leadership team. She started as a seventh-grade English teacher upon graduation from a well-recognized teacher education program. Chris is bilingual and spent a year abroad in Costa Rica during college. She teaches ESL classes to Spanish-speaking students. She was asked to join the leadership team to support their improvement work and is excited to learn more about school leadership because she thinks she might want to be a school leader someday.

Year 2, Quarter 1

Problem Formation

In the first quarter of her second year of coursework, Ava and her inquiry group began to design an improvement science project that extends throughout their research classes. Their work starts in the fall with problem formulation. Ava's program requires the four leaders in each inquiry group to work as a NIC, so they need to agree on a problem each member faces in their respective schools. This focus on a common problem gives them experience working across schools to harness shared learning. The program instructors have a few requirements for the shared problem, based on Hinnant-Crawford's and Anderson's 5S Model for Problem Formation (2022).

1) It must be a significant problem that focuses on equity, inclusion, accessibility, and social justice.
2) The problem must be leadership-centric (as opposed to an instructional problem tackled at the teacher/teacher team level or a district-wide problem).
3) The scope of the problem should be at the school level, and the improvement team will consist of only school-based leaders and teachers.

The group felt good about those parameters but struggled to understand how they could bring together their individual school goals, district priorities, and the input of their school community to come up with a shared problem that would be authentic to each of their contexts. The group knew the importance of user input through empathy interviews and felt uncomfortable going too far into defining their shared problem without multiple perspectives from within the school community. The group also knew they were all too busy and had too much to improve to spend time working on a less impactful problem to align with a common problem for their classes. Since their colleagues from their respective schools would be part of the work, it was important to focus on a problem that the improvement team and their teachers, students, and families would also identify as high leverage.

The professor suggested the inquiry group start by sharing each school's major improvement goals from their school improvement plans (SIP). Ava and her group use slightly different language to describe the plans, based on their various districts, but all schools are required by state and district policy to have a SIP. Ava went first and shared her school's two major improvement strategies, which are (a) to promote equity and unity by working to understand and educate themselves about oppression and issues of equity through their equity team and staff development, and (b) to provide support and development of all instructional staff to ensure standards-aligned and culturally responsive instruction with a particular emphasis on knowledge building and foundational skills in literacy and math through lesson and unit internalization.

Emma states she is familiar with lesson and unit internationalization and that, along with being a district priority, her school's leadership team has lesson internalization as a major improvement strategy. Luis says he has never heard of lesson and unit internalization, but he has a similar improvement goal around standards-based learning, with an emphasis on project-based learning. He shares he also has an improvement goal around promoting equity and cultural responsiveness by working more closely with his Black, Indigenous, and People of Color (BIPOC) families to make sure that the school is an inclusive space and that there are ways for the families and community to collaborate with the school to support learning. Jamie shares that she is also focused on equity and unity, and her school's improvement priority is less about culturally responsive instruction and more about culturally responsive social-emotional learning (SEL) and support for SEL.

After a long conversation about each school's goals and defining a common language, the NIC was closer to a shared problem. Ava and Emma share that lesson and unit internalization is a lesson planning process for getting clear about the purpose of a lesson or unit, exploring the priorities, and then thinking about the instructional moves that would support student needs. It is also a way to think about how existing lessons, possibly even pre-written lesson plans, could be incorporated into a unit. Jamie talks about how she is defining culturally responsive SEL, and she shares two articles from *EdWeek* and *Edutopia* with the group. Luis talks about a book he just bought called *The Pulse of PBL: Seamlessly Integrating Social and Emotional Learning,* which ties together SEL and project-based learning.

The group is starting to get excited about the synergy emerging between each of their schools' improvement goals. Luis shares that at first, it felt daunting to find a common problem. He was hesitant about finding overlap as the only rural, middle school leader in the group. However, he says, "In many ways, our schools and their problems are more similar than they are different."

In the cohort's course on equity in the first year, they read Khalifa's *Culturally Responsive School Leadership* (2018) book. Ava's inquiry group agreed that the ideas from that book had an impact on how they selected SIP goals for that year.

The group felt like the book gave them a common definition of what it meant to address cultural responsiveness in their school; this made it easier to work together. Ava's group thought the common norms and working agreements established as part of their coursework were paying off as they navigated this conversation and came to a common agreement about how to proceed.

Ava's inquiry group decided to focus on increasing cultural competency, culturally responsive teaching, and inclusive school practices within each of their schools and across their NIC. The inquiry group defined the NIC's common problem to be a lack of culturally responsive and inclusive teaching and school practices. However, each group member wanted to address different aspects of the problem. Over several classes, the professor walked the students through a process of how to plan and conduct empathy interviews; the professor gave them time to practice with each other. The group also shared out the local data, or data specific to their school's context (e.g., attendance data, discipline data, achievement data, school culture survey data) from each of their schools. These data were disaggregated; the inquiry group used these data to create their improvement goals and therefore, the data helped inform the problem. Ava's team had done an equity audit and saw those results as an important source of data. The professor gave Ava and her group an equity-focused data conversation protocol to help guide their sharing. They worked independently on systems and process maps for their own school and shared those with each other. Then, the group reviewed Khalifa's (2018) book as well as other sources of research knowledge to see how to define a lack of culturally responsive teaching and school practices and to inform the causes and possible strategies of their common problem. After reaching out to the community of leaders within each group member's district, they also shared learning from other schools that had grappled with the same problem (e.g., practice expertise or analogous settings). These activities helped the NIC understand the problem, and they looked forward to repeating the activities with their improvement teams at their respective schools.

After reviewing the data, the NIC did an activity where they divided the data among the four group members: Ava reviewed the empathy interview data; Luis summarized the notes from the research and practice knowledge; Jamie looked at the systems and process maps; and Emma explored the local data from each school. The NIC went through and wrote their insights from that data on sticky notes, and then did an affinity mapping activity where each of them went around one by one and shared what they had written on the sticky notes. Pretty quickly, they started to see trends in the data and began to group ideas into themes. Then, the NIC took those themes and transferred them to a big piece of paper on the wall that had a picture of the bones of a fish drawn on it. On one end of the fish (the head) was a box where they wrote their problem, then on the end of each of the bones, they wrote the themes from their affinity mapping. From there, the NIC had an in-depth conversation about the root causes of each of those themes, often referring to ideas on the sticky notes, which they would stick on the big piece of paper. The conversations brought up new ideas as well, which they added to a sticky note and stuck on the bone under the theme. Some of the sticky notes didn't quite make sense as causes. For those sticky notes, they would complete a *five whys* to see if there were any causes related to the insights that belonged on their fishbone. When Ava's group was done, the fishbone looked like Figure 1.1.

At this point the professor made them stop, and she gave them homework. Each NIC member had to review the fishbone they had completed and come to the next class with answers to the following prompts:

1) Which of these causes are within the power of the school?
2) Do any of the causes demonstrate deficit thinking, and if so, how do they need to be reframed?
3) Do they see any bias in their root causes? Whose perspective is missing?
4) Have we looked at the root causes with a DEIAJ lens?

At the next class, Ava's group shared their responses to the prompts. In their discussion, Luis noticed a root cause that stated, "the parents aren't actively involved in teaching and learning." When he reviewed the fishbone using the reflection questions, he felt like that statement was made with a deficit lens. Luis asked the group, "Without asking the families about their experience, how do we know how the families felt about teaching and learning and the families' roles in it?" Ava felt a little embarrassed because she had been the one to add that cause to the insights. When they first started talking about whether it was deficit thinking, her initial response was to want to be defensive, but she reminded herself of what she had learned in her class about leadership dispositions. Instead, she decided to be honest and share her feelings of discomfort with the group. Emma shared that she didn't notice the deficit thinking at first either and that she is still growing to understand what it means to be "asset based." Together, they agreed to reframe the cause with an emphasis on the system and the school's practices and structures and not the individual families.

Jamie brought up that the group used the word "parents" throughout their fishbone, but that many students live in different family formations, which might include living with a relative who is not the parent. By using parents instead of families, the group wasn't being thoughtful to all their students' experiences. Emma also noted that some students are in foster homes or other types of living arrangements that might not include their biological parents or families but temporary guardians. Together, the group decided to use the term "family/families" when talking about the student's households. They reinforced their value of being inclusive of the diversity of life experiences present in their school communities. Based on this conversation, they revised the fishbone to say, "the school doesn't know the role that families feel they play in their student's learning" instead of "the parents aren't actively involved in teaching and learning." They discussed why the new phrasing of the cause was also better because it reframed the cause to be something in the control of the school. Ava and her group discussed how the greatest area for growth as leaders was their relationship with their families and communities. The revised fishbone in Figure 1.2 reflected these changes.

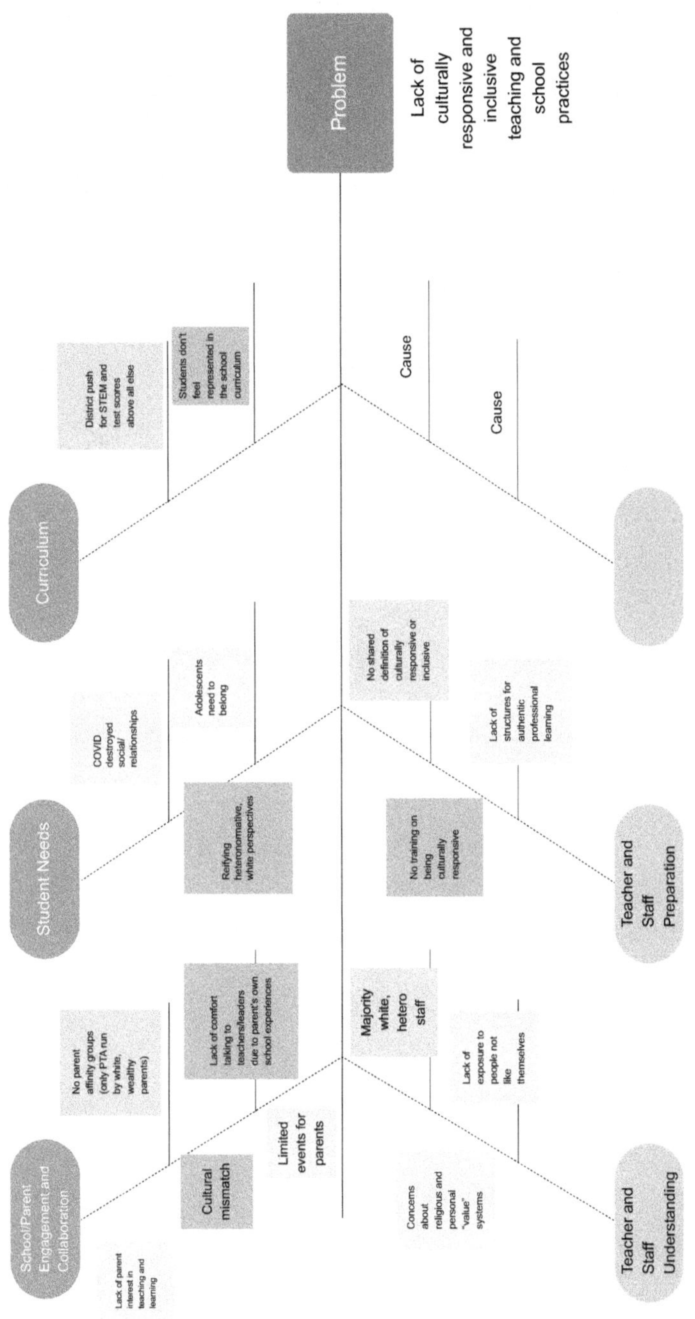

Figure 1.1 A Fishbone Diagram for the NIC.

Source: Created by the author.

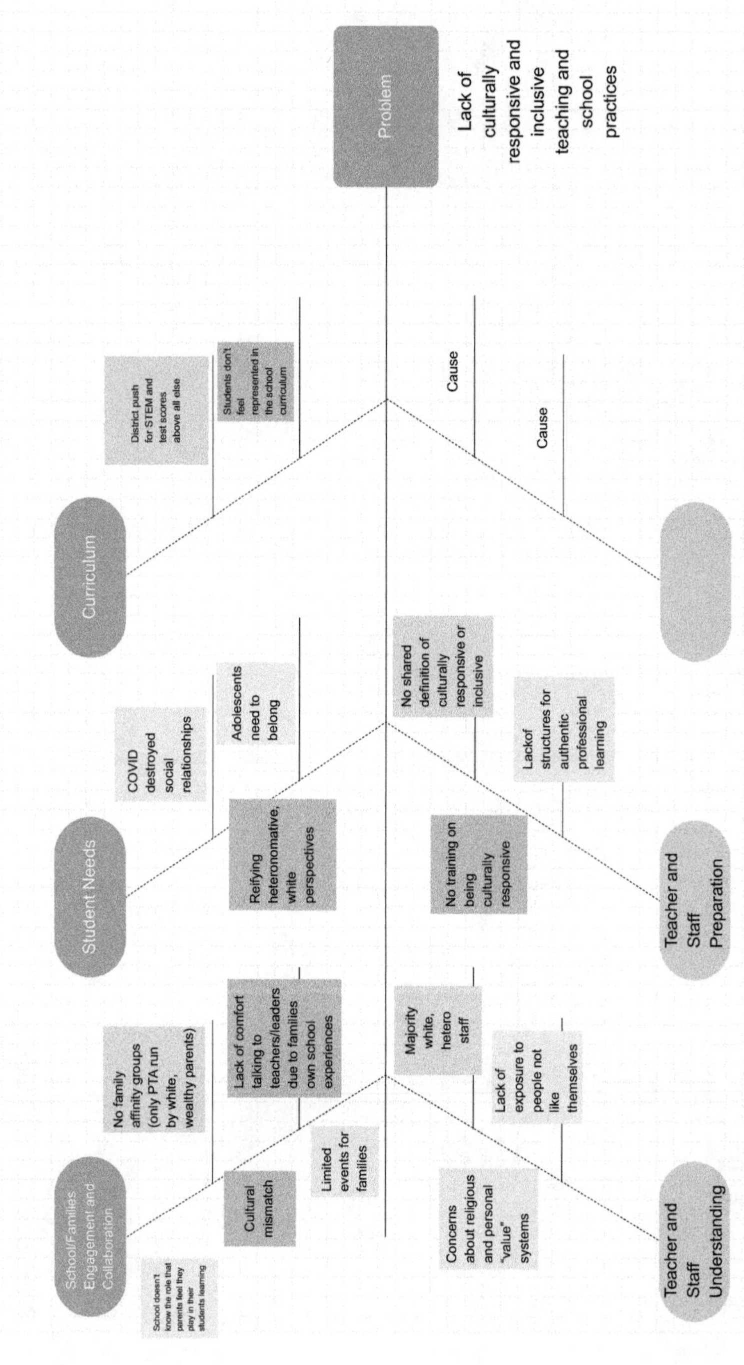

Figure 1.2 Revised NIC Fishbone After Equity Reflection.

Source: Created by author.

From there, the professor gave them several weeks to do these same activities at their respective schools. She gave the following list of "notice and reflect" questions to help guide data collection for understanding the problem that would exploit variation, take a systems lens, elevate user voices, and focus on DEIAJ.

- Empathy
  - Whose voices do we need at the table to understand how the system is producing current outcomes?
  - How does my identity and role in this project affect how and what people share with me?
  - What do people in this community identify as their needs?
  - How do I maintain awareness of my biases and challenge those biases to see this community as they see themselves?
- Local Data, Systems, and Process Data
  - How is our organization (policies, procedures, practices, priorities, personnel) contributing to the problem of practice (intentionally or unintentionally)?
  - What facets of our system (policies, procedures, practices, processes, culture, climate) are oppressing certain populations?
  - How do systemic oppression and/or privilege affect this community, and how does that relate to this project?
  - Where do we have the most leverage to intervene?
- Practice and Research Knowledge
  - What are the assumptions represented in the research?
  - Is this research and practice knowledge informed by a DEIAJ lens?

Together the inquiry group had gone through these same questions, so each member felt ready to lead the work at their schools and to guide this dialogue. The group talked about their dispositions in their leadership class, so they had been developing their improvement mindset to be humble, transparent, honest, and reflective. They discussed how that informed their empathy interviews.

After brainstorming as a NIC about who to ask empathy interview questions to make sure they had multiple perspectives, they all agreed that they would talk to at least

- Five family members of a student from a marginalized group
- Three students per grade (6–8) who identified with a marginalized group and who were not excelling or failing but were doing average with academics (e.g., C students)
- All their teachers
- Relevant support staff.

Each member of the inquiry group could add other interviewees to their list based on their own context. Ava wanted to talk to her MHMS improvement team to see with whom they thought they should conduct additional empathy interviews.

After the fishbone activity and consultation with their school improvement teams, Ava, Luis, Jamie, and Emma each decided on a slightly narrower focus for their school's problem under the umbrella of the NIC's problem of practice (Figure 1.3):

- Ava wanted to focus on building relationships with her LGBTQ+ students in her school community to address issues of belongingness and intolerance.
- Luis also wanted to focus on building relationships in his school community through meaningful ways to support the students and interactions between his mostly white teachers and BIPOC families.
- Jamie wanted to focus on culturally responsive SEL support for all her students.
- Emma wanted to focus on feedback and observation cycles and how they supported teachers' development of culturally responsive teaching while also focusing on culturally responsive coaching cycles.

From there, they began their work with the school improvement teams. Ava's team felt that in addition to the proposed participants in empathy interviews, they should do more empathy interviews with families to understand the student

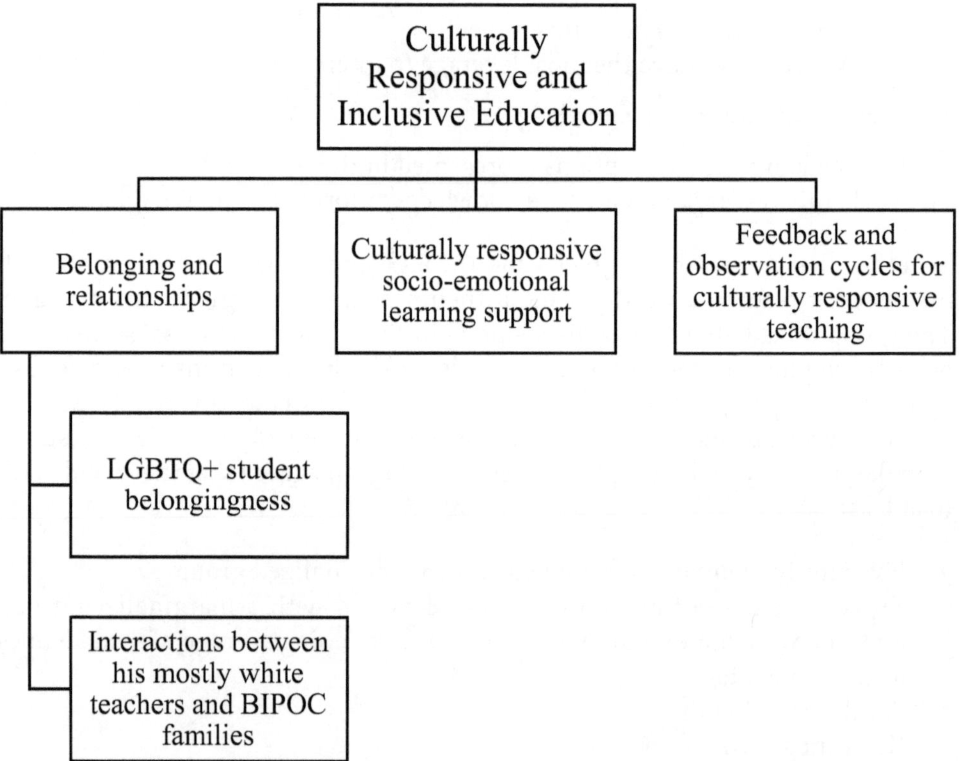

Figure 1.3 The NIC Shared Problem and School-Based Problems.

Source: Create by author.

as a whole child. They also wanted to talk to some former LGBTQ+ students who had gone on to high school. The team also thought that they should be sure to consider racial and gender diversity when they selected the students to interview.

The improvement team was not sure how to include the interviews in the school day or if they needed to ask parents' permission to talk to the students. Ava decided the team would have the student's adviser conduct the interviews, as part of advisory class, since they already had a relationship, and the team agreed to keep the questions rather broad. She asked Randy to use time in the GSA to talk about the empathy interviews with students and to provide space for them to reflect after the interviews. In addition, Ava asked Randy if they would hold focus group-like conversations with the GSA to gain even more understanding of the "user" experience. She also relied on Randy to help connect Ava to the families. She wanted to conduct those empathy interviews herself as part of getting to know her school community better, but she asked Chris to support her with the conversations with Spanish-speaking families.

The final list of empathy interview questions for current and former students was

1) How do you feel about school?
2) When do you feel most comfortable and most like yourself when you are at school?
3) When do you feel least comfortable and least like yourself when you are at school?
4) What would you most want us to know about your experience at school?

The final list of empathy interview questions for families was

1) How do you feel when your student goes to school?
2) Have you or your student ever had a bad experience at school that you would feel comfortable sharing about?
3) Has there ever been a time when your family felt particularly supported by the school?

The final list of empathy interview questions for teachers and school support staff was

1) How well do you know your LGBTQ+ students? How would you describe your relationship?
2) How do you think LGBTQ+ students feel at this school?
3) Tell me about a time when you have been inclusive of LGBTQ+ history and culture in your classes.

Ava's team had conducted an equity audit during her first year in the program, but they had not been able to make good use of that data, so she thought this would be a perfect time. The equity audit data showed that LGBTQ+ students were bullied, did not excel academically, and were overrepresented in the chronic absenteeism group. Using the same data protocol her professor had used in class, she asked Marcus to lead the improvement team through a conversation that focused on the results of the audit that specifically related to LGBTQ+ students.

Ava read extensively about equity and social justice in her program, but she didn't feel like she had a deep enough understanding of research about LGBTQ+ students, so she asked Isabella, the dean, to take some of the time allotted for professional development to familiarize herself with that research and prepare a summary. She also asked her to connect with other deans in the district to see if any of them had any practical expertise to share. Ava had also asked Randy to connect with the other GSA faculty sponsors to see if they had any resources to share with MHMS.

At first, Ava did not think that a process map would make sense for this problem, but Chris mentioned that it might be relevant to think about the process of onboarding new students and their families as sixth graders. She explained that the families' and students' feelings of belonging and inclusion are formed from those first interactions. The team agreed, so Ava asked Chris to work on creating that process map. Ava also asked the improvement team to work on a systems map and led them through a system mapping exercise as a team.

Everyone had their tasks and a few weeks to collect and organize the relevant data. Ava had to turn in her findings and insights to her professor as part of her class and wanted to make sure she had plenty of time to prepare in case the team took more than one meeting to explore the data. She planned to start the conversation at their November 1 meeting, return to data sharing at their November 8 meeting, and then lead them through the causal analysis activities (e.g., fishbone) at the next meeting on November 15. The last assignment for the quarter was to turn in her fishbone as well as the group's reflection on the equity-focused questions about root cause analysis from class. MHMS's improvement team's fishbone looked like Figure 1.4.

Year 2, Quarter 2

The NIC came back to the winter quarter after completing data collection to understand the problem in each context, the fishbone diagrams, and other causal analysis activities. The group shared those data with each other and had a chance to push each other's thinking. During the first week of class after sharing their individual school's fishbone diagrams, the NIC was ready to design a shared driver diagram or theory of improvement. It didn't take long because they had done so much to understand the problem collectively and at their schools. The NIC's initial driver diagram looked like Figure 1.5.

Ava and the NIC spent the next class thinking about this idea of practical measures and deciding on measures for their shared improvement goal that would capture their overall desire to increase cultural competency, responsiveness, and inclusion. The NIC talked about a shared system of measures, so they could learn across the schools, and settled on what they called a *Culturally Responsive Equity Ranking Survey* as a common way to track their aim across all the schools. They

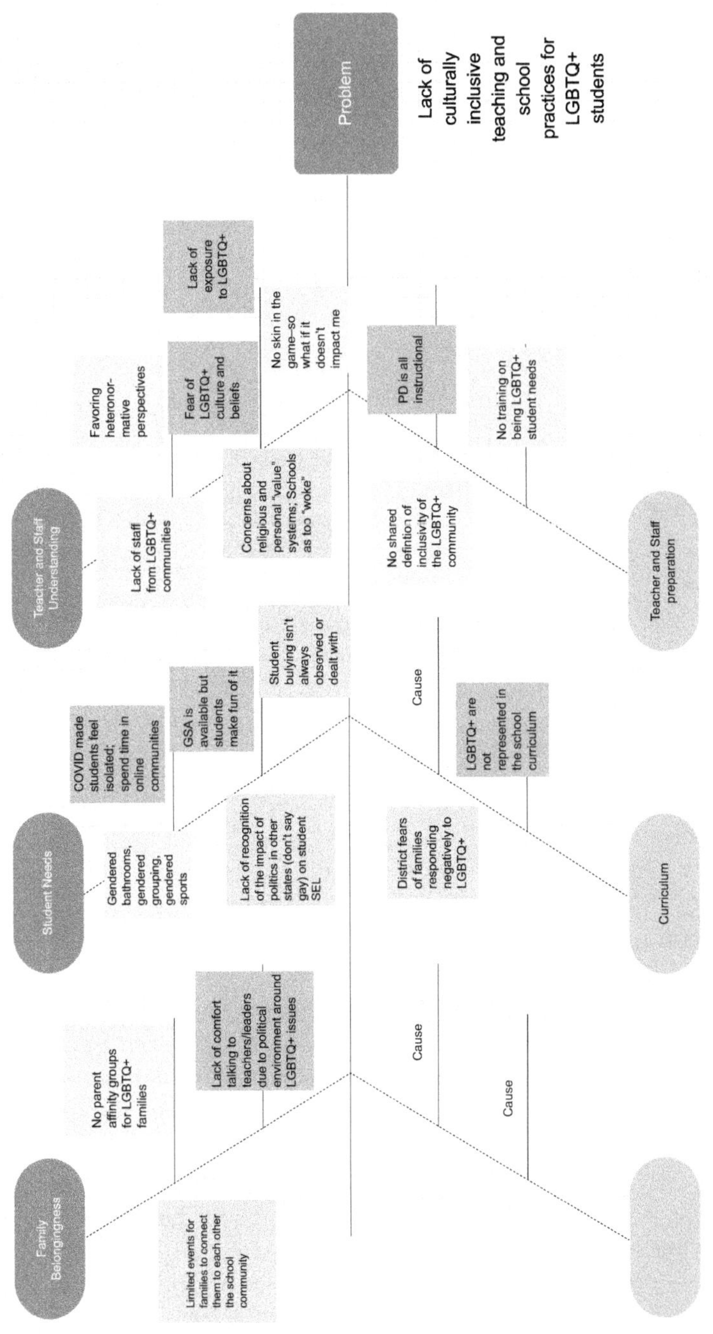

Figure 1.4 MHMS Fishbone Diagram.

Source: Created by author.

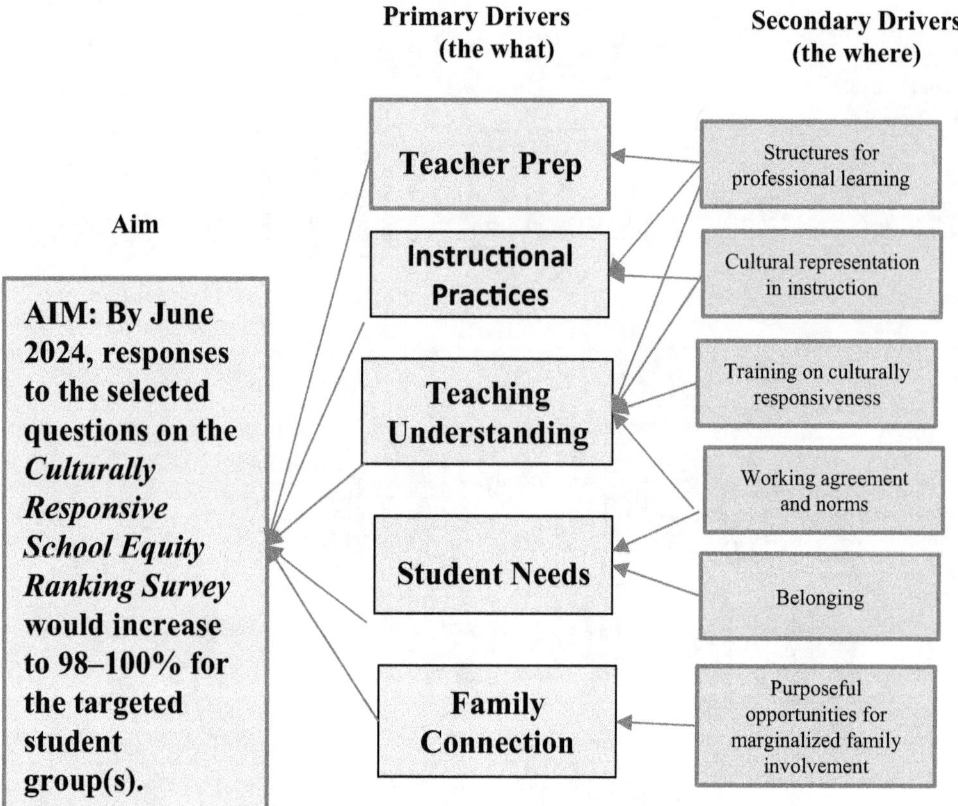

Figure 1.5 NIC Driver Diagram.

Source: Created by author.

built the survey using existing sub-scales from other surveys and questions they developed as a NIC that would capture each of their goals. The NIC agreed to incorporate a common question to see if they were all engaging in the process into students' Friday exit slips in their English classes.

The professor asked the students to come back next week with driver diagrams for each of their individual schools. The next step was to figure out a system of measures and start coming up with change ideas, so they would have time to build out prototypes and prepare for PDSA cycles in the spring. Ava knew that the educators in her school were familiar with data and measures since data-driven decision-making had been a district priority. MHMS already had a structure and protocol for data conversations. However, Ava realized her school relied on lagging data, such as end-of-the-year state test data and some interim assessments. Ava was going to need to design professional learning activities to teach the group about practical measures that were

- Embedded in daily work (easy lift)
- Rapid (quick feedback)

- Based on predictions (predict results in advance)
- Informative (reveals how the change is working)
- Responsive (captures small changes and uncovers who the change is/isn't helping)
- Theirs (open, honest reflection aimed at improvement).

Ava's professors emphasized that practical measures should not be evaluative but for learning and help

- Track the progress you want to make
- Answer your questions about the problem and add clarity to your questions
- Understand if the changes being made are an improvement
- Keep asking, "What works? For whom? Under what conditions?"

Avs wanted them to start thinking like improvers, which involves asking the following questions:

- How will we know if the changes we are making are improvements?
- Are we moving from our current to ideal state?
- What would success (or our ideal state) look like?
- What evidence should I collect for immediate decisions (PDSA), and what evidence should I plan to collect for judging long-term progress (Aim)?

Ava learned that measurable improvement requires time (and routines) to reflect on the data you are collecting to ensure that improvement is happening. She planned to start with simple ideas for practical measures like using exit tickets or short conversations with students to understand improvement. She planned to share great resources she had adapted from New York City Public Schools Improvement Science handbook (Table 1.2)

Ava led the data conversation with her school improvement team. Marcus had recently read the book *Street Data* (Safir & Dugan, 2021). In addition to noting how the book didn't speak favorably of improvement science, he noted that the book had given him some great ideas to think about student-centered practical measures that MHMS could use to support their work. Marcus offered to lead the team through a data conversation before they determined the system of measures. He was excited to share new approaches and tools including,

- The value of empathy interviews with students or parents or feedback interviews to understand change ideas;
- How they could conduct listening campaigns with stakeholders inviting them to focus groups or community pulse surveys;
- Skills for facilitating a fishbowl dialogue or Kiva circle;
- The process and benefit of student-led community walks or following a student or students for a day spending time shadowing those you're designing for; noting details and quotes and asking them questions for clarity.

Table 1.2 Types of Measures

List of Existing Potential Practical Measures	*Outcome Measures*	*Driver Measures*	*PDSA Measures*
Classroom observation checklist, rubrics, or recordings		x	x
Classwork and student projects		x	x
Homework			x
Exit tickets			x
Student assessments		x	x
Logs and journals		x	x
Checklists and rating Scales	x	x	x
Interviews	x	x	x
Surveys of students, teaching, families, etc.	x	x	x
District measures (culture surveys, state assessment data, etc.)	x		
Administrative data (disciplinary referrals, grades, attendance)	x	x	

Note: Adapted from *Types of Measures, NYCDOE Improvement Science Handbook.*

Source: *WeTeachNYC*

The MHMS group created their theory of improvement and captured it in the driver diagram in Figure 1.6 along with associated measures.

Year 2, Quarter 3

Ava felt anxious because the spring quarter was beginning. The feeling crept in that she had not improved anything yet. Despite months of learning about the problem with her NIC and her school improvement team, there had not yet been a change in practice, structures, or processes. She wanted to jump to solutions. Her professors had taught her a new term, solutionitis, and she was aware she was prone to that condition. She paused and noticed her tendency to focus on outcomes and how that was part of the white supremacy culture (Okun, 1999) she had read about in her class. She had to change her mental model around how change occurs in systems.

This approach was a pivot from how she and her team usually solve problems. She usually wanted to solve the problem quickly, due to the urgency and direct impact on students' lives. She knew the staff looked to her to solve problems; waiting to hear ideas for how to address the problem and then weighing in on her ideas and putting a change into place immediately without the depth of thought she had put into the problem using improvement science. She had a conversation with Marcus the week before, and he shared that the teachers felt included in the

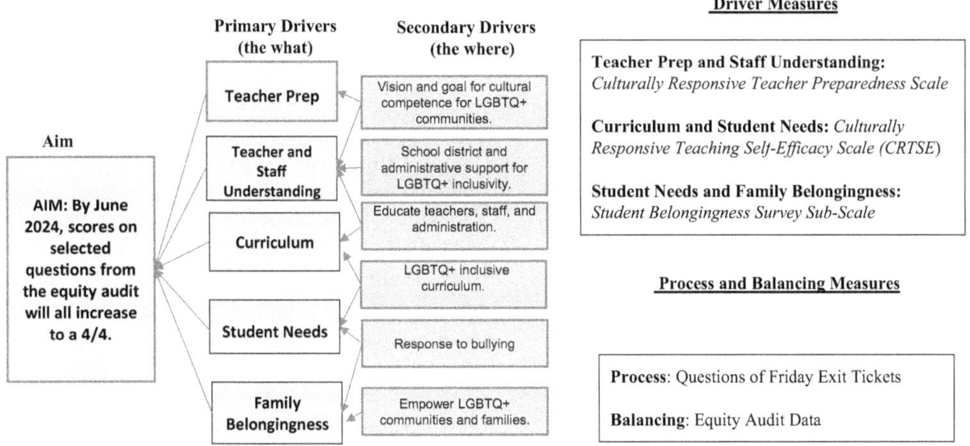

Figure 1.6 MHMS Theory of Improvement with Measures.

Source: Created by Author

problem-solving process in new ways and that his mid-year check-ins suggested teachers felt the school was more collaborative and felt more trust in the leaders and each other. Teachers mentioned that they liked how transparent the leadership team was about what they were doing, why, and to what end. They also liked being asked about their experiences as a teacher and felt like their input was included in the theory of improvement for the school. Through slowing down, Ava was making a shift toward sharing decision-making with the group, and the school improvement team was more aligned and intentional than they had ever been. Although she had always had a SIP, the improvement science process brought this improvement plan to life in new and exciting ways.

Ava's team decided to start with a simple change to a structure, figuring that she and her improvement team would build their muscles for conducting and measuring change ideas through PDSA cycles before they tried to understand the even messier mindset work. They wanted to start with "Teacher Preparation" as the first driver. The change idea tested was a *pronoun campaign*. The team thought it would be the first step toward increasing awareness of the LGBTQ+ community for teachers and students. The PDSA cycle followed the process in Table 1.3.

The improvement team found that the idea was too superficial and took too much time to implement with little improvement. A few weeks in, they decided to abandon that change idea and test a new idea.

The team had to resist the urge to force a failed idea. They talked as a group. Marcus shared he was embarrassed about lack of impact of the unsuccessful change idea. Chris shared her feelings of inadequacy and concerns she had about become a teacher leader. The team agreed failing was hard to accept. They decided that if they were going to create a learning culture at the school, then they had to be honest and transparent and create feelings of psychological safety (Edmondson et al., 2016) around a failure. At the next professional

Table 1.3 MHMS's First PDSA Cycle.

Step in Cycle	*Description of Step*	*Ava's Improvement Team Notes*
PLAN	What is the change idea you want to try? And when? What are the steps to implement the change idea? Who is responsible for the test?	The school will hang posters on the wall and dedicate a bulletin board to pronouns. Ava and Chris will make the posters. Isabella and Randy will create the bulletin board. Marcus will create exit slips to collect information on the change idea.
DO	Carry out implementing the change idea. Collect data.	The team created the posters and hung them all over the school. They also created a bulletin board with a brief history of pronouns, an explanation of why they matter, and a list of pronouns.
STUDY	What do you notice from your data? How did the results align with what you thought was going to happen during the test?	To study the change ideas, they asked English teachers to give an exit slip about pronouns to their students on three consecutive Fridays. Marcus would collect them and rack responses to see if they changed over time. They also planned to give the same exit slip to teachers after each PD section.
ACT	Do you adopt, adapt, or abandon?	After 1 week, they collected the student responses, and students were not paying attention to the bulletin boards. (10% of students and 5% of teachers indicated they had noticed the posters and read them). They decided to adapt the idea for week two and add an announcement to the morning announcements. They tracked responses for another week. No one noticed and there was little change (12% of students and 10% of teachers indicated they had noticed their posters and read them). They decided to try for one more week and see if more time changed the results. It did not, so they abandoned the idea.

development session with the teachers and the staff, the improvement team decided to share what they had tried, how it didn't work, and what they had learned from trying. The improvement team wanted to emphasize that learning comes from failed attempts at change as well-making the failure essential to the improvement process. Ava decided to really make the point that failure was okay by having a *We failed, but we succeeded*! celebration. Isabella suggested that the teams discuss what happened and what they had learned. Then, they would all tear up the idea into little pieces of paper, and table by table, throw it in the recycling bin while they toasted goodbye with apple cider. Then, in small groups, each teacher would share one time they failed in the classroom, and what they learned from that experience. Ava knew that some teachers would find this "ceremony" cheesy, but she also knew she needed to mark the shift in thinking in a symbolic way.

After this first PDSA cycle, the improvement team decided to try a new change idea where they taught teachers about the use of pronouns in their professional development equity groups. The PDSA cycle is shown in Table 1.4.

The team decided to make this part of the training for onboarding new teachers and staff.

Year 3, Conducting the Dissertation in Practice (DiP)

The cohort transitioned to a group advising structure, staying in their inquiry groups but no longer organizing as a NIC. Each inquiry group member continued their improvement work but no longer had a shared theory of improvement or common measures. Ava noted that with experience the improvement process was quicker and easier than before. Ava brought the improvement team together, and they revised MHMS's theory of improvement based on any new understanding. For her DiP, Ava needed to write three chapters before proposing

Table 1.4 MHMS's Second PDSA Cycle.

Step in Cycle	*Description of Step*	*Ava's Improvement Team Notes*
PLAN	What is the change idea you want to try? And when? What are the steps to implement the change idea? Who is responsible for the test?	Teacher training about the use of pronouns. Randy and Ava would lead the professional development using lessons adapted from the *Human Rights Campaign.*
DO	Carry out implementing the change idea. Collect data.	Professional development run by Randy and Ava where Randy shared personal experiences, and they shared data about the mental health of LGBTQ+ students and the importance of pronouns.
STUDY	What do you notice from your data? How did the results align with what you thought was going to happen during the test?	Marcus and Isabella surveyed teachers on new practices related to learning and looked for them during classroom observations. This time, the survey indicated that teachers were paying attention to professional learning and were preparing to make changes to their instruction.
ACT	Do you adopt, adapt, or abandon?	After one week, they adapted and created time in PD to ask questions in a brave space. They resurveyed the teachers and 99% were now providing an option for sharing pronouns with their teachers.

the final study. Chapter one would include everything that Ava's improvement team had learned so far. Her outline for chapter one was

(1) **Background:** description of the problem area
(2) **Local Problem Area and Organizational System:** description of the school and district, a summary of *local data* related to the problem, the *demographics, and characteristics* of people central to understanding the problem; and a *description of the researcher's role, influence, and positionality*
(3) **Understanding the Problem:** description of what was learned from improvement tools to understand the problem, see the system, recognize variation, and identify root causes, including *empathy data, systems,* and *process mapping*
(4) **Causal Analysis Focus Area:** description of the root causes of the problem using fishbone diagrams or other causal analysis tools
(5) **Statement of Problem of Practice:** clear statement of the problem, including a description of organizational issues related to the problem
(6) **Significance of the Problem of Practice:** description of why this was an important problem to solve and who was being impacted by the problem
(7) **Research Questions:** What is the overarching research question of the study? What is the question you are trying to answer? (e.g., How do we improve the learning environment for LGBTQ+ youth and children of LGBTQ+ families?)
(8) **Theory of Improvement:** display and describe the aim and the drivers.

Ava felt ready to write her introductory chapter; she had already summarized all her team's improvement work, telling the story of the work they had done the year before, the insights they had gleaned, their progress so far, and the next driver they wanted to tackle. She thought a blind spot in the first year of working on this problem was not designing change ideas to support students who may not identify as LGBTQ+ but were from LGBTQ+ families. The improvement team realized that supporting families more broadly would be the next driver to focus on, and Ava decided that she would document that process and the learning for her DiP.

Ava's chapter two summarized the literature for each driver with a focus on family and community relationships with LGBTQ+ families, and then it included a section on interventions or change ideas that others have found to help solve the problem. She reviewed what the change ideas suggested and/or tested in the literature. At the end of this section, she shared a revised driver diagram that was informed by the literature and included research-based change ideas (Figure 1.7).

The third chapter of her proposal was a methods section. She needed to explain her research plan including the (a) implementation timeline, (b) school-level improvement team, (c) overview of meetings and actions of the improvement team, (d) PDSA cycle plan, and (e) overarching research questions and inquiry questions tied to each change idea. She also needed to share the methods and measures including (a) practical improvement measures (aim, process, driver,

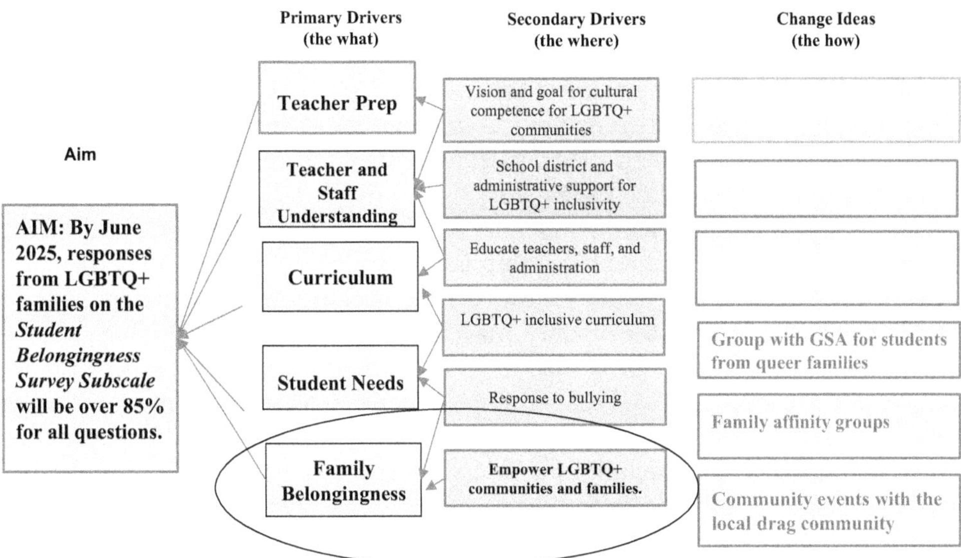

Figure 1.7 Revised Theory of Improvement for MHMS 4.0.

balancing), (b) instruments used in data collection and data collection approach, (c) data collected during PDSAs, and (d) plan for analysis of data.

The professor asked the inquiry group to create a list of questions about the proposal for the instructor. Ava and the group grappled with how to plan a study when the nature of continuous improvement was that things were always changing. Emma asked how she could leave room for growth and meet the expectations of a proposal to complete the DiP. Jamie asked how she could propose a set of change ideas and stay true to the iterative nature of the process. Luis wanted to know what would happen if he learned new information through the PDSA cycles that changed the course of action. Ava needed to reflect on how she could be sure she was staying authentic to MHMS's needs and not allowing her expectations for her doctorate to guide the work of her school. Ava's professor helped the group navigate those questions.

Ava and her inquiry group all defended their proposals in September, so by October, they were each ready to start testing change ideas at their schools. She had the plan to spend October through December engaged in PDSA cycles around three change ideas, spending about a month on each change idea, and then in January, she would begin writing her findings to answer her research questions.

AVA'S AHA MOMENT

One day when they were discussing the next step in their improvement process, Randy brought something to the forefront of their thinking. They were a member of the LGBTQ+ community, but they felt like they were being asked to carry the burden of being the sole representative of the community. Every time there was a question about how to approach the community, the team turned to Randy. They didn't want to be the only source of the in-group perspective, especially because they couldn't represent the range of queer experiences. In particular, Randy did not feel they could represent the trans experience or the experience of LGBTQ+ with marginalized racial identities.

Ava heard this concern and understood it, but she wanted to run her thinking by the inquiry group at the next group advising meeting. She was particularly interested in Emma's ideas about how to rely on multiple perspectives without making inclusion the work of only marginalized teachers and leaders. Emma agreed that it would be a good idea to work with an outside group because not only would the group have a broader range of perspectives to inform their change ideas, but participation would increase community involvement in school as they had read during their leadership for equity class in Ishimaru's book, *Just Schools Building Equitable Collaborations with Families and Communities* (2019). Emma provided Ava with a list of local non-profit organizations supporting LGBTQ+ teens' mental and physical health. Luis shared that he thought this was a good idea and that he had purposefully begun working with a local Indigenous organization to help him grow his understanding of the Native American experience, culture, and identity at his school.

Ava came to the next MHMS improvement team meeting with a proposal. Ava thought maybe they could use some of MHMS's budget to contract with a local non-profit that advocated for trans, gay, and nonbinary youth and families. This group, whose mission and values aligned with the school's, could organize and lead professional learning with the staff, broadening the perspectives of the team and taking the burden from Randy. The team discussed the pros and cons of that idea and decided that they would benefit from external collaboration in this next phase of the work.

Since Ava had done this before, she had figured out where the team needed support in conducting PDSA cycles. Like many other improvement teams, MHMS didn't struggle with trying a new idea but did struggle with planning out the measures that would allow the team to draw any actual conclusions from a test. Ava created a protocol to help MHMS plan for PDSA cycles and reflect on the measures before the inquiry cycles. The recent PDSA cycles were going well. Throughout the year, she tested ideas, abandoned some bad ideas, and adopted some good ones. Their final bundle of change ideas to address the driver of "Family Belongingness" was

1) Family affinity groups
2) A group within GSA for students from queer families
3) Community events co-sponsored with the local community for MHMS families, including *Drag Story Hour.*

She wrote her findings section of her DiP with the details of the PDSA cycles and the summary of trends in her aim data. After she shared the findings with her adviser in February, she worked on her chapter five or her plan of action for how this learning would be spread and scaled throughout the MHMS as well as working with Emma's school in the same district to help see if the ideas improved their practices at all. She hoped to work with district leaders from the culturally responsive and sustaining education office, such as the Director of Diversity, Equity, and Inclusion (DEI) to design professional learning that could be implemented first in all the middle schools and then the high schools. She and Emma offered their expertise to run a NIC of district-level leaders to teach them the improvement science process. In May, she passed her final oral defense.

During her defense, her committee pushed her to think about how she could expand her thinking about practical measures to use more than surveys. The committee also asked Ava to think about how she was creating a data infrastructure for the school and attending to spreading and scaling successful ideas in her school and district. The committee also pushed Ava to think more about how she set up the conditions to support continuous improvement. She was so thankful that she had the time to focus on all the things that mattered to her as a leader. Ava saw shifts in teachers' mindsets, greater student and family belonging, and better systems for authentic collaboration. Ava felt ready to lead the improvement science process without the formal support of her professors or the inquiry group, but she knew that they were always there if she ran into any questions or just needed moral support along the way.

Year 4, Enacting School Leadership Through Improvement Science

With her newly minted degree, Dr. Jackson was excited to get working on her next improvement priority. Based on everything she learned from ensuring the school's practices, policies, and social interactions were inclusive of the LGBTQ+ student community and LGBTQ+ families and based on what she learned from her NIC about culturally responsive education more broadly, she wanted her next improvement project to stay in the same general area of culturally responsive education, but she wanted to focus more specifically on student belonging for her students in MLL programming.

Ava noticed that students in MLL programming spent most of their time together and did not have many connections with other students who were not in MLL programming. When the school had an assembly, Ava observed how students sat together and that the emerging language learners sat alone and off to the side. Ava's initial impression was that the MLL students seemed disconnected from other students. Her NIC in her graduate cohort had worked on similar problems in their schools and shared the change ideas that worked with Ava. She was going to need to lead her team through exploring those ideas and adapting them for her context. She wanted to start there since she could borrow some ideas for practical measures from Luis, and they could work together to see how the idea worked in a different setting.

Over the last 2 years, MHMS developed collaborative structures for discussing school-wide issues, and they had worked on how to have courageous conversations about oppression and power. Also, MHMS was in the process of redesigning their professional learning community (PLC) for teachers to use improvement science on instructional problems. Randy was heading up the improvement work with teachers. Using PLCs to facilitate teachers learning of improvement science would set the teachers up in their departments to work on instructional challenges. This continuous approach to improvement work, which was inclusive of staff, student, and family perspectives, had created more relational trust in Ava and the leadership team, between educators, and between families and the school. Ava felt like they had created learning mindsets in the improvement team and others in the school and that the learning culture was one that recognized the learning that comes from failure. She still needed to work on her patience and was still getting used to shifting power to others. Chris wanted to work on developing a data infrastructure for teachers to collect and share common practical measures to share in their data meetings to drive improvement. Ava let Chris lead that work.

Ava's professors always told her that she needed to think about equity when she initiated the conditions (team and vision), throughout the process, and with the outcomes. Ava was excited to return to the start of the improvement science process with all her newfound learning after leading the school through a 2-year improvement process focused on LGBTQ+ youth. She understood that the work wasn't over and that she needed to keep reviewing key data over time and make sure that they onboarded new teachers and support staff so that they would understand the expectations of teaching for social justice at MHMS. Ava included the new improvement team in understanding the problem and gathered multiple perspectives through empathy interviews. The team decided that they could probably use the data from the prior equity audit because they hadn't focused on MLL students before.

Ava thought the team should focus on outcomes that would increase belonging for students in MLL programming. Marcus, Isabella, Chris, and Randy still wanted to be part of the improvement team, and the team added one family member, the mother of Louisa, an eighth grader who had been at the school since grade six, and another ELL teacher since their perspectives were key to the problem. Chris was already on the team and offered valuable input as an ELL teacher, and Isabella was a parent to a Latine student, who as a native English speaker did not participate in MLL programming, but she had come to understand their shared cultural experiences through her participation in the school's family affinity groups and through her role as dean. Logistically, this meant they needed to move the meetings to before school, so Louisa's mom and the teachers could attend. Including family on the improvement team meant that community input would be available throughout the process, including when they started testing change ideas. The team decided to start with an idea that was community-facing.

Ava paused and critically self-reflected. She first reflected on how these reflections had become such a key part of her leadership. In fact, not only did she lead herself through a set of prompts, but the teachers did so in their equity professional development led by the equity team. She couldn't believe how MHMS's measures of collective efficacy for culturally responsive education had continued to grow over time, and she looked forward to embarking on this next improvement journey to create a more inclusive school and classroom space for students with emerging English language skills.

BIBLIOGRAPHY

Edmondson, A. C., Higgins, M., Singer, S., & Weiner, J. (2016). Understanding psychological safety in health care and education organizations: A comparative perspective. *Research in Human Development, 13*(1), 65–83. https://doi.org/10.1080/15427609.2016.1141280

Hinnant-Crawford, B., & Anderson, E. (2022). 5S framework for defining problems addressed through improvement research in education. In D. Peurach, J. Russell, L. Cohen-Vogel, & W. Penuel (Eds.), *Handbook of improvement focused educational research* (pp. 297–324). Rowan and Littlefield.

Human Rights Campaign. (2023). www.hrc.org/resources/lgbtq-youth

Ishimaru, A. M. (2019). *Just schools: Building equitable collaborations with families and communities*. Teachers College Press.

Ishimaru, A. M. (2020). *Just schools: Building equitable collaborations with families and communities*. Teachers College Press.

Kachele, M., & Ragatz, M. (2022). *The pulse of PBL: Seamlessly integrating social and emotional learning*. Blend Education.

Khalifa, M. (2018). *Culturally responsive school leadership*. Harvard Education Press.

Milder, S., & Lorr, B. (2018). New York City public schools improvement science handbook. *WeTeachNYC*. www.weteachnyc.org/resources/resource/nycdoe-improvement-science-handbook/

Okun, T. (1999). *White supremacy culture*. www.dismantlingracism.org/uploads/4/3/5/7/43579015/okun_-_white_sup_culture.pdf

Safir, S., & Dugan, J. (2021). *Street data: A next-generation model for equity, pedagogy, and school transformation*. Corwin.

CHAPTER 2

What Is (and Isn't) Continuous Improvement in Education?

Chapter Highlights

1) Improvement, as currently enacted, is not working.
2) Continuous improvement is broadly defined.
3) Continuous improvement is defined in this book along three dimensions: instrumental methods, social relations, and moral values.

CHAPTER DESCRIPTION

This chapter continues from the introduction in laying a foundation for the volume by defining continuous improvement in education. The chapter draws out the shared principles that anchor approaches to continuous improvement and articulates continuous improvement principles in current standards, highlighting alignment, contrasts, and gaps. The chapter makes the argument that, while the standards provide broad legitimation of enacting continuous improvement in schools and school systems, improvement leadership requires attention to three dimensions of continuous improvement: instrumental methods, social relations, and moral values. This chapter positions PSEL Standard 10: School Improvement as a starting point for this volume, illustrating how the discrete elements of Standard 10 can be interpreted and enacted in school settings through these three dimensions.

DOI: 10.4324/9781003389279-3

INTRODUCTION: DEFINING WHAT CONTINUOUS IMPROVEMENT MEANS TO US

Improvement can mean many things to many people, and when it comes to school improvement, a lot of people at a lot of different levels want to or need to get involved. Let's be honest from the start: "school improvement" as a pursuit has a terrible reputation and, frankly, that reputation is well deserved. One of the most insightful critics of initial, large-scale efforts to reform schools and school systems in the 1980s described school improvement initiatives using the analogy of oceanic movements: "storm-tossed waves on the ocean surface, turbulent water a fathom down, and calm on the ocean floor" (Cuban, 1984, p. 237). For Cuban and many others, the surface of the ocean has to do with the flurry of initiatives in educational policy circles about how to bring about change, the water churning "a fathom down" relates to the churn of administrative responses in enacting new initiatives at the system and school levels, and the ocean floor is where all of those pronouncements and enactments are supposed to make a difference but rarely end up making a stir: teaching practice and student learning in classrooms.

Unfortunately, Cuban's depiction of school reform at the beginning of the era of wide-scale improvement initiatives is just as true today, nearly a half-century after he first wrote those words. A succession of national and state policy efforts have sought to advance educational quality and equity by promoting local accountability (e.g., Improving America's Schools Act, 1994; No Child Left Behind Act, 2002; Every Student Succeeds Act, 2015). The aims have been admirable: provide high-quality instruction, deeper learning, and access to 21st century skills to all students, especially those historically marginalized by our system of education such as students of color, students from low-income backgrounds, newly-immigrated students, and those speaking a first language other than English (Peurach, Foster et al., 2022). The means of achieving those aims were extensive and ambitious – carrots in the form of targeted resources, sticks whittled from the threat, and not infrequently the reality, of restructuring districts and schools. But achieving those admirable aims remains elusive (Reardon et al., 2019).

The fact that we have not only made churn "a fathom down" calls into question the means, and this is where continuous improvement enters the scene. Efforts to radically transform schools through turnaround have frequently shown initial promise but have all-too-frequently been impossible to sustain (Murphy & Bleiberg, 2019). Initiatives to transform entire school systems have also rarely led to the broad shifts in leadership and teaching practices initially envisioned (Rowan et al., 2009). Peurach, Foster, and colleagues (2022) in their review of large-scale improvement efforts highlight key findings from a range of research that illuminate different facets of the challenge.

1) Scholars point to the way educational research itself is conducted as deserving some of the responsibility for not providing guidance directly useful to educational practice (e.g., Bryk et al., 2015). The limited examples that have

led to sustained change show us that supporting sustained improvement in educational practice cannot depend solely on lab research but must be done in collaboration with educational professionals themselves (Bryk, 2020).

2) Transfer of practice, whether at the organizational level or the classroom level, is never direct. Rather, the spread of promising practices entails social processes of co-construction and adaptation among educational professionals and those developing the change (Datnow & Park, 2012).
3) Studies of change in schools have also found that the spread of an innovation at the classroom level must be coupled with parallel efforts to create the system-wide supports, or infrastructure, that can embed and sustain change at the organizational level (Coburn, 2003; Penuel et al., 2020).

ACTION INVENTORY 2.1 CHANGES IN YOUR ORGANIZATION REFLECTION QUESTIONS

1. What changes in education practice have been introduced into your school setting?
   a. How were those changes ushered in? By whom? Why?
   b. Did those changes result in a fundamental shift in practice over the long term? Why? Why not?
2. What is the role of leaders during changes?
   a. What dispositions, skills, approaches are effective during change? What is ineffective?
3. What is the role of educational leadership preparation programs for supporting aspiring leaders' capacity for leading changes?
4. What does continuous improvement look like and sound like in your organization?

The recent emphasis on continuous improvement has not shifted the aims of excellence and equity for all students; it has shifted the means to reach those aims by attending to the aspects of organizational change that were missing in preceding efforts to bring about change at scale in schools. That is why the PSEL culminate with Standard 10, School Improvement. The placement at the end of the PSEL is intentional, according to the *National Policy Board for Educational Administration* publication that announced the revised standards in 2015. The authors grouped the standards into three clusters, (a) instructional leadership (Standards 4 and 5), (b) professional leadership and community engagement (Standards 6 through 9), and (c) moral leadership (Standards 1 to 3).

Standard 10 stands apart. According to the authors: "The domain of School Improvement affects all of the clusters, which together reflect a theory of how educational leader practice influences student achievement" (p. 4).

Why does Standard 10 occupy such a prominent position among the other standards? The chapters that follow address this question in detail. This chapter examines the core notion of improvement behind Standard 10, the idea of *continuous improvement*. Other standards also mention continuous improvement in one of the several elements that comprise the domain covered, notably Standard 1 (mission, vision, and core values), Standard 2 (ethics and professional norms), and Standard 6 (developing professional capacity). But it is in Standard 10 that the term gets the spotlight as the key feature of the standard domain itself.

This chapter begins by teasing out what makes "continuous improvement" distinct from improvement that is not considered continuous. Making that distinction also gives us a chance to show you that there are several definitions of continuous improvement. From these, we put forward the working definition that we are using in this book. As you will see, continuous improvement is not one approach, it is many with often blurred boundaries between these. We narrow our focus to one approach that has, arguably, become synonymous with continuous improvement for many educational professionals. That approach is the same one Ava was using, which is known as "improvement science" (Bryk et al., 2015; Bryk, 2020; Hinnant-Crawford, 2020). This chapter places improvement science in the larger context of the current *improvement movement* (Peurach, Foster et al., 2022) in education and traces how the focus on continuous improvement in other sectors, notably industry and healthcare, led to greater uptake of improvement science in education. Finally, we focus on the implications for leadership and the reasons why Standard 10 offers a solid bookend for all the preceding standards.

What Is Continuous Improvement?

In the broadest sense, the notion of *continuous improvement* makes explicit the trade-offs between change as a set of tools and procedures and change as a social process. Not only does continuous improvement make these facets of change explicit, but the approach also ideally combines these synergistically and systematically to reach valued ends – educational excellence and equity. Conventional approaches to organizing and managing change in schools have tended to overemphasize the tools and procedures and underappreciate the social dimensions of change. The ubiquitous school improvement plan (SIP) and the annual planning process that accompanies it are prime examples of the ways conventional approaches to change can lead to unintended consequences. The typical annual school improvement planning process is a ritual of compliance – assembling data, completing templates, seeking approvals – but results in little practical or actual change that teachers can make within their classrooms and leaders can make within their schools. Plans are dusted off toward the end of the school year after sitting on a shelf, in a hard drive, or in the cloud untouched for most of the year. When the initial results from year-end standardized tests arrive in late summer, goals are updated, templates completed, requirements fulfilled and back into the shared drive it goes, ready to sit untouched until the next school year. This is a stark characterization, but we think you'll recognize some connections from your own experience. In fact, many of the aspiring leaders in our programs start out not ever having seen a school improvement plan before being required to ask their principals to see it in their first leadership course.

Continuous improvement is not just about having the school improvement plan; it's about the doing of school improvement. But the status quo ways that school improvement planning is frequently done stands in for the range of ways that the doing of school improvement currently has been more about fulfilling requirements than meeting the needs of students and motivating teachers and leaders to seek innovative ways to meet those needs (Stevenson & Weiner, 2021).

The phrase "continuous improvement" can make it seem like there is one approach that everybody knows and everybody uses. The reality is a lot different. There are many approaches to continuous improvement, and there are many approaches that are closely aligned but might cover only one facet of change. We would need a multi-volume encyclopedia to address all the approaches currently in use. Fortunately, several extensive resources exist to add more depth to the sketch that we offer in this book (e.g., Cohen-Vogel et al., 2019; LeMahieu et al., 2017; Peurach, Russell et al., 2022). Some of the better known approaches include design-based implementation research (DBIR) (e.g., Fishman & Penuel, 2018); community-engaged research (e.g., Bang et al., 2016); social design experiments (e.g., Gutiérrez & Jurow, 2016); and networked improvement communities (e.g., Russell et al., 2017). This book emphasizes a particular approach, *improvement science*, that is most closely associated with networked improvement communities. All these approaches, however, hold in common some basic principles.

The "continuous" in continuous improvement relates to a commonality shared among almost all approaches to improvement that fall under the "continuous" label – the introduction of rapid and repeated tests of change that involve those directly affected by the changes. In improvement science, these rapid tests of change are typically called "PDSA cycles" for the succession of steps involved, plan-do-study-act (Langley et al., 2009). These rapid cycles of local change typically follow one of several systematic methods of introducing and monitoring change so that the learning from one cycle to the next is continuous and grounded in the everyday actions of those doing the work.

One crucial facet of these grounded, rapid tests is that the succession of testing enables continuous learning not only about the problem itself but the system that produced it, yielding greater clarity about how a change leads to improvement. Moreover, that learning lodges in those who are doing the work, among others, not only researchers who are looking at the work from the outside. Close collaboration with those doing the work not only has to do with foregrounding social processes; it also has to do with a moral commitment to democratic values. This means using the tools of improvement to help clarify aims among diverse stakeholders, involving those stakeholders in the processes of understanding and carrying out change, and upholding the belief that the knowledge held by those doing the work is just as important as the knowledge of those studying the work.

No single contemporary definition of the term *continuous improvement* exists. Mark Smylie, who had a substantial role in shaping PSEL Standard 10, identified eight descriptive characteristics that efforts to promote continuous school improvement hold in common (Smylie, 2010). Based on their comprehensive review of relevant literature and change efforts in multiple sectors, Park and colleagues (2013) identified five core characteristics of quality improvement, subsequently characterized by O'Day and Smith (2016), and a more recent overview and assessment of approaches to continuous improvement (Yurkofsky et al., 2020) describes four "shared commitments" of continuous improvement (p. 404). See Figure 2.1 for the specific elements of each of these.

Common across these three sets of definitions are three interconnected dimensions that we mentioned earlier, dimensions that distinguish continuous improvement from other approaches to improvement. The first dimension has to do with the instrumental/technical character of continuous improvement as a form of inquiry. By this, we mean that continuous improvement entails the use of certain instruments, or methods, for systematic inquiry, such as the PDSA cycles mentioned in O'Day's and Smith's (2016) characterization and the iterative cycles of inquiry mentioned by Yurkofsky and colleagues (2020) and Smylie (2010). But there is also an implicit philosophical orientation that we reference in identifying one dimension of continuous improvement as *instrumental methods*. That has to do with the pragmatic orientation of continuous improvement as an approach to change, with the emphasis on the utility of the change to help people to adapt to the world around them (Dewey, 1916).

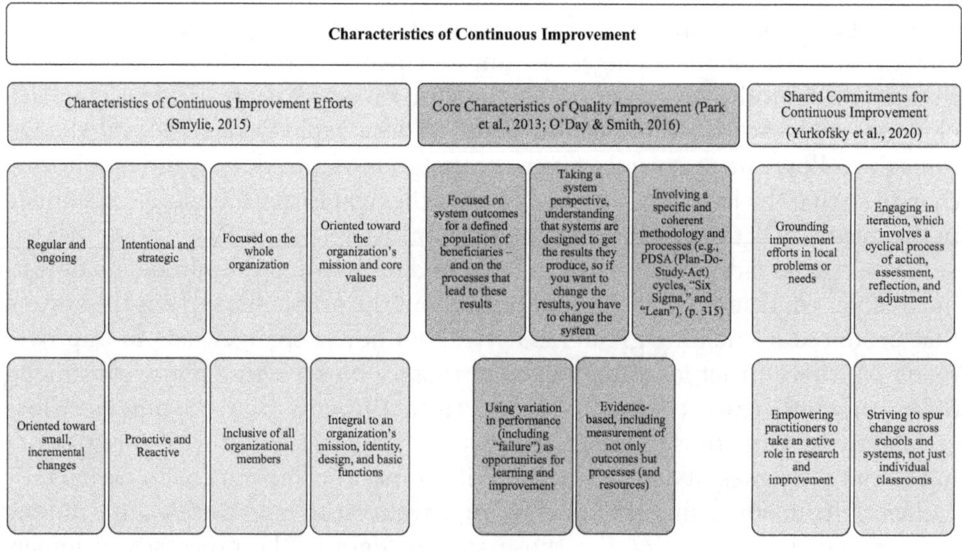

Figure 2.1 Characteristics of Continuous Improvement.

The second dimension follows from the first. Throughout all three characterizations is an emphasis on foregrounding *social relations* that are inclusive and attentive to questions of power and privilege, an aspect that arises with particular force in Yurkofsky's (2020) and colleagues' characterization of continuous improvement as "empowering practitioners" to take agency in the enterprise of improvement. The social relations dimension also highlights ways the field has evolved over the past two decades, from Smylie's focus on classrooms to the emphasis on spurring change across schools and systems. Cohen-Vogel and colleagues (2019) describe this as the "social infrastructure" of improvement, which encompasses not only the work of teacher teams in schools but now improvement teams collaborating nationally. This has led some scholars to include the term "collaborative" in front of the phrase for the label, "collaborative, continuous improvement" (O'Day & Smith, 2019).

The final dimension that we highlight is integral to the preceding two dimensions – a moral value dimension that prioritizes consideration of values and valuing as integral to the instrumental and social activities of continuous improvement. This dimension has to do with the foundation of values that orient action to certain ends. It has to do with what is "good" and "right." In improvement work, those ends focus on educational excellence, equity, and social justice. Why is this? Once you start looking for root causes and systemic conditions that impede excellence in US education, you inevitably bump up against societal conditions that yield the zip code lottery, the inevitability of achievement based on zip code, for example. Education as a social institution does not stand apart from society but is deeply enmeshed in all the rights and wrongs, the good and the bad, that make up every other aspect of our society.

The following takes each of the three dimensions of continuous improvement in turn to show how these have come to comprise what we take to be continuous improvement. For each dimension, we use the ten PSEL standard elements, 10(a) through 10(j), that comprise PSEL Standard 10 to show the expectations that the PSEL standards set in terms of the leadership of continuous improvement in education today.

CONTINUOUS IMPROVEMENT IN THREE DIMENSIONS

Instrumental Methods Dimension

Those new to continuous improvement frequently come to learn about it through its tools: fishbone diagrams, process flowcharts, driver diagrams, interrelationship digraphs, which we do discuss at various points in the following chapters and may be part of a continuous improvement toolkit or toolbox. Acknowledgment of those tools and strategies is certainly an important aspect of the leadership of continuous improvement. PSEL substandard 10(c) foregrounds the need to "develop technically appropriate systems of data collection, management, analysis, and use." The most important part of the instrumental dimension of continuous improvement is not about the tools and procedures per se or even about the skills necessary to select and apply the right tool at the right time. The instrumental dimension is about an approach to change that prioritizes the experience of developing knowledge through experimentation and the practical accomplishments that result from such experimentation.

The description of Ava's EdD program in Chapter 1 begins with a focus on tools: empathy interviews, process and systems mapping leading up to root cause analysis using affinity mapping, five whys, and a fishbone diagram. None of those tools on its own holds the prospect of transforming inequitable systems. However, when the tools are used systematically, together, and with an equity orientation, then the knowledge gleaned from an empathy interview can inform a fishbone diagram that yields new and better understanding of the system causing inequities. When Ava's group shared their reflections on their fishbone drafts, they were essentially running an informal experiment, testing their individual knowledge about what was going on in each of their schools against the collective knowledge of the team and the prompts set by the teacher. In this example, and fundamentally in improvement work, it is the interaction among procedures and people that makes the difference, that actually yields the experience of developing knowledge.

In common parlance in education nowadays, the tools and procedures of continuous improvement aim to uncover not "what works" for every student under every circumstance, but "how and why does this work and/or not work, for whom, to what extent, in what respects, in what circumstances and over what duration?" (Westhorp, 2014, p. 4). In this perspective, variation becomes the core issue to understand and explore through iterative experimentation, not to design out of the system by identifying the silver bullet solution that works for all in every circumstance.

The specific focus on local integration and efficacy maps to two of the nine PSEL elements that comprise Standard 10, the first and the sixth. The sixth element, PSEL Standard 10(e), highlights the use of "situationally-specific strategies for improvement." Leaders who take on board this orientation do so through attention to variation and experimentation. The first standard identifies effective leaders as those who "seek to make school more effective for each student, teachers and staff, families, and the community." An important point to emphasize here is the use of the verb "seek." Continuous improvement is about an orientation to strategic action that continually seeks to right-size change given the needs of students, the capacities of teachers, the availability of resources, and awareness of the context all that sits within.

Such a problem-solving focus puts emphasis on thinking systemically, or seeing the system that produces the problem. Systems thinking foregrounds "interactions among structures, work processes, and norms" (LeMahieu et al., 2017, p. 15). In education, attention to structures and interaction means attending to the many different levels of the system – classroom, school, district central office, state, and federal agencies, as well as the politics and culture within and across each of these (Smylie, 2010). PSEL element 10(h) speaks directly to this, encouraging leaders to "adopt a systems perspective and promote coherence among improvement efforts and all aspects of the school."

But how do you balance such a panascopic perspective with the very local question of "how and why does this work or not work" in *this* classroom, in *this* school? One of the beauties of the instrumental methods dimension of continuous improvement is that the tools, approaches, and principles demand a constant balancing act of flaring, or zooming out, to see the system and focusing, or zooming in, to understand what is going on right here, right now through small tests of change. At its most fundamental, the leadership of continuous school improvement involves the orchestration of organizational learning that encompasses both flaring and focusing. But orchestrating that shift entails working with other people, which brings us to our next dimension, the social relations dimension.

Social Relations Dimension

Deeply connected with the instrumental emphasis of continuous improvement is a pronounced shift in social relations from vertical, hierarchical structures to horizontal, distributive structures intended to promote collaboration and collective knowledge building. These structures range from grade-level collaborative learning teams to interstate improvement networks. However, collaborative structures on their own do not automatically yield generative professional collaboration, as you may well have experienced. Shifting the professional culture of schools and school systems from the model of the independent artisan to school-wide and system-wide professional communities is no simple task (Little & McLaughlin, 1993). Fundamental to functional teaming and networking are the identities, mindsets, and beliefs of each of those engaged in the work; how these individual attributes interact together; and the ways that the interaction shapes capacity for collective efficacy (Moolenaar et al., 2012; Yurkofsky et al., 2020). The social relations dimension of continuous improvement encompasses not only the structures of collaboration, but the beliefs and professional propensities that make collaboration effective.

Professional propensities for relational interaction have to do with a person's inclinations, sensitivities, and abilities in relation to their professional work. These are what Perkins and colleagues (1993) characterize as "dispositions." Biag and Sherer (2021) apply the notion of dispositions to continuous improvement to describe a set of "improvement dispositions" that enable collective knowledge building and coherent organizational change. Their research of improvers working in NICs identifies six dispositions (pp. 16–17):

- Engaging in disciplined inquiry
- Adopting a learner stance
- Taking a systems perspective
- Possessing an orientation to action
- Seeing the perspective of others
- Persisting beyond initial improvement attempts.

These improvement dispositions are essential to cultivating an organizational culture of improvement, and nurturing such a culture depends on the fundamental attributes of effective collaboration. Two main ingredients of effective collaboration are psychological safety and relational trust. Psychological safety involves the shared perception of people's abilities to take risks in their workplace. Business researcher Amy Edmondson (2019) defines psychological safety as "a climate in which people are comfortable expressing and being themselves" (p. x). According to Edmondson (2019, p. 2),

> (I)n a psychologically safe workplace, people are not hindered by interpersonal fear. They feel willing and able to take the inherent interpersonal risks of candor. They fear holding back their full participation more than they fear sharing a potentially sensitive, threatening, or wrong idea. The fearless organization is one in which interpersonal fear is minimized so that team and organizational performance can be maximized in a knowledge intensive world.

Developing psychological safety depends on building relational trust, which research has shown is foundational to school improvement of any kind (Ford, 2014) and especially crucial to the collaborative structures that comprise continuous improvement (Bryk & Schneider, 2002). In their work on school reform in Chicago Public Schools, Bryk and colleagues (2010) identified relational trust as the glue that holds the school together as a professional community and binds the school to its local community through robust, trusting relationships with parents, caregivers, and community members. School leaders play the most important role in cultivating relational trust, as Bryk (2010, p. 27) recounts,

> Principals establish both respect and personal regard when they acknowledge the vulnerabilities of others, actively listen to their concerns, and eschew arbitrary actions. If principals couple this empathy with a compelling school vision, and if teachers see their behavior as advancing this vision, their personal integrity is also affirmed.

One of the key ingredients of effective leadership is the principal's ability to build psychological safety through relational trust. Relational trust serves as the mortar for making "school more effective for each student, teachers and staff, families, and the community" (PSEL Standard 10[a]). Combined with the improvement dispositions, building relational trust orients the school toward improvement by fulfilling what standard element 10(c) requires: "Prepare the school and the community for improvement, promoting readiness, an imperative for improvement, instilling mutual commitment and accountability." The improvement dispositions, coupled with psychological safety built through relational trust enable school leaders to fulfill standard element 10(i): "Manage uncertainty, risk, competing initiatives, and politics of change with courage and perseverance, providing support and encouragement, and openly communicating the need for, process for, and outcomes of improvement efforts."

Crucial to the social relations dimension of continuous improvement is the capacity of *leaders* to develop *leadership* throughout their organization, not only in instructional staff, but throughout the building, in students as well as parents and caregivers, custodians and foodservice workers, social workers and school psychologists. For example, the school district of Menomonee Falls, Wisconsin, used improvement science along with other approaches to continuous improvement to involve every employee and every student in their effort to "get better at getting better" (see Bryk, 2020, Chapter 6, "Transforming a School District").

Central to the social relations dimension of the leadership of continuous improvement is the animation of agency of all involved, the "orientation to action" highlighted in the improvement dispositions. In their promotion of improvement science, the Institute of Healthcare Improvement (IHI) is to healthcare organizations what the Carnegie Foundation for the Advancement of Teaching has become for educational organizations. In fact, Carnegie learned important lessons from IHI in the development of its own approach to continuous improvement in education, networked improvement science (Bryk et al., 2015). In its effort to promote improvement science in healthcare organizations, IHI has created a *Psychology of Change Framework* (Hilton & Anderson, 2018) that centers the development of agency: "the ability of an individual or a group to choose to act with purpose." This *Framework* (Hilton & Anderson, 2018, p. 9) highlights five key elements that animate agency for improvement:

- Co-design people-driven change: Those most affected by change have the greatest interest in designing it in ways that are meaningful and workable to them.
- Co-produce in authentic relationship: Change is co-produced when people inquire, listen, see, and commit to one another.
- Distribute power: People can contribute their unique assets to bring about change when power is shared.
- Adapt in action: Acting can be a motivational experience for people to learn and iterate to be effective.
- Unleash intrinsic motivation: Tapping into sources of intrinsic motivation galvanizes people's individual and collective commitment to act.

Attention to these principles and the social relations dimension more broadly enables leaders both to "assess and develop the capacity of staff" (PSEL Standard 10[f]) and to engage everyone in a collaborative and "ongoing process of evidence-based inquiry, learning, strategic goal setting, planning, implementation, and evaluation" as PSEL Standard 10(d) requires.

Moral Values Dimension

The moral values dimension of continuous improvement interweaves with the preceding two dimensions of instrumental methods and social relations. The question of values and valuing is fundamental to any effort that uses the term "improvement," whether or not these values are made explicit. Values immediately enter the conversation as soon as you ask, "Improvement for what? Improvement for whom? Who benefits? Who loses?" When you ask those questions, you are in the territory of discerning moral values. Chapter 4, "Equity-Oriented Continuous Improvement," provides a rich foundation for the value orientation that we take in this volume, one that foregrounds equity and social justice as the imperative moral foundation for the improvement work that we do as educators. The grounding in values of equity and social justice offers the foundation for leaders to be effective in their search to "make school more effective for each student, teachers and staff, families and the community," as PSEL Standard 10(a) insists.

The emphasis on equity and social justice as keys to defining improvement and making schools more effective for all demands something more of individual and collective agency, which we highlighted in the preceding section. It demands *moral agency*, the ability to act toward those ends that realize, "what is good, right, true, and beautiful – that shape current and possible meaning making, positioning, and relations" (Bang et al., 2016, p. 29). When you complete a school improvement plan to meet the requirements laid down by your district and then put it back up on the shelf until the next annual cycle, you are neglecting your moral agency as an educator to use the planning process itself as a means of nurturing and sustaining moral agency throughout your school. Moral agency entails making the hard decisions that enable all students to thrive, especially those who have been historically and systematically marginalized by our existing approaches to education.

CONCLUSION

This volume is an attempt to provide current and aspiring leaders scaffolds for nurturing and sustaining improvement mindsets and organizational cultures of improvement that foster continuous organizational learning and improvement. We have identified three dimensions of continuous improvement and illustrated these dimensions by drawing connections with the elements of PSEL Standard 10. Each dimension maps onto each of the standard elements. Subsequent chapters detail connections across both the NELP and PSEL standards with specific aspects of continuous improvement.

Take a moment to organize your thinking related to continuous improvement. How might you complete Action Inventory 2.2?

SUPPORT MATERIAL

ACTION INVENTORY 2.2 GETTING ORIENTED TO CONTINUOUS IMPROVEMENT

What is continuous improvement?	What improvement isn't continuous improvement?
Examples of continuous improvement	Current wonderings or questions you hope are answered throughout the book?

Continuous Improvement

NELP and PSEL Connection Box for Educational Leadership Faculty

Effective educational leaders act as agents of continuous improvement to promote each student's academic success and well-being.

– PSEL Standard 10: School Improvement

BIBLIOGRAPHY

Bang, M., Faber, L., Gurneau, J., Marin, A., & Soto, C. (2016). Community-based design research: Learning across generations and strategic transformations of institutional relations toward axiological innovations. *Mind, Culture, and Activity, 23*(1), 28–41. https://doi.org/10.1080/10749039.2015.1087572

Biag, M., & Sherer, D. (2021). Getting better at getting better: Improvement dispositions in education. *Teachers College Record, 123*(4), 1–42. https://doi.org/10.1177/016146812112300402

Bryk, A. S. (2010). Organizing schools for improvement. *Phi Delta Kappan, 91*(7), 23–30.

Bryk, A. S. (2020). *Improvement in action: Advancing quality in America's schools.* Harvard Education Press.

Bryk, A. S., Gomez, L. M., Grunow, A., & Lemahieu, P. G. (2015). *Learning to improve: How America's schools can get better at getting better.* Harvard Education Press.

Bryk, A. S., & Schneider, B. L. (2002). *Trust in schools.* Russell Sage Foundation.

Bryk, A. S., Sebring, P. B., Allensworth, E., Easton, J. Q., & Luppescu, S. (2010). *Organizing schools for improvement: Lessons from Chicago.* University of Chicago Press.

Coburn, C. E. (2003). Rethinking scale: Moving beyond numbers to deep and lasting change. *Educational Researcher, 32*(6), 3–12. https://doi.org/10.3102/0013189X032006003

Cohen-Vogel, L., Harrison, C., & Griffard, M. R. (2019). *Organizing for continuous improvement in education.* Oxford Bibliographies. https://doi.org/10.1093/obo/9780199756810-0229

Cuban, L. (1984). *How teachers taught: Constancy and change in American classrooms, 1890–1980.* Longman.

Datnow, A., & Park, V. (2012). Conceptualizing policy implementation: Large-scale reform in an era of complexity. In *Handbook of education policy research* (pp. 348–361). Routledge.

Dewey, J. (1916). *Democracy and education: An introduction to the philosophy of education.* Macmillan.

Eddy-Spicer, D., & Gomez, L. (2023). Accomplishing meaningful equity. In D. J. Peurach, J. L. Russell, L. Cohen-Vogel, & W. Penuel (Eds.), *The foundational handbook on improvement research in education* (pp. 89–110). Rowman & Littlefield.

Edmondson, A. C. (2019). *The fearless organization: Creating psychological safety in the workplace for learning, innovation, and growth.* John Wiley & Sons.

Every Student Succeeds Act, 20 U.S.C. § 6301 (2015). www.congress.gov/bill/114th-congress/senate-bill/1177

Fishman, B., & Penuel, W. (2018). Design-based implementation research. In *International handbook of the learning sciences* (pp. 393–400). Routledge.

Ford, T. G. (2014). Trust, control, and comprehensive school reform: Investigating growth in teacher-teacher relational trust in success for all schools. In D. Van Maele, P. B. Forsyth, & M. Van Houtte (Eds.), *Trust and school life* (pp. 229–258). Springer. https://doi.org/10.1007/978-94-017-8014-8_11

Gutiérrez, K. D., & Jurow, A. S. (2016). Social design experiments: Toward equity by design. *Journal of the Learning Sciences, 25*(4), 565–598. https://doi.org/10.1080/10508406.2016.1204548

Hilton, K., & Anderson, A. (2018). *IHI psychology of change framework to advance and sustain improvement.* Institute for Healthcare Improvement. www.ihi.org/resources/Pages/IHIWhitePapers/IHIPsychology-of-Change-Framework.aspx

Hinnant-Crawford, B. N. (2020). *Improvement science in education: A primer.* Meyers Education Press.

Improving America's Schools Act, P.L. 103–382 (1994).

Ishimaru, A. M., & Bang, M. (2022). Solidarity-driven codesign. In *The foundational handbook on improvement research in education* (p. 383).

Langley, G. J., Moen, R. D., Nolan, K. M., Nolan, T. W., Norman, C. L., & Provost, P. L. (2009). *The improvement guide: A practical approach to enhancing organizational performance* (2nd ed.). Jossey-Bass.

LeMahieu, P. G., Bryk, A. S., Grunow, A., & Gomez, L. M. (2017). Working to improve: Seven approaches to improvement science in education. *Quality Assurance in Education, 25*(1), 2–4. https://doi.org/doi:10.1108/QAE-12-2016-0086

Little, J. W., & McLaughlin, M. W. (1993). *Teachers' work: Individuals, colleagues, and contexts.* Teachers College Press.

Moolenaar, N. M., Sleegers, P. J. C., & Daly, A. J. (2012). Teaming up: Linking collaboration networks, collective efficacy, and student achievement. *Teaching and Teacher Education, 28*(2), 251–262. https://doi.org/https://doi.org/10.1016/j.tate.2011.10.001

Murphy, J., & Bleiberg, J. F. (2019). *School turnaround policies and practices in the US: Learning from failed school reform*. Springer.

No Child Left Behind (NCLB) Act of 2001, Pub. L. No. 107–110, § 101, Stat. 1425 (2002).

O'Day, J. A., & Smith, M. S. (2016). Quality and equality in American education: Systemic problems, systemic solutions. In *The dynamics of opportunity in America: Evidence and perspectives* (pp. 297–358).

Park, S., Hironaka, S., Carver, P., & Nordstrum, L. (2013). *Continuous improvement in education*. http://admin.issuelab.org/permalink/resource/15280

Penuel, W. R., Riedy, R., Barber, M. S., Peurach, D. J., LeBouef, W. A., & Clark, T. (2020). Principles of collaborative education research with stakeholders: Toward requirements for a new research and development infrastructure. *Review of Educational Research, 90*(4), 627–674. https://doi.org/10.3102/0034654320938126

Perkins, D. N., Jay, E., & Tishman, S. (1993). Beyond abilities: A dispositional theory of thinking. *Merrill-Palmer Quarterly, 39*(1), 1–21.

Peurach, D. J., Foster, A. T., Lyle, A. M., & Seeker, E. R. (2022). Democratizing educational innovation and improvement: The policy contexts of improvement research in education. In D. J. Peurach, J. L. Russell, L. Cohen-Vogel, & W. Penuel (Eds.), *The foundational handbook on improvement research in education* (pp. 211–240). Rowman & Littlefield.

Peurach, D. J., Russell, J. L., Cohen-Vogel, L., & Penuel, W. R. (Eds.). (2022). *The foundational handbook on improvement research in education*. Rowman and Littlefield.

Reardon, S. F., Weathers, E. S., Fahle, E. M., Jang, H., & Kalogrides, D. (2019). *Is separate still unequal? New evidence on school segregation and racial academic achievement gaps (Rep.)*. Center for Education Policy Analysis, Stanford University. http://cepa.stanford.edu/wp19-06

Rowan, B., Correnti, R., Miller, R. J., & Camburn, E. M. (2009). School improvement by design: Lessons from a study of comprehensive school reform programs. In G. Sykes, B. L. Schneider, D. N. Plank, & T. G. Ford (Eds.), *Handbook of education policy research* (pp. 637–651). Routledge; American Educational Research Association.

Russell, J., Bryk, A., Dolle, J., Gomez, L., Lemahieu, P., & Grunow, A. (2017). A framework for the initiation of networked improvement communities. *Teachers College Record, 119*(6).

Smylie, M. A. (2010). *Continuous school improvement*. Corwin Press.

Stevenson, I., & Weiner, J. M. (2021). *The strategy playbook for educational leaders: Principles and processes*. Routledge.

Westhorp, G. (2014). *Realist impact evaluation: An introduction*. Overseas Development Institute. www.odi.org/sites/odi.org.uk/files/odi-assets/publications-opinion-files/9138.pdf

Yurkofsky, M. M., Peterson, A. J., Mehta, J. D., Horwitz-Willis, R., & Frumin, K. M. (2020). Research on continuous improvement: Exploring the complexities of managing educational change. *Review of Research in Education, 44*(1), 403–433. https://doi.org/10.3102/0091732x20907363

Yurkofsky, M. M., & Peurach, D. J. (2023). The paradox of leading amidst uncertainty: Maintaining balance on an unstable beam. *Journal of Educational Administration*. (Advance online). https://doi.org/10.1108/JEA-09-2022-0168

CHAPTER 3

Enacting Leadership Through Continuous Improvement

Chapter Highlights

1) Leadership through improvement science provides a process for making schools effective and equitable.
2) Through continuous improvement, leaders set the direction for the organization, build relationships and trust, develop professional capacity, secure accountability, and address inequities.
3) Improvement science aligns with turnaround leadership but pushes leaders to be strategic in contrast to encouraging unrealistic timelines for change.
4) Improvement science should encourage (a) collaborating on a team; (b) empathizing and teacher, student, and community voice; (c) seeking and valuing multiple perspectives and user experience; (d) asking questions, observing, curiosity, and challenging bias; (e) focusing collective efforts to analyze, interpret, refine, reframe, work past assumptions, identify core issues, and make meaning to define problems of practice; (f) redefining data collection and analysis for improvement through PDSA cycles; and (g) gathering feedback, reflecting, revising, refining, learning, and moving forward.

CHAPTER OVERVIEW

This chapter explains how engaging in improvement science holds the potential for enacting successful leadership practices (Hitt & Tucker, 2016; Leithwood, 2012) linked to school improvement (Leithwood et al., 2004; Grissom et al., 2021). The implementation of systematic approaches to quality improvement and the core

DOI: 10.4324/9781003389279-4

principles of improvement science can support the development of many of the leadership practices that research has identified as important for cultivating student success and school improvement (Bryk et al., 2015). As Lewis and Diamond (2015) highlight, we know a lot about what to change in schools, but we are lacking how to implement such changes. Improvement science holds the potential to inform what we know about leadership with how we improve schools.

INTRODUCTION: LEADING IMPROVEMENT OR BEING LED BY IMPROVEMENT?

As a leader, you have been involved with and made an array of decisions. Some were minor (e.g., what block of time should you dedicate to checking emails), others were high stakes (e.g., how should you speak with a veteran teacher needing to change their practice, should a student be suspended for an infraction, how to ensure all students have access to grade-level content during a pandemic). Principals and other school leaders face daunting decisions every day, and those decisions hold important consequences for everyone in the school.

We know a great deal about the leadership practices that most likely lead to the best outcomes for students and for schools overall. Unfortunately, we know less about *how* a leader carries out improvement practices during daily decision-making and actions. The improvement science process offers insight into how to develop and implement the practices tied to school success (Bryk et al., 2015).

Core principles, processes, and tools of improvement science are actionable ways to develop and perform the leadership practices necessary for transformative (e.g., Shields, 2017) and transformational (e.g., Leithwood) school improvement. Improvement science processes hold the potential to cultivate research-based leadership practices directly related to school improvement, including "school turnaround practices"[1] practices believed to make marked improvements in a school's trajectory. By implementing improvement science in their schools with integrity to the process, leaders like you can develop leadership practices that researchers and practitioners find effective to nurture equity-centered school improvement. This chapter maps the correspondence between leadership practices and dispositions aligned with the NELP and PSEL standards with the practices and dispositions of improvement science (Figure 3.1).

WHY LEADERSHIP?

Before launching into the standards, let's first get clear about a foundational notion – why leaders matter. We focus on leadership because without the presence of an effective leader no school has undergone large-scale improvement (Duke, 2004). Researchers have established leadership matters for school success and effectiveness based on various outcomes, including, but not limited to

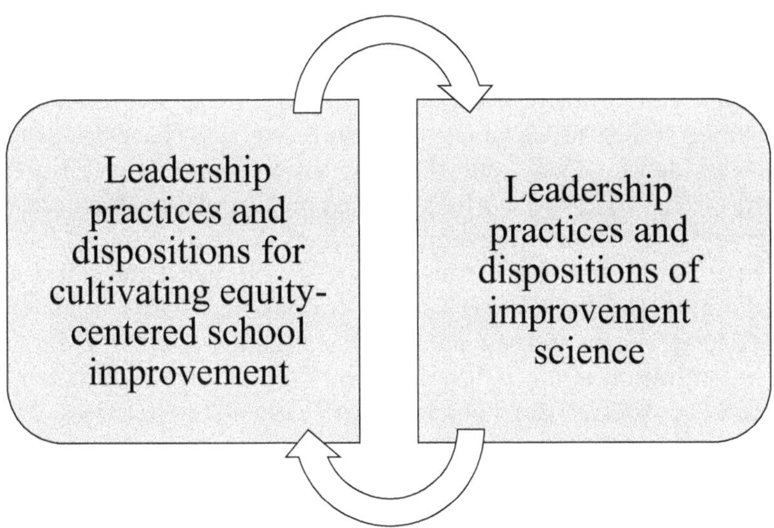

Figure 3.1 The Relationship Between Leadership Practice and Improvement Science.

Source: Created by author.

student learning (Grissom et al., 2021). Although effective leadership is essential in all schools, leadership effects are usually the largest in those schools with the greatest need for change (Murphy & Meyers, 2008). Until recently, researchers estimated that principals' (direct and indirect) effects on student learning accounted for about a quarter of total school effects. This is second only to classroom instruction (Leithwood et al., 2004). An updated estimate provided by Grissom and colleagues (2021) emphasized that leaders may be more important than previously suggested due to the impact a principal has on each student versus the impact of an individual teacher who serves fewer students. They found that replacing an ineffective principal with an effective principal could lead to three additional months of student learning.

Successful leadership practices are the actions leaders, such as principals or superintendents, or leadership teams, including assistant principals, teacher leaders (e.g., deans, department chairs), take that result in supportive working conditions, a healthy school climate, high-quality instruction, strategic resource management and decision-making, and student learning and engagement (Grissom et al., 2021; Hitt & Tucker, 2016; Leithwood, 2012). Successful leadership practices increase student learning and/or are tied to student outcomes through other factors, including teacher-level factors such as (a) better instruction (PSEL and NELP Standard Four); (b) collective efficacy; (c) teacher working relationships; (d) teacher commitment; and (e) teacher retention and student-level factors, such as (f) student engagement (PSEL Five and Eight and NELP Standard Five); and (g) cultural responsiveness (PSEL Five, Three, and Eight and NELP Standards Three and Five) (Cosner & Jones, 2016; Hitt & Meyers, 2018; Hitt & Tucker, 2016; Khalifa et al., 2016; Louis et al., 2010; Supovitz et al., 2010).

SUCCESSFUL SCHOOL LEADERSHIP PRACTICES

Successful leadership practices for school improvement have been the topic of evidence-based studies as well as reviews synthesizing a broad body of research. Some reviews identified key leadership dispositions and actions (Hitt & Tucker, 2016; Leithwood, 2012) while others focused on the relationship between effective leadership and school improvement (Bryk et al., 2010; Hitt & Meyers, 2018; Murphy et al., 2006, Murphy & Meyers, 2008). Leithwood and colleagues spent decades defining the most effective transformational school leadership practices for positive school and student outcomes (Leithwood, 2012; Leithwood et al., 2010a; Leithwood et al., 2010b; Leithwood et al., 2004; Louis et al., 2010). This synthesis of successful school and district leadership practices was adopted by the province of Ontario, Canada, called the Ontario Leadership Framework (OLF), anchoring the Ministry of Education's definition of high-quality leadership for school improvement. Leithwood's research served as a key component of a recently developed leadership framework synthesized by Hitt and Tucker (2016). We focus on the OLF and the Hitt and Tucker framework connecting leadership for school improvement and improvement science processes. Additionally, we include equity-focused leadership frameworks that more explicitly advance equity such as culturally responsive leadership (Khalifa, 2018), social justice leadership (Theoharis, 2007), and transformative leadership (Shields, 2017).

The research base supporting the OLF and the Hitt and Tucker framework influenced the development of the PSEL and NELP standards (Young & Anderson, 2020). We use the NELP and PSEL standards to structure our discussion of leadership practices and improvement science processes. Specifically, this chapter examines

- PSEL and NELP Standards One, that draw upon research on leadership practices around setting direction (Leithwood, 2012) through mission, vision, and continuous improvement.
- PSEL Six and Seven and NELP Standard Seven focus on the research around leadership practices that develop people and relationships (Leithwood, 2012) through professional capacity and professional community, including a focus on relational trust.
- PSEL Standard Ten that draws on research around the importance of leadership practices that secure accountability (Leithwood, 2012) through a data-driven, continuous improvement approach.
- PSEL and NELP Standards Three around securing equity, inclusion, and cultural responsiveness, which are not explicitly found in either the Leithwood or Hitt and Tucker frameworks but are essential to improvement (Khalifa et al., 2016; Shields, 2017; Theoharis, 2009).

The remainder of the chapter explores these standards in turn, discussing the research foundations and drawing connections with improvement science processes.

ENACTING LEADERSHIP THROUGH IMPROVEMENT SCIENCE

A commitment to a continuous improvement methodology, such as improvement science, cultivates research-based leadership practices at the building level. Leadership practices are leadership behaviors and actions that result in more successful schools. They are not inherent to or predicated on specific leadership traits; instead, they are learned (Leithwood, 2012). Think about Ava Jackson. She grew over the years as a principal, constantly learning new things about herself and new ways to lead. With attention and work, leaders can continuously improve their practice because practice and skills can be learned. This section summarizes standards-aligned, research-based leadership practices, including practices emphasized in the "turnaround" leadership literature. We describe leadership practices and connect the practices to improvement science, including connections to the core principles of improvement. We conclude with a set of recommendations for practicing leaders. Figure 3.2 provides a summary of the upcoming section.

Setting Direction: PSEL Ten and NELP Standard One – Mission, Vision, and Continuous Improvement

One of the most heralded leadership practices related to school improvement is setting direction. Leadership practices that set direction ensure a shared purpose across the organization (Hitt & Meyers, 2018; Hitt & Tucker, 2016; Leithwood, 2012; Supovitz et al., 2010). A robust body of literature (Young & Anderson, 2020) suggests that the school's purpose, often conveyed as a mission and vision, must be developed collectively, stated clearly, and communicated with all stakeholders (Hitt & Meyers, 2018; Hitt & Tucker, 2016; Public Impact, 2008, 2016). Leaders must gather varied perspectives by actively asking questions and acting upon stakeholder feedback (Hitt & Tucker, 2016). That feedback should be reflected in the vision. The use of that feedback should be transparent when sharing the vision and mission with the school community.

Evidence suggests that leaders must move beyond an aspirational vision to a focused, specific, and shared vision with goals measured by both progress and outcome measures (Cosner & Jones, 2016; Hitt & Meyers, 2018; Hitt & Tucker, 2016; Jackson et al., 2018; Robinson et al., 2008). Progress measures are data points to track advancement toward specific goals, and outcomes measures are data points to determine when goals are met. Improvement-focused leaders use those vision-aligned organizational goals to make data-informed action plans that address persisting problems within the school (Duke et al., 2013; Hitt & Meyers, 2018; Hitt & Tucker, 2016; Public Impact, 2008, 2016).

To have a shared vision and to successfully implement an action plan, a leader establishes common expectations and mental models throughout the school or establishes common ways of defining successful teaching and learning upholding equity, diversity, inclusion, and social justice (Finnigan, 2011; Foldy et al., 2008; Leithwood, 2012). You can use Action Inventory 3.1 to help you reflect on your school's vision and mission. Setting direction ensures an actionable vision that

<table>
<tr><th>Core Principle</th><th>Turnaround Practices</th><th>IS Processes/Actions</th><th>IS Tools</th><th>Leadership Practices</th></tr>
<tr><td>Make the work problem-specific and user-centered.</td><td>• Gather and act upon stakeholder feedback
• Help staff personally see and feel the problems students face
• Actively ask questions and listen to the answers
• Time commitment to problem identification and full cycles of joint learning</td><td rowspan="3">1) Understand the problem. Delve deeply into multiple perspectives and user experience. Ask questions, observe, be curious, and challenge bias.
2) Focus collective efforts to analyze, interpret, refine, reframe, work past assumptions, identify core issues, and make meaning to define problems of practice.
3) Generate change ideas and build prototypes to explore possible paths towards solutions.</td><td rowspan="3">▪ Empathy interviews
▪ Process and system map(s)
▪ Review of scholarly research
▪ Practice expertise (analogous settings)
▪ Root cause analysis (e.g., affinity maps, fishbone diagram)
▪ Data protocols</td><td rowspan="3">Setting Direction
o Focused, specific, and shared vision
o Collective purpose
o Common mental models
o Action plan based on data
Developing People
o Foster adult learning
o Encourage collective responsibility for learning
o Provide individualized support
o Require staff to change—not optional
o High levels of collaboration and communication
o Structures and opportunities for teachers to collaborate
Securing Accountability
o High expectations for students and faculty
o Regular reflection
o Measure and report frequently
Securing Equity
o Focuses on equitable practices and structures.
o Disrupt systems of inequity</td></tr>
<tr><td>Variation in performance is the core problem to address.</td><td>• Challenge the status quo and reflect on practice</td></tr>
<tr><td>See the system that produces the current outcomes.</td><td>• Systemic strategist
• Need based allocation of resources
• Implement high leverage strategies</td></tr>
<tr><td>Anchor practice improvement in disciplined inquiry.</td><td>• Analyzes school & student performance data.
• Measures and reports progress frequently and publicly
• Funnels more time & money into tactics that get results; halts unsuccessful tactics</td><td>4) Experiment with potential solutions, test prototypes, and learn from every iteration</td><td rowspan="2">▪ Aim statement
▪ Outcomes measures
▪ PDSA cycles
▪ Driver measures
▪ Process measures</td><td rowspan="2"></td></tr>
<tr><td>We cannot improve at scale what we cannot measure.</td><td>• Acts in relentless pursuit of goals not just progress</td><td>5) Gather feedback, reflect, revise, refine, learn, and move forward</td></tr>
</table>

Figure 3.2 Improvement Science Principles, Turnaround Practices, Processes, Tools, and Leadership Practices.

Source: Created by author.

ACTION INVENTORY 3.1 SENSEMAKING THE VISION AND MISSION

While this is an activity you could do individually, we recommend completing it with others on your improvement team.

1. What is the vision of your organization (e.g., school, district)?
2. What is the mission of your organization (e.g., school, district)?
3. In each, underline or star the key parts (i.e., the core terms, non-negotiables) of the vision and mission.
4. Fill out the chart:

Underlined/Starred Term in Vision and/ or Vision	Aligned current school efforts	How aligned effort is formally assessed (e.g., measured qualitatively or quantitatively)?	Notes related to future efforts and measures:	Identify areas of leadership alignment to Figure 3.2 A. Core Principles B. Turnaround Practices C. DI Process/Actions D. DI Tools E. Leadership Practices
Example: belonging	homeroom pack (includes leadership development for students and mentoring)	end-of-year questionnaire (Likert scale)	Gather narratives from students, teachers, and teachers	A. User Centered B. Gather and use feedback C. Experiment with potential solutions D. Empathy interviews E. Focus on equitable structures

creates common expectations to be communicated widely throughout the school community. Successful leaders inspire all key stakeholders, including families and the community, to support major changes guided by the vision, mission, and goals, (Hitt & Meyers, 2018; Hitt & Tucker, 2016; Public Impact, 2008, 2016). A leader, both in turnaround spaces and not, must act as an "architect" of change by being a systemic strategist (Candelarie & Korach, 2018). A systemic strategist regularly conducts needs assessments and inquiry cycles to determine the areas in the system, including both the areas of strength and areas of opportunity, that need to be addressed. They implement high-leverage strategies that result in improvement in that system, as measured by data (Hitt & Meyers, 2018; Jackson et al., 2018). Systemic leadership practices ensure a needs-based allocation of resources, including funding, staffing, and support (Cosner & Jones, 2016; Hitt & Tucker, 2016; Robinson et al., 2008). By having a systems lens, the leader aligns resources to needs and strategies.

You might take a position as a principal of a school. During those first few months, you spend time getting to know teachers, students, and the community. A vision for the school preceded you, and you are committed to understanding that vision and seeing if it still resonates with the school community. You may conduct one-on-one conversations with teachers asking them what they like about the school, what they see as the visions, and what they see as priorities. You might recruit your leadership team to help you with this effort. Together, you capture the highlights of the responses you hear in brief memos. You might conduct a listening tour with families by either inviting them into the school to provide input or going to their homes and neighborhoods to gather an understanding of their experiences at the school. You might create a short survey and ask students to provide responses to a few prompts about what is important to them in a school.

With this information, you and your leadership team could convene, along with teacher leaders and community leaders, to share summaries of collected data. Or, as a group, you might use a data protocol to unearth insights. Then, you would collectively update your vision statement. You would share that vision with the community in a newsletter, at family nights, in faculty meetings, and on the website. You create a forum for feedback and maybe even provide additional information on how you developed the vision statement.

Once that vision is in place and reflects stakeholder feedback, you will want to set improvement goals for the year, even upcoming years. This small set of three to five goals should align with the vision. If the vision includes the expectation of project-based learning for all students, you need to set goals to develop teachers' pedagogical practices with a focus on culturally responsive education and project-based learning, unpack standards and construct a curriculum that covers those standards with a focus on projects and mastery, and create structures for collaboration between and across grade levels. Then think about the data you needed to see if progress is made toward pedagogical capability, standards-based education, and professional collaboration. Finally, allocate financial, time, and human resources to implementing that vision and reviewing progress toward your goals. The number of goals you set should be manageable in the timeframe (usually an academic year) and should help you focus as a school (Meyer et al., 2023).

ACTION INVENTORY 3.2 VISION TO ACTIONABLE GOALS

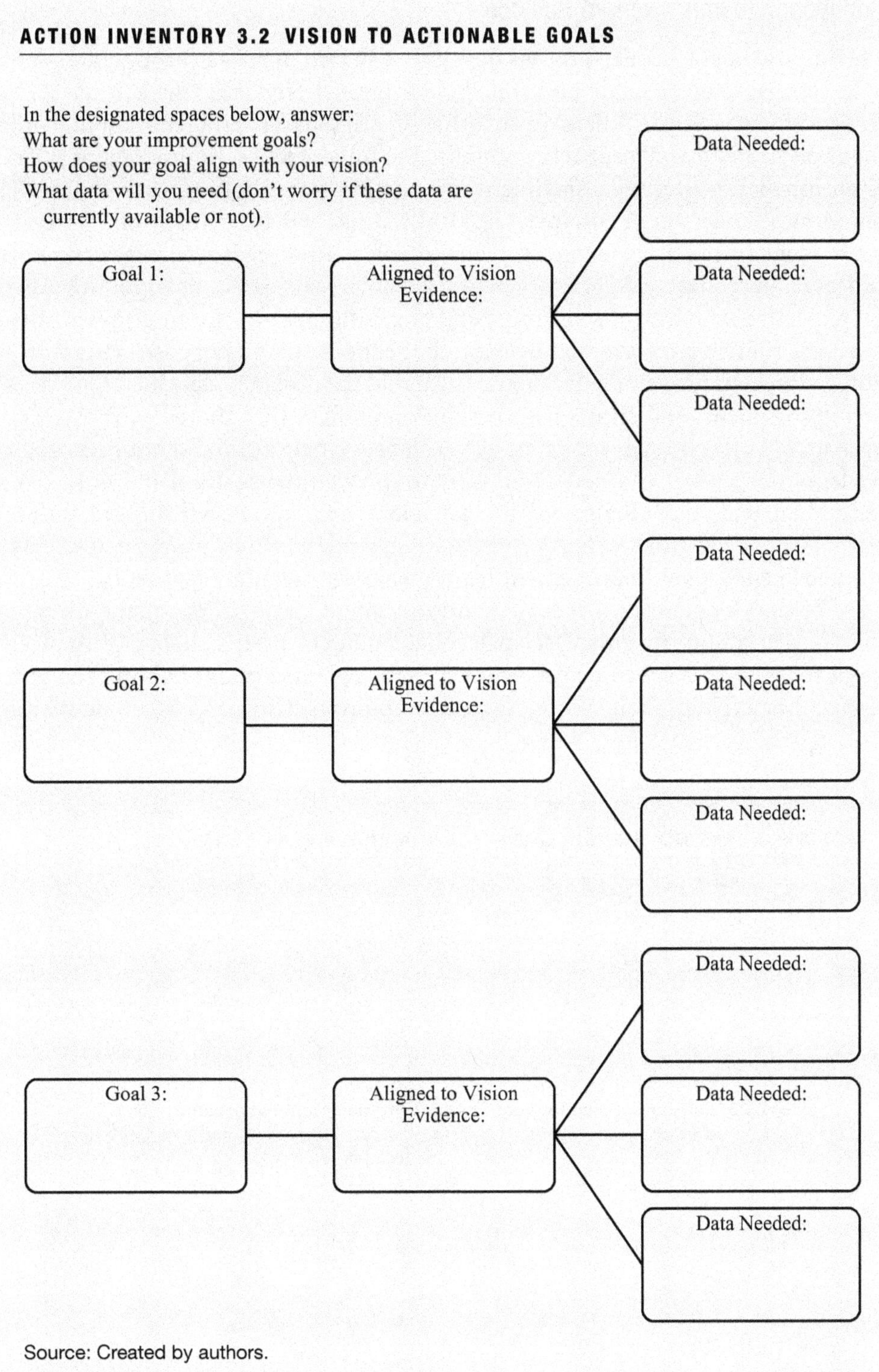

Source: Created by authors.

Connection to Improvement Science

The improvement science process develops a shared purpose through an actionable plan, aligned to goals and stakeholder or user feedback (Bryk et al., 2015). Improvement science differs from other inquiry-based problem-solving in its focus on strategy and feedback, as opposed to linear tactics. Improvement science is an interactive, iterative, flexible way to action plan aligning with short-cycle planning (Stevenson & Weiner, 2020). Leaders, and their team of improvers, must identify precisely what problem to solve. Root cause analyses based on process and systems mapping, reviewing scholarly research, recognizing practical expertise in analogous settings, and engaging in empathy interviews are all practices that help inform and develop the school's shared purpose. This work is done with an improvement team to ensure that the problem identification, theory or improvement, and strategies for solutions reflect that shared purpose. Look back at Ava's intentional selection of her improvement team. Sometimes when a leader builds a team, the leader will want to consider the position and skills of the individual, and you will also want to consider who might be willing and enthusiastic to engage in this work. As Ava began to work on a new problem at MHMS, she added additional improvement team members, including a parent.

The development of a theory of improvement can help to set the direction for the school. Improvement science relies on developing a theory of improvement focused on a specific problem that maps out the system holding the problem and is explicit about the goals of the improvement process, as defined by

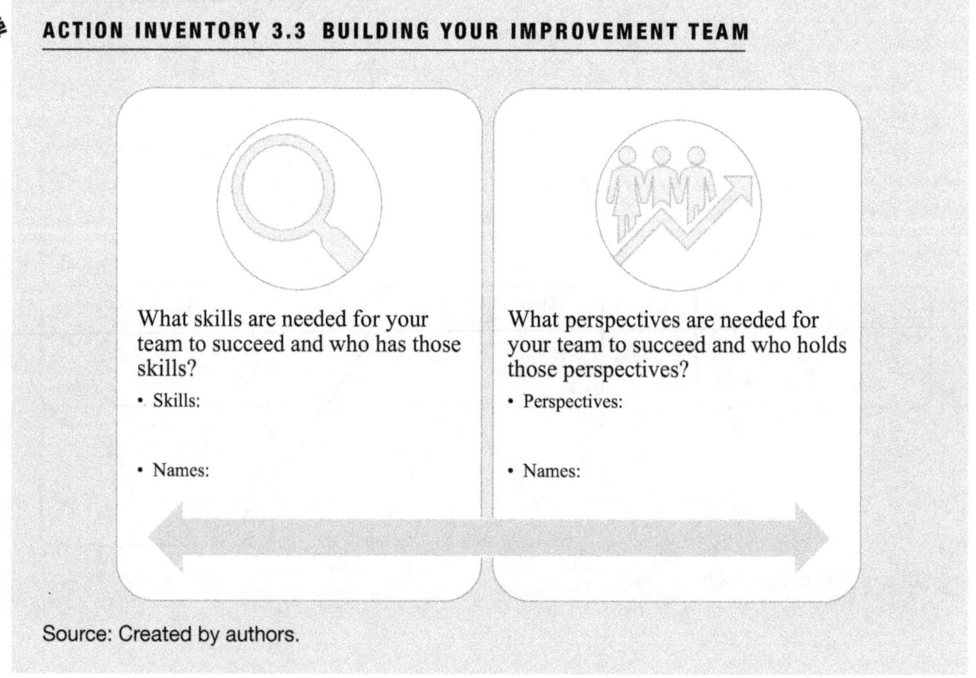

SUPPORT MATERIAL
ACTION INVENTORY 3.3 BUILDING YOUR IMPROVEMENT TEAM
What skills are needed for your team to succeed and who has those skills?
• Skills:
• Names:
What perspectives are needed for your team to succeed and who holds those perspectives?
• Perspectives:
• Names:

Source: Created by authors.

the aim and drivers. Through the process of creating and revising a theory of improvement, improvers establish a problem-specific aim that states the goal of the work and identify metrics for measuring progress toward that aim, which results in an actionable plan. The theory of improvement includes drivers, or high-leverage structures, practices, or systems that, if addressed, result in progress on the specific problem. The improvers identify metrics, or practical measures, associated with those drivers that measure the success of different actions. These actions are strategies or change ideas related to the identified drivers and the problem addressed in the aim. This theory of improvement must be based on an understanding of the problem. Through that process, common mental models are built, and common expectations are defined. Think back to when Ava and her NIC created their own survey to measure progress toward the aim of cultural responsiveness and inclusion in their classrooms and schools. This survey was informed by Khalifa's (2018) work on culturally responsive leadership and helped them created common operational definitions of what it would mean to "solve" their shared problem.

User-Centered and Problem-Specific

One core principle of improvement science argues that problem-solving is user-centered and problem-specific, centering the importance of feedback and shared purpose. Users need to be engaged throughout the process, gathering data while emphasizing user engagement throughout the improvement process: (a) in empathy interviews or other empathy exercises like empathy mapping, (b) through gathering feedback as change ideas are being scaled up and shared across a network of classrooms or schools, and (c) by surfacing assumptions or double-loop learning (feedforward) to inform next cycle of data gathering (Collinson & Cook, 2007). Empathy interviews ensure approaches to problem definition and problem-solving are user-centered; these data capture the experiences of users to inform the aim statement, drivers, and change ideas to address those drivers. We will discuss empathy interviews later in Chapter 6. Ava and her team created empathy interview questions for students, staff, and families to understand the experience of LGBTQ+ students at MHMS.

Engaging in empathy interviews, leaders are presented with opportunities to ask questions, get feedback, and respond (in a humble, non-defensive way). In addition to better understanding how stakeholders, such as teachers, support staff, and students, experiencing a problem, user data ensures the student perspectives are captured. Leaders help staff personally see, feel, and believe the problems students and families face, and empathy interviews do just that (Hitt & Meyers, 2018; Public Impact, 2008, 2016).

See the System

The next core principle is to see the system that produces the current outcomes. Seeing the system is part of being a "systemic strategist" (Candelarie

& Korach, 2018). Developing a theory of improvement to address a specific, identified problem relies on seeing the system and responding strategically. Leaders identify what they believe to be high-leverage strategies; this is inherent to the process of seeing the system by gathering data to define the problem and developing a theory of improvement with an aim, drivers, and change ideas. There is nothing specific about resource allocation in the improvement science process, but improvement science helps allocate resources toward a specific problem by aligning resources with the theory of improvement. Ava used her resources to hire outside community groups to support the development of change ideas.

To create improvement goals and strategies aligned with the mission and vision of the school, improvers, improvement teams, and leaders need to be able to see how the problem is "held in place" by the system (Kania et al., 2018). You need data like the interviews described earlier, as well as other types of local data, practical and research-based knowledge, and systems and process mapping (Hinnant-Crawford, 2020). Ava and her team collected equity audit data, other local data, and process mapping data that captured the experience of new families onboarding at MHMS. Ava and her NIC also read about systemic oppression, which helped them understand the need to focus on systems. These data help them to see the system. Process mapping lays out the steps connected to the problem and then identifies possible bottlenecks, redundancy, or wasted resources within that process. A systems map collects data on key aspects of the system, such as the instructional, operational, human resources, governance, student support, and information/communication systems and asks improvers to recognize challenges and identify the levels of those challenges (instructional, institutional, and system or district level). To understand the system, a leader could conduct an equity audit, a force field analysis, or other types of needs assessments that focus on multiple areas across the organization like the ones collected in a systems map. A force field analysis looks at the forces propelling a school toward its goals and the ones restraining your goals. An equity audit considers equity data from the classroom to school level across instruction, school culture, resource allocation, and other school practices and policies to understand how marginalized groups are impacted differently. These data, regardless of how you explore the system, inform a causal analysis such as affinity mapping, five whys, and fishbone diagrams. These processes help to dig deeper and identify the root causes of problems that then create a theory of improvement that identifies primary and secondary drivers based on root causes or areas for improvement to meet an overall goal or aim.

Securing Equity: PSEL and NELP Standards Three (Equity and Cultural Responsiveness)

Leaders are responsible for creating equitable structures and systems in schools (Khalifa, 2018; Galloway & Ishimaru, 2017). Leaders must disrupt systems of inequity and address the influence of structural racism on educational opportunities (Candelarie & Korach, 2018; Shields, 2017). Shields (2017) writes about the need for transformative leadership in a "VUCA" world. A VUCA world is volatile, uncertain, chaotic, and ambiguous, and it requires leaders who are prepared to face challenges by doing things differently and disrupt the current system, as well as to change the mindsets of people within the system, with an enduring focus on equity. Successful leaders reflect on existing practices to challenge the status quo by naming assumptions and biases underlying the need for improvement and designing new, more just approaches (Candelarie & Korach, 2018). This notion of equity leadership will be explored in-depth in Chapter 4 and includes critical self-reflection; comfort with leading equity conversations and equity work; a focus on

ACTION INVENTORY 3.4 VUCA REFLECTION QUESTIONS

1. What skills do you currently have that will help you lead in a VUCA world?
2. What talents do you currently have that will help you lead in a VUCA world?
3. Which colleagues have different talents than you could help you navigate a VUCA world?
4. Which colleagues have different skills than you could help you navigate a VUCA world?
5. Draft which of the three areas listed below, might you want to improve upon, what could improvement look like in that area, and is one strategy to make progress on that area?

    a. Willingness to disrupt
    b. Regular critical self-reflection
    c. Able to name assumptions of biases you hold
    d. Leading small group conversations around equity
    e. Leading large group conversations around equity
    f. Developing relationships with families
    g. Developing relationships with communities
    h. Connecting families/communities with others in the school or district

Area you want to improve upon:	What would improvement in this area look like for you?	Strategies to improve and make progress:

inclusion, disrupting oppression, and redesigning liberatory systems, structures, and practices; and listening and including families and communities (Khalifa, 2018; Galloway & Ishimaru, 2017; Shields, 2017; Theoharis, 2007).

Connection to Improvement Science

One of our colleagues regularly reminds leaders that, "Kids can't wait, y'all." The problem at the center of the improvement science process must reflect the importance of naming barriers to equity and working to dismantle those barriers. Because all students are counting on educators, all improvement work must focus on equity, and if that is not the focus, the leader must intentionally make equity and inclusion central to the vision, measure and monitor it regularly, and prioritize equity and inclusion moving forward. Improvement science asks people to uncover the underlying systems and structures leading to inequity. By infusing equity as an orientation throughout the process, from identifying and understanding the problem to spreading and scaling change ideas, promoting equity will naturally emerge from improvement.

Attend to Variation

The third core principle is the need to attend to variation in performance by determining what works (or doesn't), for whom, and under what conditions (Bryk et al., 2015). Data analysis for improvement science is configured to identify and address variation, not aggregation, by looking at the range of data, considering the outliers, or breaking data down by students, teachers, and demographics. Ava and her MHMS improvement team used equity audit data to see variation in LGBTQ+ students' opportunities at school, which resulted in revealing the LGBTQ+ disproportionality in discipline, academics, and the chronic absenteeism groups. The status quo is maintained by approaching problems in the aggregate instead of identifying variation in results. To challenge the status quo, leaders must try to understand where and why variation exists and address those specific causes. If Ava and her team had not done an equity audit that looked at the variation in student experience and outcomes, they may have missed that the LGBTQ+ community was impacted differently than other students. A leader must ensure that variation in performance is not based on variation in opportunities available to students or teaching practices that benefit or burden certain groups of students more than others. To identify inequitable processes and structures, it is imperative to understand what is (or is not) working, for whom, and under what conditions to identify groups that may be marginalized by existing systems and structures and then orient improvement toward creating more equitable processes and structures (Bryk et al., 2015; Hinnant-Crawford, 2020).

Developing People and Relationships: PSEL Standards Six and Seven and NELP Standard Seven (Professional Capacity of School Personnel, Professional Community for Teachers and Staff, and Building Professional Capacity)

People are the core of schools. The way people are cultivated to teach, learn, lead, and improve is essential to school success. A successful leader develops faculty and staff in service of an instructional vision to meet the needs of each student and to ensure learning growth and outcomes (Cosner & Jones, 2016; Hitt & Tucker, 2016; Jackson et al., 2018; Leithwood, 2012; Public Impact, 2008, 2016). Professional capacity and a professional community are supported by relational trust and fostering collective responsibility. These concepts are discussed in detail in Chapter 9.

Professional Capacity

A school leader must develop the teachers' capacity, which in turn has the most direct impact on student learning and well-being. If teachers and staff feel efficacious and supported by the leader, they tend to be better educators, stay in positions longer, and feel better about workplace conditions (Grissom et al., 2021). Successful leaders (a) provide models of best practices and beliefs (Hitt & Meyers, 2018; Hitt & Tucker, 2016; Leithwood et al., 2010; Public Impact, 2008, 2016), (b) foster adult learning (Leithwood, 2012; Garet et al., 2001), (c) offer intellectual stimulation (Murphy et al., 2006), and (d) provide individualized support (Hitt & Tucker, 2016). We will discuss specific professional capacity foci in greater detail in Chapter 8.

Professional Community

A leader can develop a professional culture by establishing structures and opportunities for teachers to collaborate (Hitt & Tucker, 2016). Leaders enhance collaboration and accountability and develop collective responsibility through communities of practice (Hitt & Meyers, 2018; Hitt & Tucker, 2016). These professional communities are often guided by data-informed decision-making or foci like deeper learning (Schildkamp, 2013), standards-based instruction (Gregory & Kuzmich, 2014), professional learning based on specific topics like culturally responsive pedagogy (Irby, 2021), or improvement teams (Russell et al., 2017).

Collective Responsibility

Collaboration results in sharing leadership with teachers and staff (Hitt & Meyers, 2018; Hitt & Tucker, 2016; Park et al., 2019). Research establishes the importance of developing the organization to encourage collective responsibility for learning (Hitt & Tucker, 2016). Leadership practices that encourage collective responsibility include (a) gathering staff to explore data in open, transparent meetings, (b) fostering collective leadership and teacher participation in decision-making, and

(c) ensuring time commitment to problem identification and full cycles of joint learning (Hitt & Meyers, 2018; Hitt & Tucker, 2016; Public Impact, 2008, 2016).

Relational Trust

Another important condition for improvement, related to developing people and relationships, is relational trust (Bryk et al., 2010; Bryk & Schneider, 2002; Candelarie & Korach, 2018; Hitt & Tucker, 2016). Relational trust is trust in the competence of, confidence in, and optimism about the leader and teachers (Bryk & Schneider, 2002). Trust is also about reliability, consistency, honesty, transparency, and openness (Tschannen-Moran, 2014). These are the behaviors and practices that inspire people to work together to improve. These and other leadership considerations (and tools) are explored in more detail in Chapter 8. In Bryk's and Schneider's (2002) influential research on trust in schools, they found relational trust, "fuels the multiple strands of the school change process and thereby contributes to improved student learning" (p. 121).

Connection to Improvement Science

Engaging professionals in improvement science provides the opportunity for growth and learning tied to a specific problem and the collective and collaborative approach to improvement; a leader is simultaneously learning to improve the specific problem while also learning how to approach improvement in general. Ava's EdD program was set up to teach them about leadership, helping them to recognize the problems in the school system, while also teaching them a methodology for approaching those problems. Professional learning about improvement science methods and specific strategies that address classroom-based and school-wide problems creates better instructional and educational experiences for students.

Improvement science seeks to find best practices within a school's context and to share the learning from those practices throughout the school. This process ensures members of the improvement team, as well as other relevant staff and faculty, engage in collective learning. Learning is directly relevant to daily work and specific to an identified problem; this is essential for adult learning. This approach engages each member of the improvement team in problem-solving. Beginning with gathering data to define the problem and using disciplined inquiry to solve the problem, the learning is also intellectually stimulating and meant to meet unique, individualized needs of adults and students in context. Ava and her team demonstrated a genuine interest in improving outcomes for LGBTQ+ students through unraveling the different root causes and drivers of the problem.

The existence of learning communities is enhanced through the improvement science process. Improvement science is designed to be a collaborative activity. The improvement science process relies on an improvement team working together on solving the problem. As change ideas are being tested, many members of the school community are asked to engage in the work. Improvement science distributes the responsibility to lead improvement from the sole purview of the principal to the collective purview of the entire improvement team and other key stakeholders in the school community. Think about how Ava's MHMS improvement team divided up data collection to understand the problem and then brought that information back together as they consolidated insights. That is a learning community. Sometimes, improvement science is engaged in networked improvement communities or NICs, where multiple schools address a similar problem by collectively defining their theory or improvement and sharing lessons from testing ideas throughout the network. Ava and her classmates utilized this NIC structure to share knowledge gained from their individual schools, to share learning about improvement processes, and to share each member's personal growth as an equity-oriented leader. We will cover more about NICs in Chapter 7 on spreading and scaling.

Committing to the core principles and phases of improvement, the staff is dedicated to the change effort. The improvement science process, by nature, focuses on documenting progress and including key users in the framing of the problem and determining solutions, and it encourages influential stakeholders to support change readily. The improvement science process supports joint learning through PDSA cycles and tracking progress toward the aim (Penuel et al., 2020). By the end of Ava's DiP, Marcus shared that the teachers in the building felt increased commitment to the problem and to each other from being part of the change effort in deliberate and transparent ways.

The improvement science process encourages increased belief in the competence of improvers, confidence in the work, and optimism about the improvement work by tracking success and failure along the way. Improvement science produces change reliably and consistently at scale where the team shares, respects, and addresses both failure and success; this encourages honesty. The work is done in a transparent manner to be clear about what worked, for whom, and under what conditions (Hitt & Meyers, 2018). Engaging in root cause analysis (See Chapter 5) requires staff and members of the leadership team(s) to have transparent conversations about all factors in the school's/organization's control related to a problem. Lastly, process and outcome measures are tracked, shared, and discussed; disciplined inquiry makes explicit the goals behind a change idea being tested, the goals of the test itself, and the results of the test. Time is set aside to share out on progress and to allow user feedback throughout the process; this is an open-air approach to discussing improvement. Communicating with the school community is encouraged in improvement science and is essential to building relational trust.

The improvement science process encourages risks. Testing of change ideas is built on the premise we may be "possibly wrong and definitely incomplete." A PDSA cycle is an opportunity to figure out what is working to develop sustainable change ideas. The process relies on relational trust and builds that trust, as reported by the teachers at MHMS. Reframing educator practice from always having the right answers to problems to iterating, not only solves problems but learns from the failed attempts; there is more consistency, reliability, and encouragement of honest conversations about what is and isn't working.

Securing Internal Accountability: PSEL Standard 10 (School Improvement)

Securing accountability ensures high expectations for students and faculty (Hitt & Tucker, 2016; Leithwood, 2012; Murphy et al., 2006). This accountability is not compliance-based accountability. We reframe accountability from an externally driven model that focuses disproportionately on test scores and creates punitive measures to respond to underwhelming results. This framing of accountability is more about holding yourself and those you lead to a set of high expectations and striving toward collective goals.

Leaders ensure internal accountability or make sure educators recognize that growth and improvement are central to their job (Elmore, 2005; Fullan & Quinn, 2019; Public Impact, 2008, 2016). Problem-solving is the responsibility of all leaders in the building, and the improvement team must share responsibility for the improvement process (Public Impact, 2008, 2016). Leaders must seek to solve problems that are leading to disparities in the education systems (Jackson et al., 2018; Public Impact, 2008, 2016). Accountability can be maintained through regular reflection (Public Impact, 2008, 2016). A leader should measure and collect data, personally analyze school and student performance data, and report progress frequently and publicly (Public Impact, 2008, 2016).

Successful leaders commit resources, such as time and money, to strategies that attain results while stopping committing to unsuccessful strategies (Grissom et al., 2021; Public Impact, 2008, 2016). In the scenario presented earlier in the "Setting Direction" section, the leadership and improvement team created a shared vision and aligned goals. One goal may ensure all students are demonstrating reading competency by the end of third grade based on the formative literacy assessments adopted by the district (e.g., iStation, Dynamic Indicators of Basic Early Literacy Skills [Dibels]). A leader may discover from literacy scores that the system wasn't serving Latine students effectively. To secure accountability, a leader would disaggregate the data by students, teachers, and skills and discover that Latine students are not spending enough time independently decoding grade-level passages. The leader sets expectations that all teachers provide time for 30 minutes of reading at home and then commit resources to build a library of books that are of high interest and represent diverse cultures. Then, teachers will create homework lessons that focus on reading independently and give regular checks for understanding and assessments of the skill gaps identified in the disaggregated data. The collaborative learning structure for teachers, such as a professional learning community, would provide time to reflect on the learning and share successful strategies for students who are struggling to find the time to read or need additional support.

School leaders are more effective when they communicate an ideal future state through a positive vision (Public Impact, 2008, 2016) (i.e., answering Langley's and colleague's [2009] question, How will we know a change is an improvement?). By building a systems approach to addressing problems and an action plan, leaders can consider a set of tested actions or strategies to achieve the vision (Public Impact, 2008, 2016). The turnaround literature argues early wins in the improvement process encourage ongoing engagement in the improvement effort and help to build a coalition of people who actively want to solve the problem (Hitt & Meyers, 2018; Murphy & Meyers, 2008; Meyers & Hitt, 2018; Public Impact, 2008, 2016).

Connection to Improvement Science

The improvement science process is based on a model of improvement that aims to address what is working or not and for whom (Langley et al., 2009). That process frequently measures progress through small cycle testing and exploring how those data can be used to make decisions. Improvement science offers principles and approaches for regular reflection on practice at all levels of the school. From seeking user voices and a deep dive into local data to the testing of small, change ideas, critical reflection is essential to the improvement science process. Reflection is based on data collected and at the systems level to frame the specific problem and develop an improvement aim. By tracking process and outcome data, improvement science positions leaders and leadership teams with formative, ongoing data to share with the school community and stakeholders. Consider what Peterson and Carlile (2019, p. 173) emphasize in their chapter, "Preparing School Leaders to Effectively Lead School Improvement Efforts." They write,

> When the tools and processes of these initiatives [i.e., PLCs, culturally proficient schools, PBIS] fail to result in student success, a common leadership response is to increase accountability measures, demand consistency of meeting agendas or protocols, or to otherwise blame the teachers or school leaders for the failure. A significant departure in IS, however, is that the teachers identify the goal, investigate potential interventions, collect, and interpret data on their interventions and determine whether to continue the intervention or adjust it based on their particular context. When a solution is not working, the variability of context is considered as a potential reason for failure (Lewis, 2015), rather than placing blame on the failures of teachers and school leaders.

Disciplined Inquiry

The next core principle is to anchor improvement in disciplined inquiry, or engage in quick, iterative cycles of improvement. A PDSA cycle allows improvers to learn fast, fail fast, and improve quickly (Bryk et al., 2015). Learning about the success or failure of a change idea or strategy must happen because of disciplined inquiry and inform subsequent steps. Through PDSA cycles, leaders learn what works in context and what does not. The use of PDSA cycles to test new ideas and experiment with improvement strategies is a manifestation of leadership practices identified to be effective for turnaround leaders. The PDSA process allows leaders to act, to test promising strategies that may have been successful in other contexts or new ideas that have emerged from the school stakeholders, and to determine effectiveness in the current school context.

PDSA cycles, due to their rapid nature, facilitate early wins by documenting success at a smaller scale and continue to measure that success as a change idea or improvement strategy is scaled up. To ensure resources are used effectively, ideas are tested at a small scale through these PDSA cycles before scaling and spreading (Francera & Bliss, 2011). Some ideas fall flat or fail altogether, like the "pronoun campaign" that Ava and her improvement team tried in Chapter 1. Practical measures are available to track that failure, and ineffective ideas can be abandoned before taking up too many resources. Testing ideas to adapt, adopt, or abandon new strategies and by tracking progress toward the aim, improvers can may connect their disciplined inquiry to progress toward improvement goals. The marriage of an improvement goal or aim, a plan for getting there, and measures of progress and outcomes ensure a positive vision of future school results.

Embrace Measurement

The last core principle we connect to in this chapter is the need to embrace measurement since educators cannot improve at scale what they cannot measure (Bryk et al., 2015). This analysis may be done alongside a team of leaders and teachers, but the improvement science process requires a collaborative approach to gathering and consolidating qualitative and quantitative data; the leader is part of that process, although maybe not necessarily in charge of the process (Public Impact, 2008, 2016). The improvement science process requires an aim statement, like a SMART goal, that defines a positive and successful solution to a specific problem, and it requires that the improvement process continues until that goal is met. It also emphasizes collecting a system of measures beyond measuring the outcome of the change to understanding the process, capturing the progress toward individual drivers, and identifying balancing measures, or unexpected ways in which the changes may be affecting the system. Perhaps, most importantly, the process also includes measures for individual change ideas that help the leader to understand what is working and why. All these measures may take the form of quantitative or qualitative data, helping to understand the improvement process.

Take a look at Action Inventory 3.5. The left side of the action inventory captures data from an example. Let's say a new policy requires teachers to follow a certain protocol for lesson planning. You've been told by one of your supervisors that it has been vetted and is based on best practice. However, you come to learn that it seems like the protocol is too laborious or not aligned with pedagogical training (as measured by feedback interviews with the teachers), the time taken to complete the protocol (measured by timing the teachers using the protocol) might take away from the teacher's ability to provide individualized instruction to their students (as measured by a tally sheet of time spent with students), and it results in an unintended consequence (as measured by a decrease in unit grades). Measuring the process of implementing the lesson planning protocol, the student outcomes, data from PDSA cycles, and balancing measures of unintended consequences, the protocol can be improved and iterated until it works for all teachers, under all conditions. How might you complete the right side of the action inventory to capture different types of data and data sources that can then guide your and your team's future action?

ACTION INVENTORY 3.5 USING MULTIPLE SOURCES OF DATA TO GUIDE ACTION

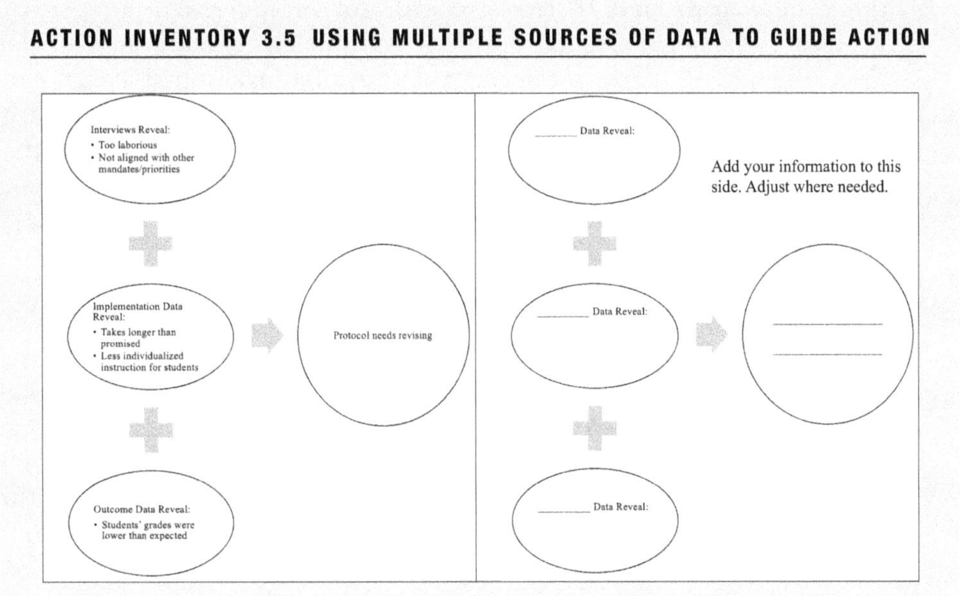

RECOMMENDATIONS

School leaders who commit to a continuous learning approach are likely to find a process that supports and amplifies effective leadership practices. They (a) collaboratively set direction for the mission, vision, and goals of a school through developing a working theory of improvement collectively, with all stakeholders; and they (b) build internal accountability and secure external accountability through disciplined inquiry to test strategies that align with the school's purpose. School leaders may also use an improvement science approach to (c) develop people and relationships through collaborative learning and a collective commitment to change. From understanding the problem and the system that surrounds it to a working theory of improvement to an open exploration of data, leaders create a culture of professional learning in which teachers feel valued and engaged. Finally, if purposeful about approaching improvement science with an equity stance and recognizing variation in the system, this approach can also serve to (d) secure equity for students that have been historically underserved in our schools, such as students of color, students with LGBTQ+ identities, students with varying religious or national backgrounds, and students with disabilities.

Here are the key recommendations for practicing leaders based on this chapter.

1) **Take a new approach to develop leadership practices.** Live the improvement principles. Leadership can be enacted through improvement science that provides a process to make schools more effective and equitable. A continuous improvement process results in better leadership practices, and ultimately, more effective, and equitable outcomes for teachers, staff, students, and the community.

2) **Take a new approach to turnaround.** Turnaround, as it is presently conceived, is rare. Turnaround practices lead to change, and improvement science aligns with many of the competencies of a turnaround leader, particularly the emphasis on improvement. However, most schools identified as needing to "turn around" are in need of more strategic, reflective, iterative change, rather than rapid improvement. Change takes time, and for a school to turn around and sustain change, there needs to be a multi-year process and commitment to embedding strategic responses into the school's system (Fullan, 2001).
3) **Take a systems approach.** Take a systems-thinking approach: learn fast, and create feedback loops (e.g., PDSA cycles) to ensure transparency and collective responsibility for change. Drastic disruption puts organizations at even greater risk (Hitt & Meyers, 2018; Murphy & Meyers, 2008; Meyers & Smylie, 2017). Strategic, situational, and incremental change is more effective. It is not enough to state a vision. Improvers must tightly align the vision to the improvement process and create an actionable plan that considers the current and ideal state of the organization. An improver can be a "systemic strategist" and architect of change instead of an "impromptu responder" trying to build student academic success and well-being in the absence of a plan.
4) **Take a new approach to collective learning.** Improvement science encourages (a) working collaboratively on a team; (b) forefronting empathy and teacher, student, and community voice; (c) delving deeply into multiple perspectives and user experience; (d) asking questions, observing, being curious, and challenging bias; (e) focusing collective efforts to analyze, interpret, refine, reframe, work past assumptions, identify core issues, and make meaning to define the problem of practice; (f) redefining data collection and analysis for improvement through PDSA cycles; and (g) gathering feedback, reflect, revise, refine, learn, and move forward. A leader needs to make space for this learning to take place.
5) **Take a new approach to accountability.** Simply increasing the pressure on educators is unlikely to bring about real improvements (Mintrop & Sunderman, 2009; Mintrop & Trujillo, 2005). Using data to plan and implement improvement leads to stronger outcomes than using data to hold individual educators accountable. Lead to learn and to improve, not just evaluate. By determining an aim or set of goals to track within the context of a theory of improvement, the focus shifts from the outcomes to the strategy for achieving those outcomes.

CONCLUSION

Improvement science is worth pursuing in the ongoing quest for school improvement. We suggest many ways the process could encourage effective leadership practices for all leaders as well as those leaders who feel the pressure of "turnaround" leadership.

ACTION INVENTORY 3.6 APPLYING THE KEY RECOMMENDATION

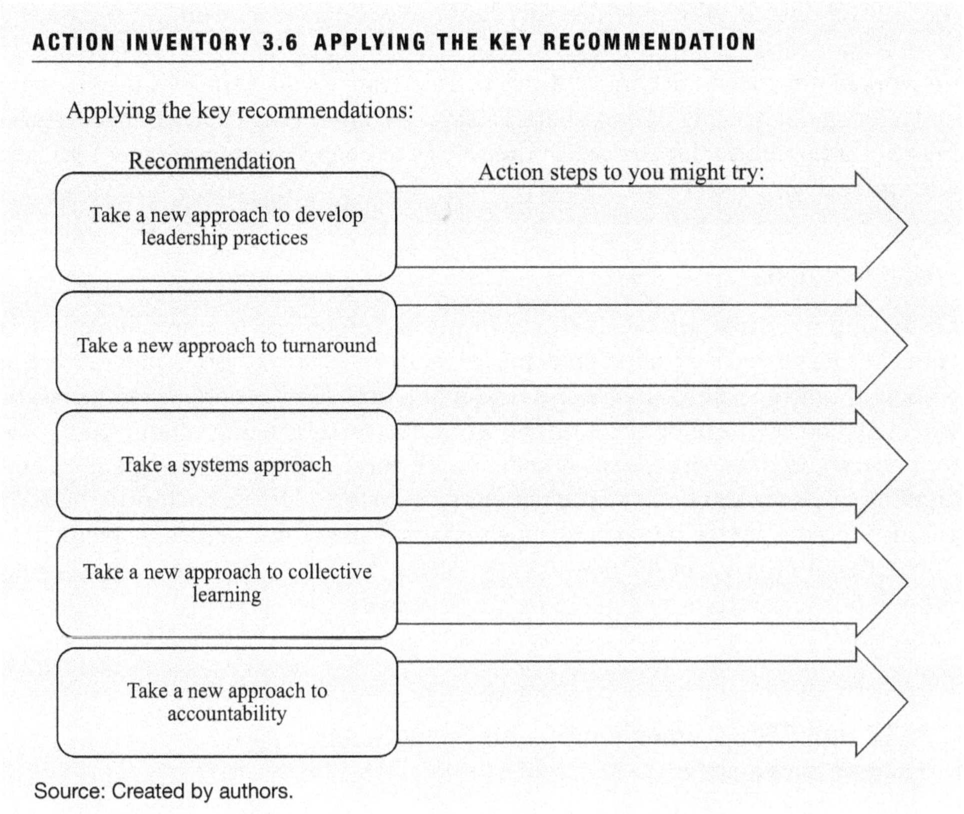

Applying the key recommendations:
Recommendation
Action steps to you might try:
Take a new approach to develop leadership practices
Take a new approach to turnaround
Take a systems approach
Take a new approach to collective learning
Take a new approach to accountability

Source: Created by authors.

Moral Values

Schools need effective leaders to facilitate the improvement of teaching and learning in service of equity. Leaders are responsible for creating a vision and mission, developing people, building relationships and trust, securing equity, and ensuring accountability. As leaders, rethinking accountability through continuous improvement by focusing on systems, leadership development, and collective learning, leads to lasting change instead of sporadic reform.

Instrumental Methods

Embedded in the core principles, processes, and tools of improvement science are many of the effective leadership practices missing from many unsuccessful improvement initiatives. The improvement science process is responsive to what we know about improvement and to facilitate leadership practices or actions that lead to improvement is incumbent on leaders clearly defining the process. Members of the organization need to learn the process and apply it authenticity to the process (Bryk et al., 2015). Learning and doing improvement science depends upon (a) leadership dispositions, (b) existing school climate and working conditions, (c) district and school culture (e.g., does it allow for failure, does it allow for slowing down to accelerate learning), (d) existing mental models about improvement and student learning, (e) the existence of networked improvement communities to accelerate the learning, (f) the struggle and tension of agreeing upon a shared aim while also being context-specific, and many other potential influences on the ability to engage in improvement science with integrity.

Social Relations

Leadership practices are conducive to initial engagement in improvement science. Leaders need to understand more about whether schools engage in the work without the initial existence of these practices (e.g., collaboration, trust) or whether they can develop through the work. Research is being conducted to better understand those practices associated with successful initial engagement and ongoing implementation of improvement science (e.g., Orr & Lochmiller, 2019). We also recognize that personal dispositions may also influence the implementation of the improvement science process (Hitt et al., 2018; Leithwood, 2012), and those will be important to explore in future research.

NELP and PSEL Connection Box for Educational Leadership Faculty

This chapter aligns closely with PSEL Standards One and Ten and NELP Standard One. These standards focus on the development and implementation of a mission, vision, and the use of continuous improvement, specifically related to fundamental priorities and "core set of values and priorities" (NCPEA, 2018). NELP Building Standard Ten, "Mission, Vision, and Improvement," highlights the need "to collaboratively lead, design, and implement a school mission, vision, and process for continuous improvement that reflects a core set of values and priorities that include data, technology, equity, diversity, digital citizenship, and community".

The leadership practices and outcomes of an improvement science process align with the following areas included in the standards: (a) ethical decision-making and professional norms (PSEL and NELP Standard Two); (b) equity, inclusiveness, and cultural responsiveness (PSEL and NELP Standard Three); (c) learning and instruction, including curriculum and assessment (PSEL and NELP Standard Four); (d) caring and support for students as well as meaningful engagement of families and community (PSEL Five and Eight and NELP Standard Five); (e) operations and management (PSEL Nine and NELP Standard Six); and (f) professional capacity and professional community for teachers and staff (PSEL Six and Seven and NELP Standard Seven).

NOTE

1. Turnaround is a commonly accepted term for rapid, dramatic school improvement or change, often with sanctions for not making a specific amount of progress in a specified amount of time. Although we prefer terms like "school renewal" (Goodlad, 1998), we will use turnaround in this chapter because that is how the research informing the practices highlighted in this chapter conceptualized their research.

BIBLIOGRAPHY

Bryk, A. S., Gomez, L. M., Grunow, A., & LeMahieu, P. G. (2015). *Learning to improve: How America's schools can get better at getting better.* Harvard Education Press.

Bryk, A. S., & Schneider, B. (2002). *Trust in schools: A core resource for improvement.* Russell Sage Foundation.

Bryk, A. S., Sebring, P. B., Allensworth, E., Luppesco, S., & Easton, J. Q. (2010). *Organizing schools for improvement: Lessons from Chicago.* The University of Chicago Press.

Candelarie, D., & Korach, S. (2018). High octane instructional leadership: The attributes of turnaround leaders. In C. S. Bingham, P. Egelson, & K. Sanzo (Eds.), *Research-based instructional practices of effective principals* (pp. 111–130). Information Age Press.

Collinson, V., & Cook, T. F. (2007). *Organizational learning: Improving learning, teaching, and leading in school systems.* SAGE Publications, Inc. https://doi.org/10.4135/9781452225890

Cosner, S. (2009). Building Organizational Capacity Through Trust. Educational Administration Quarterly, 45(2), 248–291. https://doi.org/10.1177/0013161X08330502

Cosner, S., & Jones, M. F. (2016). Leading school-wide improvement in low-performing schools facing conditions of accountability: Key actions and considerations. *Journal of Educational Administration, 54*(1), 41–57. http://doi.org/10.1108/JEA-08-2014-0098

Duke, D. L. (2004). *The challenges of educational change.* Allyn & Bacon.

Duke, D. L., Carr, M., & Sterrett, W. (2013). *The school improvement planning handbook: Getting focused for turnaround and transition.* Rowman & Littlefield Education.

Elmore, R. F. (2005). Accountable leadership. *The Educational Forum, 69*(2), 134–142. https://doi.org/10.1080/00131720508984677

Finnigan, K. S. (2011). Principal leadership in low-performing schools. *Education and Urban Society, 44*(2), 183–202. http://doi.org/10.1177/0013124511431570

Foldy, E. G., Goldman, L., & Ospina, S. (2008). Sensegiving and the role of cognitive shifts in the work of leadership. *The Leadership Quarterly, 19*(5), 514–529. https://doi.org/10.1016/j.leaqua.2008.07.004

Francera, S., & Bliss, J. (2011). Instructional leadership influence on collective teacher efficacy to improve student achievement. *Leadership and Policy in Schools, 10,* 349–370. http://10.1080/15700763.2011.585537

Fullan, M. (2001). *Leading in a culture of change.* Jossey-Bass.

Fullan, M., & Quinn, J. (2019). *Coherence: The right drivers in action for schools, districts, and systems.* Corwin Press.

Galloway, M., & Ishimaru, A. (2017). Equitable leadership on the ground: Converging on high-leverage practices. *Education Policy Analysis Archives, 25,* 2. https://doi.org/10.14507/epaa.25.2205

Garet, M. S., Porter, A. C., Desimone, L., Birman, B. F., & Yoon, K. S. (2001). What makes professional development effective? Results from a national sample of teachers. *American Educational Research Journal, 38*(4), 915–945. https://doi.org/10.3102/00028312038004915

Goodlad, J. I. (1998). *Educational renewal: Better teachers, better schools.* Jossey-Bass.

Gregory, G. H., & Kuzmich, L. (2014). *Data driven differentiation in the standards-based classroom.* Corwin Press.

Grissom, J. A., Egalite, A. J., & Lindsay, C. A. (2021). *How principals affect students and schools: A systematic synthesis of two decades of research.* The Wallace Foundation. www.wallacefoundation.org/principalsynthesis

Hinnant-Crawford, B. N. (2020). *Improvement science in education: A primer.* Myers Education Press.

Hitt, D. H., & Meyers, C. V. (2018). Beyond turnaround: A synthesis of relevant frameworks for leaders of sustained improvement in previously low-performing schools. *School Leadership & Management, 38*(1), 4–31. http://doi.org/10.1080/13632434.2017.1374943

Hitt, D. H., & Tucker, P. D. (2016). Systematic review of key leader practices found to influence student Achievement: A unified framework. *Review of Educational Research, 86*(2), 531–569. http://doi.org/10.3102/0034654315614911

Hitt, D. H., Woodruff, D., Meyers, C. V., & Zhu, G. (2018). Principal competencies that make a difference: Identifying a model for leaders of school turnaround. *Journal of School Leadership, 28*(1), 56–81. https://doi.org/10.1177/105268461802800103

Irby, D. J. (2021). *Stuck improving: Racial equity and school leadership.* Harvard Education Press.

Jackson, K. R., Fixsen, D., & Ward, C. (2018). *Four domains for rapid school improvement: A systems framework* [The Center for School Turnaround at WestEd]. WestEd. www.wested.org/rd_alert_online/framework-strengthens-states-school-improvement-and-turnaround/

Kania, J., Kramer, M., & Senge, P. (2018). *The water of systems change.* FSG. https://policycommons.net/artifacts/1847266/the-water-of-systems-change/2593518/CID:20.500.12592/8wz3hz.

Khalifa, M. A., Gooden, M. A., & Davis, J. E. (2016). Culturally responsive school leadership: A synthesis of the literature. *Review of Educational Research, 86*(4), 1272–1311. https://doi.org/10.3102/0034654316630383

Langley, G. J., Moen, R. D., Nolan, K. M., Nolan, T. W., Norman, C. L., & Provost, P. L. (2009). *The improvement guide: A practical approach to enhancing organizational performance* (2nd ed.). Jossey-Bass.

Leithwood, K. (2012). *Ontario leadership framework with a discussion of the leadership foundations.* The Institute for Education Leadership, OISE. www.education-leadership-ontario.ca/en/resources/ontario-leadership-framework-olf

Leithwood, K., Harris, A., & Strauss, T. (2010a). *Leading school turnaround: How successful school leaders transform low performing schools.* John Wiley & Sons.

Leithwood, K., Patten, S., & Jantzi, D. (2010b). Testing a conception of how school leadership influences student learning. *Educational Administration Quarterly, 46*(5), 671–706. https://doi.org/10.1177/0013161X10377347

Leithwood, K., Seashore-Louis, K., Anderson, S., & Wahlstrom, K. (2004). *How leadership influences student learning*. Wallace Foundation. www.wallacefoundation.org/knowledge-center/Documents/How-Leadership-Influences-Student-Learning-Executive-Summary.pdf

Lewis, C. (2015). What is improvement science? Do we need it in education? *Educational Researcher, 44*(1), 54–61. https://doi.org/10.3102/0013189X15570388

Lewis, A. E., & Diamond, J. B. (2015). *Despite the best intentions: How racial inequality thrives in good schools*. Oxford University Press.

Louis, K. S., Leithwood, K., Wahlstrom, K. L., Anderson, S. E., Michlin, M., & Mascall, B. (2010). *Learning from leadership: Investigating the links to improved student learning*. Center for Applied Research and Educational Improvement/University of Minnesota and Ontario Institute for Studies in Education/University of Toronto. www.wallacefoundation.org/knowledge-center/Documents/Investigating-the-Links-to-Improved-Student-Learning-Executive-Summary.pdf

Meyer, F., Bendikson, L., & Le Fevre, D. M. (2023). Leading school improvement through goal-setting: Evidence from New Zealand schools. *Educational Management Administration & Leadership, 51*(2), 365–383. https://doi.org/10.1177/1741143220979711

Meyers, C. V., & Hitt, D. H. (2018). Planning for school turnaround in the United States: An analysis of the quality of principal-developed quick wins. *School Effectiveness and School Improvement, 29*(3), 362–382. http://doi.org/10.1080/09243453.2018.1428202

Meyers, C. V., & Smylie, M. A. (2017). Five myths of school turnaround policy and practice. *Leadership and Policy in Schools, 16*(3), 502–523. http://doi.org/10.1080/15700763.2016.1270333

Mintrop, H., & Sunderman, G. L. (2009). Predictable failure of federal sanctions-driven accountability for school improvement: And why we may retain it anyway. *Educational Researcher, 38*(5), 353–364. http://doi.org/10.3102/0013189x09339055

Mintrop, H., & Trujillo, T. (2005). Corrective action in low performing schools: Lessons for NCLB implementation from first-generation accountability Systems. *Education Policy Analysis Archives, 13*(48). http://doi.org/10.14507/epaa.v13n48.2005

Murphy, J., Elliott, S. N., Goldring, E., & Porter, A. C. (2006). *Learning-centered leadership: A conceptual foundation*. Learning Sciences Institute, Vanderbilt University.

Murphy, J., & Meyers, C. V. (2008). *Turning around failing schools*. Corwin Press.

National Policy Board for Educational Administration. (2015). *Professional standards for educational leaders 2015*. Author. www.npbea.org/psel/

National Policy Board for Educational Administration. (2018). *National Educational Leadership Preparation (NELP) program standards: Building level*. www.npbea.org

O'Day, J. A., & Smith, M. S. (2019). *Opportunity for all: A framework for quality and equality in education*. Harvard Education Press.

Orr, M. T., & Lochmiller, C. (2019, November). *Examining improvement leadership at the individual, school, and setting levels*. Paper presented at the meeting of University Council of Educational Administration.

Park, J.-H., Lee, I. H., & Cooc, N. (2019). The role of school-level mechanisms: How principal support, professional learning communities, collective responsibility, and group-level teacher expectations affect student achievement. *Educational Administration Quarterly, 55*(5), 742–780. https://doi.org/10.1177/0013161x18821355

Penuel, W. R., Riedy, R., Barber, M. S., Peurach, D. J., LeBouef, W. A., & Clark, T. (2020). Principles of collaborative education research with stakeholders: Toward requirements for a new research and development infrastructure. *Review of Educational Research, 0*(0), 0034654320938126. https://doi.org/10.3102/0034654320938126

Peterson, D. S., & Carlile, S. P. (2019). Preparing school leaders to effectively lead school improvement efforts: Improvement science. In R. Crow, B. N. Hinnant-Crawford, & D. T. Spaulding (Eds.), *The educational leader's guide to improvement science: Data, design, and cases for reflection* (pp. 167–182). Meyers Press.

Public Impact. (2008, 2016). *School turnaround leaders: Competencies for success: Part of the school turnaround collection from Public Impact.* Public Impact. https://publicimpact.com/school-turnarounds/turnarounds-within-schools/turnaround-competencies-and-actions-principals-and-teachers/

Robinson, V. M. J., Lloyd, C. A., & Rowe, K. J. (2008). The impact of leadership on student outcomes: An analysis of the differential effects of leadership types. *Educational Administration Quarterly, 44*(5), 635–674. http://doi.org/10.1177/0013161X08321509

Russell, J., Bryk, A., Dolle, J., Gomez, L., Lemahieu, P., & Grunow, A. (2017). A framework for the initiation of networked improvement communities. *Teachers College Record, 119*(6), 1. https://doi.org/https://doi.org/10.1177/016146811711900501

Schildkamp, K., Lai, M. K., & Earl, L. M. (2013). *Data-based decision making in education: Challenges and opportunities.* Springer.

Shields, C. M. (2017). *Transformative leadership in education*: Equitable and socially just change in an uncertain and complex world. Routledge.

Stevenson, I., & Weiner, J. M. (2020). *The strategy playbook for educational leaders: Principles and processes.* Routledge.

Supovitz, J., Sirinides, P., & May, H. (2010). How principals and peers influence teaching and learning. *Educational Administration Quarterly, 46*(1), 31–56. https://doi.org/10.1177/1094670509353043

Theoharis, G. (2009). *The school leaders our children deserve: Seven keys to equity, social justice, and school reform.* Teachers College Press.

Tschannen-Moran, M. (2014). *Trust matters: Leadership for successful schools.* John Wiley & Sons.

Young, M. D., & Anderson, E. (2020). *The research base for the National Educational Leadership Preparation (NELP) standards: Building level.* NPBEA. www.npbea.org/wp-content/uploads/2018/11/NELP-Building-Standards.pdf

CHAPTER 4

Equity-Oriented Continuous Improvement

Chapter Highlights

1) Integration of equity with improvement as a function of the overall orientation of improvement approach.
2) Strong equity, not thin equity will change systems.
3) Equity as a lens: individual, interpersonal, organizational, institutional.
4) Equity as a process: inclusion of cognitive diversity and multiple perspectives.
5) Equity as a capability: what people can be and do.
6) Initiating conditions, processes, and outcomes must include strong equity.

CHAPTER OVERVIEW

This chapter explores the ways equity, social justice, and cultural responsiveness are core orientations to value dimensions of improvement by raising questions regarding what is defined as "improvement," who advances the selected articulation of "improvement," and how educators engage the process of "improvement." This chapter argues that continuous improvement offers the potential to address systemic and structural inequities but only if that orientation is continuously and explicitly interrogated. The chapter highlights three crucial moments in the trajectory of improvement during which concerns around social justice are particularly salient: initiating conditions, the processes of improvement, and the outcomes or substantial insights. This chapter poses the question, "Improvement of what?" at each of these three moments. It is indeed the choice of "what" to improve along with how and by whom

DOI: 10.4324/9781003389279-5

that choice is made that determines if and how a given instance of continuous improvement bends toward "strong equity" (Cochran-Smith et al., 2017). The chapter draws out the leadership implications of embracing equity as a central precept of continuous improvement, as suggested by the NELP and PSEL standards, through examples and discussion of barriers and challenges confronted in equity-oriented continuous improvement initiatives. If you want to deepen your understanding of culturally responsive education, we provide examples of anti-oppressive teaching practices and school practices that affirm the assets of communities of color and other marginalized groups in the sources listed at the end of this chapter.

Introduction: The Potential of Continuous Improvement for Equity Orientation

Equity, social justice, and cultural responsiveness are well-documented as necessary for improving schools (Diem & Welton, 2020; Hinnant-Crawford, 2021; Irby, 2021). These concepts are part of the espoused mission and vision statements and improvement priorities in many schools and districts. Due to concern about facing the reality of racial oppression, in other schools and districts, these terms may be feared. In those communities and in communities throughout the United States, such concepts are open to scorn, resistance, and at times, outright attack.

Leaders seek to change systems through equity and social justice to empower oppressed groups and communities, such as, but not limited to, Black students, students with disabilities and cognitive diversity, students identifying as LGBTQ+, students with emerging English language skills, and students from underrepresented cultural groups such as the Asian American and Pacific Islander (AAPI) and Latine communities or oppressed religious groups like Muslim or Jewish students. Whether you personally feel excited, traumatized, hesitant, beleaguered, or curious when you begin reading a chapter about equity, public school educators are responsible for setting up the conditions to provide the best education for *each* and *every* student in the school community. Empirical insights and practical concerns reinforce the view that *each* student cannot be served by our schools and districts unless schools change policies, practices, structures, and systems that have systemically limited opportunity for some groups while upholding dominant white cultural values at the expense of other cultural values (e.g., Irby, 2021).

ACTION INVENTORY 4.1 INTRODUCTION REFLECTION QUESTIONS

1. How do you currently see the relationship between equity and improvement?
2. What are your current wonderings connected to the relationship between equity and improvement?

Continuous improvement approaches, such as an improvement science methodology, are not inherently about equity and social justice. In fact, there are some scholars and practitioners who view the theoretical foundations and practical implications of a continuous improvement approach as being at odds with culturally responsive and justice-oriented approaches to school change (Capper, 2018; Horsford et al., 2019; Safir & Dugan, 2021). We address those critiques in more detail later. Here, we want to develop a shared understanding of the potential of continuous improvement for orienting toward equity. To shift systemic problems in education, we believe the methodology of improvement science lends itself to a solid grounding in equity and to addressing social justice concerns (Eddy-Spicer & Gomez, 2022). Our own research and experience demonstrate improvement science can and should be equity-oriented, but it requires deliberate activation of the core principles to increase social justice and ensure cultural responsiveness (e.g., Anderson et al., forthcoming; Anderson et al., under review: Biag, 2019; Eddy-Spicer & Gomez, 2022; Hinnant-Crawford, 2020; Hinnant-Crawford et al., 2021, in press; Ishimaru & Bang, 2022).

Improvement without a focus on equity will fail to solve deeply entrenched problems in school systems because most root causes of our systemic problems in education (e.g., funding, discipline, academics) are tied to structural inequities, oppression, biases, and deficit thinking (Hinnant-Crawford et al., in press; Koretz, 2008; Martínez & Spikes, 2020). Oppression is defined as "a combination of prejudice and institutional power that creates a system that regularly and severely discriminates against some groups and benefits other groups" which can be "in the form of limitations, disadvantage, or disapproval" (National Museum of African American History and Culture 2023, np). That prejudice is often the result of bias, how we see the work through our own cultural views and experiences, and deficit thinking. Deficit thinking is holding "students from historically oppressed populations responsible for the challenges and inequalities that they face" (Davis & Museus, 2019, p. 119). This oppression is embedded in the larger political, social, and economic systems, and as a result, is built into the education system creating structural inequalities (e.g., Gorski, 2011; Davis & Museus, 2019). Improvement science lends itself to unlearning these biases to correct systems that oppress.

Defining Equity, Social Justice, and Cultural Responsiveness

Equity or educational equity is about "each child receiving what they need to develop to their full academic and social potential" (National Equity Project, 2021). This definition is seemingly simple, but there is a lot to unlearn, critically reflect upon, and restructure in order to create the conditions within the school system that ensure each student reaches their full potential. The National Equity Project suggests that for leaders to ensure equity in our schools, they must "transform our organizations" by "directly addressing and eliminating the current inequities that limit the success or failure of students based on identity" (np). The goal of educational equity is to no longer need to talk about an achievement gap because we have closed opportunity gaps by meeting marginalized student needs, recognizing their gifts and talents, affirming their culture, and working to mitigate the inequities in broader society (e.g., Gay, 2000; Ladson-Billings, 2021; Lindsey et al., 2018).

Equity is often discussed in concert with social justice. Social justice is the goal of addressing inequities born out of a lack of access or unfair conditions. Sensoy and DiAngelo (2009) define "social justice-oriented approaches in education" as actions that "actively address the dynamics of oppression, privilege, and isms, recognizing that society is the product of historically rooted, institutionally sanctioned stratification along socially constructed group lines that include race, class, gender, sexual orientation, and ability" (p. 350). Educators must learn and accept that schools perpetuate society's oppression; some taken-for-granted practices and structures of school culture, curriculum, and teaching practices lead to inequity and limit justice (Biag, 2019). Scholars and researchers have explored this idea in-depth; suggestions for further reading are found at the end of this chapter.

Leadership for social justice, as described in professional standards (e.g., PSEL 3, NELP 3), must involve each person being critically reflective and recognizing the role of oppression in our current education system (Hinnant-Crawford et al., in press; Khalifa, 2018). Some sources of inequity may be improvable at the school level. For other sources, the onus of change will involve larger political and social responses within and outside the education system. We ask that improvers not only recognize they are embedded in that larger system but also that they see where they can make changes within their school to create more social justice.

Educators in socially just and equitable schools demonstrate cultural responsiveness. The Culturally Responsive Education (CRE) Hub shares the following definition of a culturally responsive education system. It states,

> CRE advances equity and social justice by (a) centering and valuing students' cultures and identities, (b) using rigorous and relevant curriculum, and anti-oppressive teaching practices, (c) building strong, positive relationships between students, families, and school staff, and (d) supporting students to develop the knowledge, skills, and vision to transform the world toward liberation.
>
> (CRE Hub, 2022, np)

Thinking about equity and improvement, we often focus on gaps, such as the "achievement gap" between marginalized groups of students (by cultural, social, and economic factors) and white, middle to upper-class students. Even reframing the achievement gap as an opportunity gap – placing the onus on education systems, not students and families – fails to recognize that our school systems favor certain ways of being and knowing that do not build on the strengths of marginalized groups who have "funds of knowledge" (González et al., 2006) and "community cultural wealth" (Acevedo & Solorzano, 2021; Yosso, 2005; Yosso & Burciaga, 2016) beyond those forms of capital valued in a "white supremacist" school culture (Irby, 2021, Kendi, 2019; Liu et al., 2019). Community cultural capital wealth includes aspirational, navigational, social, linguistic, familial, and resistant capitals, and funds of knowledge that are types of knowledge developed and nurtured within a community or cultural group (Yosso, 2005). To transform our schools, we need to be aware of the ways we value some cultural groups' assets (e.g., white, middle-class, male culture; Christian culture; gender-conforming, heterosexual culture; ableist culture) intentionally or unintentionally over others. We must change systems to be more inclusive of all cultural groups and their assets. A culturally responsive education system values these forms of capital and limits systems of oppression through developing relationships with students and families, building the values of equity and social justice in teachers and students.

Being culturally responsive is not just sponsoring a "multicultural" event at the school or changing bulletin boards to celebrate Black pioneers during Black History month – although those gestures of inclusivity can add richness to the culture of schools. Nods to inclusion are defined as thin equity (Cochran-Smith et al., 2017; Eddy-Spicer & Gomez, 2022). Being culturally inclusive incorporates all cultures of the school community into the fabric of the school when discussing policies (e.g., attendance, behavior), teacher practices, curriculum, decision-making processes, leadership structures, conflict management, and all other aspects of schooling.

Defining Leading for Strong Equity

The concept of equity can be thought of in three ways: as a lens, as a process, and as a capability. First, equity is a lens when it is used to make sense of systems, structures, and practices at individual, interpersonal, and organizational levels. Generally, a lens is a framework or viewpoint to filter our understanding and make sense of the world. Equity as a lens means we see the world through definitions of equity, social justice, and cultural responsiveness, and we seek to recognize inequities, injustice, and white-centric practices when approaching improvement work.

We may consider equity when approaching a problem, such as concerns over discipline practices in schools being subjectively applied and overly punitive for certain groups. We may seek to understand how bias and deficit thinking influence decisions about classroom management and how forms of social capital and cultural assets are ignored or diminished. The lens of equity applies to educators' interaction with students and families, causing us to be critically reflective as we track discipline practices looking for trends and exploring biases.

Ava and her team used equity as a lens for their improvement work around both LGBTQ+ and MLL students. She framed all conversations from asset-based perspectives and sought to understand and uphold the assets of the respective cultures, interrogating their existing beliefs, and identifying where learning was necessary. When we consider changes in discipline practices, we could engage the lens of equity to do a school-wide equity audit to see how those trends play out across the school, exploring variation at the organizational level. Engaging an equity lens at a higher systems level could be expanding data collection to encompass multiple schools and sharing out these learnings across the district to work on creating more equitable discipline practices.

Second, equity is a process. We will talk more about how equity is part of the process of improvement science later in this chapter. For now, we want to consider that the equity lens translates into practices that advance equity, such as the inclusion of cognitive diversity, racial diversity, and multiple perspectives in all aspects of a process (Wilhem, forthcoming).

Ava ensured equity in the process of improvement. Her problem was about belongingness and inclusivity, and she led the work with those same values at the forefront. She was inclusive of multiple perspectives on her improvement team, during empathy interviews, and throughout the testing cycles; Ava and her team also sought community perspectives. Then, they listened. Listening is one of the most important parts of the process (Zumpe & Aramburo, in press). Then she acted upon that learning.

Third, equity is defined as a capability. An individual or group's ability to do equity work is dependent on what they can know and do based on their own intercultural development, knowledge of oppression, power, and privilege, and critical self-reflection related to those concepts. Capabilities also include a level of understanding about inequity and how to both engage in and facilitate conversations about diversity, equity, inclusion, justice, ability, and racism. Jabbar and Childs (2022) argue that "deeper engagement with critical perspectives, methodologies, epistemologies, and frameworks is necessary to engage historically marginalized and disempowered people as active collaborators in the improvement process" (p. 242). These are the types of capacities essential for equity.

Ava gained capabilities as an equity leader in her coursework where her professors exposed her to readings and uncomfortable, important conversations about the implications of racism, white supremacist culture, oppression, social justice, deficit thinking, cultural responsiveness, and current inequities. She, as a school leader, then made it a priority to develop those capabilities in her staff through professional learning. It was not an option whether Ava's staff was going to treat the LGBTQ+ students and families in just and fair ways: they were going to do so. She made it central to the school's improvement plans, mission, and vision.

Equity as a lens, process, and capability must all be considered to enact equity-oriented improvement science. Equity-oriented improvement science must commit to strong equity rather than weak equity (Cochran-Smith et al., 2017; Eddy-Spicer & Gomez, 2022). Improvement science without embracing a "strong equity" orientation will reproduce inequities and fail to address deeply entrenched problems. Strong equity has several characteristics related to equity capability and are included in Figure 4.1.

Strong equity emphasizes transforming systems through intentional action. We mentioned at the start of this chapter that equity and related concepts are embedded in many espoused mission statements. Many districts have created a district-level position to lead DEIAJ work, or they require school faculty to attend professional development – possibly sponsored or created by district

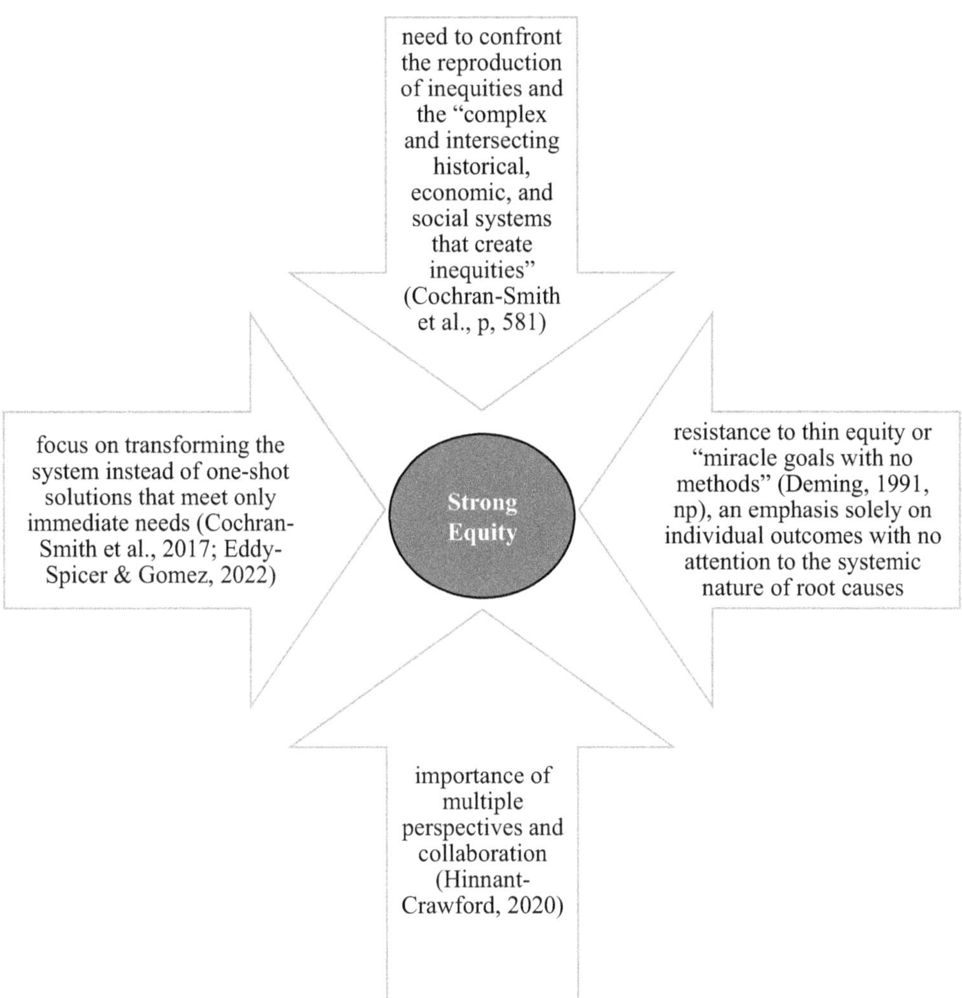

Figure 4.1 Characteristics of Capability for Strong Equity.

Source: Created by author.

DEIAJ leaders. Most districts stated major improvement goals address "closing the achievement gap" or increasing equity in other ways. These structures and practices are welcomed but limited. Without a commitment to unlearning, critically reflecting upon, and restructuring mindsets and beliefs to disrupt systems in schools and districts, we are practicing thin equity. Eddy-Spicer and Gomez (2022) expand on strong equity in improvement science by positing the "pragmatic arc of moral agency." Moral agency is how improvement leaders attend to equity and social justice and create the conditions for improvement infused with such values. These conditions for improvements include social relations (initiating), organizing processes, and structures for substantive insights (outcomes).

To come back to our example related to discipline practices, let's explore what a thin versus strong equity process would be. For instance, the leaders collected data and analyzed trends through an equity lens and found that Black males were twice as likely to be sent out of the classroom for the same behaviors exhibited by white male students. When we think about how to frame these data and spearhead a response, or equity as a process, we have traditionally thought it was necessary to make more rules or rethink the consequences (equity as capability), possibly asking teachers to keep students in the classroom and give detention instead. You might even think an equity response would be to stop after-school detention because students aren't responding to it, can leave easily, and might have family or work obligations. Lunch detention could be assigned since it is easy to find students in the lunchroom if they don't attend on their own, and it is during the school day, so it won't interfere with family obligations, extracurriculars, or after-school employment. Maybe improvers recognized that their Black students are culturally highly relational and have also built in one-on-one meetings with the school leader who handles discipline to talk through what happened and why. These are the types of responses that nod to equity but are still representative of a white-dominant ideology or thin equity.

Strong equity instead explores discipline practices through an equity lens by recognizing first that Black males have faced oppression historically, which has led to distrust of authority. These students have witnessed Tyre Nichols, George Floyd, Briana Taylor, and countless others mistreated by the members of society who are supposed to protect us all. Second, taking a top-down, authoritative approach triggers responses to the ways Blackness has been criminalized. There is a school-to-prison pipeline documented, and it impacts Black males disproportionately (Okilwa et al., 2017). Finally, students are aware of who is being disciplined and why, which creates greater tensions between students of color and white students and creates deficit thinking among the white students. A strong equity lens leads to different responses that go beyond moving detention to change the discipline system. A strong equity response would include students and families exploring why this disparity is happening, sharing their experiences with the discipline policy at the school, and designing new, more equitable, just responses to student discipline that reflect the values, culture, and experiences of Black families.

Critiques of Improvement Science: Can It Be Equitable?

Some people, even some of you, may ask if improvement science can be socially just if it has roots in structures of inequity. Improvement science comes from a long tradition of continuous improvement in which some methods are believed to be rooted in a structural-functional epistemology (Capper, 2018) (See Chapter 2). This critique suggests that improvement science is about getting "back" to some desired state in which the dominant cultural view and related systems (e.g., white, ableist, heterosexual, middle-class) are "ideal," and those struggling within the system are "negatively labeled and segregated into separate programs" (Capper,

2018, p. 36). Capper argues the "gap" at the heart of the problem in improvement science is a gap between how marginalized students meet up to dominant expectations. The power of improvement science resides in collectively naming a gap between the current (dominant) and ideal (equitable and socially just) state and using inclusive and aspirational approaches to strive for new ways of being that disrupt long-standing systems of inequity. Although we recognize there are aspects of our educational system that favor a dominant culture and limit the value of other forms of cultural capital (e.g., Yosso, 2005), an improvement science methodology, with a focus on root causes and exploring systems and variation, offers the opportunity to problem-solve in ways that can shift the system to be more inclusive of marginalized identities, particularly by including multiple voices in the process and rethinking definitions and measures of success.

The improvement science methodology has been brought to the education sector by philanthropic organizations such as the Carnegie Foundation and the Gates Foundation (Horsford et al., 2019); these intermediary influences on the education systems are seen as a threat and are believed to have undue power to guide educational policy. There are concerns that these large philanthropic funders emphasize top-down approaches to leading schools and are influenced by other disciplines like business that do not share key characteristics or values with schools. The process has roots in many organizations, including healthcare, that bear similarities to the problems in schools, i.e., a failure to address problems and to disrupt systems of inequity that lead to negative outcomes for those we serve – patients and students (Langley et al., 2009).

Although we share these same concerns about outside influences in the education system, we believe improvement science is inherently a bottom-up response to what has long been a top-down approach to school improvement and reform (Bryk et al., 2015; Fishman & Herrenkohl, 2022). This method is rooted in local context, focused on the stakeholder groups within the school community, and is based on learning from failure, in contrast to the top-down, competitive models to which it is being compared. While outside philanthropic agendas driving change in education is problematic, the funding that such organizations commit to exploring the use of improvement science for equity in education, university-district partnerships for preparing leaders for continuous improvement, and the potential of networks to catalyze systems change has been instrumental in providing the training, space, and forums for discussions that allow educational researchers, leaders, and teachers to take up equity-focused improvement initiatives.

A shift from the impression of improvement science as being at odds with equity is one that emphasizes a critical pragmatist epistemology (Herr & Anderson, 2014) – born from the justice-oriented theoretical underpinnings of action research and the continuous quality improvement of Deming (See Chapter 2). Improvement science does not have to be situated in opposition to equity, but instead can expand possibilities to make systematic and systemic changes to forward equity. Jabbar and Childs point our "improvement science has been conducted using conventional assumptions . . . a common underlying assumption, however is that policies and practices are race neutral" (Jabbar & Childs, 2022, p. 244). Ignoring the implications of race and other forms of oppression and marginalization most certainly will perpetuate the status quo. However, potential exists to disrupt systems. Hinnant-Crawford (2020), writing about being a Black woman who endorses equity-oriented improvement science, mentions that the hesitation that social justice scholars have about continuous improvement models like improvement science often results in a reluctance to engage. She also argues the methodology's potential for making a lasting change when undertaken with equity at its core. Hinnant-Crawford and others, including our author team on this book, work on the integration of equity with improvement as a function of the overall orientation of the improvement approach (e.g., Anderson et al., forthcoming; Anderson et al., under review Biag, 2019; Eddy-Spicer & Gomez, 2022).

Equity-Oriented Improvement Science

You may understand the call for strong equity, social justice, and cultural inclusion, but still ask, "what is equity-oriented improvement science" and "how can improvement science change the system to promote strong equity?" To enact strong equity by centering equity on continuous improvement, the National Equity Project suggests that improvers and designers do the following:

- Prioritize the approach to the work (initiating social relations, organizing processes, and developing structures for substantive insights).
- Create flexible processes (such as design thinking and improvement science).
- Develop equity leadership habits that see-engage-act, in which leaders see and recognize oppression, critically reflect and engage with that oppression, and plan to understand and act on that learning.
- Emphasize noticing and reflecting on the equity orientation as part of the phases or steps of improvement (engage users, formulate problems, see the system, design a theory of action, test change ideas, measure progress and outcomes, and spread and scale those ideas).
- Cultivate liberatory design mindsets (equity mindsets that orient the work toward equity and liberation that will be explained throughout this chapter).

Equity cannot be an add-on but must be integrated into each phase of improvement science.

Equity-oriented improvement science elaborates the core principles of improvement science to not just consider, but to center equity. The process starts by seeing the system, attending to variation, and being user-centered and problem-specific. Although the emphasis on the core principles of disciplined inquiry and embracing measurement are key to ensuring equity through collecting data on improvement, those processes cannot effectively happen until the initial problem framing is clear and deeply understood, and the organization of the work has set the stage for socially-just improvement science. These core principles should look familiar from Chapter 2; however, here we will expound upon them to frame each with a strong equity orientation.

Seeing the System

You must see the system within which the problem is embedded. School systems are built on structural racism; inequity is built into the system. There are almost no adaptive problems in our education system today that aren't, at least in part, connected to racist or socially stratified structures and systems as well as policies and systems that marginalize people of color, Indigenous peoples, people with disabilities, students identifying as girls/women or members of the LBGTQ+ community, non-Christian religions, and other groups. The National Equity Project (2023) states that

> At the core of liberatory design are a set of beliefs: racism and inequity have been designed into systems and thus can be redesigned; designing for equity requires the meaningful participation of those impacted by inequity; and equity-driven designs require equity and complexity-informed processes.

Notice how the National Equity Project's words inject hope into the work. It is possible – because the systems are designed – to redesign them. They offer this call to action so that we may lead changes. It is important to remember that it was through the design of ideas to address perceived problems that we created the inequitable, racist systems that we must now design solutions to disrupt. As the saying goes, nothing changes if nothing changes.

Attending to Variation

Another core principle of improvement science is attending to variation or asking what works for whom under what conditions (Langley et al., 2009) through exploring systems and structures and how individuals fare within those systems and structures. Variation, and the ways students are offered different opportunities for success, are related to equity. Variation in data reveals where inequities in the system manifest or are caused. Until we can name the ways in which the educational experiences are different for different people based on specific identity and cultural markers, we cannot address equity. Our understanding of variation and equity must be pushed to understand how dominant groups' values are represented in that variation and the measures of success as we also must understand the conditions underlying differing opportunities. Although disaggregating data is important to discover a variation, an equity-oriented approach recognizes that to design solutions that will meet the needs of all students, we must not just focus on "subgroups" and "gaps." Instead, we must also look for outliers and trends to reveal the conditions that lead to some students being more successful than others by exploring variation to highlight the successes and resilience of marginalized populations and look at trends of "positive deviance" (LeMahieu et al., 2017; Pascale et al., 2010) or examples of classrooms or schools that have been successful with the problem. Designing with that consideration of variation in mind will help to ensure "strong equity."

User-Centered and Problem-Specific

Another core principle of improvement science is that you must be user-centered and problem-specific. This focus defines a problem, determines what is "improvement," and explores exactly whose values are reflected in defining "improvement." Being user-centered should mean the improvers gather multiple perspectives about how the problem makes each person think and feel. It is important to talk to a diverse group of people and include their perspectives not just in the problem definition but also in the design of solutions, development of practical measures, and scaling up of ideas. Power dynamics must shift from leaders as experts to leaders as facilitators of a full understanding of a problem that is informed by teachers, students, families, and communities. This shift involves accepting we will be better at solving problems if we find out how others experience the problem, especially those whose perspectives are marginalized (Ishimaru & Bang, 2022). The perceived power dynamics currently suggest that leaders have answers, however, leaders must spearhead this shift through intentional modeling and communication to invite other voices to be contributors and valued in improvement.

Disciplined Inquiry, Measurement, and Scaling Up

Two additional core principles of improvement science are related to the role of outcomes and the iterative nature of testing change ideas to fail fast and learn from those "failures" to ensure that students are being given the opportunities necessary to transform the system and eliminate inequitable practices (National Equity Project, 2023). Some of you may be hearing "testing change" and "failing fast" and may wonder how those ideas square up with the history of oppressed groups being "tested on" or may wonder if we are suggesting that failing these groups is acceptable. The tolerance of failing fast through iterative testing is intended so we no longer fail our students of color, students with disabilities, and other marginalized students. Making systemic change is a large undertaking: testing and iterating allow us to learn about the conditions for change and the results of the change itself, while questioning and critiquing the power structures and revealing implications for social justice as we seek lasting solutions to entrenched problems.

Central aspects of continuous improvement are embracing measurement and engaging in disciplined inquiry. Measurement is important for upholding an equity orientation for several reasons. Without data (i.e., qualitative and quantitative), we cannot know what our impact is on students and how their experiences may vary. These data are closely connected to the work and give an understanding of process and experiences through a reflective process. Qualitative data, "street data" (Safir & Dugan, 2021), and data capturing inequities beyond just "gaps" in test scores are valid practical measures that capture the experience of multiple perspectives, maintain a critical lens, emphasize assets and other forms of capital, and interrogate existing systems, structures, and practices. Data should reveal who is being impacted and should consider the disaggregated impact on groups.

These data should be shared with others tackling the same problems through a NIC to accelerate wide-scale transformation; this is the last core principle of improvement science. Scaling up needs to include practical measures of the impact of these new ideas on marginalized communities. There is still the possibility – even with equity, justice, and inclusion at the forefront of the process up to this point – to inadvertently return to oppressive systems by not considering how all members of the community interact with the changes. That iterative process of testing can be done deliberately to measure the differing impact across grades, classrooms, and community members; this will reduce negative impacts when spreading change. Also, continuing to gain multiple perspectives at each phase of the process, including full implementation, will help to measure the impact and ensure strong equity.

Three Crucial Moments in the Arc of Improvement

To uphold this commitment to equity and to challenge the aforementioned critiques, this section describes three crucial moments in the improvement trajectory during which these core principles and concerns around equity, social justice, and cultural responsiveness are particularly salient: namely, initiating social conditions, the processes of improvement, and the outcomes or accomplishments of improvement. Strong equity is dependent on the equity lens, process, and capability at these crucial moments.

Initiating Social Conditions

Improvement work begins by bringing together a design team of improvers who work together throughout the process – from defining a problem and understanding a problem, to developing a theory of improvement, to testing change ideas and deciding what to spread and scale. An equity-oriented approach to improvement starts by setting up team norms, dynamics, and processes that recognize the needs of individuals, develop collaborative habits, and explore power. Eddy-Spicer and Gomez (2022) label this an orientation to process that includes interpersonal interactions; group actions; organizational routines, such as collective processes and collaborative routines; and the explicit acknowledgment of power.

Orientation to the process is the "setup" for the work. Think about when you are preparing for a project from building a new deck to baking a multi-layered cake. Before you start, you collect the ingredients and tools you need to be able to complete the project. You also might need to ask for help and include others in the project. You would ask your friends with skills in building or baking to join you, which requires acting in a group or being clear about the roles and routines that will guide the project. You set up the space to be conducive to the task at hand. The ingredients and tools for improvement science are those interpersonal interactions and collective processes. Leaders, like a builder or the baker, must establish collaborative systems and structures with an orientation toward equity and recognition of power structures (Ainscow et al., 2016; Galloway & Ishimaru, 2020; NEP, 2023). Look at Action Inventory 4.2, which lists some of the items needed for the earlier examples. Brainstorm an initial list of what and who you will need to help you set up the conditions for successful equity-focused improvement efforts and capture those ideas in the space. You will probably add and adjust to this list as you bring additional teammates into the work and as you learn more about the problem of practice on which you want to improve. At the end of Ava's story, they added a parent and additional ELL teacher to her improvement team as the focus shifted to MLL students.

Practices and structures for open communication about inequities and the role that educators play in oppression, to name and address deficit thinking and biases, and to engage in critical self-reflection are required (Biag, 2017; Eddy-Spicer & Gomez, 2022). The team should ensure diverse perspectives and include people who are closest to the problem: students directly impacted by the problem or teachers in the grades or subjects where the problem is most obvious. An improvement team with an equity orientation includes leaders, teachers, support staff, and potentially students, family members, and/or other community members. The team needs to be structured to support psychological safety and relational trust and must emphasize exploring power structures and engaging in critical reflection. This stage "requires a significant amount of humility in the sharing of power for the improvement process to be equitable" (Hinnant-Crawford, 2022). For instance, if the principal is on the improvement team, norms, expectations, working agreements, and ways of working must be established to allow for everyone's voice to have dedicated space in the process without fear of repercussions. Intentional modeling and example-setting by the principal are key to assuring no repercussions. Setting norms for the team that attend to power dynamics, trust, and so forth will be important for upholding equity. Those enabling conditions and the leader's role in developing them are further explained in Chapter 9.

Eddy-Spicer and Gomez (2022) describe a future orientation that emphasizes the reason for the work, engendering change, and the development of specific capabilities, practices, and identities. Improvement work cannot be done without a vision for where improvement goes and why and for whom this improvement is needed. There must be goals and predictions for how the change will be an improvement and how the systems, structures, and practices will ensure greater equity. The model for improvement, introduced by Langley and updated by Hinnant-Crawford and colleagues (2021), should explore the following: (a) What are we trying to accomplish, and *who benefits (and who does not)*? (b) What change might we introduce and why and *whose values are represented and who takes on the burden of the change*? and (c) How will we know a change is an improvement and *whose values are represented and who defines what is an improvement*? To explore to whom it benefits, whose values are upheld, and who defines improvement and carries the burden of change, you need data about the human experience of improvement and change; this leads to the process of improvement.

ACTION INVENTORY 4.2 SETTING UP YOUR IMPROVEMENT SPACE

Baking a Cake

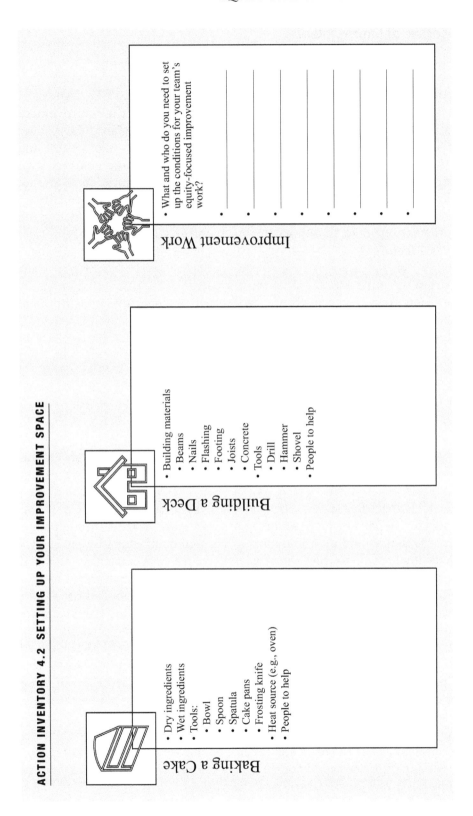

- Dry ingredients
- Wet ingredients
- Tools:
  - Bowl
  - Spoon
  - Spatula
  - Cake pans
  - Frosting knife
- Heat source (e.g., oven)
- People to help

Building a Deck

- Building materials
  - Beams
  - Nails
  - Flashing
  - Footing
  - Joists
  - Concrete
- Tools
  - Drill
  - Hammer
  - Shovel
- People to help

Improvement Work

- What and who do you need to set up the conditions for your team's equity-focused improvement work?
- ____________________
- ____________________
- ____________________
- ____________________
- ____________________
- ____________________
- ____________________
- ____________________

The Processes of Improvement

Each stage of the improvement science process must be infused with equity and social justice. The liberatory design model helps to understand what improvement infused with equity and social justice looks like (Anaissie, 2021). This model includes mindsets and modes that help the improvement team maintain an equity orientation. One practice embedded in the improvement process is to "notice and reflect." To utilize the process of notice and reflect, the team establishes norms, creates a process for and comfort with dialogue about inequity, and explores data to highlight inequity. The National Equity Project has created prompts for teams to discuss equity and social justice at each stage of the improvement process. For example, during the problem formation stage, liberatory design requires you to notice and reflect upon several factors:

- Identity: Who am/are I/we? Who are our users?
- Power: How are we respectively situated (relative to opportunity, institutional power)?
- Context: What is our situation, our equity challenge? What barriers are in the way of achieving equitable outcomes?

(Anaissie, 2021)

Ava and her team embedded these types of notice and reflect questions from NEP into her team's process of understanding the problem, which took place in Chapter 1.

The team starts by identifying a problem. Most people begin the improvement science process in one of two ways: either they have a problem and bring together a team to tackle that problem, or they have a team determine what problem they would like to address. Regardless, the work starts by understanding the problem via looking at variations in data, exploring processes and systems through mapping exercises that should illuminate inequities, and doing empathy interviews that include anyone who touches the problem (e.g., teachers, students, and families). Empathy interviews, introduced in Chapter 3, are short conversations that ask how teachers, students, and families experience the problem and what their experience of the problem looks like and feels like, which gains their perspective on the causes of the problem (Bryk et al., 2015; Hinnant-Crawford, 2020; Kelley & Kelley, 2015; Nelsestuen & Smith, 2020). Empathy interviews, when done with an equity orientation, include groups with limited power whose voices may not be regularly captured (i.e., the C student who disappears between those excelling and those failing, the Black parent who works during parent meetings and who has never been heard, etc.).

Power is diffused through the inclusion of multiple perspectives beginning with the development of the team and the use of empathy interviews, but it can't stop there. Hinnant-Crawford (2022, February 15) explains in her podcast called *Improvement as a Tool for our Collective Liberation,*

It is all about honoring all voices from the beginning to the end, from problem definition, from seeing the system. Because people from different perspectives see different parts of the system, from understanding the variation. You've got to have a multiplicity of voices throughout . . . And you've got to be intentional about giving minoritized and marginalized voices space and power, especially when there is a perceived power differential. And if you don't do that, you can't have an equitable improvement process.

ACTION INVENTORY 4.3 WHO DO WE SEEK FOR HELP ON AN IMPROVEMENT PROJECT?

Role	4 (always)	3 (sometimes)	2 (rarely)	1 (never)	Not Applicable
Principal					
Assistant Principal(s)					
School Counselor					
Social Worker					
School Psychologist					
Teacher Leaders					
Teachers					
Instructional Coaches					
Paraeducators					
Front Office Staff					
Cafeteria Staff					
School Safety Staff					
Buildings and Grounds Staff					
District Representatives					
Student Leaders					
Students (who do not hold school-based leadership roles)					
Family Members (who are typically involved in school events)					
Family Members (who are not typically involved in school events)					
College or university representatives					
Community members					
External experts					

Review your answers to the chart in Action Inventory 4.3. Where are opportunities to flatten power dynamics, reduce deficit thinking, and strengthen relationships? For instance, when a caregiver is asked to give input on something at the school, is it typically the same person who volunteers at the school? Who can attend school events? Do you also invite collaborative, listening opportunities with caregivers who are, for any number of reasons, perhaps not at as many school events? You may also want to think about situations in which inviting voice is a part of the work and when it is not. It is not unusual for a building leadership team, for example, to be the group to work on addressing a problem in school. This is likely a very talented group of educators. How might that group deepen their understanding of a problem in their school through admitting where their limitations in understanding lie and to whom they might go for additional information? While working on LGBTQ+ belongingness, Ava used resources from the Human Rights Campaign to design professional development and reached out to a local advocacy group to support family belongingness.

Teams need to be thoughtful and honest about the systems and structures to be interrogated. Organizational problems must be addressed to ensure the work of improvement is socially just and focused on gaps in opportunity built into the structures, practices, systems, and spaces within a school. Use Action Inventory 4.4 to start to practice identifying how structures and practices are connected to different adaptive problems in your school, the variation in opportunity or whose needs are being met and whose needs are being ignored, and shared values that focus on shifting the opportunity structure.

ACTION INVENTORY 4.4 VARIATIONS IN OPPORTUNITIES WITH CORRESPONDING SYSTEMS AND PRACTICES

Opportunity Gap	Corresponding System	Corresponding Practices
Example: All multilingual (ML) students are pulled out of instructional time to practice the English language.	ML policy in the district requires students who are ML (regardless of their English language abilities) to be taught by an ML teacher. This teacher serves multiple schools and is at the school 3 hours a week.	• Registration and evaluation of students who are ML • Schedule of classes • Viewing students (through a limited and deficit lens) • Schedule of personnel • Consultation (or lack thereof) with parents

The Outcomes of Improvement

Another crucial moment for an equity orientation is in how you define the outcomes of improvement. Focusing on outcomes ties back to what the improvement is for and who defines improvement. To have an equity orientation to outcomes, you must be thoughtful about what is focused on and whether the problem is targeting an underserved, marginalized group or ensuring their needs are met in the system. The improvement team must ask if this is focused on all students, does it ensure that the progress is tracked across marginalized groups to attend to variation? Then if it is not working for everyone, how can we rethink the problem or change idea(s) to be more targeted? A strong equity orientation toward outcomes goes even further than focusing on underserved, marginalized groups. It gives care and attention to those groups in the definition of measures and the review of data, and this ensures their perspective is present in the definition of culturally relevant outcomes (Eddy-Spicer & Gomez, 2022).

Measurement in improvement science tracks an aim statement or measurable goal (like a SMART goal). We introduced you to aim statements in Chapter 3 and discuss data and measurement in more detail in Chapter 6. The process of tracking an aim statement ensures attention to the data necessary to measure outcomes for all students; tracking should be explicit about goals for marginalized students. Traditionally, improvement science has focused on outcomes measured by achievement indicators like tests or grades. Since success in these spaces is essential to improvement in our current system that emphasis makes sense. However, equity-oriented improvement should focus less on measures built on inequitable structures. Liberatory and resilient systems can have a more explicit focus on changing complex systems and "system conditions that increase its capacity to bring about more equitable outcomes and experiences," as opposed to just focusing on outcomes like closing the opportunity gap (NEP, 2022). In other words, outcomes are not only about test scores but about changing the way the school functions, addressing underlying systems and structures as a proposed outcome of improvement. Leaders may ask, "How might educational leaders shift the outcome measure to capture changes in the system?" For instance, the leader is trying to understand if the new discipline system is working to decrease disparity in discipline responses. In addition to gathering data to measure the gap between the current (disproportionate discipline responses) and ideal (proportional responses to discipline) through collecting numbers and comparing the number of Black males disciplined before and after the change idea was implemented. The leader might also have a monthly check-in with a student who had been impacted by the old policy, to see if this experience at school is improving overall.

Leading for Equity-Oriented Improvement Science

Leading improvement science is equity-oriented by integrating aspects of culturally responsive school leadership (CRSL) (Khalifa, 2018; Khalifa et al., 2016) and by using liberatory design mindsets and practices (Anaissie, 2021). Equity, social justice, and culturally responsive education are part of CRSL. Three of the areas of CRSL pertain most directly to the initiation and process of improvement science: (a) self-reflection on leadership behaviors, (b) promoting cultural responsiveness, and (c) engaging families in Indigenous contexts. These skills can be developed by creating capacity for culturally responsive pedagogy, professionally developing teachers in culturally responsive pedagogy, creating teams of teachers to work together on culturally responsive school leadership, exploring data to see gaps, and helping teachers reform both curriculum and assessment to be culturally responsive. These concepts all connect to the standards for school leaders (e.g., PSEL) and for programs preparing leaders (e.g., NELP) that state that leaders are responsible for creating an inclusive school culture that ensures socially – just, equitable, and culturally competent educational spaces; recognizes and challenge bias; and collaborates and engages with communities and families. Liberatory design mindsets help leaders and other improvers ensure they work toward strong equity. Liberatory design mindsets also include ways of orienting oneself to improvement work that center strong equity, ultimately leading to the liberation of oppressed groups. These mindsets undergird the actions of improvement leaders.

CRSL must self-reflect on leadership behaviors, acting with cultural competence and responsiveness, ensuring each student is treated fairly, respectfully, and with an understanding of each student's culture and context. CRSL must evaluate, design, cultivate, and advocate for a supportive and inclusive school culture.

A CRSL self-reflects on leadership behaviors by embracing social justice and inclusion in the ways mentioned earlier and reflection during improvement efforts will help you and your team stay accountable to being leaders in culturally responsive and liberatory ways. Action Inventories 4.5–4.7 are anchoring protocols you can utilize during your and/or your team's reflection that includes both CRSL and liberatory design elements that overlap with the practice of reflection.

Leaders must also promote cultural responsiveness, which is defined in the standards as,

> developing student policies and addressing misconduct in a positive, fair, and unbiased manner, confronting and altering institutional biases . . . associated with race, class, culture, language, gender and sexual orientation, and disability of special status; evaluating, cultivating, and advocating for equitable access to educational resources and opportunities that support the educational success and well-being of each student; and evaluating, cultivating, and advocating for equitable, inclusive, and culturally responsive instruction and behavior support practices among teachers and staff.

CRSL to promote cultural responsiveness involves building relationships, promoting a vision for inclusion, challenging exclusionary policies, acknowledging and valuing cultural and social capital, and using data to discover and track disparities. Similarly, liberatory design mindsets that align most closely with promoting cultural responsiveness are building relational trust, working with fear and discomfort, working to transform power, and focusing on human values. Action Inventories 4.5, 4.6, and 4.7 can help your team reflect on these practices.

Culturally responsive school leaders must engage families in Indigenous contexts. This is defined in the PSEL and NELP standards as recognizing, respecting, and employing each student's strengths, diversity, and culture as assets for teaching and learning; collaboratively engaging families in strengthening student learning in and out of school; collaboratively engaging and

ACTION INVENTORY 4.5 REFLECTING ON THE PRACTICE OF CRITICAL REFLECTION FOR EQUITABLE IMPROVEMENT

Week of

This week my / my team's improvement efforts were focused on

In relation to CRSL, our team…	
Accepted local identities by being open to learning about other cultures and adapting behaviors and beliefs to the cultures of the school community.	We did this when… We could have done it when… Next week we could…
Practiced critical consciousness by reflecting critically on actions, decisions, and beliefs.	We did this when… We could have done it when… Next week we could…
Involved family and communities in assessing CRSL in schools by gathering input from the community on actions and decisions.	We did this when… We could have done it when… Next week we could…
Challenged whiteness by recognizing that whiteness is the dominant culture, which presents challenges for non-white communities.	We did this when…. We could have done it when….. Next week we could…
Conducted equity audits by gathering information through data collection on how practices, structures, and systems currently promote equity or inequity.	We did this when…. We could have done it when….. Next week we could…
Led with courage by being willing to take risks for what is just and to come up with change ideas that disrupt the status quo.	We did this when…. We could have done it when….. Next week we could…

In relation to liberator design mindsets, our team…	
Practiced self-awareness by constantly reflecting on your own beliefs, biases, cultural experiences, and impact on others to situate your experience in understanding.	We did this when… We could have done it when… Next week we could…
Recognized oppression by learning, accepting, and acting on the role of oppression in our political, social, and economic structures, systems, and practices, understanding their impact on schools.	We did this when… We could have done it when… Next week we could…
Embraced complexity by learning, accepting, and acting on the fact that the system is complex and interrelated, that improvement is hard to see, attain, and sustain, and that the work may never be done.	We did this when… We could have done it when… Next week we could…
Exercised creative courage by being willing to take risks for what is just and to come up with change ideas that disrupt the status quo (same as above).	We did this when…. We could have done it when….. Next week we could…
Took action to learn by admitting there is a lot you still need to know and actively educate yourself to accelerate intercultural development.	We did this when…. We could have done it when….. Next week we could…

Source: Created by author.

ACTION INVENTORY 4.6 REFLECTING ON THE PRACTICE OF PROMOTING CULTURAL RESPONSIVENESS FOR EQUITABLE IMPROVEMENT

Week of

This week my / my team's improvement efforts were focused on		In relation to CRSL, our team… In relation to liberator design mindsets, our team…	
Built relationships by creating connections between the various individuals and communities in your school community.	We did this when… We could have done it when… Next week we could…	**Built relational trust** by acting in ways that promote honesty, trust, transparency, and a willingness to admit areas of competence and areas of growth.	We did this when… We could have done it when… Next week we could…
Promoted a vision for inclusion by creating the conditions for all cultures to be welcomed in your school community unless they restrict the cultures of others.	We did this when… We could have done it when… Next week we could…	**Worked with fear and discomfort** by acting with humility, vulnerability, and honesty to get out of your comfort zone and understand both your orientation to the culture and other people's culture.	We did this when… We could have done it when… Next week we could…
Challenged exclusionary policies by approaching discipline and other policies (e.g., gifted) with the intention to be inclusive.	We did this when… We could have done it when… Next week we could…	**Worked to transform power** by recognizing that you are part of the power structure and being willing to share that power with others traditionally left out of power structures, all the while focusing on the collective.	We did this when… We could have done it when… Next week we could…
Acknowledged and valuing cultural and social capital by recognizing the assets of other cultures and embedding those assets into practices, policies, structures, and systems.	We did this when…. We could have done it when….. Next week we could…	**Exercised creative courage** by being willing to take risks for what is just and to come up with change ideas that disrupt the status quo (same as above).	We did this when…. We could have done it when….. Next week we could…
Used data to discover and track disparities by valuing multiple types of data, including qualitative data, basing decisions in data and tracking data to understand the impact of those decisions on marginalized groups.	We did this when…. We could have done it when….. Next week we could…	**Focused on human values** by prioritizing human beings needs, fears, feelings, and struggles and approaching human change with compassion.	We did this when…. We could have done it when….. Next week we could…

Source: Created by authors.

ACTION INVENTORY 4.7 REFLECTING ON THE PRACTICE OF ENGAGING WITH FAMILIES FOR EQUITABLE IMPROVEMENT

Week of **This week my / my team's improvement efforts were focused on**		**In relation to CRSL, our team…** **In relation to liberator design mindsets, our team…**	
Developing positive relationships with the community by bringing the community into the school and interacting in ways that develop collaboration and collectivism	We did this when… We could have done it when… Next week we could…	**Resisting deficit images** by avoiding stereotypes of community members that may conjure negative thoughts and emotions for the leader and the community.	We did this when…. We could have done it when….. Next week we could…
Finding spaces for school and community to overlap by reducing isolation in schools by engaging oppressed communities into school until they feel less dissonant.	We did this when… We could have done it when… Next week we could…	**Nurturing others and sharing information** by caring for the community and being transparent about challenges, growth, and the journey to improvement.	We did this when…. We could have done it when….. Next week we could…
Serving as an advocate and activist by supporting community needs whenever possible.	We did this when… We could have done it when… Next week we could…	**Seek liberatory collaboration** by collectively working with communities and families the school serves and including them as partners.	We did this when… We could have done it when… Next week we could…
Embracing the community as an informative space by gathering input, such as empathy interviews from community members to inform decision-making and improvement.	We did this when…. We could have done it when….. Next week we could…	**Attend to healing** by recognizing that people are complex and sensitive and, at times, traumatized. Space needs to be made to process those feelings.	We did this when… We could have done it when… Next week we could…
Connecting directly with students by gathering input, such as empathy interviews from students to inform decision-making and improvement by allowing for student's voices.	We did this when…. We could have done it when….. Next week we could…	**Share, don't sell** by inviting people into the work and letting them experience improving	We did this when… We could have done it when… Next week we could…

Source: Created by author.

cultivating relationships with community members, partners, and other constituencies for the benefit of school improvement and student development; and collaboratively engaging the larger organizational and policy context to advocate for the needs of their school and community (Ishimaru & Bang, 2022; Khalifa, 2018). CRSL to engage families in Indigenous contexts must develop positive relationships with the community, find spaces for school and community to overlap, serve as an advocate and activist, embrace the community as an informative space, connect directly with students, resist deficit images, nurture others, and share information.

The liberatory design mindsets that align most closely with engaging families in Indigenous contexts are seeking liberatory collaboration, attending to healing, and inviting people into the work. Action Inventory 4.6 can help your team reflect on these areas.

Table 4.1 shows the alignment between the PSEL and the NELP standards, the core principles of the improvement science process, and the culturally responsive leadership framework, as well as the liberatory design mindsets.

Barriers and Challenges Confronted in Equity-Oriented Continuous Improvement Initiatives

Equity-oriented improvement will not transform an organization if the right conditions don't exist to explore one's own position of power and privilege; identify systems, structures, and practices that perpetuate inequities; and allow for discussions about inequities that lead to productive approaches to changing norms, practices, and routines. If you are not careful, you may fall into an "equity trap" or take an "equity detour," only practicing thin equity instead of the strong equity defined in this chapter (see Gorski, 2019; McKenzie & Scheurich, 2004). By engaging in critical reflection, you may realize your equity work is more performative, espoused but not enacted, or may continue to perpetuate the status quo. NEP (2021, np) states equity efforts stall because of the following:

- The equity lens isn't deep enough. There is a focus on diversity and inclusion instead of systemic oppression. This concept is similar to the idea of thin equity vs. strong equity discussed earlier in the chapter.
- People fail to recognize the messiness and complexity of improvement and take a traditional accountability route to equity.
- People are dominated by white culture. They use traditional structures, don't engage in critical dialogue, aren't creative, are focused on urgency instead of lasting change, and create great ideas but don't ensure leadership is on board with the solutions.
- There is a lack of trust, especially across groups with differential power. Trust and relationships need to be developed to navigate the discussions and changes associated with improving equitable, socially just, and culturally competent schools.

Table 4.1 Alignment between Standards, Culturally Responsive School Leadership, Liberatory Design Mindsets, and Improvement Science.

CRSL	*Liberatory Design Mindsets*	*NELP*	*PSEL*	*Improvement Science Process*
Self-reflect on leadership behaviors – Accepting local identities – Practicing critical consciousness – Involving family/communities to assessing CRSL in schools – Challenging whiteness – Conducting equity audits – Leading with courage – Embracing social justice and inclusion	– Practice self-awareness – Recognize oppression – Embrace complexity – Take action to learn – Exercise creative courage	Evaluate, design, cultivate and advocate for supportive and inclusive school culture. **(3.1)**	Act with cultural competence and responsiveness. **(3g)** Ensure each student is treated fairly, respectfully, and with an understanding of each student's culture and context. **(3c)**	– Understand the problem and be user-centered – See the system – Attend to variation
Promote cultural responsiveness – Build relationships – Promote a vision for inclusion – Challenge exclusionary policies – Acknowledge and value cultural and social capital – Use data to discover and track disparities	– Build relational trust – Work with fear and discomfort – Work to transform power – Focus on human values	**Evaluate, cultivate, and advocate for:** – equitable access to educational resources and opportunities that support the educational success and well-being of each student. **(3.2)** – equitable, inclusive, and culturally responsive instruction and behavior support practices among teachers and staff. **(3.3)**	Address matters of equity and cultural responsiveness in all aspects of leadership. **(3h)** Develop student policies and address misconduct in a positive, fair, and unbiased manner. **(3d)** Confront and alter institutional biases . . . associated with race, class, culture, language, gender and sexual orientation, and disability of special status. **(3e)**	– Disciplined inquiry – Embrace measurement (and attend to variation through that data)

(*Continued*)

Table 4.1 (Continued)

CRSL	*Liberatory Design Mindsets*	*NELP*	*PSEL*	*Improvement Science Process*
Engage families in Indigenous contexts – Develop positive relationships – Find spaces for school and community to overlap – Serve as an advocate and activist – Community as an informative space – Resist deficit images – Nurture others and share info – Connect directly with students	– Seek liberatory collaboration – Attend to healing – Share, don't sell – invite people in	**Collaboratively engage:** – families in strengthening student learning in and out of school. **(5.1)** – and cultivate relationships with community members, partners, and other constituencies for the benefit of school improvement and student development. **(5.2)** Collaboratively engage the larger organizational and policy context to advocate for the needs of their school and community. **(5.3)**	Recognize, respect, and employ each student's strengths, diversity, and culture as assets for teaching and learning. **(3b)** Infuse the school's learning environment with the cultures and languages of the school's community. **(3f)**	– Understand the problem and be user-centered – See the system

It is important to mention that we recognize that an equity orientation is not always welcomed by teachers, leaders, school boards, and communities. Some of the factors that stall equity-oriented improvement are not in the school leaders' control. Currently, if you are in a geographic region that won't allow educators to discuss equity explicitly or where policymakers have enacted policies that limit the rights of groups of students, then, to maintain the necessary focus on equity, you need to navigate that political tension and the potential ramifications of resisting those policies very carefully. You also need to keep your job for your sake and for the students for whom you are trying to improve the system. It is not easy work and cannot be approached without the foresight to recognize barriers will arise, but equity-oriented improvement science is the right work for leaders and schools to transform organizations to be successful and to meet the needs of each student.

Equity as an Orientation

Hopefully, you see why we say that an equity orientation is not only important for leading improvement in schools, but that improvement science is a means for pursuing problem-solving to transform organizations. You may be left wondering what equity-oriented improvement science look would like in practice. We suggest some steps to take to lead this work. These steps come from a framework created by Anderson et al. (forthcoming) and are anchored in liberatory design mindsets to support a NIC seeking to create equitable outcomes for marginalized students: students with disabilities, students with English as a second language, students living with low socioeconomic status, and students of color in high school math.

1) **Engage in critical self-reflection and recognize how one is complicit in structural racism and inequity.** This aligns with the liberatory design mindset of "practice self-awareness." An equity-oriented improvement process includes critical reflection through self-awareness. An improver needs to interrogate deficit beliefs and biases and must understand equity as it relates to marginalized groups of students and families. Hinnant-Crawford explained:

    > The other piece – and not just humility – is this real critical reflection, and it's hard. Because it is a lot easier to look at data than it is to look in the mirror and see how you might be perpetuating injustices or oppressions within the process by dismissing certain voices. And so when you want to focus more on a data point than the voice of the person whose data point that is, that makes the whole process jaded. And in many ways, it invalidates it" (Brandi Hinnant-Crawford, hthUnboxed, February 15, 2022).

    Space needs to be made to be critical and to reflect on the role each individual plays in an inequitable system. Making space for critical reflection can involve individual reflection such as making time to journal, voice memo, or just think and jot notes about how your leadership is impacting equity on a daily or weekly basis (like what the Action Inventories invite you to do). These spaces can be more collective and can include a formal or informal network of leaders who meet regularly to discuss and reflect on leadership moves related to equity. Group members can bring dilemmas to the table or share their personal reflections and gather feedback and support. As a leader, you could also join or lead a school-based or district-based equity team with a structured agenda for exploring and acting on equity issues.

2) **Question norms and practices that lead to inequities, including creating a culture that invites a dialogue about issues of equity, social justice, and cultural competency. Approach data analysis with equity, social justice, and cultural competency lenses and explore norms, practices, and routines that are the cause of inequities.** This aligns with the liberatory mindsets of "build relational trust," "work with fear and discomfort," "recognize oppression," and "embrace complexity." The team working on improvement and the whole school community must establish norms and patterns of communication that create space for the kind of open, honest, and personal conversations required. There is discomfort in questioning inequities, exploring oppression, and examining the role each person plays in the systems of oppression. This discomfort must be recognized and supported. Addressing deep problems that challenge equity and social justice and that change systems, structures, and practices is complex work, must be named by the leader to "acknowledge the confusion and discomfort present in our work" (NEP, 2022, np). The team will be more likely to capture that complexity, name the oppression, and question existing norms and practices with equity-oriented data.
3) **Develop and uphold an inclusive, anti-oppressive, and anti-racist school environment for all that is inclusive of the community for all marginalized groups.** This aligns with the liberatory mindsets of "focus on human values," "attend to healing," and "work to transform power." The work is about humans and about the need to transform systems, structures, and practices in ways that recognize the humanity of people, making space for the experiences and stories of all users and community members. The school needs to invite the community into conversations and solutions (Khalifa, 2018) and "attend to [the communities'] well-being and healing on an ongoing basis" (NEP, 2022, np). Making space for healing includes regular check-ins, protocols for having difficult conversations, and attending to trauma. Power dynamics are at play: between members of an improvement team, between leaders and teachers, and between educators and families (interpersonal). Those power dynamics must be interrogated and reimagined to create equitable change. As part of developing an inclusive environment, power must be shared. Through working together on problems, there are opportunities to hear multiple perspectives and make space for those perspectives in decision-making.

4) **Make equity, social justice, and cultural competency central to the improvement process from the beginning and ensure school-wide equity-oriented practices.** This aligns with the liberatory mindsets of "seek liberatory collaboration," "exercise creative courage," "take action to learn," and "share, don't sell – invite people in." This work is meant to be done in teams, and those teams should include the perspective of traditionally marginalized groups. We can collaborate in ways that perpetuate oppression and power structures, or we can collaborate in ways that are truly inviting everyone to the table, validating experiences, and recognizing various forms of strength or capital. The improvement science process involves creating a theory of improvement that names the key drivers in the systems and aligns change ideas to those drivers. Those change ideas are tested and iterated until solutions are designed to be scaled up and spread through the school or district. The ideas tested should seek to transform systems. By being creative and addressing oppression, "we must act courageously to imagine possibilities beyond the confines of the dominant culture" and "cultivate an environment that inspires curiosity and courage to think, feel, and act creatively" (NEP, 2022, np). By approaching the work with collaboration, humility, and a focus on inclusion, people will seek to join the work.

One school with which an author works serves as an example of how to apply such recommendations. The school identified a problem of practice: they wanted to increase student engagement in a culturally responsive manner. Through empathy interviews and reviewing data, systems, and processes, the school realized there were challenges associated with this problem; to practice strong equity, they needed to move away from compliance-based practices, support their students of color in transitioning from dependent to independent learners, and needed to focus on academic excellence for Black students. They reached these beliefs through critical self-reflection where the instructional leadership and improvement team realized that although they were knowledgeable about culturally responsive education, they may not be practicing it. They began to question their coaching model, evaluation model, and data-driven instruction (DDI) model. This led to four interrelated change ideas. One, they revisited the evaluation process, and instead of relying on the score-based, district-provided system, they decided to have teachers involved in the decision about their own growth. Two, the leadership team recognized oppression stemming from the evaluation system as a driver of change; to address this, they implemented a teacher-led goal-setting process focused on the instruction of a group of five Black students who were on the cusp of academic success. Three, the school created vertical DDI learning labs to increase teachers' voices, recognize expertise, and enhance learning from each other. Four, they video recorded lessons and reflected on them, planning for the next steps in small groups. This process transformed the power and sought liberatory collaboration. At the same time, they had Culture Friday where they engaged in a book group on *Culturally Responsive Teaching and the Brain* by Hammond (2014). They changed the structure of coaching meetings to reframe the teacher as the expert. The coach and teacher now work together to determine the next steps for increasing outcomes for the target group of five students for whom they are goal setting and discussing as the focus on the taped lesson in DDI meetings. These change ideas require them to practice self-awareness, transform power, and build relational trust by creating inclusion with equity at the center.

Now that you've finished reading this chapter, go back to Action Inventory 4.1 and review your responses and then capture any new insights or rethinking in Action Inventory 4.8.

ACTION INVENTORY 4.8 CONCLUSIONS REFLECTION QUESTIONS

1. Now, how do you currently see the relationship between equity and improvement?
2. Did any of your wonderings connected to the relationship between equity and improvement get addressed? Which ones and how so?
3. What are your new wonderings connected to the relationship between equity and improvement?

CONCLUSION

Moral Values

Equity work is the moral obligation of educators and must be prioritized at each phase. Regardless of where you are on your journey toward intercultural development and cultural competency, developing an equity orientation, and upholding social justice beliefs and action, you will want to approach improvement by recognizing there is oppression, inequity, and injustice in the education system. You, as an individual in that system, are not responsible for the whole system, but you are responsible for the students, families, teachers, and community that you serve. Your job is making equity, justice, and culturally responsive education norm in your school and district and disrupting those existing systems of stratification, gaps in opportunity, and the marginalization of your students who are non-white, non-Christian, non-heterosexual, or marginalized based on other identity markers.

Social Relations

Equity-oriented, socially-just, and culturally responsive improvement science requires attention to social relations. Improvers must consider how they interact with others within the existing power structures, must work in collaboration toward collective beliefs and practices, and must create a culture that invites a dialogue about issues of equity, social justice, and cultural competency. Attending to power structures, leaders of improvement must include multiple perspectives throughout the process and must be inclusive of Indigenous communities. Processes will need to be interrogated to ensure that norms and habits uphold equity.

Instrumental Methods

Focus on equity in measures and outcomes. Those measures should uplift the voices of people impacted by the problem and solutions, and they should consider the goals and intentions of the cultural groups within the school community. Variation is key to understanding how the problem impacts different groups of students, and the types of measures used should capture the multiple experiences of stakeholders.

This chapter is only an introduction to the issues and concepts related to diversity, equity, inclusion, and social justice relevant to the topic of grounding continuous improvement with, through, and in equity. Within the space of this chapter, we sought to introduce key concepts like oppression, stratification, bias, deficit thinking, privilege, power, and cultural capital. To deepen your equity as a capability, here is a list of resources to consult:

- Diem, S., & Welton, A.D. (2020). *Anti-racist educational leadership and policy: Addressing racism in public education* (1st ed.). Routledge.
- Gay, Geneva. (2000). *Culturally responsive teaching: theory, research, and practice*. Teachers College Press.
- González, N., Moll, L. C., & Amanti, C. (Eds.). (2006). *Funds of knowledge: Theorizing practices in households, communities, and classrooms*. Routledge.
- Hammond, Z. (2014). *Culturally responsive teaching and the brain: Promoting authentic engagement and rigor among culturally and linguistically diverse students*. Corwin Press.
- Khalifa, M. A. (2018). *Culturally responsive school leadership*. Harvard Education Press.
- Ladson-Billings, G. (2021). *Culturally relevant pedagogy: Asking a different question*. Teachers College Press.
- Ladson-Billings, G. (2022). *The dream keepers: Successful teachers of African American children*. John Wiley & sons. (3rd Edition).
- Lindsey, R. B., Nuri-Robins, K., Terrell, R. D., & Lindsey, D. B. (2018). *Cultural proficiency: A manual for school leaders*. Corwin Press.
- Love, B. L. (2019). *We want to do more than survive: Abolitionist teaching and the pursuit of educational freedom*. Beacon Press.
- Muhammad, G., & Love, B. L. (2020). *Cultivating genius: An equity framework for culturally and historically responsive literacy.*
- Radd, S. I., Generett, G. G., Gooden, M. A., & Theoharis, G. (2021). *Five practices for equity-focused school leadership*. ASCD.
- Singh, A. A. (2019). *The racial healing handbook: Practical activities to help you challenge privilege, confront systemic racism, and engage in collective healing*. New Harbinger Publications.

- Singleton, Glenn E. (2014). *Courageous conversations about race: A field guide for achieving equity in schools*. Corwin.
- Valencia, R.R. (Ed.). (1997). *The Evolution of Deficit Thinking: Educational Thought and Practice* (1st ed.). Routledge.
- Valencia, R. R. (2019). *International deficit thinking: Educational thought and practice*. Routledge.

NELP and PSEL Connection Box for Educational Leadership Faculty

In addition to PSEL Standard 10, this chapter aligns closely with PSEL and NELP Standards Three and NELP Standard Five. These standards focus on the development and implementation of a mission and vision and the use of continuous improvement, specifically related to a "core set of values and priorities" (NCPEA, 2018). The standards for school leaders (i.e., PSEL) and for programs preparing leaders (i.e., NELP), state that leaders are responsible for creating an inclusive school culture that ensures just, equitable, and culturally competent educational spaces; recognizing and challenging bias; and collaborating and engaging with communities and families. NELP Standard Three "Equity, Inclusiveness, and Cultural Responsiveness" states, "Candidates who successfully complete a building-level educational leadership preparation program understand and demonstrate the capacity to promote the current and future success and well-being of each student and adult by applying the knowledge, skills, and commitments necessary to develop and maintain a supportive, equitable, culturally responsive and inclusive school culture." PSEL Three is related directly to NELP Standard Three. PSEL Three suggests leaders should: (a) shape and maintain a safe, caring, healthy, inclusive, and responsive school environment; (b) develop, implement, and evaluate equitable guidelines, procedures, and decisions; (c) ensure that each student has equitable access to resources, relationships, opportunities, and supports necessary for success; and (d) support the development of responsive and equitable practices among teachers and staff. This chapter discusses specific PSEL and NELP components of the third NELP and PSEL standards that connect equity concerns and continuous improvement. Equity and cultural responsiveness are also present in PSEL and NELP Standards 4 (Learning and Instruction) and NELP Standard 6 and PSEL Nine (Operations and Management). Finally, since equity and improvement cannot be done without including families and communities, NELP Standard 5 on community and external leadership states that candidates should, "understand and demonstrate the capacity to understand and engage families, communities, and other constituents in the work of schools and the district and to advocate for district, student, and community needs." Working with and in the community is essential for equity.

BIBLIOGRAPHY

Acevedo, N., & Solorzano, D. G. (2021). An overview of community cultural wealth: Toward a protective factor against racism. *Urban Education, 0*(0). https://doi.org/10.1177/00420859211016531

Ainscow, M., Dyson, A., Goldrick, S., & West, M. (2016). Using collaborative inquiry to foster equity within school systems: Opportunities and barriers. *School Effectiveness and School Improvement, 27*(1), 7–23. http://10.1080/09243453.2014.939591

Anaissie, T., Cary, V., Clifford, D., Malarkey, T., & Wise, S. (2021). *Liberatory design.* www.liberatorydesign.com

Anderson, E., Cunningham, K. W., & Richardson, J. W. (Forthcoming, 2023). Sustaining continuous school improvement: A framework for transformative organizations. In E. Anderson & S. Hayes (Eds.), *Continuous improvement: A leadership process for school improvement.* Information Age Publishing.

Anderson, E., Cunningham, K. W., & Richardson, J. W. (under review). Framework for implementing improvement science in a school district to support sustainable growth.

Anderson, E., Cunningham, K. W., & Richardson, J. W. (Forthcoming, 2023). Sustainingcontinuous school improvement: A framework for transformative organizations. In E. Anderson & S. Hayes (Eds.), Continuous improvement: A leadership process for schoolimprovement . Information Age Publishing.

Bang, M., Faber, L., Gurneau, J., Marin, A., & Soto, C. (2016). Community-Based Design Research: Learning Across Generations and Strategic Transformations of Institutional Relations Toward Axiological Innovations. Mind, Culture, and Activity, 23(1), 28-41. https://doi.org/10.1080/10749039.2015.1087572

Biag, M. (2017). Building a village through data: A research-practice partnership to improve youth outcomes. *School Community Journal, 27,* 9–27.

Biag, M. (2019). Navigating the improvement journey with an equity compass. In R. Crow, B. Hinnant-Crawford, & D. T. Spaulding (Eds.), *The educational leader's guide to improvement science: Data, design and cases for reflection* (pp. 91–124). Myers Education Press.

Bryk, A. S., Gomez, L. M., Grunow, A., & Lemahieu, P. G. (2015). *Learning to improve: How America's schools can get better at getting better.* Harvard Education Press.

Capper, C. A. (2018). *Organizational theory for equity and diversity: Leading integrated, socially just education.* Routledge.

Cochran-Smith, M., Baker, M., Burton, S., Chang, W. C., Cummings Carney, M., Fernández, M. B., . . . Sánchez, J. G. (2017). The accountability era in US teacher education: Looking back, looking forward. *European Journal of Teacher Education, 40*(5), 572–588. https://eric.ed.gov/?id=EJ1159379

CRE Hub. (2022). *Culturally responsive education.* EIROC at NYC Metro Center. https://crehub.org/

Davis, L., & Museus, S. (2019). What is deficit thinking? An analysis of conceptualizations of deficit thinking and implications for scholarly research. *Currents, 1*(1), 117–130. http://dx.doi.org/10.3998/

Diem, S., & Welton, A. D. (2020). *Anti-racist educational leadership and policy: Addressing racism in public education* (1st ed.). Routledge.

Eddy-Spicer, D., & Gomez, L. M. (2022). Accomplishing meaningful equity. In D. J. Peurach, J. L. Russell, L. Cohen-Vogel, & W. R. Penuel (Eds.), *The foundational handbook on improvement research in education* (pp. 89–110). Rowman & Littlefield.

Fishman, B., & Herrenkohl, L. R. (2022). Equitable learning. In D. Peurach, J. Russell, L. Cohen-Vogel, & W. Penuel (Eds.), *Handbook of improvement focused educational research* (pp. 47–66). Rowan and Littlefield.

Galloway, M. K., & Ishimaru, A. M. (2020). Leading equity teams: The role of formal leaders in building organizational capacity for equity. *Journal of Education for Students Placed at Risk (JESPAR), 25*(2), 107–125. https://doi.org/10.1080/10824669.2019.1699413

Gay, G. (2000). *Culturally responsive teaching: Theory, research, and practice.* Teachers College Press.

González, N., Moll, L. C., & Amanti, C. (Eds.). (2006). *Funds of knowledge: Theorizing practices in households, communities, and classrooms.* Routledge.

Gorski, P. C. (2011). Unlearning deficit ideology and the scornful gaze: Thoughts on authenticating the class discourse in education. *Counterpoints, 402,* 152–173. www.jstor.org/stable/42981081

Gorski, P. C. (2019). Avoiding racial equity detours. *Educational Leadership, 76*(7), 58–61.

Hammond, Z. (2014). *Culturally responsive teaching and the brain: Promoting authentic engagement and rigor among culturally and linguistically diverse students.* Corwin Press.

Herr, K., & Anderson, G. L. (2014). *The action research dissertation: A guide for students and faculty.* Sage Publications.

Hinnant-Crawford, B. N. (2020). *Improvement science in education: A primer.* Myers Education Press and Spaulding.

Hinnant-Crawford, B. N. (2022, February 15). *Improvement as a tool for our collective liberation, with Dr. Brandi Hinnant-Crawford.* https://hthunboxed.org/podcasts/s3e14-improvement-as-a-tool-for-our-collective-liberation-with-dr-brandi-hinnant-crawford/

Hinnant-Crawford, B. N., Lett, E. L., & Cormartie, S. (forthcoming) Improvement: Critical dispositions for equitable improvement. In E. Anderson & S. Hayes (Eds.), *Continuous improvement: A leadership process for school improvement.* Information Age Publishing.

Hinnant-Crawford, B. N., Nazario y Colon, R., & Davis, T. W. (2021). Who is involved? Who is impacted? Teaching improvement science for educational justice. In D. T. Spaulding, R. Crow, & B. N. Hinnant-Crawford (Eds.), *Teaching improvement science in educational leadership* (pp. 17–41). Myers Education Press.

Horsford, S. D., Scott, J. T., & Anderson, G. L. (2019). *The politics of education policy in an era of inequality: Possibilities for democratic schooling.* Routledge.

Irby, D. J. (2021). *Stuck improving: Racial equity and school leadership.* Harvard Education Press.

Ishimaru, A. M. (2019). From family engagement to equitable collaboration. *Educational Policy, 33*(2), 350–385. https://doi.org/10.1177/0895904817691841

Ishimaru, A. M., & Bang, M. (2022). Solidarity-driven codesign. In D. J. Peurach, J. Russell, L. Cohen-Vogel, & W. R. Penuel (Eds.), *The foundational handbook on improvement research in education* (pp. 383-402).

Jabbar, H., & Childs, J. (2022). Critical perspectives on gthe contexts of improvemtn research in education. In D. J. Peurach, J. L. Russell, L. Cohen-Vogel, & W. R. Penuel (Eds.), *The foundational handbook on improvement research in education* (pp. 241–262). Rowman & Littlefield.

Kelley, T., & Kelley, D. (2013). *Creative confidence: Unleashing the creative potential within us all.* Currency.

Kendi, I. X. (2019). *How to be an antiracist.* Penguin.

Khalifa, M. A. (2018). *Culturally responsive school leadership.* Harvard Education Press.

Khalifa, M. A., Gooden, M. A., & Davis, J. E. (2016). Culturally responsive school leadership: A synthesis of the literature. *Review of Educational Research, 86*(4), 1272–1311. https://doi.org/10.3102/0034654316630383

Koretz, D. M. (2008). *Measuring up*. Harvard University Press.

Ladson-Billings, G. (2021). *Culturally relevant pedagogy: Asking a different question*. Teachers College Press.

Ladson-Billings, G. (2022). *The dream keepers: Successful teachers of African American children* (3rd ed.). John Wiley & Sons.

Langley, G. L., Moen, R. D., Nolan, K. M., Nolan, T. W., Norman, C. L., & Provost, L. P. (2009). *The improvement guide: A practical approach to enhancing organizational performance* (2nd ed.). Josey-Bass.

LeMahieu, P. G., Lee, N., & Gale, D. (2017). Positive deviance: Learning from positive anomalies. *Quality Assurance in Education, 25*(1), 109-124. https://doi.org/doi:10.1108/QAE-12-2016-0083

Lindsey, R. B., Nuri-Robins, K., Terrell, R. D., & Lindsey, D. B. (2018). *Cultural proficiency: A manual for school leaders*. Corwin Press.

Liu, W. M., Liu, R. Z., Garrison, Y. L., Kim, J. Y. C., Chan, L., Ho, Y., & Yeung, C. W. (2019). Racial trauma, microaggressions, and becoming racially innocuous: The role of acculturation and White supremacist ideology. *American Psychologist, 74*(1), 143. https://doi.org/10.1037/amp0000368

Love, B. L. (2019). *We want to do more than survive: Abolitionist teaching and the pursuit of educational freedom*. Beacon Press.

Martínez, D. G., & Spikes, D. D. (2020). Se Acabaron Las Palabras: A post-mortem Flores v. Arizona disproportional funding analysis of targeted English Learner expenditures. *Educational Policy*. https://doi.org/10.1177/0895904820917370

McKenzie, K. B., & Scheurich, J. J. (2004). Equity traps: A useful construct for preparing principals to lead schools that are successful with racially diverse students. *Educational Administration Quarterly, 40*(5), 601–632. https://doi.org/10.1177/0013161X04268839

Muhammad, G., & Love, B. L. (2020). *Cultivating genius: An equity framework for culturally and historically responsive literacy*. Scholastic, Inc.

National Equity Project. (2023). *Equity tools*. www.nationalequityproject.org/resources/tools

National Museum of African American History and Culture. (2021, December 28). *Social identities and systems of oppression*. Smithsonian. https://nmaahc.si.edu/learn/talking-about-race/topics/social-identities-and-systems-oppression

National Policy Board for Educational Administration. (2015). *Professional standards for educational leaders 2015*. Author. www.npbea.org/psel/

National Policy Board for Educational Administration. (2018). *National Educational Leadership Preparation (NELP) program standards: Building level*. www.npbea.org

Nelsestuen, K., & Smith, J. (2020). Empathy intervieww. *The Learning Professional, 41*(5), 59. https://du.idm.oclc.org/login?url=www.proquest.com/scholarly-journals/empathy-interviews/docview/2469852826/se-2

Okilwa, N., Khalifa, M. A., & Briscoe, F. (2017). *The school to prison pipeline: The role of culture and discipline in school* (N. Okilwa, M. A. Khalifa, & F. Briscoe, Eds.). Emerald Publishing.

Pascale, R. T., Sternin, J., & Sternin, M. (2010). *The power of positive deviance: How unlikely innovators solve the world's toughest problems*. Harvard Business Press.

Patton Davis, L. & Museus, S. (2019). What Is deficit thinking? An analysis of conceptualizations of deficit thinking and implications for scholarly research. *Currents, 1*(1), 117-130. http://dx.doi.org/10.3998/ currents.17387731.0001.110

Radd, S. I., Generett, G. G., Gooden, M. A., & Theoharis, G. (2021). *Five practices for equity-focused school leadership.* ASCD.

Safir, S., & Dugan, J. (2021). *Street data: A next-generation model for equity, pedagogy, and school transformation.* Corwin.

Sensoy, O., & DiAngelo, R. (2009). Developing social justice literacy: An open letter to our faculty colleagues. *Phi Delta Kappan, 90*(5), 345–352. https://doi.org/10.1177/003172170909000508

Singleton, G. E. (2014). *Courageous conversations about race: A field guide for achieving equity in schools.* Corwin.

Valencia, R. R. (Ed.). (1997). *The evolution of deficit thinking: Educational thought and practice* (1st ed.). Routledge.

Valencia, R. R. (2019). *International deficit thinking: Educational thought and practice.* Routledge.

Wilhelm, A. G., Gray, D. S., & Crosby, E. O. (In press). Building capacity for continuousimprovement: Iterating to center racial equity in a PK-8 community school. In E.Anderson & S. Hayes (Eds.), Continuous improvement: A leadership process for schoolimprovement . Information Age Publishing.

Yosso, T. J. (2005). Whose culture has capital? A critical race theory discussion of community cultural wealth. *Race Ethnicity and Education, 8*(1), 69–91. https://doi.org/10.4324/9781003005995-8

Yosso, T. J., & Burciaga, R. (2016). Reclaiming our histories, recovering community cultural wealth. *Center for Critical Race Studies at UCLA Research Brief, 5,* 1–4. www.ccrse.gseis.ucla.edu/publications

Zumpe, E., & Aramburo, C. (In press). Developing enabling conditions for continuous improvement: Building foundational team "habits of mind." In E. Anderson & S. Hayes (Eds.), *Continuous improvement: A leadership process for school improvement.* Information Age Publishing.

PART II

How Do We Enact Continuous Improvement?

CHAPTER 5

Problem Identification and Framing

with Brandi Hinnant-Crawford

Chapter Highlights

1) Problem formulation is important for improvement. Selecting the wrong problem can limit improvement.
2) Understanding the problem and the system surrounding it is key to solving that problem.
3) This process can and should be applied to complex, adaptive, wicked problems.
4) The 5S Model of Problem Formulation can be used to guide problem selection.

CHAPTER OVERVIEW

This chapter discusses how to begin continuous improvement by framing a problem of practice as an opportunity for adaptive change. Complex problems cannot be solved without being identified and defined. We discuss a model for problem formulation that considers five major dimensions: significance (focus on equity and/or efficiency), source, substantive focus, scale, and scope (Hinnant-Crawford & Anderson, 2022). Schools can develop a deeper understanding of the problem by unearthing assumptions and uncovering the "real" problem (Mintrop, 2016) and by using epistemologies for equity (e.g., Khalifa, 2018). Leaders effectively facilitating efforts to focus on problem identification and framing results in more manageable, impactful, and successful improvement. Furthermore, the chapter discusses the tools used in the process for identifying the root causes of a problem

DOI: 10.4324/9781003389279-7

and explores challenges in problem identification and framing as related to those five major dimensions.

We will reference many tools to help you make a thoughtful, grounded, and informed decision in selecting the problem. These include

- Empathy interviews (user-centered approach to problem identification)
- Local data (aggregated and disaggregated to understand what works for whom and capture variability)
- Equity audits (local data exploring equitable access)
- Systems and process mapping (maps providing a visual of the system to identify areas of concern, bottlenecks, and breakdowns)
- Research knowledge (how has the problem been framed in research?)
- Practical knowledge (how has the problem been framed and solved in analogous settings and what do those closest to the problem know about the problem?)
- Root cause analysis based on empathy data, local data, research, and practice knowledge (e.g., affinity mapping, fishbone diagrams, five whys)

We will not describe tools in detail. The tools are used by Ava in Chapter 1, and the procedures are described in more detail in the toolbox chapter (Chapter 8). You don't need to use all these tools, although we would encourage getting familiar with each tool. Your selection of problem-formulating tools will be based on your problem and your context.

Introduction: Problem-Solving in Improvement Science

Improvement science is a "problem-solving approach centered on continuous inquiry and learning" (Institute for Education Science, 2017, np). Improvement is the response to a problem or a gap between the ideal state of your school and the current state of your school. When that gap persists over time, the problem is entrenched or "wicked," a problem difficult or impossible to solve due to the complexity of its interconnections (Rittel & Webber, 1973). We are sure everyone reading this book could come up with a list of wicked, entrenched problems they face daily. These problems are sharp and jagged. They impact people in harmful ways. They can block and stop goals and priorities from being met. Part of leadership is being able to not only identify but deliberately name these as things to address, even if they have not been explicitly named before. You can use Action Inventory 5.1 to practice this. Articulate some of those sharp, jagged, wicked problems below in Action Inventory 5.1.

Deeply entrenched problems, embedded in the oppressive systems we described in Chapter 4, are adaptive challenges: to be solved they require shifts in both thoughts and actions (Heifetz et al., 2009). Before an improvement team can solve a problem of practice, they must define the nature of the problem. For continuous improvement to have the greatest impact on students, teams should select wicked, entrenched problems that are adaptive challenges (Argyris & Schön, 1996; Heifetz et al., 2009;

Senge, 2006). Adaptive challenges are tenacious, multifaceted, ill-structured, or vague (Dunn, 2018; Gomez et al., 2016; Gutiérrez & Penuel, 2014; Mintrop, 2016; Perry et al., 2020; Rittel & Webber, 1973). These challenges or problems persist over time because they require a response that not only involves changing systems, structures, and practices but also shifting mindsets, assumptions, and beliefs.

ACTION INVENTORY 5.1 NAME SOME OF THE WICKED, ENTRENCHED PROBLEMS YOUR SCHOOL FACES

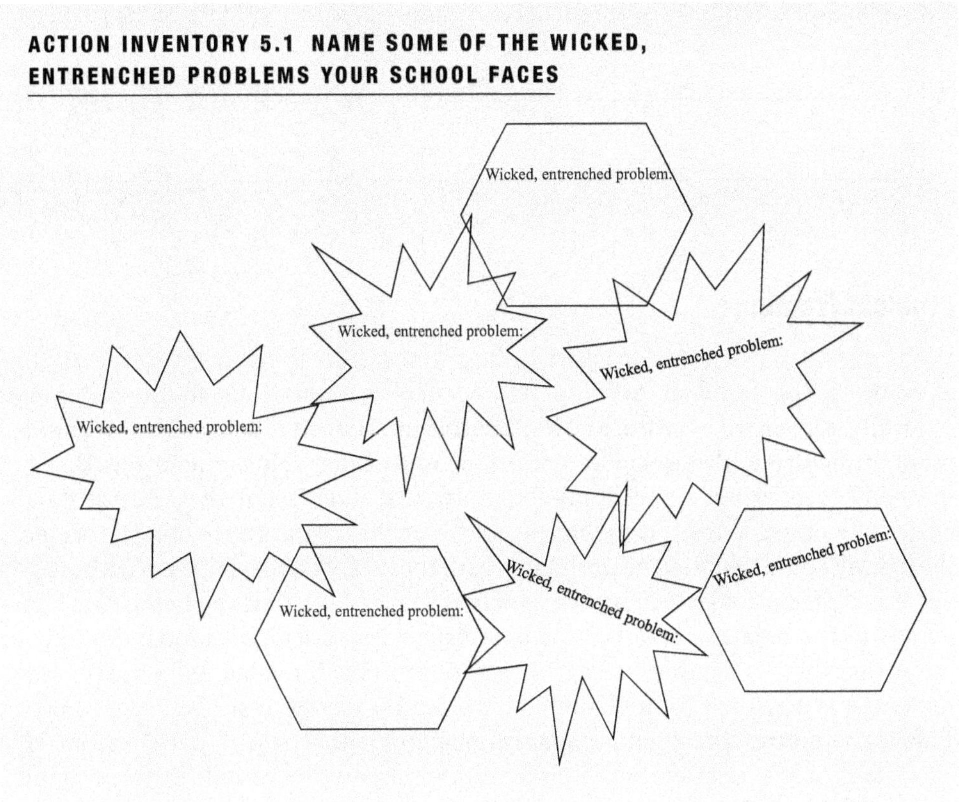

To change the system, one needs to see the system. The nature of problems ripe for continuous improvement emerges from complex systems through inquiry processes (Mintrop, 2016). Problems are aspects of complex systems, so even problem framing is iterative and ongoing. Clarity on the true nature of the problem only becomes apparent through testing. The systems, and the problems embedded in them, evolve with time and require constant and continuous attention.

These systems-embedded improvement problems need adaptive solutions. Adaptive solutions respond to the complexity of the problem (Heifetz et al., 2009). To determine adaptive solutions, the problem must be clearly framed. Solving adaptive problems also requires multiple coherent and aligned strategies that may take time to design and measure. This is not simple work. We encourage you to embrace the challenge! Think about some of the problems you are considering dedicating efforts to address. Take a moment to make sure they are adaptive by completing Action Inventory 5.2.

ACTION INVENTORY 5.2 CHECKLIST: IS THIS PROBLEM ADAPTIVE?

Problem to potentially address	Is it . . . tenacious?	Is it . . . multifaceted?	Is it . . . ill-structured?	Is it . . . vague?

Problem Framing

What does it mean for a problem to be framed with the system in view? How is framing the problem different from current approaches to improvement? Typically, a group of educators notices a problem, such as a lack of student engagement, difficulty with teacher retention, or unfulfilled achievement outcomes in math. They may have anecdotal conversations about what they notice during leadership or grade team meetings. Usually, at this point, the group shares ideas they think could address the problem; then, they select a response either based on perceived group consensus or the hunch of the leader, often the principal. Those people in the meeting or other formal leaders are tasked with letting everyone know that there is a new system, process, or protocol intended to fix the problem. Everyone is expected to implement this solution for the rest of the school year. This is the normal process for engaging the problem.

The problem is often left ill-defined and largely anecdotal. Problem definition and formulation are based on the personal experiences of those people in the room during the conversation. This approach does not consider all staff experiences or multiple perspectives about the problem and solution(s). Everyone is being asked to implement a solution, but some of the staff may not agree that the stated problem is, in fact, a problem. Other staff members may agree about the problem but not have confidence in the newly brainstormed solution. Some educators may fear the solution will only be a temporary fix or this problem and solution will only be a priority for the school until another new idea takes precedence. Regardless of their perspective on or experience with the problem, teachers are asked to implement the new system, structure, process, or protocol in their classroom for the rest of the year. For that reason, and often rightfully so, teachers may choose to ignore the strategy and continue with their own approach.

Educators are frequently asked to implement new solutions to solve perceived problems in the system; however, the number of initiatives that the average educator may be asked to engage in (and then move on from) over several years in the classroom can be overwhelming and frustrating. Initiative fatigue is a common experience in schools and can limit engagement of key stakeholders in implementing solutions (Freedman, 1992). Schools have long been expected to respond to the introduction of solutions, instead of being asked to help define and solve their own problems. For instance, the introduction of a new curriculum; the hot, new education book that everyone is mandated to read; or the professional development whose topic or focus is determined by the district are put forth as responses to perceived needs in the system, but they may not actually be addressing the right problem, making them harder to implement and easy to ignore.

Problem Framing Through Improvement Science

Now, consider instead the use of a problem-focused, user-centered approach to problem-solving. This process of problem identification is multi-staged and nonlinear. Instead of a small group of well-meaning individuals having a brief discussion during a meeting and coming up with a solution, that same group, using improvement science, begins the process by engaging in understanding the problem, like Ava and her NIC and the school improvement team did in Chapter 1. After initial conversations about perceptions of a problem, the improvement team members engage in a process to deepen their understanding and widen their perspectives. For example, the team would refer to existing research to explore the context surrounding the problem and practical knowledge, like analogous settings, to see how other schools have dealt with the problem.

The leaders would also engage in systems mapping and/or process mapping to get a sense of how things are currently working and where the organizational breakdowns may be limiting desired outcomes. This improvement process would include gathering local data to understand the problem and looking at those data in ways that highlight variations in trends. Instead of just looking at all attendance data as an average to understand problems with attendance, the team would look across grades, classrooms, demographics, and times of the day/year. The team may categorize students into low absenteeism, moderate absenteeism, and chronic absenteeism groups and then look at trends within those groups across the variables mentioned earlier. Other tools that might support problem framing and help to identify variation in the system may be a needs assessment or an equity audit.

Most importantly, the team would talk to others, gathering multiple perspectives on the problem. Most frequently, this is done through empathy interviews or short conversations focused on understanding how people are experiencing the problem. These questions should be human-centered and capture feelings so the questions ensure user engagement. Empathy interviews ask people to tell their stories and to share what works for them under what conditions, giving teachers and other community members opportunities to add their voices to the process, thereby humanizing how the problem is conceptualized and understood (Khilji, 2021).

The improvement team would take all this information and reconsider their interpretation of the problem. In many cases, the team would revise their initial problem statement to be more specific or to adjust the focus of the problem. These data may guide the team to focus on a group of students who are most impacted by the problem or to target emphasis within the problem area. For instance, Ava's school had a problem with school culture, discovered due to a few reports of student fights, harassment, and bullying. Through gathering detailed information, the team came to realize that students from the LGBTQ+ community were disproportionately impacted by bullying and involved in fights. Ava and her team figured that within the problem area of school culture, the focus needed to be on creating an inclusive culture for LGBTQ+ students, specifically the trans community. The school designed solutions that addressed the inclusive culture for trans students instead of creating something broader, like a new "code of conduct" for the school.

The process of data collection can help the team frame the problem. For example, in one elementary school we've worked with, the improvement team began their improvement science process by framing their problem as *special education students are not successful in their classes due to the schedule.* Do you notice how they thought they had the reason figured out too? They embarked on data collection and invited teachers to participate in empathy interviews about the schedule. No one agreed to participate. The team began to explore why nobody participated. The administration had a trusting relationship with the teachers; they didn't think that was the reason for the lack of participation. The teachers were generally willing to collaborate and had some collective responsibility for the students in the school, so the desire to participate didn't seem to be the reason. At their next school professional learning session, the team led a whole-staff activity to simulate the data collected in one-on-one empathy interviews. When the improvement team gathered multiple perspectives, the team quickly learned the problem wasn't significant to their colleagues; the teachers simply didn't agree that the schedule was the issue. Furthermore, based on experience, the teachers didn't feel they needed to give input on the schedule. As had always been common practice, the administration would change the schedule, and the teachers would implement it. What the teachers were concerned about, which emerged through empathy interviews, was student and teacher relationships, particularly between teachers and students with special needs. Once they reframed the problem to focus on relationship-building, the teachers were on board and motivated to be part of the solution. The schedule was a driver of the problem because that very schedule made relationship-building more difficult, but it was no longer viewed as *the* problem.

Systems Thinking and Leading Problem Framing in Improvement Science

Fundamentally, problem framing focuses on the systemic nature of problems. Systems thinking has roots in organizational theory and should undergird the problem-framing process. A systems thinking approach brings people, processes, interactions, leadership, mental models, and feedback loops together to understand how organizations operate (Senge, 2006). Improvement science in education is based on systems thinking; it examines systems in districts and schools to determine what can be changed to yield different, more equitable, outcomes.

Systems thinking invites opportunities for improvers to "zoom out" so they might observe from the proverbial "balcony" to get a sense of what is going on the "dance floor" (Heifetz et al., 2009). A systems-thinking approach to problem framing looks at where and how elements of the organizational system or processes – the individuals on the dance floor –intersect, and then it zooms in to focus on an area of the system for close observation and interrogation to then pull back again to the balcony view and so on. Zooming in-and-out and back-and-forth perspective-taking is a consistent reminder the system is the focus of improvement; it is not oriented to individual instances. Improving the system targets how the organization, processes, norms, expectations, and policies work together.

To change systems though, we need to change mental models. Senge and Sterman (1990) noted the challenge of integrating leaders' understanding, or mental models, related to organizational work, stating, "Challenging mental models is testing for internal and external validity. Once team members have gone public with their mental models, they can begin to discover internal inconsistencies and contradictions with data and others' knowledge" (Senge & Sterman, 1990, p. 1010). They highlight why dedicating time to articulating how different people understand the system is important, and a valuable exercise for those in leadership positions, as well. Senge and Sterman add, "Experienced managers often have accurate perceptions of causal structure and decision-making process. Nonetheless, they often draw erroneous conclusions about what happens with different parts of a system, each of which they may understand in isolation, interact" (p. 1010). A systems understanding of the problem through zooming in and out, honoring all voices, and exploring the variation throughout the system will lead to a more fully defined and fully framed problem.

Problem Formulation in Improvement Science

You may wonder more about the process of problem formulation. The improvement science approach is about slowing down – in service of being intentional and thorough – to solve problems, include multiple perspectives, and respond to the system. However, that process is also a lot of work, and it will take time and energy from educators within and outside the school building. How can a school identify the types of high-leverage, system-level, adaptive challenges that should become the focus of their work? The problem of practice that needs to be addressed is at the center of improvement science; therefore, the identification, definition, and framing of the problem are all core decisions to be made.

The 5S Model for Problem Formulation

Problem formulation includes deciding which problem to address, making sense of the causes and reasons for that problem, taking a systems approach to defining the problem, and framing that problem in the context of the school. Hinnant-Crawford and Anderson (2022) created a 5S model for problem formulation that can help improvers to make sense of how to approach the problem. They explain

> To avoid selecting the wrong problem . . . it is essential to explore the **significance** and **source** of the problem. Centered in this purpose and focused on the roots of the problem, improvers must narrow to a **substantive focus** for developing solutions to the problem. When focusing on the problem and solutions during problem delineation, it is helpful to identify the **scope** of the problem or where in the system the problem lies. By determining where in the system in which the problem is located, it will help to define the problem and ensure that the targeted solutions address the problem. Finally, in problem definition, it is important to develop a team that spans those organizational levels and includes the voices of those closest to the problem, those with practical and scholarly knowledge to address the problem, and those who can summon the necessary resources to solve the problem or determine the correct **scale** to ensure multiple perspectives.
>
> (Hinnant-Crawford & Anderson, 2022, p. 304)

Significance, source, substantive focus, scope, and scale are the five aspects of problem formulation and definition. Let's get into each of these elements, explaining how a leader would address those elements and discussing some possible challenges that might emerge within each element.

Source – The What?

The source of the problem is arguably the most important aspect of the improvement science process. To solve a problem, you must understand why and where the problem is occurring, that way you can design solutions that address the problem's root causes. Finding the source is the only way to create lasting solutions. You may notice water dripping into your basement and puddling on the floor. (a) You could clean up the water and hope it doesn't return; or (b) you could replace a valve near the leak to stop the water from flowing on the floor. Neither of those solutions would get to the source of the problem, which is a leaky pipe in the wall behind the upstairs shower. (c) To solve the problem at its source, you need to remove the tile, open a hole in the wall, remove the existing pipe, replace that pipe, put in new hardware, close the hole, and retile the wall. This solution is far more complex than just mopping up the water and has more steps, but it will address the system and solve the problem for a sustained period. The problems we need to solve in schools require the same approach to finding the source and solving the root(s) of complex problems. Identifying the source of the problem is common in our approach to problems in life, but, for some reason, it can be overlooked in adaptive problem-solving in schools.

Although educators operate at each level of the system, a systems perspective runs counter to defining problems within individuals. Solutions that simply ask individuals to "be better" when they are working in flawed environments with problematic conditions, such as our school systems, will not work, as we mentioned in Chapter 3. In his 2016 New York Times blog article, titled "How Asking Five Questions Allowed Me to Eat Dinner with My Kids," Charles Duhigg recounts that digging deep and locating the root of why his family was not able to eat dinner together allowed them to fix the family routine. By getting at the root, his family did not resort to getting everyone to dinner on time by pointing fingers or directing one another to go faster or be better. Instead, they made a change to their system (i.e., their routine) to set themselves up for success. Interrelated processes, programs, practices, and mindsets drive improvement efforts – not individuals.

However, individuals are embedded in systems. Interrogating the beliefs and understanding of the system stakeholders, such as those impacted by the problem as well as the leaders who guide the system, is critical to identifying the source, but it is but challenging. Hinnant-Crawford (2022), a leading improvement scholar, shared in the hthUnboxed podcast that stakeholder voices across the system throughout the improvement process are key:

> It is all about honoring all voices from the beginning to the end, from problem definition, from seeing the system. Because people from different perspectives see different parts of the system, from understanding the variation. You've got to have a multiplicity of voices throughout. And you've got to be intentional about giving minoritized and marginalized voices space and power, especially when there is a perceived power differential. And if you don't do that, you can't have an equitable improvement process.
>
> (Hinnant-Crawford, 2022, np)

This systems approach begins when defining the problem. Variance reveals what is or is not working for whom and under what conditions; variance leads to the source (Bryk et al., 2015; Hinnant-Crawford, 2022; Langley et al., 2009). Explicit attention to how one positions oneself relative to others can reveal assumptions about whose system you are currently seeing. The voices of individuals within the system can be an important data source that helps round out improvers' and leaders' understandings of the current problem; but the leadership needs to engage in critical reflection (Khalifa, 2018) to gain an understanding of their own and their team's views, assumptions, and interpretations of the system.

ACTION INVENTORY 5.3 CRITICAL REFLECTION QUESTIONS

1. Where am I and my team members located in the system?
   a. Are there areas of the system not represented in our team? What should we do about that?
2. What people or groups of people in our school or district have been prioritized?
3. What people or groups of people in our school or district have been ignored?
4. How are problems typically framed?
5. How will we take an assets-based view and avoid a deficit perspective of the problem and those who experience the problem?
6. What assumptions am I carrying with me about the problem?
7. How willing am I to learn, admit, and then address my own limitations?

Having done this work with leaders and schools, we have seen the importance of exploring the source of the problem through multiple perspectives. One school we have worked with wanted to improve differences in outcomes on literacy assessments between students of color and white students in K–2 grade. The improvement team knew they wanted to focus on phonics and phonemic awareness since the principal was a literacy teacher, and the district had named phonics instruction as an effective literacy strategy. Using traditional approaches to problem-solving, the team "solved" the problem by pulling out students for one-on-one instruction with the literacy specialist and having a whole-staff professional development on phonics.

Through exploring the problem differently using empathy interviews and local data, the improvement team came to realize two important elements: (a) pulling out students to "catch them up" was creating gaps in understanding that left them further behind. One source of the problem was the model of instruction, which separated struggling students from their classmates. This approach was well-intentioned but did not address the reason the students were struggling. (b) They also learned that students who loved to read in kindergarten didn't have the same love for reading in second grade, indicating another area to explore to solve the problem. They needed to dig deeper to see what was happening with instruction and curriculum in those early grades that turned off kids from reading.

They also learned that the professional development being offered was not meeting teachers' needs, but the teachers were embarrassed to admit it. The model for professional development was insufficient for preparing teachers to teach phonics and phonemic awareness, concepts they were not familiar with, and they had not been trained for in their teacher education programs. They didn't want to admit this to the principal, indicating underdeveloped relational trust was another source of the problem. By going underneath the surface to understand the source of their gaps in outcomes, the improvement team was able to design solutions addressing the real problem. They created a professional development model that allowed reading interventionists to model a 10-minute lesson and support teachers in that lesson in their classroom, and they created a push-in model with the reading interventionists that used reading blocks to support struggling readers without the student missing other content.

Challenges With Source

The process of root cause analysis builds team dynamics and consensus about a problem. However, there may be a lack of agreement over the problem and its roots. Some team members may place the onus on students and families, others may focus on schools and educators. Additionally, the source of the problem may be dependent on where each improver is in the system. Root cause analysis is like professional development: it can't be "one and done;" it must be continuous, informed not just at the beginning of the process but be ongoing.

Some team members may need more training in social justice and equity to ensure they are seeing the racial, economic, ableist, and heteronormative structures and practices undergirding the problem. There are a few areas in which determining the source can unearth deficit thinking. We defined deficit thinking in Chapter 4. As a reminder, deficit thinking is viewing the problems that marginalized groups are facing because of their own personal deficits. During a root cause analysis activity, a team member may look to explain the source of the gap in literacy discussed earlier as the result of parents of color not reading with children at home. This is a deficit response and evidence of concerning beliefs about racial groups. As the leader, you will need to be prepared to address deficit thinking, including, for example, causes identified as inherent to a group of students/families, problems failing to recognize assets, or a focus on achievement gap versus opportunity gap. One suggestion is to remind the group before engaging in the root cause analysis that this activity is about determining problems in the system not determining problems in individual people or their communities and that "causes" should be in the locus of control of individuals within the school and should be focused on the school system.

Before embarking on this work, your team should utilize epistemologies for equity to develop norms of collaboration and core values that center on equity, social justice, inclusion, and anti-racism (Khalifa, 2019). Scholars such as Singleton (2012, 2014) provide models of how to have the types of conversation necessary to center those values. We will talk more about his framework for courageous conversation in Chapter 9. Valencia (2019) provides a model for taking an asset-based view of schooling by recognizing the strengths of marginalized groups of students, as opposed to framing differences as a deficit. Ava and her improvement team created solutions to bullying and belonging of LGBTQ+ students that centered on celebrating the students' culture – bringing drag events into the school community – instead of banning difference at MHMS. Schools may need to seek skilled facilitation of conversations about equity, social justice, inclusion, and anti-racism that engage improvement work in a way that addresses deficit thinking and changes systems of oppression. Ava and her team sought support from local LGBTQ+ advocacy groups after struggling to think of impactful change ideas.

Another potential area for concern is that the group will "simulate" that they are working to understand causes (i.e., go through the motions of improvement science), but they already have a solution in mind. Solutionitis is the tendency to want to jump to solutions without being sure the problem is properly identified (Bryk et al., 2015). Educators may seek causes to validate existing ideas instead of truly uncovering assumptions and exploring data sources (Mintrop, 2016). This tendency to move toward solutions without taking time to understand problems and uncover beliefs about the problem is socialized into those of us in the education system. We are always seeking to fix problems with haste since there is an urgency in providing the best experience for the kids in schools today; however, that urgency is also built into the accountability systems that define kids, teachers, leaders, and schools according to scores on tests, determining their future based on these scores, adding pressure into the system.

A mistake is to not include multiple perspectives in the data or bring multiple voices to the table for the causal analysis. We see the parts of the system we interact with most frequently, and, especially as the leader, who is traditionally expected to have answers, we can extrapolate from our narrow perspective, leaving out causes we may not be able to see. To understand all the sources of the problem, the improvement team must engage in meaningful activities, such as empathy interviews and causal analysis activities such as fishbone diagrams to deeply explore the problem.

Finally, the team may get stuck in analysis paralysis Bryk et al., 2015. They get trapped in the phase of understanding the problem, and then they get stuck there for too long, failing to respond to the problem. Although we want to be thoughtful and informed about the problem before designing solutions, a working theory of improvement is a living document that will be informed by future learning and revised to incorporate new thinking. Engaging in the improvement science process will deepen how the school defines and frames the problem, and the improvement team needs to make space to return to conversations about the root cause throughout the iterative process.

ACTION INVENTORY 5.4 DO THIS, NOT THAT

Instead of ______,	do this: ______.
focusing on individuals	focus on the system and processes (e.g., the conditions) resulting in the problem
accepting lack of agreement about the problem of focus	engage in collaborative root cause analyses
accepting deficit thinking and perspectives	redirect to connect to values of equity, social justice, inclusion, and anti-racism
jumping to solutions	help the team take the necessary time to thoroughly explore the problem through multiple perspectives and data sources

In Action Inventory 5.4, reflect on whether your current practices are in the left column or right column, and what steps you need to take to have all your responses in the right column.

Significance – The Why?

Central to the process of problem definition and identification is significance – how will we solve a long-standing, entrenched problem? Not all problems deserve the attention an improvement science methodology requires. You should be solving a wicked problem whose solution advances equity and social justice, creates improved learning and working conditions, and/or serves the academic and non-academic needs of the whole child. If you think back to the school described earlier that wanted to work on the schedule as a problem of practice, you can see how *significance* is important. That school was trying to solve something they thought was causing the problem (the schedule) rather than using systems thinking to recognize the interconnections that make the challenge adaptive. That school confused a technical problem (the schedule) with an adaptive challenge (student and faculty relationships), leading to insignificant solutions. Also be aware that when addressing wicked, entrenched, and adaptive challenges, sometimes technical problems emerge as symptoms of a more complicated issue at hand. In other words, don't ignore the technical problems, but use them to help you know where to potentially dig deeper.

Hinnant-Crawford and colleagues (2021) amend the model of improvement (what are we trying to accomplish, how do we know if the change is an improvement, and what change might I introduce and why?) to incorporate issues of power, normativity, and impact (See the discussion in Chapter 4). They expand on this model to suggest that when figuring out what you are trying to accomplish, you must consider who it benefits and why it is important. They argue that when figuring out how we will know if that change is an improvement, we need to think about who defines what it means to improve and whose values are being represented. Finally, they remind us that when you think about what changes to introduce, you must consider whose values and ideas are incorporated into that change and who bears the burden of implementing the change.

To understand why the problem is significant and to approach that problem to make positive change or improvement, it is important to focus on the problem with an equity-oriented systems lens and focus on variation in experiences, inclusions, and opportunities (i.e., systems and structures resulting in inequitable outcomes). A significant problem should not reinforce negative stereotypes about groups of students, reinforce existing unsuccessful practices, or exacerbate existing inequities. It should disrupt systems.

Challenges With Significance

Engaging a significant problem can be a struggle for some improvement teams. In some cases, the focus is on technical aspects of the organization (e.g., the schedule in the example earlier). Operational tasks are essential to running and managing an effective school but may not require the attention an improvement science process gives to the problem. Adaptive problems require shifting mindsets along with shifting actions and procedures. You will want to question if the problem is high leverage and interrogate if the problem is adaptive. Focusing on improvement also means that you need to have some agreement on what improvement is and the potential impacts on (in)equity and (in)efficiency. Think about the types of problems that Ava, Luis, Emma, and Jamie defined and framed in Chapter 1; these problems sought to change mindsets as well as behaviors aiming to create more equitable and just schools.

Another potential challenge is the level of disruption and innovation necessary for making real change. Ensure enabling conditions necessary to make disruptive shifts to entrenched problems are present or can be attended to (discussed in detail in Chapter 9). With a significant problem like persistent gaps in outcomes between groups of students, solutions will need to recognize the central role of whiteness in our schools and elevate the voices of Black and Brown students (Irby, 2021; Khalifa, 2018). Several of Ava's NIC group members, including Luis, recognized that to create belonging and inclusivity in their schools, they needed to create a space that reflected the values, beliefs, and cultures of all students.

Substantive Focus – The What/How

The next consideration for problem formulation is the substantive focus of the problem. The PSEL standards for leaders and the NELP standards for preparation programs are aligned around the major areas to be developed, evaluated, and improved in schools: (a) vision and core values, (b) professional norms, (c) equitable and culturally-responsive practices, (d) coherent systems of learning, (e) school culture, (f) professional capacity and culture, (g) relationships with families and community, and (h) operational systems. Table 5.1 provides a description of these areas of focus.

No matter what area a school identifies to be significant, the improvement team will use a social justice and equity lens to explore the problem. For instance, if you identify *teachers needing to learn new instructional strategies for math (professional capacity)* as the problem, then you will want to explore how those strategies are informed by what we know about culturally responsive learning, how the professional culture supports each teacher's learning of those strategies, and how that knowledge may impact the existing strategies in the classroom. These foci included in the standards are often interconnected and one area: *professional capacity* might be a driver of an instructional problem of ineffective pedagogy (*coherent systems of curriculum, instruction, and assessment*); *core values* may be a driver of the problem of disproportionate outcomes in discipline practices (*equity and culturally responsive practices*).

Table 5.1 Substantive Focus for Problem Formulation Guided by Professional Standards.

Substantive Focus	*PSEL*	*NELP*
Vision and Core Values	Core values that define school culture (child-centered, high expectations and support, equity and social justice, openness, caring, and trust) (1d)	Evaluate the school mission and vision (1.1)
Professional Norms	Norms of personal conduct, relationships, decision-making,	Evaluate ethical and legal decisions (2.2); follow and

(*Continued*)

Table 5.1 (Continued)

Substantive Focus	*PSEL*	*NELP*
	and stewardship or resources (2a); integrity, fairness, trust, collaboration, perseverance, and learning (2b); democracy and individual freedom (2d); interpersonal and communication skills, socio-emotional insights, and understanding of student and staff backgrounds (2e); ethical and professional behavior (2f)	design laws, policies, rights, and regulations (6.3)
Equity and Culturally Responsive Practices	Practices that are fair, respectful, and inclusive (3a); employ strengths, diversity, and culture (3b); promote equitable access (3c); guide student behavior practices (3d); confront and alter biases, deficit-based schooling, and low expectations (3e); act with cultural competence and responsiveness (3g)	Ensure equitable access (3.2); equitable, inclusive, and culturally responsive instruction and behavior support (3.3)
Coherent Systems of Curriculum, Instruction, and Assessment	Systems that promote the mission, vision core values, embody high expectations, align with standards, and are culturally responsive (4a); promote love of learning, habits of learners, identities of learners, and a healthy sense of self (4b); promote effective pedagogy consistent with child development and student needs (4c); strength-based, differentiated, and personalized learning (4d); use of technology (4e); valid assessments (4f); and data use (4g)	Provide technology-rich curriculum and other supports and academic and non-academic systems (4.1); design and promote high quality and equitable academic and non-academic instructional practices and systems (4.2); coordinate coherence among practices, resources, and services that support equity, digital literacy, and school's academic and non-academic systems; ensure culturally responsive and accessible assessments (4.3); create coherent and systematic curriculum, instruction, technology, data systems, and assessments (4.4)
School Culture	School environment that is safe, caring, and healthy (5a); has coherent systems of academic and social supports, services, extracurricular activities, and accommodations (5a); promotes relationships (student to adult, student to student, school to community) (5d); cultivates and reinforces school engagement (5c); ensure each student is known and cared fro (5b); and creates a culturally relevant learning environment (5f)	Evaluate supportive and inclusive school culture (3.1)

(*Continued*)

Table 5.1 (Continued)

Substantive Focus	*PSEL*	*NELP*
Professional Capacity and Culture	Instructional capacity and professional practice that (6d, 6f); promotes personal and professional health and well-being (6g); encourages personal growth/work-life balance (6i); recruits and retain educationally effective faculty (6a); develops professional knowledge (6c); and delivers actionable feedback through research-anchored systems of supervision (6e) Professional culture of engagement, commitment (to vision, mission, equity, whole child), communication, collaboration, and collective responsibility and efficacy and mutual accountability (7c, 7b, 7d); open, productive, caring, and trusting working relationships (7e); opportunities for individual and collective learning (7f, 7g)	Evaluate professional staff capacity needs (7.1); ensure systems of supervision and support and evaluation to promote improvement and success (7.4)
Relationship with Families and Community	Relationships with families that are positive, collaborative, and productive (8b); regular and open with two-way communication (8c); work in partnership with and in the community (8e, 8f)	Engage with community (5)
Operation and Systems	Monitor operation and systems (9a); strategically manage resources (9b, 9c, 9d)	Evaluate existing school improvement processes (1.2); evaluate management, communication, tech, school-level governance, and operation systems (6.1); create a data-informed and equitable resourcing plan (6.2)

Challenges With Substantive Focus

As the improvement work takes hold, the capacity to maintain multiple foci expands; but in the beginning, you must determine one area of improvement. With the complexity of the current education system and the number of challenges educators face daily, committing time and human resources to a substantive focus is of great importance. Recognizing if the substantive focus and significance of that focus are high leverage enough can be difficult. A school team or hub can create structures for knowing when you have identified the wrong problem. The reactions of the faculty, students, and families, such as the school that had selected to focus on the schedule, can help the improvement team determine if the focus is important to members of their community. Also, starting with a needs assessment or equity audit helps to elicit priorities, as it did for Ava and her team in Chapter 1.

The problem should align with priorities outlined in school improvement plans and other strategic planning documents that the leadership team creates with the assistance of district partners like instructional superintendents. It can be difficult to be user-centered and stay in alignment with system goals (e.g., district strategic plan). Schools may find the problem or problems they most want to tackle are not aligned with district priorities. Schools' localized concerns should take precedence over the vision of the district. Using localized concerns as the basis for formal school improvement goals helps keep the focus central to the school's daily activities. Action Inventory 5.5 can help guide your team on selecting a problem on which to focus efforts..

SUPPORT MATERIAL

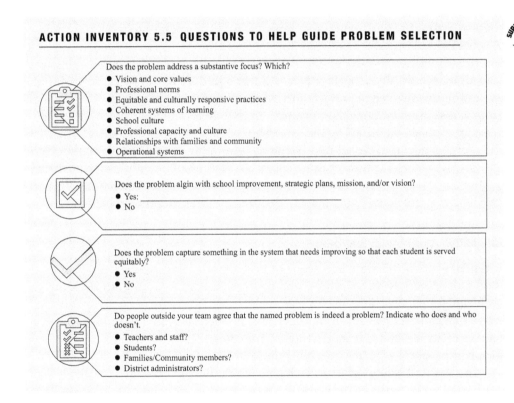

ACTION INVENTORY 5.5 QUESTIONS TO HELP GUIDE PROBLEM SELECTION

Does the problem address a substantive focus? Which?

- Vision and core values
- Professional norms
- Equitable and culturally responsive practices
- Coherent systems of learning
- School culture
- Professional capacity and culture
- Relationships with families and community
- Operational systems

Does the problem algin with school improvement, strategic plans, mission, and/or vision?

- Yes: ______________________
- No

Does the problem capture something in the system that needs improving so that each student is served equitably?

- Yes
- No

Do people outside your team agree that the named problem is indeed a problem? Indicate who does and who doesn't.

- Teachers and staff?
- Students?
- Families/Community members?
- District administrators?

Scope – The Where?

Scope considers where the boundaries of the problem's impact are located. Some problems are based in the classroom and relate to individual teachers. Some are classroom-centric but common within a department or subject area. Other problems may be school-wide problems, such as responses to discipline or the school's relationships with the community. If the scope fits any of these three areas, the problem is likely bounded to an individual school. A problem, such as the disproportionate representation of students of color who have been issued suspensions across all high schools, is bounded at the district level. These problems may be experienced by all schools in the district or by multiple schools within the district. A problem can also be found across multiple districts or at the state or federal level, as is often the case with issues of teacher recruitment and retention. Understanding the "where" of the problem helps improvement teams know who to involve and to what to direct improvement efforts.

Scale – The Who?

The scale in problem formulation focuses on who needs to be involved in defining and solving the problem (which may be at the scope of a single school, several schools, a district, or a state). Scale, here, is different from the spread and scale discussed in Chapter 7. This scale refers to who defines and solves the problem, which may be at the team level, school level, multi-school level, or district level, or it may involve partnering with external organizations, such as non-profits or universities. A school-based improvement team may address the problem within and throughout the school (i.e., the scope). The scope of the problem may be shared across several schools, a whole district, or across schools in different districts requiring the scale of those involved in problem formulation to be widened to include individuals from across organizations. For instance, an individual site may join a NIC to solve a shared problem identified by the leadership team(s) or a group of schools/districts may forge a new networked improvement community to solve a shared problem. The problem identification, at the scope of a school or a NIC, could also be done in partnership with outside organizations, like non-profits or university-district partnerships who are actively involved in defining and framing the problem.

Challenges With Scale and Scope

Challenges with the scale and scope of problem identification largely have to do with balancing power, priorities, and process (Figure 5.1). In both deciding the scale and scope, decisions need to be made about the locus of control. One challenge that can occur in selecting the "right" problem is who determines the problem: Is it site-based? Is it district-led or mandated? Is it the role of the hub (e.g., group of people that facilitate a NIC, more in Chapter 7) that leads the NIC?

Leaders will make difficult decisions when the local context outweighs network goals. Particularly in a NIC structure, it can also be difficult to balance between taking a user-centered/context-driven process for problem identification and the role of NIC and identification of shared problems. What happens when users at your school site determine a root cause that doesn't resonate with the rest of the network? How can you focus on the local needs and contribute to group learning? Also, what happens if you have committed to a NIC and realize that your priorities are elsewhere? Look at Figure 5.2. Reflect on which areas in the 5S model may be the biggest challenges your team will need to face during this work. Note why you identified those areas as potential challenges.

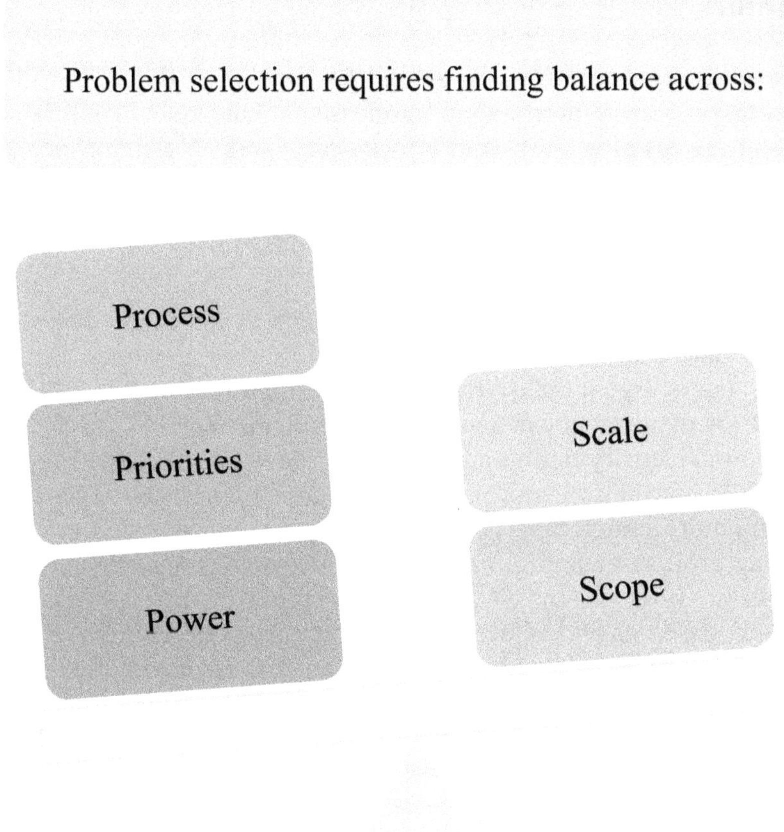

Figure 5.1 Finding Balance in Problem Framing.

Source: Created by author.

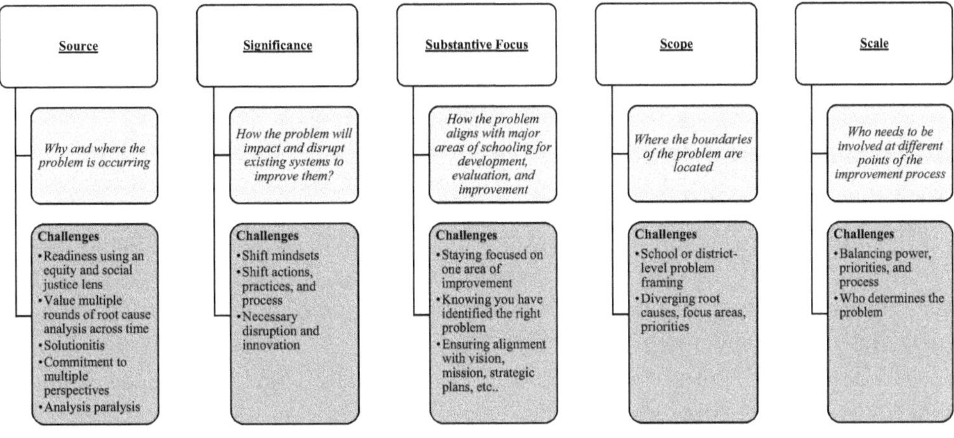

Figure 5.2 5S Definitions and Challenges.

Source: Created by the author.

CONCLUSION

Problem identification and framing should be done with thoughtful diligence or an orientation toward personal and professional characteristics that support learning and improvement. An equity focus can result in a more manageable, impactful, and successful continuous improvement process. There are some important recommendations to consider when engaging in problem identification and formation:

1) Avoid solutionitis by deeply studying the problem and the system that produces it. Take time to walk through the 5S process and resist jumping to answers due to urgency. Take time to define and formulate the problem that will address that urgency in a more sustainable manner.
2) Know how to identify, define, and frame high-leverage, DEIAJ-focused problems while considering multiple stakeholder perspectives. Use the tools that help us to understand problems, including empathy interviews, systems and process mapping, practical and research knowledge, and causal analysis.
3) Make sure the focus of the improvement matters to your school. The improvement science process is a commitment of time and resources. Tie the process to a major improvement strategy in your school improvement plan and tackle an adaptive, wicked problem that will make your school more inclusive and improve instruction for each student, particularly marginalized students and families.
4) Focus on causes within the school's locus of control, understanding what is happening within your school and not placing blame for the problem outside of the school while also recognizing that some problems may be out of your control.
5) Narrow the focus of the problem to ground inquiry in specific problems and create problem-focused solutions. Time spent problem framing will lead to a theory of improvement that aligns your change ideas or solutions to the roots or drivers of the problem.

Instrumental Methods

As we mentioned at the start of this chapter, there are many tools associated with problem identification and framing. These tools help guide the improvement team toward adaptive problems by exploring the causes of the problem, the variation of the problem, and defining the system or processes that "hold the problem in place" (Kania et al., 2018).

To determine the problem, an improvement team needs to make sense of what they learned through the data, empathy interviews, research and practice, and mapping exercises to help identify initial ideas about the root causes of the problem. Root causes are areas of the system that are underlying the problem or the unaddressed reasons allowing the problem to persist. Think back to the example of traditional approaches to improvement – the solution is brainstormed by a small group of people in a meeting. They are not likely to address the underlying cause of the problem, but instead, at best, they may put a band-aid on the problem.

Your team should engage in root cause analysis activities, such as affinity mapping, the five whys, the fishbone diagram, or a combination of activities. These tools are ways to explore the underlying reasons for the problem. We will talk more about these tools in Chapter 8 and provide examples of their use from Chapter 1. From there, design an aim statement, create a theory of improvement, identify drivers of the problem identified, and design change ideas linked to those drivers. This process for identifying and framing the problem leads to deeper understanding and more targeted responses.

Social Relations

Problem identification should be done collaboratively. The people on the improvement team should represent diverse perspectives. The collection of data to understand the problem should maximize variation in experiences among educators, students, and families. To work together in ways that will lead to meaningful and significant improvement, the improvement team and school community must attend to the culture of collaboration and be prepared to lead conversations about inequity and injustice that may require skilled facilitation. People outside the building may be involved in problem identification, including improvement coaches from partner organizations or district liaisons who help to identify school priorities. The principal will need to be able to navigate the group within these social relations to ensure there is agreement on the problem, adherence to the problem identification process, and attention to the source, significance, and substantive focus of the problem.

Moral Values

As stated in the PSEL and NELP standards, all improvement and leadership work should be undertaken in service of better learning outcomes and well-being for all students in the school community. Defining the problem should have equity and social justice at the forefront as defined and explored in Chapter 3. The problem-framing process should be based on the core values of the school and should align with Standard 2 of the PSEL standards. In addition to placing students at the center of education and accepting responsibility for each student's academic success and well-being, these standards suggest a leader must lead continuous improvement work and specifically the selection of a problem with (a) ethical and professional personal conduct, relationships with others, and decision-making . . . according to the professional norms of integrity, fairness, transparency, trust, collaboration, perseverance, learning; (b) values of democracy, individual freedom and responsibility, equity, social justice, community, and diversity; and (c) social-emotional insight and understanding of all students and staff members' backgrounds and cultures.

NELP and PSEL Connection Box for Educational Leadership Faculty

In addition to PSEL Standard 10, this chapter aligns closely with PSEL and NELP Standard Three and NELP Standard Five. These standards focus on the development and implementation of a mission and vision and the use of continuous improvement, specifically related to a "core set of values and priorities" (NCPEA, 2015). The 2015 PSEL standards state, "Educational leaders evaluate when they collect, synthesize, and assign value to data to help diagnose problems, monitor progress, and make decisions about the extent to which a project/policy/procedure meets identified goals/objectives or about the quality of performance and how it might be improved" (NCPEA, 2015).

BIBLIOGRAPHY

Argyris, C., & Schön, D. (1996). *Organizational learning II: Theory, method, and practice.* Addison-Wesley Publishing Company.

Bryk, A. S., Gomez, L. M., Grunow, A., & Lemahieu, P. G. (2015). *Learning to improve: How America's schools can get better at getting better.* Harvard Education Press.

Duhigg, C. (2016, March, 10). How asking five questions allowed me to eat dinner with my kids. *The New York Times.* https://archive.nytimes.com/well.blogs.nytimes.com/2016/03/10/how-asking-5-questions-allowed-me-to-eat-dinner-with-my-kids/

Dunn, W. N. (2018). *Public policy analysis: An integrated approach* (6th ed.). Routledge.

Freedman, M. (1992). Initiative fatigue. *Strategic Change, 1*(2), 89–91. https://doi.org/10.1002/jsc.4240010205

Gomez, L. M., Russell, J. L., Bryk, A. S., LeMahieu, P. G., & Mejia, E. M. (2016). The right network for the right problem. *Phi Delta Kappan, 98*(3), 8–15. https://doi.org/10.1177/00317217166772

Gutiérrez, K. D., & Penuel, W. R. (2014). Relevance to practice as a criterion for rigor. *Educational Researcher, 43*(1), 19–23. https://doi.org/10.3102/0013189x13520289

Heifetz, R. A., Linsky, M., & Grashow, A. (2009). *The practice of adaptive leadership: Tools and tactics for changing your organization and the world.* Harvard Business Press.

Hinnant-Crawford, B. N. (2020). *Improvement science in education: A primer.* Spaulding.

Hinnant-Crawford, B. N. (2022, February 15). *Improvement as a tool for our collective liberation, with Dr. Brandi Hinnant-Crawford.* https://hthunboxed.org/podcasts/s3e14-improvement-as-a-tool-for-our-collective-liberation-with-dr-brandi-hinnant-crawford/

Hinnant-Crawford, B. N., & Anderson, E. (2022). Improvement-focused educational research action: Scholars, scholarship, and setting. In L. Cohen-Vogel, W. Penuel, D. Peurach, & J. Russell (Eds.), *Handbook of improvement research in education.* Rowman & Littlefield.

Hinnant-Crawford, B. N., Nazario y Colon, R., & Davis, T. W. (2021). Who is involved? Who is impacted? Teaching improvement science for educational justice. In D. T. Spaulding, R. Crow, & B. N. Hinnant-Crawford (Eds.), *Teaching improvement science in educational leadership* (pp. 17–41). Myers Education Press.

Institute for Education Science. (2017, December). *Introduction to improvement science.* Regional Educational Laboratory Program. https://ies.ed.gov/ncee/edlabs/regions/west/Blogs/Details/2

Irby, D. J. (2021). *Stuck improving: Racial equity and school leadership.* Harvard Education Press.

Kania, J., Kramer, M., & Senge, P. (2018). *The water of systems change.* FSG. https://policycommons.net/artifacts/1847266/the-water-of-systems-change/2593518/CID:20.500.12592/8wz3hz.

Khalifa, M. (2018). *Culturally responsive school leadership.* Harvard Education Press.

Khilji, S. E. (2021). An approach for humanizing leadership education: Building learning community & stakeholder engagement. *Journal of Management Education, 46*(3), 439–471. https://doi.org/10.1177/10525629211041355

Langley, G. J., Moen, R. D., Nolan, K. M., Nolan, T. W., Norman, C. L., & Provost, L. P. (2009). *The improvement guide: A practical approach to enhancing organizational performance.* John Wiley & Sons.

Mintrop, R. (2016). *Design-based school improvement: A practical guide for education leaders.* Harvard Education Press.

National Policy Board for Educational Administration. (2015). *Professional standards for educational leaders 2015.* Author. www.npbea.org/psel/

National Policy Board for Educational Administration. (2018). *National Educational Leadership Preparation (NELP) program standards: Building level.* www.npbea.org

Perry, J. A., Zambo, D., & Crow, R. (2020). *The improvement science dissertation in practice: A guide for faculty, committee members, and their students.* Stylus, Inc.

Rittel, H. W., & Webber, M. M. (1973). Dilemmas in a general theory of planning. *Policy Sciences, 4*(2), 155–169.

Senge, P. M. (2006). *The fifth discipline: The art and practice of the learning organization.* Currency.

Senge, P. M., & Sterman, J. D. (1990). *Systems thinking and organisational learning: Acting locally and thinking globally in the organisation of future* (pp. 1007–1022). www.systemdynamics.org/conferences/1990/proceed/pdfs/senge1007.pdf

Singleton, G. E. (2012). *More courageous conversations about race.* Corwin Press.

Singleton, G. E. (2014). *Courageous conversations about race: A field guide for achieving equity in schools.* Corwin Press.

Valencia, R. R. (2019). *International deficit thinking: Educational thought and practice.* Routledge.

CHAPTER 6

Data for Improvement and Disciplined Inquiry

Chapter Highlights

1) Disciplined inquiry involves practical and consistent measurement.
2) Various types of data may need to be collected and analyzed during improvement work.
3) How data are organized and stored (i.e., data infrastructure) will need to be intentional, explicit, and systematized.
4) Data collection and organization may look different for different levels in the system (e.g., district level, school building level, classroom level).
5) Making sense of and then effectively communicating information gleaned from data to the broader stakeholder groups is important to garner buy-in and sustain momentum.

CHAPTER DESCRIPTION

The role of data is key in understanding both the problem of improvement and the steps improvers take to address the problem. There are different considerations to attend to when collecting, reflecting upon, and utilizing data. This chapter will discuss the types of useful data (e.g., quantitative, qualitative, practical measures) and how those data might be collected, organized, and leveraged to forward improvement work. Attention given to data infrastructure will be a necessary element as the data need to be gathered, interpreted, and organized in a systematic way to track and communicate the improvement work accurately and effectively. Further, evidence finds its utility when improvers and their stakeholders have collective understanding of the data and improvement process. This chapter

DOI: 10.4324/9781003389279-8

will describe reporting and communication structures for sharing data with the collective as well as strategies that will help improvers emphasize the importance of data collection processes and interpretation of evidence. Data for improvement and data for accountability will be juxtaposed so district, state, and school level leaders have guidance on which data are appropriate for which purpose and why. This will lead to a discussion within the chapter of how school leaders can communicate their improvement work effectively using data, deepening stakeholders' understanding of progress and the process of improvement science.

INTRODUCTION: A DELUGE OF DATA

Quick! Think of two pieces of data you use or reference at work. Got them? Okay, now think about what these data look like. What do these data tell you? What is missing from what these data are telling you? Keep these data in mind while reading this chapter and assess and critique the role these data play (or don't play) when engaging in continuous improvement processes.

The role of data and disciplined inquiry bring the science into improvement science because improvers take the humble, learner stance of "Have we really got it right?" (Bryk, 2020, p. 88). The word data is plural for datum which is "a piece of information . . . an assumption or premise from which inferences may be drawn, or a fixed starting point of a scale or operation" (Oxford Languages, 2022). What's different about data for improvement? Aren't data just data? Isn't improvement science just data-based or data-informed decision-making that stems from pilot testing something? The short answer? . . . Not exactly. In this chapter we will grapple with how the concept of data is threaded across the PSEL and NELP standards, what data "counts" in improvement work, and how to use data to answer question three in the model of improvement: *How will we know that a change is actually an improvement?* (Langley et al., 2009). We will weave in leadership considerations related to how leaders facilitate and approach efforts around data for improvement.

Data and Educational Leadership Standards

The professional standards (PSEL and NELP) reflect data's importance. For example, the PSEL mentions data use in four of the ten standards. Look at Action Inventory 6.1. How does your team currently use data in relation to your mission and vision, for instructional improvement, or to support your messaging to audiences inside and outside the school? What sort of organizational data infrastructure and approach do you and your team have?

With such a broad range of uses, it's no wonder data are often seen as the solution to all issues. And it is no wonder that leadership preparation programs, like the one Ava is in, have overhauled their programs to prepare students for the deluge. The NELP leadership preparation standards include the centrality of growing leadership students' capacities for using data to establish a mission and

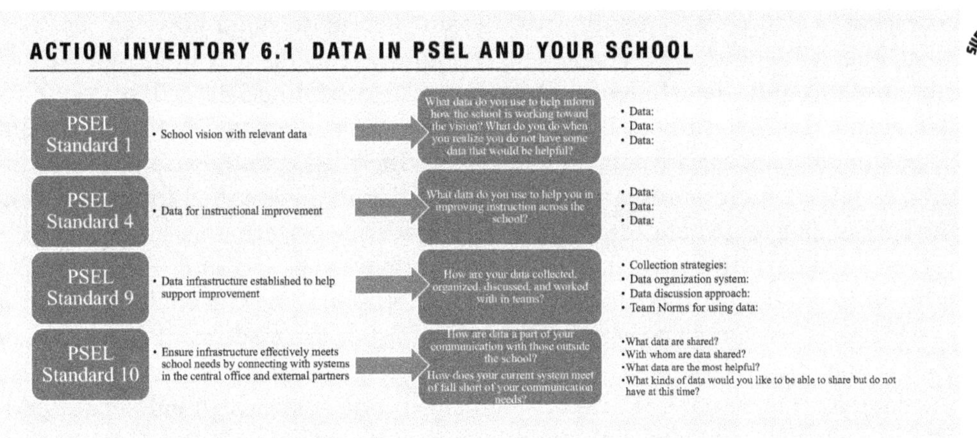

SUPPORT MATERIAL

vision and guide improvement. Data use is frequently given pride of place in the sequence of activities that encompass improvement, including in standards. For example, NELP Standard 1.2 notes, "Program completers understand and demonstrate the capacity to lead improvement processes that include data use, design, implementation, and evaluation." The phrasing suggests a linear sequence that presumably begins with data collection and moves on to data use as the first steps in a process that would conclude with evaluation. And this is the way many school planning processes are completed – by amassing all available data and then sorting it into the appropriate categories according to already-defined priorities. Continuous improvement, as we define it in this book though, entails a different take on data because measuring stuff alone doesn't improve anything. Data without action misses the point.

Catching the Data Wave

Coburn and Turner (2011) note that action related to data is impacted by the organizational context and the practices surrounding the available data. Schools and school districts are awash in data, as was suggested in the beginning of the chapter. Hinnant-Crawford (2020) discusses the notion of schools and DRIP; meaning that schools and districts are "data rich, but information poor." In other words, schools have numerous pieces of data or sources of data, but a deep understanding of what all of those data mean, how those data might be used together to make sense of the school, the limitations of the existing data, or what to do next according to the data may not be entirely clear. The past two decades' emphases on performance-based outcomes and standardized testing as the benchmark of school performance have brought a tsunami of quantitative data. These data typically measure academic performance, as measured by standardized tests, linking student learning outcomes to the performance of school systems, individual schools, and controversially, each leader and teacher in a school (Bryk, 2015; Ravitch, 2011).

Schools also collect quantitative measures to understand how families feel about the school (family engagement data), how students feel in school (school climate data), and what student well-being is like (discipline data, SEL scales). This has meant that educational leaders at all levels are inundated with assessment data, climate data, survey data, to name a few. In addition to these multiple measures of school success, researchers and practitioners have called for broadening the base of data to include not only numeric academic performance but also observational and narrative data that captures experience (e.g., Dixon & Palmer, 2020; hthUnboxed, 2021; Hinnant-Crawford, 2020). We imagine you could list several specific categories of data you are asked to collect or are made available to you at your school. School leaders could likely fill many physical and virtual boxes with the data you have access to! Take a moment to reflect on which data (e.g., MAP scores) you and your team typically reference and complete Action Inventory 6.2.

Label the open boxes with those data you typically or most frequently reference and discuss. Label the closed boxes with data that you think are available in your school, but you do not reference as much. You can also organize your answers in a way that makes visual and organizational sense for you and your team. For instance, perhaps the size of the boxes below indicates how much or how important different sources of data are valued. After you label the boxes, mark which data you and your team need to utilize more to get a deeper picture of what is going on in your context. Do those data already exist, or do you need to do some data collection? How might you intentionally, authentically, and meaningfully bring the boxes of data you identified into your improvement work?

With attention paid to data, why is it so challenging to find robust examples of data being used effectively? And by "effectively," we mean guiding improvements in the school, such as teacher development and student learning, including improvements to the conditions of learning for all children, especially those who come from families and communities who have been underserved in education and opportunities. Despite the surfeit of data, little has been put to practical use and more often data occupies a symbolic role in ensuring compliance with mandates, including the ritualistic enactment of school improvement planning to demonstrate that the school does have a plan, even though the plan may lack specific strategies to enact systematic improvement or improving systems and structures in order to improve other outcome data in realizable ways (see Chapter 10). What is your data strategy?

You Can't Improve at Scale What You Can't Measure

Ava's team wanted to improve the lack of culturally inclusive practices for their LGBTQ+-identifying students. In their improvement work, data were leveraged to help inform not only that the problem existed but how to begin addressing the problem. And as data revealed additional places to explore and gather more data, the team was willing to do so (Meyer, 2022). The fourth improvement principle (Carnegie, 2023) suggests measurement is necessary to determine how changes impact the system in positive, negative, and in unintended ways.

ACTION INVENTORY 6.2 FILLING YOUR DATA BOXES?

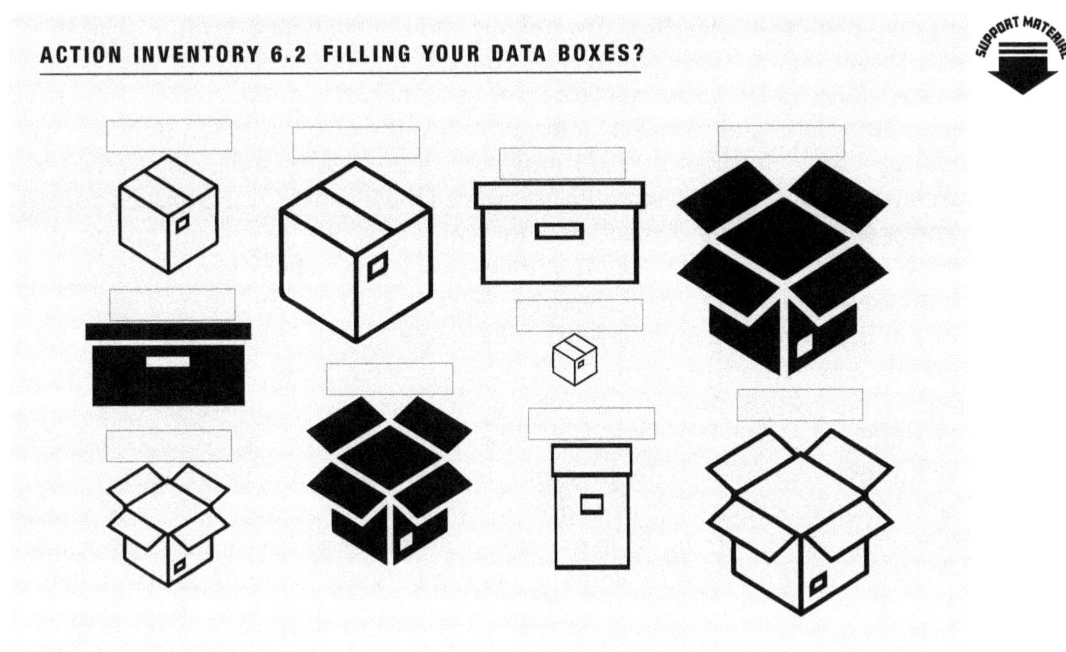

Let's take a moment before we go further to define what we even mean by data and data for improvement. Given that you are already an educator, you have a working definition of data. You likely have caught the data wave and use data regularly in your practice. Think back to those two pieces of data you identified at the top of this chapter. Were they both quantitative? We bet many of you answered yes to that question. We want to be clear; it is important that you have valuable quantitative data on which to lean. But we also want to encourage you to not limit yourself in how you accept what "counts" as data or how data can be used.

Very often, those in conversation about educational data or continuous improvement limit themselves. First, they may limit themselves in the types of quantitative data used. There is a burgeoning field of quantitative analysis that centers equity in collection and analysis (i.e., QuantCrit). An example of QuantCrit work is presented by Hinnant-Crawford and colleagues (2023) who offer a scale for measuring asset-based pedagogy. QuantCrit evidence may be particularly helpful for improvers since improvers aim to address those systems and structures that are not effective for specific populations.

The second way those in conversation about educational data or continuous improvement limit themselves is by focusing solely on quantitative data and dismissing the role of qualitative data. Qualitative data are particularly important when understanding inequitable experiences of those in our systems, our community. Contrary to what we have heard some educators claim, qualitative data can absolutely be valid . . . there are simply different ways qualitative data and quantitative data are determined as such; whereas validity with quantitative data is about the appropriateness of the measure (i.e., does the scale measure what is intended to measure free of bias), qualitative data are valid when meeting standards of trustworthiness (i.e., the data is not skewed by the researchers beliefs) (Glesne, 2011). So, data for improvement can mean quantitative data and qualitative data. Don Berwick, a leader in healthcare quality and improvement, explicitly spoke to this in a 2021 hthUnboxed podcast episode. He offered some examples of practical measures and reminded the listeners, "measurement doesn't always mean numbers. Reflection is measurement. Stories are measurement . . . sometimes numbers help. And if numbers are going to help, you have to have to know how to interpret them" (Berwick, 2021).

An informed strategy related to collecting and interpreting both quantitative and qualitative data will be important in forwarding the disciplined inquiry of your improvement work. You use quantitative data, like assessment scores, to decide on how students captured learning in a subject or grade level. You collect qualitative data using observation skills to identify students or staff who are having a hard day, who are disengaged, or who seem enthusiastic and connected. You use qualitative data to identify strengths in teachers and students such as leadership potential, senses of humor, levels of empathy, or communication skills. You lean on qualitative

ACTION INVENTORY 6.3 WHAT COUNTS AS DATA REFLECTION QUESTIONS

1. What types of data do you typically think of when you think of data for improvement?
   a. How might you extend your thinking about data?
2. Take a moment and think about the extent to which you value certain types of data over others and why that might be.
3. If you were to expand your acceptance and valuing of different types of data, how might that help you in improving problems of practice in your own context(s)?
4. Are there narratives, reflections, and stories that could help deepen your understanding of something – be it the problem itself, the quantitative data you have, or the context?
   a. How should those data be captured and organized? By whom?
5. How are data organized in your school? What types of data are there? Who knows about the data? How might your data need to be organized more effectively?
6. Think about your leadership preparation program. How did your program talk about data (e.g., data-informed decision-making)? How does the preparation program and your working context align in data use? What does this mean for you as an improver?

data when listening to teachers, students, and families and the stories they share. Another piece of good news is that your skills in interpreting different types of data (i.e., qualitative and quantitative) will be leveraged in enacting improvement science approaches. Opportunities to systematize how qualitative and quantitative data are gathered and organized is a step your team will need to make.

According to Langley and colleagues (2009), there are some categories of data that are particularly helpful for improvement: (a) continuous measurements (measured over time), (b) counts of observations, (c) documentation of what people think and feel, (d) rating scales, and (e) ranking categories. Think about Chapter 1, when Ava and her NIC decided to use existing sales to create a survey to measure equity practices as an outcome of their work at their individual schools. After gathering data, your team will need to interpret the data you have. Anderson and colleagues (forthcoming) highlight how to approach data analysis with an equity lens. They suggest leaders aim to

> ensure quality of social interaction (matters of trust, power, and professional identity) during data use, facilitate data conversations that are safe but honest, design interactions with colleagues to provide and discuss data pertaining to racial and other equity gaps, interrogate what kinds of data are missing and make a plan to gather those data, utilize racially disaggregated data in an authentic way, and use data in a systemic, reflective manner.

Committing to an interpretative lens will invite you and your team to directly address problems to make the educational experience more effective for all students.

Embrace Measurement: Practical Measures Are Our Data Treasures

Doesn't the word *practical* evoke good feelings? A harbinger for realistic use, practical means, applicable, uncomplicated, helpful. Practical measures are available in a timely manner, are easily accessible, and straightforwardly understood. Practical measures and improvement science approaches go hand in hand as these measures capture the "learning in and through practice to improve outcomes in the context of everyday practice" (Yaeger, n.d., p. 3), Practical measures reveal where improvement areas exist, build understanding of both the problem and system, surface how different groups of people might be experiencing the problem, and reveal how to recognize if a change is indeed an improvement. They inform action, are drawn from our social and organizational routines, and stem from trust and openness. They operationalize an improvement team's working theory of improvement and are connected to the processes and outcomes that your team wants to change. Practical measures help reveal if the system underwent change and can inform if how subsequent outcomes follow the change. (Bryk et al., 2015).Action Inventory 6.4 offers some examples of what practical measures might be and then invites you to reflect on your experience with or plans to engage with these data.

One improvement effort that exemplifies the use of practical measures is the Building Teaching Effectiveness Network (BTEN) initiative (See Hannan

ACTION INVENTORY 6.4 EXAMPLES OF PRACTICAL MEASURES

Examples of Practical Measures		
Qualitative	**Quantitative**	**Examples of how qualitative data can be transformed into quantitative measures**
• Empathy interviews • Data from iterative testing cycles • Narratives • Feedback • Observations • Equity audit • Listening sessions • Fishbowl dialogue • Kiva circle • Community walks • Shadowing a student	• Data from iterative testing cycles • Community pulse surveys • Equity Audit • School based data (e.g., enrollment, discipline, attendance, climate survey data, assessment scores) • Efficacy levels	• Salience of an experience in empathy interviews on a scale from 1-3 • Number of people who give positive or negative feedback related to an experience

Practical Measure Example	Have used	Have heard of it but not used it	Additional information (e.g., How will you get these data? Who is well-positioned to gather and analyze these data?)
Empathy interviews			
Data from iterative testing cycles			
Narratives			
Feedback			
Observations			
Equity Audit			
Listening sessions			
Fishbowl dialogue			
Kiva circle			
Community walks			
Shadowing a student			
Community pulse surveys			
School based quantitative data			
Efficacy			

Source: Created by authors.

et al., 2015). An example of how the improvers in this network gathered practical measures was when they asked a specific, but simple question about the improvement work, which involved dedicated meetings to share feedback. Of the change idea, the improvement team asked, "Did the feedback meeting happen?" By asking this question, it helped the team be positioned to make a claim about the initiative implementation and processes. These measures are often referred to as process measures (Bryk et al., 2015; Hinnant-Crawford, 2020).

Practical measures include multiple types of data (i.e., qualitative and quantitative) from multiple sources (e.g., existing school-based data, feedback data, interview data, observational data). Not too long ago, we heard a panel discussion about improvement science and equity in education. The panelists, Brandi Hinnant-Crawford and Ben Daley, encouraged improvers to accept and use stories, experiences, opinions, and qualitative assessments to be indicators of change or measurement. The panelists encouraged embracing qualitative indicators and using them as practical measures for understanding improvement alongside quantitative data.

"Learning often comes from understanding themes and patterns in the data" (Langley et al., 2009, p. 30). When collected, organized, or displayed effectively, and then used purposefully and consistently, practical measures can pave the feedback loop for your team's efforts and serve as a mechanism for generating learning because qualitative and quantitative measures are evidence and evidence helps determine if the change is making a positive difference. Educators are already strong at the skills needed for collecting practical measures.

> Teachers are encouraged to look for embedded evidence. They are asked to observe real-time formative data and not wait for summative data. The question we engage to check for a change in improvement science is not "if" the change worked or did not work, but "how" the change worked and what we learned from it.
>
> (Milder & Lorr, 2018, p. 1)

At the end of the day, your team will use practical measures to know if your change idea worked, is working, how it is working, and if the implemented change is working as your team anticipated and planned for it to work (Hinnant-Crawford, 2019, 2020). While we've dedicated space to describing practical measures, it might also be helpful to include what practical measures are not. In other words, what are impractical measures? Since improvement efforts answer the question "How will I know if a change is an improvement?", ill-defined data, data that take too long to collect or to analyze (e.g., end-of-year assessment data, enrollment data), or data that are disconnected or superfluous to what your improvement focus is are each impractical measures for the purposes of improvement. These data still may be useful, just not for this specific context of working to improve the exact problem you are trying to address.

Let's frame this into an example; if your team is making a change to how student-family conferences are organized and using the PDSA cycle to organize iterative tests on a developed conference protocol, state assessment data will not be helpful. Conference attendance data, although the topic seems connected, would also not be helpful. Instead, data that captures how many minutes the student spoke versus the number of minutes the teacher spoke would be helpful. Qualitative feedback data from caregivers, teachers, and students related to their experience using the protocol would be helpful. These data would help inform the team if the conference protocol was leading to improving the quality and effectiveness of the conference. Notice how the data that would be helpful are practical, relatively easy to gather, are timely, and are directly connected to the targeted improvement element (i.e., conference protocol).

Our Data Look Different for Some People!: How Variation Guides Focused Improvement

Once again, the questions What works, for whom, and under what conditions? What is not working, for whom, and under what conditions? are questions of variation. How are different people in different parts of the system experiencing something? If there are differences in data, that is evidence that people are having different experiences.

The term "variation" in quantitative conversations typically refers to how much different variables impact the statistical outcome measured in the analysis. For instance, the variable *years of teaching experience* may impact (or statistically correlate with) a certain set of outcome data – like how a student will do on a state standardized test – to a different degree than the variable *family income*, which may impact outcome data to a different degree than *age*. Variation, as applied to quantitative outcome data, is regularly used when describing large-scale educational testing data, such as assessment data connected with policy requirements. In these conversations, variation is used to examine and explain differences in outcome data between and within reporting groups or reveal ways policies impact different groups of students inequitably (e.g., Martínez & Spikes, 2020); and in this way, attuning to variation can be helpful because it can signal inequities in educational opportunities (Koretz, 2008). As Koretz (2008) notes, "educational inequities are the root of much of the performance variation in the United States" (p. 139). In a localized context – such as a classroom, school, district, or network – variation may be explored using sophisticated statistical methods, and variation may be also explored by leveraging the practical expertise of those engaged in the improvement process. The practical expertise educators bring when identifying and interpreting variation will likely take the front seat when conducting small, iterative tests of change; whereas analysis with larger quantitative data sets may take the front seat when understanding the problem more broadly as it appears in a wider range of settings or when improvements result after numerous tests of change have taken place and the change idea scales.

In both large data sets and in data sets with a smaller group of participants (e.g., tests of change), outcome data can vary for different reasons and in different ways. Variation is a clue for improvers about their system because it reveals that either the implemented change is impacting different elements or individuals within the system differently or that the change itself was implemented differently by those testing the change (Bryk et al., 2015; Hinnant-Crawford, 2020; Perry et al., 2020). Variation, however, can be leveraged to better position improvers, like a school principal, to continue to refine, to continue to test, to continue to improve. Keep in mind that variation when stress testing changes for a system (or a group or even an individual), especially in the early stages, is inevitable. Iterating on the tested changes aim to minimize variation while also aiming for the whole of the group or organization to "skew right," which means that a clearer understanding of the system that produces(ed) variation, coupled with testing change ideas then implementing effective change ideas, results in improvement for all who encounter the issue.

ACTION INVENTORY 6.5 REFLECTION QUESTIONS

1. In what ways can data be used as a tool? In what ways can data be used as a weapon?
2. How could observations stemming from how data reveal variation lead to deficit-based conclusions? What strategies could be employed in order to avoid, subvert, or redirect deficit-based interpretations?
    a. What type of organizational environment is present in each of these?
    b. What type of leadership is present in each of these?

As introduced earlier, how data are collected and organized help improvers assess if a change is making an improvement. There are several ways you might organize and display data for your team's analysis such as, but not limited to, stories or illustrative quotes from interviews, word clouds, timelines, counts of data (e.g., UNC university libraries, 2023), frequency of a qualitative observation), scatter diagrams, pareto charts, and run charts (see Hinnant-Crawford, 2018; Langley et al., 2009). Think about the experience you or your team have in using any of the ideas in Action Inventory 6.6 and if there are opportunities to use these in your current work.

As you probably gathered from Action Inventory 6.6, there are many resources that describe the strategies in much more detail, so we will include additional resources and share how one of the teachers at Ava's school used a run chart tool to help her solve a problem. Using a graph with both X and Y axes, run charts are used to capture data across time. Because they includes a temporal element, they offers a visual of a "before and after" of when a change idea is implemented (Institute for Healthcare Improvement, 2023c). The improvement team will need

ACTION INVENTORY 6.6 ORGANIZING DATA IN VISUAL DISPLAYS

Type of Data Display	Assessment of Potential Use for Current Problem of Practice
Timeline (UNC Libraries, n.d.)	☐ Already used for this problem of practice ☐ Need to use for this problem of practice ☐ Not needed for this problem of practice ☐ Not sure; I need more information
Wordcloud (UNC Libraries, n.d.)	☐ Already used for this problem of practice ☐ Need to use for this problem of practice ☐ Not needed for this problem of practice ☐ Not sure; I need more information
Frequency Table (IHI, 2023a)	☐ Already used for this problem of practice ☐ Need to use for this problem of practice ☐ Not needed for this problem of practice ☐ Not sure; I need more information
Scatter Diagram (IHI, 2023a)	☐ Already used for this problem of practice ☐ Need to use for this problem of practice ☐ Not needed for this problem of practice ☐ Not sure; I need more information
Run Chart (IHI, 2023c)	☐ Already used for this problem of practice ☐ Need to use for this problem of practice ☐ Not needed for this problem of practice ☐ Not sure; I need more information
Pareto Chart (IHI, 2023a)	☐ Already used for this problem of practice ☐ Need to use for this problem of practice ☐ Not needed for this problem of practice ☐ Not sure; I need more information
Histogram (IHI, 2023a)	☐ Already used for this problem of practice ☐ Need to use for this problem of practice ☐ Not needed for this problem of practice ☐ Not sure; I need more information

a data strategy to collect and plot data consistently in order to get the most out of this tool. A simple example was completed by one of the teachers at Ava's school. ELL teacher, Chris Butler, was practicing some improvement science strategies on her own. So, while Chris hoped for zero student tardies, she was noticing that regularly there were students marked tardy to her third period. So, she started to track some data. Over 3 weeks she captured baseline tardy data and logged it using a run chart generator (see IHI, 2023c). Two things popped out to her when she did this. She noticed and circled a run (i.e., a group of three data points below the median value that indicate a potential trend), but by and large she noticed variation illustrated by the dramatic up-and-down nature of the connected points on the graph. This led her to see that on Mondays, Wednesdays, and Fridays, she had more students tardy to her third period than on Tuesdays and Thursdays.

Since Chris had some baseline data and interpretations from which to work, she began to think about the question set: What is working, for whom, and under what conditions? But she asked the inverse: What is not working, for whom, and under what conditions? She hypothesized that something was not working related to the second and third period transition. She dug a little deeper and learned that "for whom" was actually a consistent group of students who were late. In other words, when someone was tardy on Mondays, Wednesdays, or Fridays, it was one of five students. She still needed to learn more, so she had a brief conversation with the five to try to understand what was going on. From her conversations she discovered that all five students were in second period together and that on Mondays, Wednesdays, and Fridays, their second period class spent time in the science or computer labs resulting in more clean-up or wrap-up responsibilities or steps. Chris visited her colleague, Alex, whose classroom was on the opposite side of the school building who taught those students in second period. Their conversation allowed both Chris and Alex to learn more about why her students were late to third period those days. Together, the two teachers strategized how they might ensure that the students could get to third period on time while also participating fully in second period. They tried an intervention (i.e., a change idea) and noticed the tardies to third period, while improved, did not fully rectify the situation. So, at the beginning of week six, they adapted their initial strategy and over the course of that sixth week, they made notable progress where they had a run of all the days that week recording below the median; there were only two tardies recorded instead of the 14 from week one. Their next steps are to

Chris's Run Chart

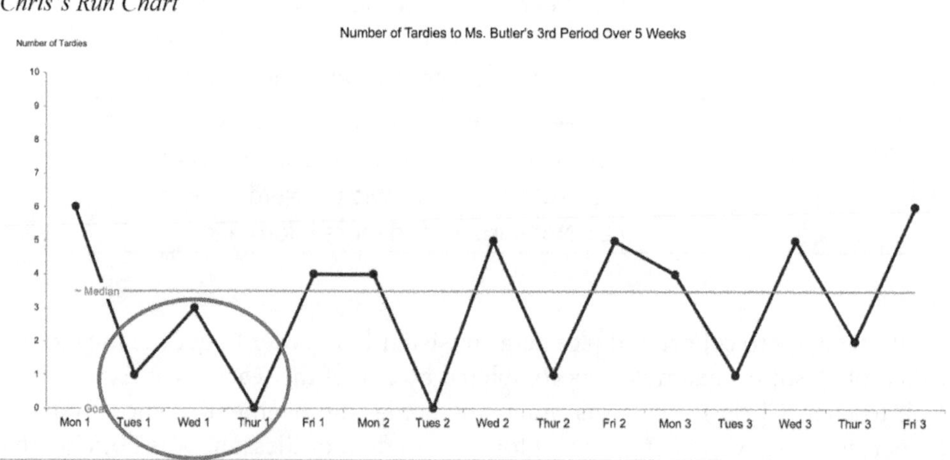

Figure 6.1 Chris's Run Chart.

Source: Created by author.

consult with the students and determine another adaptation to their intervention to reach a goal of zero tardies.

Chris thought about variation and improvement and recognized the salience of what Berwick meant when he said, "Think of improvement as the enterprise of making invisible variation visible for the purpose of learning." Chris learned through paying attention to variation and to the system leading to varying outcomes for that group of students. Instead of simply telling those students they needed to be faster in getting to class, she took the time to learn about the problem. She took time to examine what was not working for her students and collaboratively adjusted the conditions under which her students were navigating. In other words, she demonstrated how to improve the system for a long-term solution instead of blaming people.

Recall that when Chris and Alex put together a strategy that they thought would work, they implemented it, continued to collect data, and then examined the data to see how it was going. They noticed an opportunity to adapt the strategy and tried again, collecting data along the way. This type of incremental work that involves purposeful data collection and implementing small change ideas and adjusting based on ongoing data collection and analysis is something called disciplined inquiry. One of the hallmark approaches to disciplined inquiry in improvement science is the PDSA cycle. You read about the PDSA cycles Ava's team completed, and we will go into more detail about how to engage in PDSA cycles in Chapter 8, but in a nutshell, it is a process like Chris led. Take a look at Action Inventory 6.7 that features the four parts of a PDSA cycle where we give you a definition of what happens during each stage of the PDSA cycle. Select each action Chris completed at the corresponding stage.

The data collected before and during PDSA cycle work help reveal when there is variation that helps improvers understand what is working for whom and under what conditions while it also allows improvers to learn what is not working, for whom, and under what conditions. Variation can be a strong litmus test to identify the specific conditions leading to inequitable systems.

Number of Tardies

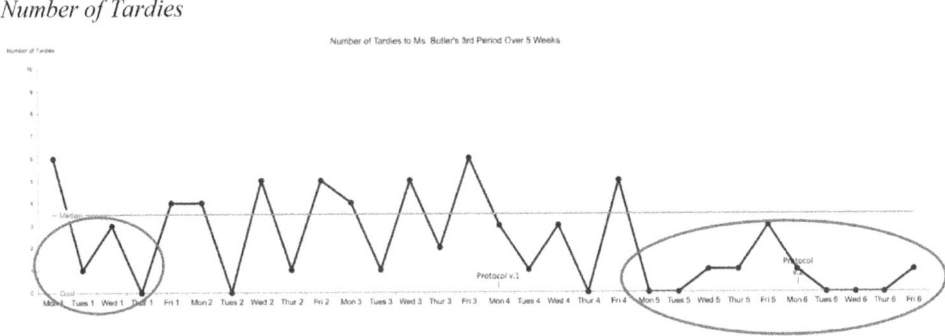

Chris thought about variation and improvement

Figure 6.2 Number of Tardies.

Source: Created by author

ACTION INVENTORY 6.7 DISCIPLINED INQUIRY: PDSA CYCLE STAGES

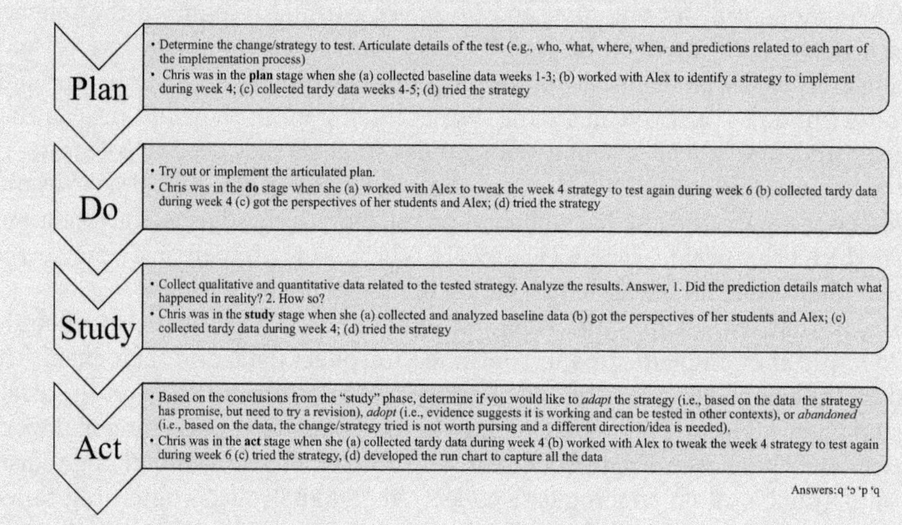

Plan
• Determine the change/strategy to test. Articulate details of the test (e.g., who, what, where, when, and predictions related to each part of the implementation process)
• Chris was in the plan stage when she (a) collected baseline data weeks 1-3; (b) worked with Alex to identify a strategy to implement during week 4; (c) collected tardy data weeks 4-5; (d) tried the strategy
Do
• Try out or implement the articulated plan.
• Chris was in the do stage when she (a) worked with Alex to tweak the week 4 strategy to test again during week 6 (b) collected tardy data during week 4 (c) got the perspectives of her students and Alex; (d) tried the strategy
Study
• Collect qualitative and quantitative data related to the tested strategy. Analyze the results. Answer, 1. Did the prediction details match what happened in reality? 2. How so?
• Chris was in the study stage when she (a) collected and analyzed baseline data (b) got the perspectives of her students and Alex; (c) collected tardy data during week 4; (d) tried the strategy
Act
• Based on the conclusions from the "study" phase, determine if you would like to adapt the strategy (i.e., based on the data the strategy has promise, but need to try a revision), adopt (i.e., evidence suggests it is working and can be tested in other contexts), or abandoned (i.e., based on the data, the change/strategy tried is not worth pursing and a different direction/idea is needed).
• Chris was in the act stage when she (a) collected tardy data during week 4 (b) worked with Alex to tweak the week 4 strategy to test again during week 6 (c) tried the strategy, (d) developed the run chart to capture all the data
Answers:q 'ɔ 'p 'q

Source: Created by the author.

Data Infrastructure

So far we've covered the importance of collecting and analyzing different types (i.e., qualitative, quantitative, practical measures) of data. We've also mentioned the importance of having a strategy for your data. What we have not yet discussed is the elements of a data infrastructure to help your team identify, collect, organize, display, store, and capture your analysis over time. Imagine you had no closets in your home. Imagine not only do you not have closets, but you also have no cabinets. What would your home look like? Cabinets and closets bring order to our clothing and accessories and other household items. There are designated places for different types of items. For instance, you may hang shirts in a closet located in or near a bedroom. You probably store plates and bowls in a cabinet in the kitchen. Building a purposeful categorical infrastructure in your home helps you stay organized. It also can guide decision-making. You can open your cabinet and see if you need to do laundry, need to buy more plates, or if you have ingredients on hand. Building a purposeful data infrastructure helps your improvement team stay organized and facilitates decision-making. Data infrastructures include the types of data needed for addressing a problem of practice, the norms your team uses surrounding how data are used, as well as how data are organized for your team.

As you move through this book, you will come to a more detailed description of what is needed in your data infrastructure in Chapter 9. Leaders can help improvement teams build a data infrastructure by asking clarifying and probing questions related to what data the team have and what other data are helpful to have. Educators are very attuned to paying attention to outcome measures (e.g., test scores, climate survey data), but other measures are important because other data can be indicators, or the breadcrumbs, that lead to the outcome data. When engaged in continuous improvement processes, the breadcrumb data are clues (i.e., evidence) to your team about how the improvement efforts are going, how effective the changes are, for whom, and under what conditions. Having systems to organize and make sense of data is necessary.

Data and Improvement Science Stages

We want to take a moment to briefly describe how data can be sought and interpreted at different stages or phases of improvement: problem identification, understanding the problem, developing a theory of improvement, improving the problem through a disciplined inquiry process (i.e., testing), then scaling. See Figure 6.3.

Identifying a Problem

Paying attention to existing data signals where a problem exists. Chapter 5 already covered how to use data to both identify and frame a problem. Local data will be helpful here because local data are readily available and offer preliminary evidence that there is a problem in the system. These data can also be used by the improvement team as baseline data. Baseline data serve as a comparison point when changes to the system are implemented and tested (Hinnnat-Crawford, 2019).

Understanding a Problem

Data help improvers understand the problem they are hoping to address (also addressed in Chapter 5 in detail). When improvers engage in the understanding the problem phase, they use data such as interview data, local data, equity audit data, literature and research, stories from people, and systems data to try and identify root causes that lead to the problem. During this stage, data are used in a purposeful way to not only illuminate where a problem exists, but also

Stages of Data

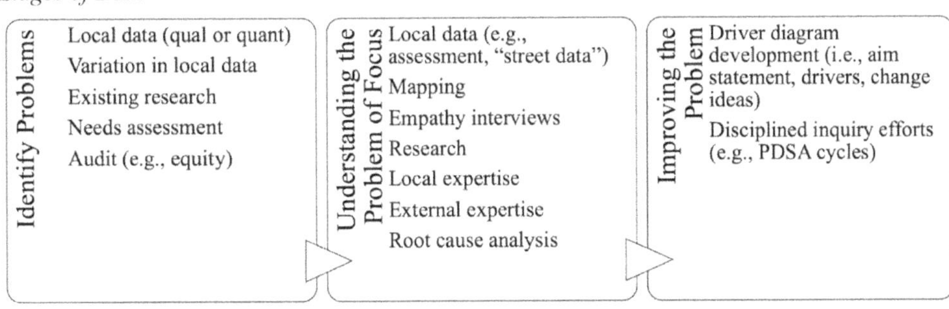

Figure 6.3 Stages of Data.

Source: Created by author

different sources of data can help improvers to make sense of the problem from multiple angles; this includes how those impacted by the problem experience it. For instance, if you have a lot of quantitative data about students not getting to class on time, you will need to add data to help deepen your understanding – you will need to get the perspectives from those who are not getting to class on time (via empathy interviews, for example).

Theory of Improvement

After identifying and understanding a problem, the next steps are to create a theory of improvement that will include a clear aim statement or a succinct statement of what the team hopes to change, by when, for whom, and with what measures (or how they hope to solve the problem). One tool that in improvement science helps teams visually see their theory of improvement is that of the driver diagram (Described in Chapter 8). The driver diagram contains an improvement aim, the organizational elements that connect to the aim, and possible change ideas to test to meet the aim.

That aim statement is the ultimate outcome of the improvement work or a measurable way to mark progress toward a solution to the identified problem. The aim is contingent upon certain areas of influence within the school system or the drivers of the problem. These three to five aspects of the school system drive the problem and can drive the solution. Within those primary drivers, some improvement teams like to get even more granular and name the secondary drivers to structures or processes within the primary driver that make up that driver. Then the team begins to brainstorm changes (systems, processes, structures, practices, or protocols) that they hope will address the drivers and lead to improvement, as measured by the aim as well as measures of the individual drivers. The theory of improvement then succinctly captures how improvement can be made: If we introduce [this change idea], then it will improve [these drivers], which will lead to progress on our aim (Carnegie Foundation for the Advancement of Teaching, 2018).

An intentional conversation with your team will need to take place to connect your theory of improvement to measures. The improvement question – how will we know a change is an improvement? – will anchor this discussion. Improvement teams need to be specific about what improvement looks like and what data or look-fors your team will use to determine progress toward the aim (Carranza et al., 2018).

Improving a Problem

Different data are used in the PDSA cycle. It begins with planning, not with data collection. It's in the planning that we set forward our initial ideas about what data might be useful and how we might use specific data types to see if changes improve a problem. In a sense, even in the planning stages of improvement, we are lifting up what we hope to see and also force improvers to confront – as one teacher put it – "Does the data I'm collecting actually match the interpretations I'm making?" (Julie, featured teacher in the hthUnboxed podcast episode: "Continuous Improvement: Teacher Induction").

How your team decides to measure progress on improving the problem has implications for your work. And as your understanding of improving the problem evolves, your measurement system may also evolve; you may change it based on what you're learning and how practical the measures are. In your improvement journey, embrace the opportunity to test and iterate your measurement system. Building your data and measurement systems will likely cover areas such as how to get change ideas to happen effectively and reliably where variation becomes a non-issue as well as what data are necessary to determine if identified drivers are being meaningfully impacted by tested change ideas.

Scaling Improvement

Scaling improvement will be informed by a system of measures. The multiple measures you may draw upon could include leading and lagging indicators, outcome measures, driver measures, balancing measures, process measures, and PDSA data (see, e.g., Hinnant-Crawford, 2020). Data stemming from your disciplined inquiry are your source when determining when and how to scale change ideas. Change ideas are those interventions or changes your team predicts will make an improvement to your system and then, because you test them on a small scale through an approach like a PDSA cycle, you have confidence in the promise of that change idea. You have measures that allow you to confidently say you are on the right track. As your team engages in scaling tests moving, for example, from one classroom, to one grade level, to one school, to multiple schools, data from PDSA cycles will guide your direction. This is because during the study and act portion, you will use data to compare to your predictions from the plan phase to then decide if your team should (a) adopt the change to scale or continue to scale, (b) adapt the change to make a modification and test, or to (c) abandon the change since the test revealed the change idea did not go well and is not worth pursuing. An important thing to notice in scaling is that decisions are informed by the data you planned to collect as part of your system of measures.

Leadership and Data

Leaders of improvement build shared meaning through data. With the improvement team, there are different approaches that can help you as a leader refine or establish new norms for how you and your team use data for improvement. First, remember that there will likely be anxiety around conversations of data, especially if teachers are used to data being a tool for judgment, evaluation, guilt, or shame rather than as a tool for discovery or learning. Therefore, leaders are responsible for nurturing a safe, trusting environment. Leaders for improvement who dispel fear and instead build and nurture trust among those in the organization are perhaps one of the most important conditions for examining and reducing variation. Consider this 2013 quote from The W. Edwards Deming Institute:

> The data gathered are a result of the system. If the system creates fear among employees the chances of tainted data increases. Another way Deming stated this is where there is fear you do not get honest figures. If the system creates incentives to have the data look good to get promotions or bonuses or credit the chances of tainted data increases. If the system doesn't use good operational definitions to define how to collect the data the chances of tainted data increases (Hunter, 2013).

It is imperative for you as an educational leader to see data for improvement in a very specific way. Data for improvement purposes are used for *learning*. Data for improvement are not used for *judgment*. Data for learning invites collaborative conversations, sensemaking, and a willingness to explore what is going on in the system that is leading to the data presented. Data for judgment could include evaluation on personnel's performance, connected to merit pay, used to point blame on individuals, and may not be approached with support and care. If you are in an organizational space where evidence (i.e., data) is or has been used to guilt, shame, or call out people, then this approach needs to shift; if you are the leader, the responsibility of this shift lies on your shoulders. Lasting improvement will not come from this approach. In a similar way that Steven Tozer mused, "You can't fire your way to increased test scores," you cannot data shame your way to improvement. Fear will impede or block learning (Berwick, 2021). Leaders should not rationalize a fear-based approach by hiding behind comments like, "I am leading with the data," or "Well, it's what the data say," or "I'm just telling the truth." This is not to say people are not held accountable or responsible in an organization. Accountability is necessary; in a learning organization, productive accountability will require leaders to set up the conditions so that increasing trust, openness, and collective understanding around data will take intentional precedence over guilt and shame (see, for example, Brené Brown's research). Second, leaders help facilitate meaning making when interpreting data and what the data reveal about current systems and the improvement necessary for those systems (Park, 2018). Further, meaning making should avoid blaming and instead be grounded in the values your team and organization hold such as excellence, equity, humility, and integrity. Third, leaders need to recognize two types of boundaries. One boundary relates to what the data can tell you and what the data cannot tell you. Although extrapolating from existing data can happen with care, take time to pause and reflect with your team if the data are being used appropriately and where the limits of the data are. Leaders need to help the improvement team know when to stop collecting more and more data and to move forward with the improvement work – avoiding analysis paralysis (Bryk et al., 2015). One consideration IHI (2023c) offers is to determine when additional data will not yield any new information.

The other boundary relates to the scope and sphere of influence your team has over the improvement work. Therefore, ensure that the data on which you are focused are situated within your sphere of influence.

Data can help tell the story of your improvement. See Action Inventory 6.8 for some questions to consider related to data and communication. Leaders can leverage data to communicate about the improvement work, especially with those who are external to the improvement group. Perhaps some data can demonstrate a before and after story of improvement, highlight the important learning that came from a failed test of change, or even data related to the improvement team's efforts (e.g., meeting times, number of PDSA cycles, the number and types of empathy interviews the team completed).

ACTION INVENTORY 6.8 COMMUNICATING IMPROVEMENT WORK USING DATA

1. Who would you like to share the improvement work with? What data might that audience be most interested in learning? Why?
2. What does your team consider to be the most compelling quantitative data related to your improvement work?
3. What does your team consider to be the most compelling qualitative data related to your improvement work?
4. What data demonstrate an asset-based view of those in the system?

CONCLUSION

Remember, continuous improvement focuses on systems; continuous improvement is not a synonym for "increased test scores," and yes, while increased assessment scores is something that holds currency in educational policy contexts (for better or worse), continuous improvement focuses on making the system better that leads to desired results.

Social Relations

Improvement processes suggest that your team will interact with a system of measures. In other words, data from several sources help us understand the problem, understand the outcome, and what led to the outcome, like breadcrumbs on a trail. Outcome measures are relatively easy to get and pay attention to. Think of end-of-year testing, graduation rates, those types of things. However, as a leader, you will have to help your team expand, valuing more than outcome data. Data for improvement can include virtually any category of data that serves as

- evidence of variation in outcomes, processes, and experiences
- a vehicle to deeper understand the problem you are hoping to solve

- a way to better understand the system that leads to the problematic result
- measures that demonstrate improvement from a change idea is or is not made
- a way to understand the circumstances related to how the change idea was implemented.

Instrumental Methods

Sometimes the data related to these five areas are readily available (e.g., regularly scheduled assessments, as part of professional practice routines). Other times, data may need to be sought out to specifically help you in one of those areas. For example, if the problem you are hoping to solve is related to student tardiness to class, data available might include who is tardy and how often and to which classes and grades in those classes. Data that are not readily available but would be helpful in working to solve the problem might include observational or interview data with the students to better understand why a student or group of students is habitually tardy. In this case, intentional seeking out of this information will be not only helpful but critical so that assumptions about the problem or assumptions about those closest to the problem are not made.

Moral Values

For whom are you doing this improvement work? The system of measures you lean on should have an obvious connection to the aim and to improving the system to work effectively in an equitable way. The purpose of data collection, analysis, sensemaking, conversations about and use of data should always be handled with care and be user centered.

ACTION INVENTORY 6.9 CHAPTER REFLECTION QUESTIONS

1. In which areas from this chapter do you feel confident? Which areas are you hoping or needing to build your capacity? How might you build this capacity?
2. How are you thinking about data differently since reading this chapter? What are some key points you would like to be sure to "bring with you" into your practice?
3. How does your school or team
   a. currently approach data?
   b. currently approach variation?
   c. What implications related to how your school or team currently use data and variation have for you as a leader of improvement?

Additional Resources

Books

- Bernhardt, V. L. (2018). *Data Analysis for Continuous School Improvement (4th ed.)*. Routledge.
- Hinnant-Crawford, B. N. (2020). *Improvement Science in Education: A Primer.* Meyers Education Press.
- Johnson, R. S., Avelar La Salle, R. L. (2010). *Data Strategies to Uncover and Eliminate Hidden Inequities: The Wallpaper Effect.* Corwin Press.
- Peurach, D., Russell, J., Cohen-Vogel, L., Penuel, W. (Eds.) *Handbook of Improvement Focused Educational Research.* Rowan and Littlefield (See Sola Takahashi, Kara Jackson, Jon R. Norman, Marsha Ing, and Andrew E. Krum, Measurement for Improvement. Pp. 423–442 chapter specifically).
- Safir, S. and Duggan, J. (2021). *Street Data: A Next-Generation Model for Equity, Pedagogy, and School Transformation.* Corwin Press.
- Singh, A. A. (2019). *The Racial Healing Handbook: Practical activities to help you challenge privilege, confront systemic racism, and engage in collective healing.* New Harbinger Publications.

Practical Measures Resources

- Listening Sessions/Empathy Interviews: https://sites.google.com/view/design-improvement-2022/my-school
- Equity Audit (https://maec.org/wp-content/uploads/2016/04/Criteria-for-an-Equitable-School-2020-accessible.pdf)
- Fishbowl dialogue (www.facinghistory.org/resource-library/fishbowl)
- Kiva Circle (https://buildingpublicunderstanding.org/assets/files/kiva_protocol.pdf)
- Community walks (www.edutopia.org/blog/community-walks-create-bonds-understanding-shane-safir)
- Shadowing a student (https://drive.google.com/file/d/1P_E0SQNh3Q5NYo1jMqHqJzx0M7YyoLfH/view)
- Community pulse surveys (https://drive.google.com/file/d/1Nd1FGBZmhmUOywVnpn73n8a15mryagau/view)
- Data from iterative testing cycles (https://eskolta.org/wp-content/uploads/2017/02/APBI-Inquiry-Protocol-PDSA.pdf)

Other Resources

- Bennett, B. (2018). Branching Out: Use measurement trees to determine whether your improvement efforts are paying off. *Quality Progress.* Retrieved from: https://qi.elft.nhs.uk/wp-content/uploads/2018/09/QP_Branching-Out_MeasurementTree_20180901.pdf
- Boudett K.P., City E.A., Murnane R.J. (Eds.). (2013). *Data wise: A step-by-step guide to using assessment results to improve teaching and learning.* Cambridge, MA: Harvard Education Press.

NELP and PSEL Connection Box for Educational Leadership Faculty

This chapter connects to several NELP and PSEL standards. NELP standards One, Three, Four, and Seven all invite preparation programs to help leaders develop skills in determining how to foster a strong, supportive school culture and using data to help guide these efforts (NPBEA, 2018). In a similar way, PSEL standards One, Four, and Ten implore school leaders to dedicate efforts to improve systems for staff, students, and families. For instance, Standard Ten, in its focus on how to "Develop and promote leadership among teachers and staff for inquiry, experimentation and innovation, and initiating and implementing improvement," aligns with using data and disciplined inquiry for continuous improvement (NCPEA, 2015).

BIBLIOGRAPHY

Bryk, A. S. (2015). 2014 AERA distinguished lecture: Accelerating how we learn to improve. *Educational Researcher, 44*(9), 467–477. https://doi.org/10.3102/0013189X15621543

Bryk, A. S. (2020). Improvement in action: Advancing quality in America's schools. Harvard Education Press.

Bryk, A. S., Gomez, L. M., Grunow, A., & Lemahieu, P. G. (2015). *Learning to improve: How America's schools can get better at getting better.* Harvard Education Press.

Carnegie Foundation for the Advancement of Teaching. (2018). Teaching commons. https://teachingcommons.carnegiefoundation.org/auth/login/?next=/

Carnegie Foundation for the Advancement of Teaching. (2023). *The six core principles of improvement.*www.carnegiefoundation.org/our-ideas/six-core-principles-improvement/

Carranza, R. A., Weinberg, P., Senior, M. C., & Leopold, J. (2018). *Improvement science handbook.* NYC Department of Education. www.weteachnyc.org/resources/resource/nycdoe-improvement-science-handbook/

Coburn, C. E., & Turner, E. O. (2011). Research on data use: A framework and analysis. *Measurement: Interdisciplinary Research & Perspective, 9*(4), 173–206. https://doi.org/10.1080/15366367.2011.626729

Coburn, C. E., & Turner, E. O. (2012). The practice of data use: An introduction. *American Journal of Education, 118*(2), 99–111. www.jstor.org/stable/10.1086/663272

Cosner, S. (2011). Supporting the initiation and early development of evidence-based grade: Level collaboration in urban elementary schools: Key roles and strategies of principals and literacy coordinators. *Urban Education, 46*(4), 786–827.

Datnow, A., Park, V., & Kennedy-Lewis, B. (2013). Affordances and constraints in the context of teacher collaboration for the purpose of data use. *Journal of Educational Administration, 51*(3), 341–362. https://doi.org/10.1108/09578231311311500

Dixon, C. J., & Palmer, S. N. (2020, April). *Transforming educational systems toward continuous improvement: A reflection guide for K–12 executive leaders.* www.carnegiefoundation.org/resources/publications/transforming-educational-systems-toward-continuous-improvement/

Downey, C., & Kelly, A. (2013). Professional attitudes to the use of data in England. In K. Schildkamp, M. K. Lai, & L. M. Earl (Eds.), *Data-based decision making in education* (pp. 69–89). Springer.

Earl, L., & Fullan, M. (2003). Using data in leadership for learning [Article]. *Cambridge Journal of Education, 33*(3), 383–394. www.proxy.its.virginia.edu/login?url=http://search.ebscohost.com/login.aspxdirect=true&db=a9h&AN=11794371&site=ehost-live&scope=site

Glesne, C. (2011). *Becoming qualitative researchers: An introduction* (4th ed.). Pearson.

Halverson, R., Grigg, J., Prichett, R., & Thomas, C. (2007). The new instructional leadership: Creating data-driven instructional systems in school. *Journal of School Leadership, 17*(2), 159–194.

Hannan, M., Russell, J. L., Takahashi, S., & Park, S. (2015). Using improvement science to better support beginning teachers: The case of the building a teaching effectiveness network. *Journal of Teacher Education, 66*(5), 494–508. https://doi.org/10.1177/0022487115602126

Hinnant-Crawford, B., Bergeron, L., Virtue, E., Cromartie, S., & Harrington, S. (2023). Good teaching, warm and demanding classrooms, and critically conscious students: Measuring student perceptions of asset-based equity pedagogy in the classroom. *Equity and Excellence in Education*. https://doi.org/10.1080/10665684.2023.2166446

Hinnant-Crawford, B. N. (2019). Practical measures. In R. Crow, B. N. Hinnant-Crawford, & D. T. Spaulding (Eds.), *The educational leader's guide to improvement science* (pp. 43–70).

Hinnant-Crawford, B. N. (2020). *Improvement science in education: A primer*. Meyers Education Press.

Hunter, H. (2013, February 28). Where there is fear you do not get honest figures. The W. Deming Institute. https://deming.org/where-there-is-fear-you-do-not-get-honest-figures/

Institute for Healthcare Improvement (IHI). (2023a). *Know when enough data is enough*. www.ihi.org/resources/Pages/ImprovementStories/KnowWhenEnoughDataisEnough.aspx

Institute for Healthcare Improvement (IHI). (2023b). *Tools*. www.ihi.org/resources/Pages/Tools/default.aspx

Institute for Healthcare Improvement (IHI). (2023c). *Run chart tool*. www.ihi.org/resources/Pages/Tools/RunChart.aspx?PostAuthRed=/resources/_layouts/download.aspxSourceURL=/resources/Knowledge%20Center%20Assets/Tools%20-%20RunChartTool_35cea96e-7360-4db3-94db-9c4640ab759b/Run-Chart-Template.xls

Koretz, D. M. (2008). *Measuring up*. Harvard University Press.

Langley, G. J., Moen, R. D., Nolan, K. M., Nolan, T. W., Norman, C. L., & Provost, L. P. (2009). *The improvement guide* (2nd ed.). Jossey-Bass.

Martínez, D. G., & Spikes, D. D. (2020). Se Acabaron Las Palabras: A post-mortem Floresv. Arizona disproportional funding analysis of targeted English Learner expenditures. *Educational Policy*. https://doi.org/10.1177/0895904820917370

Meyer, A. J. (2022 December 1). Swimming against the current: Resisting white dominant culture in improvement work. *hthUnboxed*. https://hthunboxed.org/unboxed_posts/swimming-against-the-current-resisting-white-dominant-culture-in-improvement-work/

Milder, S., & Lorr, B. (2018). *New York City public schools improvement science handbook*. WeTeachNYC.www.weteachnyc.org/resources/resource/nycdoe-improvement-science handbook/

National Policy Board for Educational Administration (NPBEA). (2015). *Professional standards for educational leaders national policy board for educational administration*. www.npbea.org

National Policy Board for Educational Administration (NPBEA). (2018, August). *National Educational Leadership Preparation (NELP) program recognition standards district level*, 142. www.npbea.org

Oxford Languages. (2023). Datum. Oxford English Dictionary. www.oed.com/

Park, V. (2018). Leading data conversation moves: Toward data-informed leadership for equity and learning. *Educational Administration Quarterly, 54*(4), 617–647. https://doi.org/10.1177/0013161X18769050

Perry, J. A., Zambo, D., & Crow, R. (2018). *The improvement science dissertation in practice: A guide for faculty, committee members, and their students.* Myers Education Press.

Ravitch, D. (2011). *The death and life of the great American school system: How testing and choice are undermining education.* Basic Books.

Schildkamp, K., Lai, M. K., & Earl, L. M. (2013). *Data-based decision making in education: Challenges and opportunities.* Springer. 1850–9999. www.springer.com/gb/BLDSS.

Spillane, J. P. (2012). Data in practice: Conceptualizing the data-based decision-making phenomena. *American Journal of Education, 118*(2), 113–141. https://doi.org/10.1086/663283

UNC Libraries. (n.d.). *Data visualization.* https://library.unc.edu/data/data-visualization/

Wayman, J. C., & Stringfield, S. (2006). Data use for school improvement: School practices and research perspectives. *American Journal of Education, 112*(4), 463–468.

Yaeger, D. (n.d.). *Practical measurement.* Carnegie Foundation for the Advancement of Teaching. www.carnegiefoundation.org/resources/publications/practical-measurement/

CHAPTER 7

Spread and Scale

The Promise (and Perils) of Networks and Systems Change

Chapter Highlights

1) The goal of improvement in networks is the promise to scale up instructional innovation as change bundles or packages.
2) Systems change leadership responds to variation in complex systems.
3) Networks support the spread and scale of change bundles through the analytic and social structure.
4) Implementation of spread and scale should attend to the ecological aspects.

CHAPTER OVERVIEW

This chapter tackles how to spread and scale a change idea or bundle of change ideas in a complex school system through leading systems change. Implementation practices move change through a system. Systems variation plays a role in spreading and scaling and networked learning, including the structure of the "hub" or central node of a networked improvement community (NIC). A NIC allows schools to work on shared problems, measure success, and spread learning throughout the system. Organizing for continuous improvement, implementing for organizational growth, and sustaining change for organizational development bolster the success of networked learning.

The chapter offers a perspective on the orientation of continuous improvement with the use of evidence practice, leveraging practical and local expertise.

DOI: 10.4324/9781003389279-9

We contrast this approach with long-standing notions of the researcher as an expert outsider. Collaborative research is an emerging construct of continuous improvement, often building on existing research-practice partnerships and leadership preparation partnerships. The chapter concludes with a discussion of the eight principles advanced in Penuel's and colleagues' (2020) review of collaborative research in education and the implications for the application of standards and the promotion of the spread and scale of instructional innovation.

INTRODUCTION: A NEW IDEA FOR SYSTEMS CHANGE

Spreading and scaling are terms you have probably heard before; they may even conjure up memories of a time you were told to implement a new initiative, practice, or idea into your existing practice without anyone asking your perspective. You might have been asked to help "spread" an idea that worked elsewhere or worked in an experimental setting. Depending on how long you have been in education, you might have been asked to "scale up" new district or statewide initiatives. You have probably been asked to change your curriculum and instruction (e.g., think new math, the science of reading, Common Core Standards, Next Generation Science Standards), to change your pedagogy (e.g., small groups, grading for equity, differentiation, standards-based learning, mastery-based learning, project-based learning), and to rethink your classroom or building culture (e.g., SEL learning blocks in every class, etc.). Many, if not all, of these practices and initiatives, are in good faith. Most have an empirical body of evidence showing the potential to work in some settings under certain circumstances. Nevertheless, you may be frustrated. That frustration is not from being asked to implement something new from taking up practices that align with contemporary understandings of teaching and learning. The issue might be that you are often asked, or directed, to make changes in an unfeasible time frame with insufficient resources and without attention to understanding how this novel idea fits your context (Figure 7.1).

Often, as educators, we are treated like widgets – nameless, faceless beings who, if standardized into submission, can be successful and "effective." When asked to implement new ideas, this widget mentality is lauded. Implementation with fidelity is the ideal result. If an idea is good, we want to spread it far and scale it widely. The expectation is that an idea, if implemented in a new setting just as it was in the successful setting (or with fidelity), will result in the same outcomes. In this implementation model, if an idea doesn't work, it is because the new people trying out the idea didn't replicate it exactly as done before. Improvement science asks you to rethink implementation with fidelity and focus on implementation with integrity (Figure 7.2).

Implementation with integrity involves spreading and scaling while recognizing the unique skills, assets, and contexts of educators putting the ideas into practice (Bryk, 2020; Bryk et al., 2015). To implement with integrity, you adhere to the core principles of improvement science, using the principles to help you adapt the process and the change ideas to meet local needs and systems.

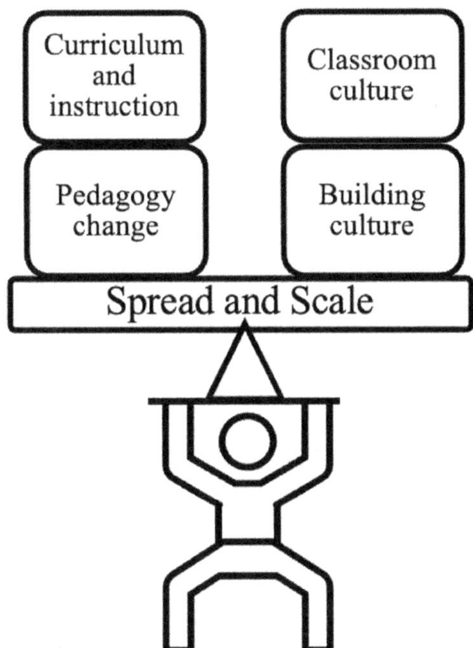

Figure 7.1 Balancing New Initiatives.

Source: Created by authors.

Figure 7.2 Implementation with Integrity.

Source: Created by authors.

Variation and Complexity

The use of improvement science in education was born out of healthcare (Berwick, 1996; Langley et al., 2009; Lewis, 2015). Although healthcare and education are different fields, they have many parallels: people helping people (social and moral) using discrete knowledge about how to help people (instrumental). Healthcare includes individual providers working independently and collectively to support the well-being of people. Collaboration in healthcare and education is essential to success, but sometimes individual needs, systems of hierarchy, inefficient systems, and lack of communication can lead to less-than-ideal outcomes. Finally, healthcare and education are part of societal systems that reproduce inequities in resources, unevenness in the quality of care, and lack of response to user-centered considerations of culture, identity, and background.

Reasons for the impact of variation on implementation in education are similar to those described by Compton-Phillips (2019) from the Massachusetts Medical Society in her assessment of variation in healthcare. First, Compton-Phillips suggests healthcare providers learn from the people around them, resulting in geographic trends in professional norms and practices. Educators are context-specific in our thinking; we become entrenched in the ways of being in our school and district, creating nearly school-by-school variation in beliefs, learning strategies, instructional practices, and school culture. We learn from other teachers and leaders in our building and district, and we create localized knowledge. Due to the variation mentioned earlier, debates arise whether evidence about the success of change ideas in one context in a classroom or school can be relevant in other contexts such as other classrooms or schools. It is largely believed that spread and scale are more useful when the contextual or demographic features are similar between two organizations because the complexity of the system has ultimately shaped unique schools or districts. Recognizing localized knowledge and context-specific experience is built into the core principles of improvement science. Yet, there can be danger due to overemphasizing the uniqueness of your context or deciding that an idea will never work for you because you can only learn new practices from similar contexts. Recognizing the impact of context on variation and implementation should not stop one from trying out a new idea based on solid evidence from elsewhere; recognition of context should lead to heightened acknowledgment of the need for continuous, experience-based learning and cyclical planning for successful spread and scale. Ava borrowed ideas from her NIC group, including from leaders in rural and urban schools that did not resemble her suburban school.

The second factor Compton-Philips (2019) uses to explain variation is that medical outcomes are tenuously related to practice, and this factor is arguably even more applicable in education than healthcare. We seek to connect learning outcomes to teaching, but evidence suggests that teaching practice is only one of many factors that lead to student learning outcomes; teaching practice is not even the most important one! We use standardized tests to measure student learning, but, as we know, the largest predictor of how a student performs on a standardized test is parents' educational level and income, suggesting there are out-of-school factors that influence how we measure classroom learning (Dixon-Roman et al., 2013; Mattern et al., 2016). Outcome measures, such as tests, are not often tied to specific learning goals, and a teacher engages in a guessing game as to what will be on a standardized test. An emphasis on the test skills necessary to perform well on standardized tests doesn't equal learning. Even when using formative assessments or assessments closely connected to learning outcomes and instructional delivery by a teacher, there is a subjectivity to those assessments; such assessments may not truly measure understanding or learning. Furthermore, "soft" skills or "noncognitive factors" are hard to measure in ways that allow them to be "outcome measures," although we know they are essential to learning (Devedzic et al., 2018; Escolà-Gascón & Gallifa, 2022; Farrington et al., 2012). It is harder to create a system-wide measure of student belonging than it is to create a standardized test based on content.

Third, Compton-Phillips (2020) describes the impact of the explosion of knowledge on variation in outcomes on healthcare. Similarly, there has been a proliferation of research on educational effectiveness, educational leadership, culture and climate, teaching and learning, and culturally responsive and socially-just education; this makes it difficult to isolate specific successful practices and creates even more variation in understanding. Making sense of the expanding body of research, including contradictions and contributions, is a demanding task. Educational research abounds with "competing theories" that "are common in the social sciences because the nature of the phenomenon being studied allows for those phenomena to be viewed from multiple perspectives, or 'lenses', each perspective could provide a reasoned and sensible explanation of the phenomenon being studied" (Anfara & Mertz, 2014, p. 3). Judging what ideas to put into practice may be dependent on your context and your beliefs. Regardless, the number of ideas presented in research and the lack of specificity available in most published research leaves much to the interpretation of educators, adding more variation to the system.

Research has repeatedly suggested the importance of educator collaboration. Some researchers and practitioners are advocating for professional learning communities or PLCs, but, even with that focus, there are many different models of what constitutes an effective PLC (e.g., DuFour, 2004; DuFour et al., 2006; Stoll & Louis, 2007). There is agreement that collaboration matters, but some educators suggest collaboration should be formal; and others suggest formal structures don't allow for natural collaboration. Some educators suggest leaders, due to power dynamics, can't collaborate in meaningful ways, and others suggest leaders need to model collaboration alongside teachers (e.g., Johnson, 2003). We share this example not to align with one of these stances but to suggest that even when drilling down to a particular practice, there are bodies of knowledge within that practice that require additional sensemaking, introducing more variation.

Variation complicates improvement. As Compton-Phillips (2020) states, "Variation in care is rarely a problem of recalcitrant doctors and nurses being unwilling to learn or resistant to change, but rather is the result of a system that has evolved to perpetuate variation" (p. 2). The opportunities for improvement in our education system are not the result of unwilling teachers and leaders but are the result of a system in which complexity is often underestimated, leading to inadequate reforms and responses overly focused on scaling "best practices" and over indexing the priority of fidelity. Improving education, like improving healthcare, involves solving complex adaptive problems in which variation is introduced with the students, the teachers, the leaders, demographics, geography, resources, and more, resulting in a wide discrepancy in educational practices and outcomes (Compton-Phillips, 2020). Greenhalgh and Papoutsi (2019) suggest "Achieving any change takes work, and it usually also involves – in various combinations – spending money, diverting staff from their daily work, shifting deeply held cultural or professional norms, and taking risks" (p. 1). Allocating resources, repurposing time, and rethinking tasks, changing mindsets and norms, and trying new things with the potential of failure are all multifaceted, creating more complexity. Action Inventory 7.1 helps you think about what might need to change related to your problem.

ACTION INVENTORY 7.1 WHAT MIGHT NEED TO CHANGE WHEN IMPROVING YOUR SELECTED PROBLEM?

Shift in which working norms?

Shift in allocation of which resources (e.g., money, time)?

Shift in which mindsets?

What is the exact problem you are trying to solve:

Shift in which organizational structures?

Shift in which routines?

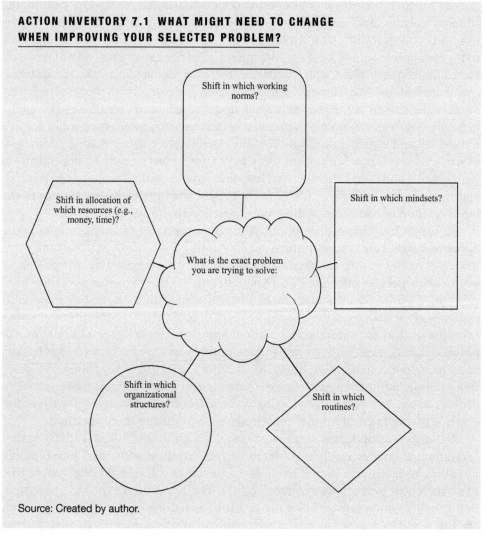

Source: Created by author.

Systems Change

Due to the complexity sketched earlier, simple, routinized responses are not enough to address improvement and solve problems; we must change the system (Compton-Phillips, 2020). Typical responses to educational problems or the types of knowledge legitimized through policy, such as the federal Elementary and Secondary Education Act (ESEA) and its subsequent reauthorizations No Child Left Behind (NCLB) and Every Student Succeeds Act (ESSA), seek human-proof solutions to problems. However, education is inherently human and complex due to its social context. An emphasis on improvement in education regularly perpetuates a myth of "silver bullet" solutions judged effective through randomized control trials (RCTs) (Rippner, 2015; Cobb & Virella, 2019). Experimental designs allow researchers to eliminate other factors that influence outcomes and isolate the effects of a specific intervention or strategy. However, this linkage may be lost when that intervention is introduced in a complex, adaptive system. Qualitative research emphasizes explaining the conditions and context of learning and prioritizes describing and analyzing the experiences of those within the system focusing on what, how, and why. These data help with spread and scale because you locate influences on strategies as well as conditions for implementation though those might fall short of measuring the impact of a complex adaptive problem. Applied researchers, such as improvement scientists isolate variables and describe experiences within contexts to lead to actionable strategies to lead to change or improvement. These data, based on both quantitative and qualitative methods, are practical measures (see Chapter 6). Making improvement is about putting together the "what works" with how it works to spread and scale change. Complex adaptive problems in complex adaptive systems require continuous improvement approaches.

Systems Change Leadership

To foster the success of spread and scale, leaders must demonstrate systems change leadership. What we mean by systems change leadership is a leadership approach that utilizes systems thinking in approaching problems of practice and change. Systems thinking in relationship to change is based on systems theory or "consists of interrelated parts that work together or in some fashion and impact each other in a process" (Vornberg, 2013, p. 806). Seeing the system or understanding the "profound inter-connectedness" (Senge, 2020, p. 57) is a core principle of improvement science.

One aspect of systems change leadership is considering the whole picture. One of our favorite visuals that emphasizes the need for this approach is based on the old trope of blind men trying to identify an elephant piece-by-piece while missing the bigger picture. An updated version of this shows various blindfolded people in white lab coats exploring different sides of an obviously annoyed pachyderm (Figure 7.3).

Figure 7.3 The Systems Elephant.

Source: *The blind men and the elephant*. Poem by John Godfrey Saxe (Cartoon originally copyrighted by the authors; G. Renee Guzlas, artist). The Buddhist text *Tittha Sutta, Udāna 6.4, Khuddaka Nikaya*, contains one of the earliest versions of the story. From *The elephant in uremia: oxidant stress as a unifying concept of cardiovascular disease in uremia* by J. Himmelfarb, P. Stenvinkel, T. A. Ikizler, and R. M. Hakim, 2002, for Kidney International, Perspectives in Renal Medicine, 62(5); 1524028

In the front a scientist touches the tusks and determines that the item he is engaging with is a spear. On the top, another scientist is touching the elephant's big floppy ears and says that they are a fan. On the side, another person touches the large, gray surface and thinks she is touching a wall. Another scientist touches the tail and thinks it is a rope; another touches the legs and thinks it is a tree, and the last one touches the trunk and thinks it is a snake. Similarly, we see the education system from each of our own perspectives, which can lead to a narrow, insufficient, or wrong understanding of the problem we are trying to solve as discussed in Chapter 5. Limited solutions do not affect much change.

Think about your experiences in school. Leaders often wonder why teachers don't see problems in the schools the same way they do, and teachers question leaders' decisions. If you put together those perspectives, as well as those held by the counselors, social workers, children, parents, deans, department chairs, teachers, and other members of the school community, you can have a more complete picture of what is happening and a better chance of implementing lasting change throughout the system. Change with integrity asks a systems change leader to develop the capacity of their team to "see the system" before, during, and after undertaking systems change.

Spread and Scale

We have talked about the impact of variation and system complexity on spread and scale, but we have not described, in detail, what we mean by those terms. In the context of improvement science, spread is sharing change idea(s) or change bundles tested for success through PDSA cycles by adopting the change idea throughout a school or multiple schools in a network. What works in one classroom through small-scale tests of change (PDSAs) might be adopted in other classrooms, using small-scale tests of change as each classroom integrates the change. At the end of Ava's story, her improvement team sought to support multilingual learning. She asked her former EdD NIC group members for a summary of the change bundles that had been used in their schools to see if they would help her identity solutions to her problem. To do so, she would adapt the ideas using PDSA cycles.

Tests of change spread across a wide variety of settings help the improvement team understand if spread is working. This spreading can include sharing ideas with different schools by less formal sharing strategies such as a community of practice (COP) or bright spotting success across a school or district. Tests of change can also be more structured where multiple sites have the same problem and share learnings in a NIC (Bryk et al., 2015; Bryk, 2020). When spreading change ideas systematically throughout an organization, you are scaling up, which "means tackling the infrastructural problems (across an {organization}, locality, or health system) that arise during full-scale implementation"(Greenhalgh & Papoutsi, 2019, p. 1). Greenhalgh and Papoutsi also recognize that "in practice the one blurs into the other" (p. 1). Spreading and scaling also focus on the process or the journey. There may be times when it makes sense to spread learning from understanding the problem, the theory of improvement, or information about what didn't work to help accelerate learning in other schools. In Ava's story, she learned that a poster campaign was ineffective for catching the attention of students and teachers. They needed the human experience to understand the importance of pronouns. This was invaluable learning that would influence future strategies for change.

Networks

Networks create opportunity for spreading and scaling improvement science learning through many schools. Working in networks is the sixth core principle of improvement science. The Carnegie Foundation for the Advancement of Teaching website says, "Embrace the wisdom of crowds. We can accomplish more together than even the best of us can accomplish alone" (np). Networks accelerate our understanding of what works and in what conditions and create a mechanism for sharing knowledge across settings such as schools. They harness the experiences of improvement teams and schools to learn together.

The goal of improvement science in a network is to successfully scale an effective change idea so other groups can benefit and improve. Improvers scale change ideas incrementally through PDSA cycles, making observations about what is happening during implementation and why it happens. The variation that results from scaling efforts reveal bottlenecks, barriers, or contextual factors not previously considered. A change idea may have yielded promising results across the elementary schools in one urban school district; however, when scaled to test in a middle school, there is no improvement; or when scaled across contexts to a rural school, the change idea was not effective. Attention to the reasons a change idea works in some settings and not others and for some students and not others help the field assess what is effective, where it is effective, and what needs to be adjusted to account for changes in new environments. If a change idea is effective in an elementary school but unsuccessful at a middle school, additional PDSA cycles can reveal how the change idea might be adapted for a new context. If adaptations lead to success in the middle school, then the change idea could be tested again in the elementary context to see if the adapted middle school change idea would still be effective. If it is effective, then variation would be low, and the field may identify a change package or bundle, solutions to a problem that works in differing contexts. Bryk and colleagues (2015) suggest, "Getting smarter about how to successfully replicate results under diverse conditions is the key analytic challenge for quality improvement" (Bryk et al., 2015). Networked learning can emerge from informal networks, such as communities of practice, or from NICs (Bryk et al., 2015; Bryk, 2020; Hannan et al., 2015; LeMahieu et al., 2017; Russell et al., 2017).

Hub Structure

A NIC is the primary type of formal network for spreading improvement science (Bryk, 2020). If improvement teams are part of a NIC, then guidance from a hub structure is necessary. A hub is a group of people who ensure the capacity for improvement, create the analytic infrastructure, meet regularly to attend to routines, and manage the scaling and spreading of change ideas within and between schools (LeMahieu et al., 2017; Russell et al., 2017).). In some cases, district managers and staff who work in a department committed to improvement and innovation may manage the hub. In other cases, external providers, such as non-profits or universities may offer hub management as a service to a district. The district managers and external providers may work together to lead a hub. Where there is greater capacity, building-level leaders like principals, assistant principals, or teacher leaders, might serve as facilitation leads for their design teams and engage in hub leadership as part of that role.

A NIC structure involves a group of schools that share a problem and share drivers of that problem. For instance, in one district where we have partnered, leaders have been working in a multi-school NIC structure for several years. The NIC is part of a national initiative based around high school math outcomes for marginalized students, including students of color, students with special needs, and students with emergent English language skills. Outcomes for these groups of marginalized students are below the average for the district and the state. During the first year of the NIC, the schools worked collaboratively, under the guidance of the hub, to collect empathy data, review research and practical knowledge, conduct process and systems mapping, and explore school and district level local data to create a shared aim and theory of improvement (captured in a driver diagram). They identified four primary drivers and accompanying secondary drivers as seen in Figure 7.4.

These drivers were identified through activities facilitating the understanding of the system and root causes, including fishbone diagrams. The hub, which included district leaders and school facilitation leads from the improvement team, brought this knowledge together.

NICs can operate in several ways. Schools in a NIC may test the same change ideas. Each school in the NIC might try out an idea and gather data and

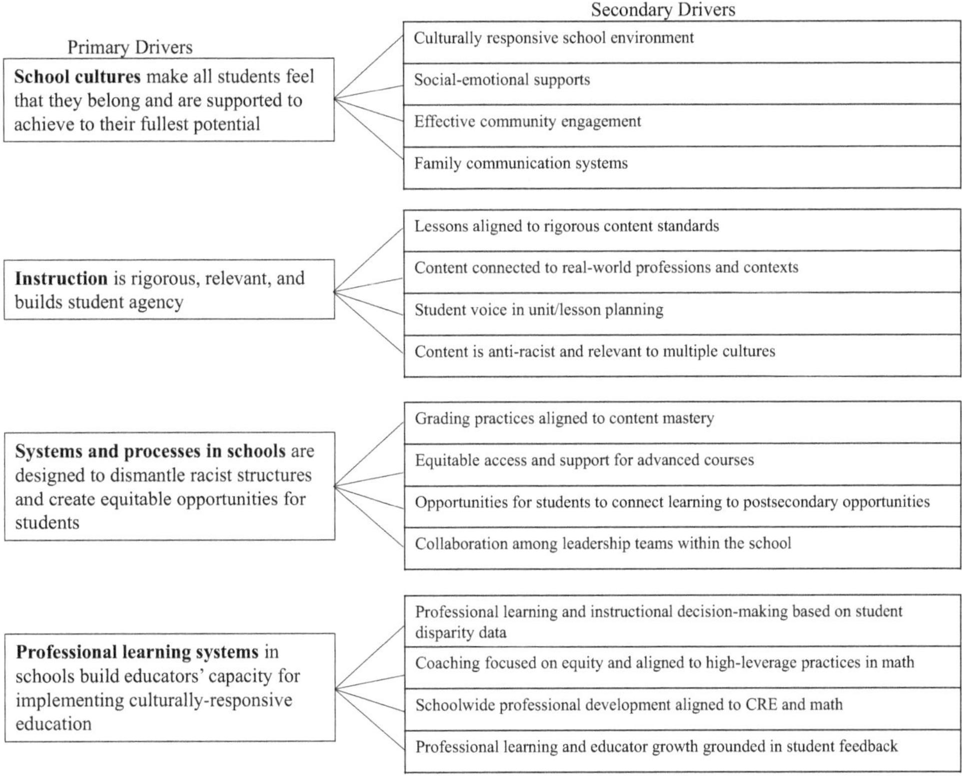

Figure 7.4 NIC Theory of Improvement.

Source: Created by the author.

iterate in their context to support the learning of all the schools. In other NICs, schools may have a catalog of change ideas to test out in their context and then share those learnings with other schools testing the same ideas. These change ideas may be co-created by the hub or the schools themselves, selected from published research, tested by the NIC, or tested by a previous group of schools in a NIC structure. In the example of the NIC we shared, schools created change ideas based on their individual context and data that aligned with the secondary drivers. Each school created the prototype of the change idea based on their existing knowledge and the support of their improvement coaches who provided summaries of research-based strategies for the school improvement teams to review. For instance, one school redesigned its grading policies and adjusted its grading scale based on the book *Grading for Equity* (Feldman, 2019). Another school created what they called "tiny projects" aligned with a school-designed framework focused on real-life math application. Yet another school created their own protocols for SEL circles and SEL lessons embedded in seminar classes.

In some NICs, the group of schools share one co-constructed aim statement. In other cases, the group has a primary aim, and each school has a sub-aim tailored specifically to the way the problem occurs in their context. The rationale for a shared aim is a shared data collection strategy that can provide more evidence of the outcomes of the change ideas across the network. The NIC that we mentioned had an overall aim to "increase the percentage of Class of 2024 Black and Latine students who demonstrate competency in mathematics to 70% or higher by EOY 2022." Individual schools were encouraged to create sub-aims based on the drivers linked to their change ideas. For instance, the school that focused on grading for equity would also have an aim of 100% of math teachers grading policies based on student mastery by EOY (i.e., end of year) 2022; they would measure this by ongoing reviews of class policies and practices and reviewing student work to see if the change ideas impacted student learning.

Spread and Scale Within a School

Spread and scale can also happen within a school. The concept is similar: there needs to be a group, like the design team or improvement team, who serves in the capacity of the hub, creating knowledge through organizing data, managing planning for tests of change (e.g., PDSA cycles), and facilitating knowledge sharing. Roles like coaches may also be involved during these processes. Within a large district, one of the authors of this book works with groups of schools to select their own problems based on an analysis of the opportunity gap in their setting. Each year, between five and ten schools are included in a network. As the external provider working with these schools, we are not the hub. There is no hub structure since we are not a NIC. Instead, the network supports schools through a coaching model and builds the internal capacity to spread and scale changes ideas or bundles of change ideas throughout the school. The coaches are active participants in their improvement team and over several years coaches guide them through understanding improvement science, and they also support them building learner stances, learning cultures, data for improvement, and adaptive processes (See Chapter 9 for detailed explanations of these concepts).

School improvement design teams in this network, in conjunction with improvement coaches, set their own aims, create their own theory of improvement, and determine, develop, and test out their own change ideas. However, the schools meet regularly and share their work and processes. Schools give each other ideas and feedback to improve their processes, and, when appropriate, they share change ideas and/or ways in which they understood their problem that would deepen other schools' understanding. This past fall, one school from the group of schools working on different problems in the network, decided to rethink its whole child support around attendance. At a network convening, the design team shared that they were addressing attendance, and one other school, which had tackled a similar problem 2 years before, offered to help. A person from the school improvement team that had addressed attendance met with the dean of school culture at the school who was just beginning to explore the problem and provided them with information about what they had tried that did and didn't work. The school shared data to support the change ideas that worked and to give the new school a way to approach tracking success. The schools learned from each other in less formal ways, but by working in community, they helped each other spread learning throughout their schools and between schools.

To summarize, Bryk (2020) suggested five commonalities of networked activity, regardless of whether the network is within a single school or across schools or districts:

1) Each network is organized around a specific problem.
2) Participants' efforts are disciplined by a shared working theory of improvement that is anchored in seeing how the system generates the unsatisfactory outcomes targeted for change.
3) The network develops and uses common measures and inquiry tools so that members can learn together and quickly share whether the changes they are testing are actually moving their system in the right direction.
4) These intentionally formed networks draw together diverse sources of expertise from practitioners, school leaders, researchers, designers, technologists, and depending on the problem, often families and students as well.
5) Participants are deliberate in consolidating the practical knowledge developing from their efforts and making it quickly accessible to still others who may further refine it as they seek to integrate it effectively in their particular contexts.

(pp. 12–13)

Bryk and colleagues (2015) point out that "no governmental or professional infrastructure currently exists for engaging educators in developing and testing . . . practice-based knowledge and synthesizing what is being learned along the way" (p. 46). It is up to the improvers to create the systems, structures, and environment for developing change ideas, testing, and learning from one another effectively.

Organizing for Continuous Improvement, Implementing for Organizational Growth, and Sustaining for Organizational Change

NICs and other forms of learning communities can be successful at spreading and scaling change ideas into the school system, but without certain conditions present at the district level, improvements may subside when the NIC is dissolved or if the change is not monitored over time for continued success. For spreading and scaling to be sustainable, the hub or district must attend to how they organize, implement, and maintain change. Figure 7.5 is from a chapter authored by two of the authors of this book.

When schools or districts plan for an improvement science approach, there are certain considerations to help guide how to organize the work for continuous improvement. Center the focus on the schools themselves and embed the process in existing improvement work to facilitate success. A system can become overwhelmed with ideas, even good ideas, and educators can feel like they are the last people consulted about what they need. To set up continuous improvement in a meaningful way, the needs, structures, and norms of schools must be considered. Take a moment to consider what you, working in your school, should keep in mind related to these and list them in the appropriate box in Action Inventory 7.2. District-wide initiatives, solely conceived of and implemented by district leaders, even when rooted in continuous improvement, will struggle to become routine practice if the focus isn't on the schools.

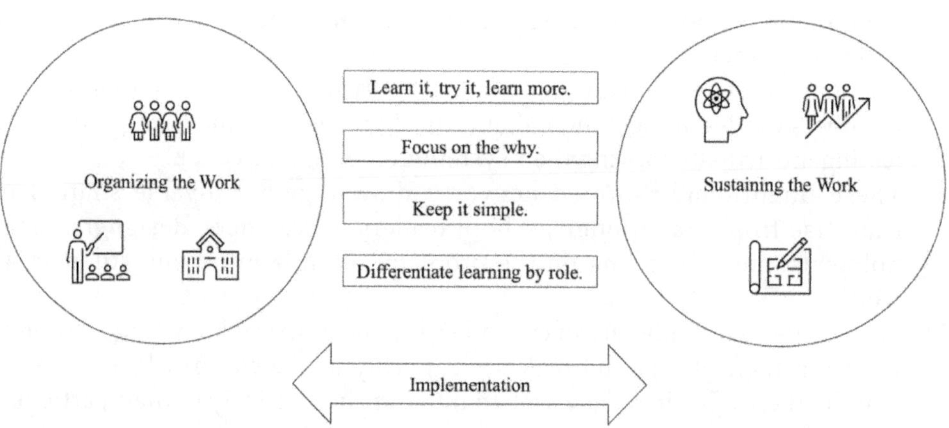
Organizing the Work
Learn it, try it, learn more.
Focus on the why.
Keep it simple.
Differentiate learning by role.
Sustaining the Work
Implementation

Figure 7.5 Framework for Organizing for Continuous Improvement, Implementing for Organizational Growth, and Sustaining for Organizational Change.

Source: Created by authors.

ACTION INVENTORY 7.2 IDENTIFYING EXISTING NEEDS, STRUCTURES, AND NORMS THAT WILL IMPACT IMPROVEMENT WORK

What are key existing needs, structures, and norms in your school?		
Existing Needs (e.g., technology, dedicated meeting time)	Existing Structures (e.g., common planning time, PLCs)	Existing Norms (e.g., collaboration, risk-taking, transparency, isolation, admit/don't admit struggles)

The work also needs to be structured with hybrid, bottom-up decision-making and top-down support (Anderson et al., under review). The locus of control needs to be at the unit of change; namely, it needs to be at the school. King and Bouchard (2011) call this a hybrid model of top-down and bottom-up structures. In a hybrid model, there are certain decisions and practices for formal leaders, such as the principal, but there is also an opportunity for "bottom-up" decision-making, in which teachers and other staff can authentically engage in improvement. Greenhalgh and Papoutsi (2019) make a similar argument about change in health care by suggesting a tight-loose-tight management style in which some aspects of the work are standardized, and other aspects are customized based on the school's context. They suggest setting goals, facilitating networks, creating data infrastructure, and determining the range of improvement tools should be held more tightly, or should be considered top-down support. The why (goals), what (measures), and when (goals and measures) should be tight. Local control of decision-making or more loose management should be applied to developing insights, making sense of the improvement process, surfacing needs, and determining the resources necessary to address those needs. The who (teachers, families, students, leaders) and how (needs and processes) should be loose or bottom-up.

Implementation in Practice

As for implementing the improvement work, Anderson and colleagues suggest the hub or district needs to focus on four areas: (a) learn it, try it, learn more; (b) focus on the why; (c) keep it simple; and (d) differentiate learning by role. The best way to engage new improvers in continuous improvement is to improve something (Bryk et al., 2015). After getting a basic understanding of the core principles and the tools of improvement (learn it), applying the process (try it), ideally with the support of a more experienced improver work, is the best way to support people in learning the process (learn more). Learning that comes from doing the work will fuel the skill and will to engage in improvement science and beckon people to continue using improvement science.

Emphasizing the reasons that the work is being done with an equity orientation engages new learners in improvement science. Ava's NIC selected a problem that focused on being culturally response and inclusive. To engage teachers and staff in their schools, each leader had to select a problem that resonated with the school. MHMS focused on LGBTQ+ students and families because that MHMS teachers and staff saw the need. Then, keep the learning simple, which is welcomed in a complex system. Don't get bogged down in the theory and the tools but get bogged down in the improvement.

Not everyone needs to understand every aspect of continuous improvement. By helping people learn what is necessary for them to participate in the improvement work without overwhelming them with all aspects of the work, you can again help reduce the complexity in an already complex system. If attention is paid to these four aspects of the improvement process during the initial implementation, the NIC or network will be in a better position to spread and scale.

Sustaining the work involves planning, specifically around coaching, knowledge management, and growth and succession planning. As we mentioned before, the key responsibility of the hub is to create analytic structures, necessary for producing the data and learning that can become knowledge. Of particular importance for spread and scale, you need a plan for how learning will be captured, shared, and codified. In addition to a knowledge management structure, there needs to be a plan for how the improvement process will be learned and shared. Coaching consistently seems to be the best model for learning improvement science; a coaching plan for what that will look like (i.e., how coaches will be prepared, and what will be the length and depth of the coach's role) is needed for sustained change. Coaches play a key role in spread. Finally, the growth and succession plan should consider the very question of spreading and scaling and what structures, systems, and practices need to be developed for an idea to spread. This plan also considers who and how will the system manage scaling. This planning is especially important in a system that faces a lot of churn with people moving throughout and outside of the system. We suggest you use Action Inventory 7.3 to help plan to sustain your improvement work.

Due to the complexity and the focus on systems thinking, a focus on implementation practices is essential for the spread and scale of the work. However, implementation is important, difficult, and hard to understand (Greenhalgh & Papoutsi, 2019). Bryk and colleagues call this spread and scale "adaptive integration" or "learning how to make things work under a variety of different organizational conditions" and then adapting the problem and solution to fit that context.

SUPPORT MATERIAL

ACTION INVENTORY 7.3 COACHING, LEARNING, SCALING CONSIDERATIONS

Coaching

1. Who will be responsible for coaching the improvement team (person inside or external to the organization)?
2. Why is this person/people the right fit?
3. When will coaches help the team?
4. Will coaches be compensated? How much?
5. How will the coach help with knowledge management?
6. How will the coach help with growth and succession planning?
7. What is the expectation for the scope of the coach's role(s) with the improvement team?

Knowledge Management

1. Our improvement work evidence and artifacts will be stored in the following place (e.g., shared folders):
2. Who has access to this information?
3. Who is responsible for sharing what?

Information to Share	Person Responsible

4. When will information be shared?

Growth and Succession Planning

1. Who is involved in spreading efforts?
2. Who is involved in scaling efforts?
3. When a member of the improvement team is replaced by a new member, how will that new member be onboarded?
4. When there is school or district level leader turnover, how soon will you communicate the improvement work with them?
5. What does the new leader need to know?
6. What steps will you need to complete to ensure the improvement efforts continue?

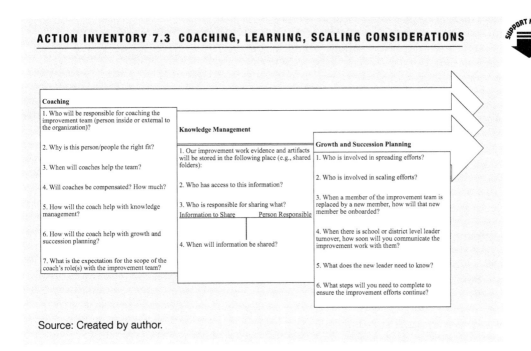

Source: Created by author.

The study of implementing new ideas through improvement is "implementation science" or "the systematic uptake of research findings and other evidence-based practices into routine practice" (p. 2). When applied to improvement science, implementation science by itself can be limited in that it focuses primarily on the technical and not the social or moral, resulting often in the approach to implementation mentioned earlier in this chapter – implementation with fidelity. Greenhalgh and Papoutsi (2019) provide a thorough description of three approaches to spread and scale, which not only consider (a) an implementation science approach but also attend to (b) complexity science and (c) social science or the moral and social aspects of implementation (Figure 7.6). They astutely point out, "As a rule of thumb, the larger, more ambitious, and more politically contested the spread challenge, the more ecological and social practice perspectives will need to supplement (or replace) 'mechanical' efforts to replicate an intervention" (p. 4). Keeping in mind the goal of improvement science should be to disrupt systems of inequity and recreate just systems, which are often politically contested; spread and scale rely on the ecological and social views.

Greenhalgh and Papoutsi (2019) introduced implementation science as an approach to spreading evidence-based interventions. The steps in implementation science, of which you will notice parallels with improvement science, are to develop an intervention, conduct small-scale tests, undergo "systematic effort to replicate it in other settings", and "{identify and deal} with barriers (which get in the way of the implementation effort) and facilitators (which potentially support it)" (p. 1). Greenhalgh and Papoutsi suggest this is a mechanical approach that, while attending to context, is focused on fidelity

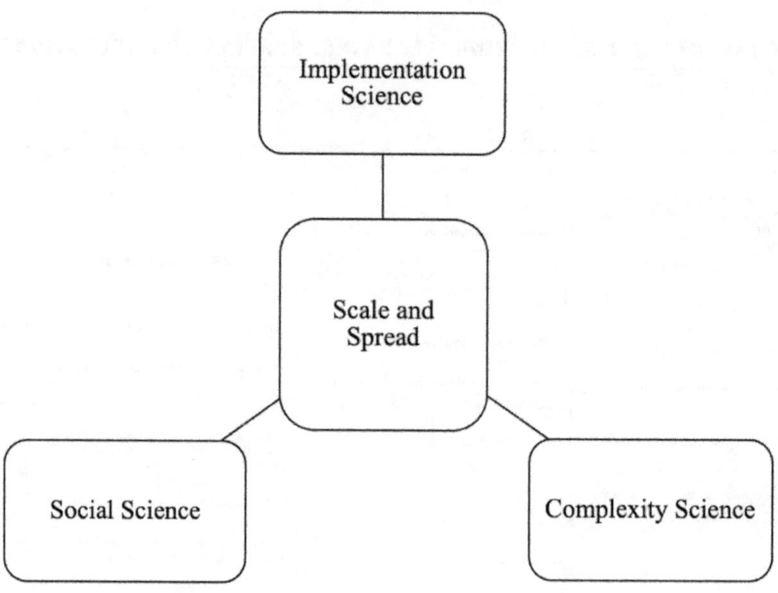

Figure 7.6 Implementing Scale and Spread.

of implementation. The context is relevant so that implementers can appreciate the context (qualitatively) to reduce uncertainty and eliminate variance (quantitatively) by creating a tight, structured model, protocol, or program that can be scaled in a complex system with consistent results. Although finding solutions to educational problems that can be replicated across schools and districts is appealing, this approach may be limited if it does not attend to the human element of change.

Taking an ecological approach, in addition to or instead of the mechanical approach, is the recognition that a "complex system is a set of things, people, and processes that evolve dynamically and can be defined in terms of their relationships and interactions" (p. 1). Greenhalgh and Papoutsi (2019, p.1) explain,

> Systems are characterized by uncertainty, unpredictability, and emergence. They adapt through self-organization (such as continuous adaptations initiated by frontline staff to allow them to complete tasks given local contingencies and availability of resources), attention to interdependencies (how the parts of the system fit together), and sensemaking (the process by which people, individually and collectively, assign meaning to experience and link it to action).

Building from this idea about self-organization, interdependence, and sensemaking, Lanham and colleagues (2013) recommend that when creating change or facilitating improvement in complex systems, you

- **Acknowledge unpredictability** – "implementation teams should tailor designs to local context and view surprises as opportunities" (p. 2)
- **Make space for self-organization** – "implementation teams should actively capture data and feed it into the adaptation process" (p. 3)
- **Facilitate interdependencies** – "implementation teams should attend to these relationships, reinforcing existing ones where appropriate and facilitating new ones" (p. 3).

This complexity approach recognizes there are various levels to the system and that the people within and between those levels also have varying perspectives and roles. There needs to be space for sensemaking within and across levels of the system and "implementation teams should encourage participants to ask questions, admit ignorance, explore paradoxes, exchange different viewpoints, and reflect collectively" (Lanham et al., 2013, p. 3). Implementers must productively develop adaptive capability in staff, attend to human relationships, and harness conflict.

Attending to complexity involves creating an understanding of the why, the how, and the what of improvement. Adaptive improvement practices handle the uncertainty and respond flexibly to the social, historical, political, racial, and organizational context of schools and school systems. The types of data necessary to address this context are narrative stories or cases that provide detailed explanations of how the strategy or change ideas work in different contexts to spread and scale with an eye on the complex nature of change, including explanations of failure and associated learnings from failure. Applying a complexity approach to implementation recognizes a focus on the moral arc of strong equity. For example, equity should not just be considered when understanding the problem or creating change ideas, but it needs to be explicitly sought and monitored when an idea is spread and scaled.

Spread and scale require attention to social science. Similar to a complex systems approach, social science recognizes connections between the individuals, teams (improvement teams, departments, whole child teams, instructional leadership teams), organizations (school), and inter-organizational (multiple schools, districts) relationships that surround the implementation process. In addition to seeking consistency and accepting unpredictability, the last approach is focused on social behavior: What do people believe? How do those beliefs translate to action? What are the patterns or social routines that result from those beliefs and actions? To spread and scale with a mind toward social science focuses on the ways the context influences social behavior and interaction through ethnographic methods that seek to understand human experience in context to understand how the implementation is influenced by professional, interpersonal, and organizational contexts. Equity considerations – such as power, liberatory collaboration, and Indigenous contexts – should be addressed with critical self-reflection and dialogue about how spreading change ideas may be responsive to or a driver of social change in an unjust system.

When leading spread and scale in your organization or system, such implementation practices with a focus on equity are a roadmap for considering how to organize the spread and to provide areas for consideration that bring promising idea(s), such as a change bundle, to scale. We suggest successful implementation would require considering all three approaches and deepening an understanding of what we are trying to spread, how the complex system will respond to that change, and how people in the system will need to be prepared for the uptake of new ideas. Bryk (2020) refers to the work of an improvement community as a "learning web." He explains that the role of the hub includes "interconnectivity," "good communications," and "healthy social relationships" (p. 186). Many good ideas have never made it into everyday educational practice because leaders have failed to recognize and attend to the social and moral in addition to the instrumental. Action Inventory 7.4 invites you to think about how you might address the social science considerations for scaling and spreading.

Research Practice Partnerships for Spread and Scale

Research practice partnerships (RPPs) support the spread and scale of both improvement science and the change ideas that emerge from the improvement science methodology. A NIC can be a type of RPP. RPPs involve those within the school system, such as school and district leaders, collaborating in partnership with a researcher, often from a university to co-capture knowledge and support change within and outside the system. In an RPP, the educators and researchers

SUPPORT MATERIAL

ACTION INVENTORY 7.4 THOUGHTFUL SCALING AND SPREADING

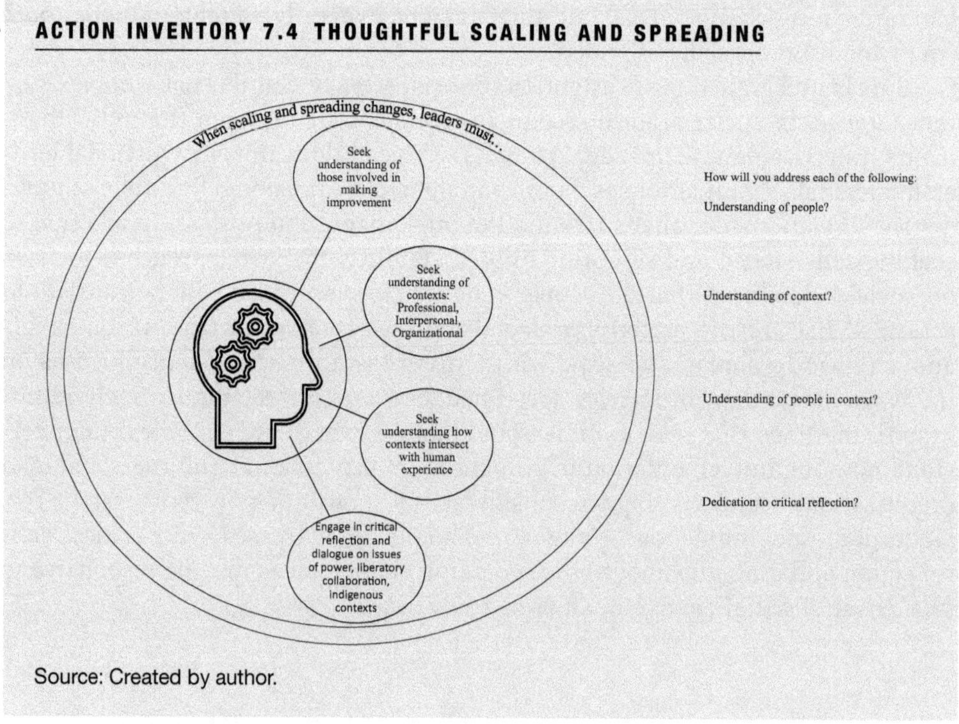

Source: Created by author.

work together to identify the problem to be solved and identify the needs of the district or school; they co-create a research agenda to meet those needs (Penuel et al., 2020). Action Inventory 7.4 supports you in planning for thoughtful spreading and scaling.

Penuel and colleagues (2020) suggest eight principles for collaborative education research, especially research in RPPs. These eight principles help ensure the focus of improvement captures contextual data and evidence necessary for spread and scale. We've translated these into *some* items you and your partners will likely need to address in your partnership work and captured these in Action Inventory 7.5. The first set of principles focuses on what the partnership is intended to do and why the organizations want to work together. First, they suggest that schools/districts and researchers need to have a sense of agency and a belief in their ability to change schools. Second, there must be an underlying belief that the value of the research is its practical application, a tenet of applied research and pragmatism. Third, the problem is at the center of the collaboration, and the nature and extent of that problem should guide the work of the partnership. Fourth, the collaboration must recognize the context of the school/district and how that context situates the problem and the conditions around the problem.

Together the partners ensure their values and beliefs align with one another around change, equity, social justice, and the assets of educators (Anderson & Lochhead, 2023). The partners must achieve their understanding of root causes, systems and process mapping, and identification of drivers together to ensure that they have a common understanding of the problem and context. Fifth, the research should also be of value to others with similar values, beliefs, contexts, and problems.

The remaining principles focus on how to collaborate. The sixth principle is that there needs to be role clarity. The research plan should situate the "expertise" of each educator and researcher and define how their roles contribute to the research. Seventh, there should be an opportunity to compare what the collaboration set out to understand and do and what they learned and accomplished. Eighth, the collaboration needs to have clear research plans, which include how they will test change ideas and identify solutions, including how that learning will become practical knowledge, how they will organize the research study, and how that learning will lead to scholarly knowledge. Outside partners, often academic researchers, bring their research perspective and help to guide the development of a research plan, sharing of learning in scholarly venues like journals and presentations. Applied researchers, often practitioners within the school or district, bring their understanding of the context, helping to shape what research will be relevant in their school/district. District (and school) leaders have a role in creating systems to allow for knowledge transfer or the collection and analysis of data to spread and scale promising change ideas that address the problem that the partnership collaboratively identified.

To illustrate what this would look like, we will return to the NIC and the network we discussed earlier in the chapter, both of which are embedded in an RPP between a university and a district. In this case, the RPP intended to capture learning about the implementation of improvement. Partners came together to conduct collaborative education research around the act of improving. The district tried many popular reforms, partnered with many outside providers, and engaged

ACTION INVENTORY 7.5 SOME TO-DO LIST ITEMS FOR PARTNERS

PK-12 Partner To-Do List	Partnership To-Do List	University Partner To-Do List
☐ Highlight team members' areas of expertise	☐ Identify a shared goal for the partnership work	☐ Highlight team members' areas of expertise
☐ Identify areas in the system for improvement and research	☐ Identify shared expectations for the role of research and improvement (e.g., practical application)	☐ Lead conversation on organizing research and improvement plans
☐ Hold deep understanding of context	☐ Role identification for each organization	☐ Facilitate improvement and research dissemination efforts
☐ Honor research methods and theory expertise from the university	☐ Establish collaboration norms	☐ Honor applied research expertise from the district
☐ Develop systems and structures to support improvement processes (e.g., root cause analysis, PDSA cycle)	☐ Establish collaboration routines	☐ Consult with IRB
☐ Other:	☐ Consolidate learning and understanding	☐ Other:
	☐ Develop an understanding of improvement science methods, approaches, priorities	
	☐ Other:	

Source: Created by author.

in many improvement strategies focused on closing the opportunity gap, but despite those efforts, improvement was not occurring district-wide. The university researcher taught and researched improvement science and served as a state provider for schools in need of improvement. The district partners led innovation and improvement efforts in the district, including the development of several district-led NICs. These partners came together around the common problem of persisting inequities in the district and the lack of sustained improvement. They explored the context and the system to develop a research agenda that would both help the district learn to improve and capture through a rigorous case study on improvement science that could be shared throughout the field. The RPP identified the following research questions:

1) How does a university/district partnership design and implement a professional learning program for school improvement, based on improvement science and liberatory design, in one western urban district?
2) In what ways, if any, do school leadership teams apply design improvement to address urgent, complex problems of practice? How are such efforts having an impact on the culture of continuous improvement at the schools as well as student outcomes?
3) What are the benefits and challenges of integrating design improvement into existing school improvement work?
4) In what ways, if any, do school leadership teams build capacity to identify high-leverage areas for improvement, implement change, and measure the

stated goals? How are such efforts having an impact on the sharing of learning and spreading effective practices within the network and beyond?
5) What are we doing to prioritize diversity, equity, inclusion, anti-racist, and just (DEIAJ) practices within the partnership and in work with schools? How are such efforts having an impact on the culture of culturally responsive mindsets and practices at the school and district levels in the district?

The partners identified data sources such as the school's root cause analysis templates, empathy interview notes, driver diagrams (all versions), change idea prototypes, PDSA notes, aim data, presentations, and other planning/meeting documents, including coaching notes from each session, field notes of coaching sessions (once per action period), field notes from professional learning sessions (recorded), evaluations from professional learning sessions, documents and notes from the partnership and NIC and COP planning meetings, and end-of-the-year interviews (teams, district leaders, coaches). The district created tracking systems to monitor small tests of change that individual schools were engaging in across their NICs. They worked together on a knowledge management system, and they created a learning trajectory to guide coaching. The university researcher provided reports and suggestions based on the data; the district team worked to apply those learnings. District and university partners presented results at national conferences and published in books and journals. This work is current and evolving. Descriptions of the partnership are available in other published writing. In this chapter, we hope to bring to life spreading and scaling efforts though this example of collaborative research and the RPP.

CONCLUSION

Changing systems is about implementing spread and scale through schools, networks, and networked improvement communities. These structures for spread and scale can include educators and researchers from the P–12 space and beyond.

Instrumental Methods

There are tools that help spread and scale change throughout a complex system. The process of spreading ideas should not take place organically; the process requires planning and monitoring. There needs to be an analytical structure to collect data and measure progress. This structure, guided by the hub or improvement team, helps track progress toward an overall aim of the improvement work, measure the impact of the change idea in different settings and at different levels of the system, and capture contextual conditions that support or hinder improvement.

Moral Values

Improvers need to recognize there is complexity and variation in the system, and they must slow down to understand the system and to recognize and understand the people working within the system before attempting to scale new ideas. To spread and scale with a focus on equity, we need to center schools and their needs. We must listen to the voices of the community to help define and refine what students and families need. This process should be a hybrid bottom-up and top-down process with priorities coming from the schools and support for developing improvement processes coming from the district and beyond.

> **NELP and PSEL Connection Box for Educational Leadership Faculty**
>
> This chapter connects to PSEL One and Ten and NELP Standard One ("Mission, Vision, and Improvement"), specifically NELP Component 1.2, which deals with the capacity to lead school and district strategic planning and continuous improvement processes that engage diverse stakeholders in data collection, diagnosis, design, implementation, and evaluation; and it deals with the substandards within PSEL Standard One that address working collaboratively to develop and enact an organizational vision that promotes the success of each student (1b) and strategically developing, implementing, and evaluating actions to achieve the vision of the school (1d). PSEL Ten includes 10d, 10g, and 10j, which encompass engaging others in inquiry, learning, strategic goal setting, planning, implementation, and evaluation for continuous improvement; developing technically appropriate systems of data collection, management, analysis, and use; connecting as needed with the district office and external partners for support in planning, implementation, monitoring, feedback, and evaluation; and developing and promoting leadership among teachers and staff for inquiry, experimentation, and innovation, and initiating and implementing improvement. Standard Ten also suggests the adoption of a district perspective to improvement and promoting coherence among improvement efforts and all aspects of school organization, programs, and services.

Social Relations

When trying to spread change, interactions matter. You must lead work around collaborative structures, team dynamics, and relationships before moving an idea through a system. Implementation cannot be people-proof because people are the system in schools. Networks are one structure that allow for social learning. RPPs create knowledge and flip the notion of "expertise" on its head. In an improvement science approach to partnering for improvement, the practitioners and researchers work together, playing on their varied strengths and assets, learning, and applying that learning to future improvement.

BIBLIOGRAPHY

Anderson, E., Cunningham, K. W., & Richardson, J. W. (under review). Framework for implementing improvement science in a school district to support sustainable growth.

Anderson, E., & Lochhead, S. (2023, April). Shared goals, methods, and learning: Partnering for equity-focused, systems-level improvement. In M. Biag & L. Gomez (Eds.), *Improving America's schools together: How district-university partnerships and continuous improvement can transform education* (pp. 219–239). Rowan and Littlefield.

Anfara, Jr., V. A., & Mertz, N. T. (Eds.). (2014). *Theoretical frameworks in qualitative research*. Sage Publications.

Berwick, D. M. (1996). A primer on leading the improvement of systems. *BMJ, 312*(7031), 619–622. https://doi.org/10.1136/bmj.312.7031.619

Bryk, A. S. (2020). *Improvement in action: Advancing quality in America's schools*. Harvard Education Press.

Bryk, A. S., Gomez, L. M., Grunow, A., & Lemahieu, P. G. (2015). *Learning to improve: How America's schools can get better at getting better.* Harvard Education Press.

Cobb, C. D., & Virella, P. (2019). The legitimization of improvement science in academe. *Systemics, Cybernetics and Informatics, 17*(1), 287–296.

Compton-Phillips, A. (2020). Spreading at scale: A practical leadership model for change. *NEJM Catalyst, 1*(1). https://doi.org/10.1056/cat.19.1083

Devedzic, V., Tomic, B., Jovanovic, J., Kelly, M., Milikic, N., Dimitrijevic, S., Djuric, D., & Sevarac, Z. (2018). Metrics for students' soft skills. *Applied Measurement in Education, 31*(4), 283–296. https://doi.org/10.1080/08957347.2018.1495212

Dixon-Roman, E., Everson, H., & Mcardle, J. (2013). Race, poverty, and SAT scores: Modeling the influences of family income on black and white high school students' SAT performance. *Teachers College Record, 115.* http://doi.org/10.1177/016146811311500406

DuFour, R. (2004). What is a professional learning community? *Educational Leadership, 61*(8), 6–11.

DuFour, R., DuFour, R., Eaker, R., & Many, T. (2006). *Learning by doing: A handbook for professional learning communities that work.* Bloomington, IN: Solution Tree.

Escolà-Gascón, Á., & Gallifa, J. (2022). How to measure soft skills in the educational context: Psychometric properties of the SKILLS-in-ONE questionnaire. *Studies in Educational Evaluation, 74,* 101155. https://doi.org/10.1016/j.stueduc.2022.101155

Farrington, C. A., Roderick, M., Allensworth, E., Nagaoka, J., Keyes, T. S., Johnson, D. W., & Beechum, N. O. (2012). *Teaching adolescents to become learners: The role of noncognitive factors in shaping school performance: A critical literature review.* University of Chicago Consortium on Chicago School Research. https://consortium.uchicago.edu/publications/teaching-adolescents-become-learners-role-noncognitive-factors-shaping-school

Feldman, J. (2019). *Grading for equity: What it is, why it matters, and how it can transform schools and classrooms.* Corwin.

Greenhalgh, T., & Papoutsi, C. (2019). Spreading and scaling up innovation and improvement. *BMJ*, l2068. https://doi.org/10.1136/bmj.l2068

Hannan, M., Russell, J. L., Takahashi, S., & Park, S. (2015). Using improvement science to better support beginning teachers. *Journal of Teacher Education, 66*(5), 494–508. https://doi.org/10.1177/0022487115602126

Himmelfarb, J., Stenvinkel, P., Ikizler, T. A., & Hakim, R. M. (2002). The elephant in uremia: Oxidant stress as a unifying concept of cardiovascular disease in uremia. *Kidney International, 62*(5), 1524–1538. https://doi.org/10.1046/j.1523-1755.2002.00600.x

Hinnant-Crawford, B. (2020). *Improvement science in education: A primer.* Spaulding.

Johnson, B. (2003). Teacher collaboration: Good for some, not so good for others. *Educational Studies, 29*(4), 337–350. https://doi.org/10.1080/0305569032000159651

King, M. B., & Bouchard, K. (2011). The capacity to build organizational capacity in schools. *Journal of Educational Administration, 49*(6), 653–669. https://doi.org/10.1108/09578231111174802

Langley, G. J., Moen, R. D., Nolan, K. M., Nolan, T. W., Norman, C. L., & Provost, L. P. (2009). *The improvement guide: A practical approach to enhancing organizational performance*. John Wiley & Sons.

Lanham, H. J., Leykum, L. K., Taylor, B. S., McCannon, C. J., Lindberg, C., & Lester, R. T. (2013). How complexity science can inform scale-up and spread in health care: Understanding the role of self-organization in variation across local contexts. *Social Science & Medicine, 93*, 194–202. https://doi.org/10.1016/j.socscimed.2012.05.040

LeMahieu, P. G., Grunow, A., Baker, L., Nordstrum, L. E., & Gomez, L. M. (2017). Networked improvement communities: The discipline of improvement science meets the power of networks. *Quality Assurance in Education, 25*(1), 5–25. https://doi.org/doi:10.1108/QAE-12-2016-0084

Lewis, C. (2015). What is improvement science? Do we need it in education? *Educational Researcher, 44*(1), 54–61. https://doi.org/10.3102/0013189X15570388

Mattern, K., Radunzel, J., & Harmston, M. (2016). *ACT composite score by income*. ACT. www.act.org/content/dam/act/unsecured/documents/R1604-ACT-Composite-Score-by-Family-Income.pdf

Penuel, W. R., Riedy, R., Barber, M. S., Peurach, D. J., LeBouef, W. A., & Clark, T. (2020). Principles of collaborative education research with stakeholders: Toward requirements for a new research and development infrastructure. *Review of Educational Research, 90*(5), 627–674. https://doi.org/10.3102/0034654320938126

Rippner, J.A. (2015). *The American Education Policy Landscape* (1st ed.). Routledge. https://doi.org/10.4324/9781315728247

Russell, J. L., Bryk, A. S., Dolle, J. R., Gomez, L. M., Lemahieu, P. G., & Grunow, A. (2017). A framework for the initiation of networked improvement communities. *Teachers College Record, 119*(5), 1–36. https://doi.org/10.1177/016146811711900501

Senge, P. M. (2020). Commentary: Why practicing a system's perspective is easier said than done. *Applied Developmental Science, 24*(1), 57–61. https://doi.org/10.1080/10888691.2017.1421429

Stoll, L., & Louis, K. S. (2007). Professional learning communities: Elaborating new approaches. In L. Stoll & K. S. Louis (Eds.), *Professional learning communities: Divergence, depth, and dilemmas* (pp. 1–14). Open University Press.

Vornberg, J. A. (2013). Systems theory. In B. J. Irby, G. Brown, R. Lara-Alecio, & S. Jackson (Eds.), *The handbook of educational theories* (pp. 805–813). IAP Information Age Publishing.

PART III

What Is Leading Continuous Improvement?

CHAPTER 8

Building a Toolbox for Leading Continuous Improvement

Chapter Highlights

1) Reflect on leadership dispositions related to guiding improvement.
2) Employ collaborative team structures using distributed leadership.
3) Protocols (e.g., PDSA templates, driver diagrams) help to develop practices and patterns of behavior.
4) Garnering "buy-in" (commitment, collective responsibility) will be necessary.

CHAPTER DESCRIPTION

This chapter seeks to offer practical tools for leading and enacting continuous improvement. Guidance is provided on how to establish conditions for improvement such as collaborative structures, a trusting culture, and alignment with organizational priorities. The chapter also presents a comprehensive toolbox that supports the transfer of learning from a preparation program or professional learning experience to leading improvement in schools. This toolbox can be adapted for district or school settings as well as non-education spaces.

INTRODUCTION: THE IMPORTANCE OF THE TOOLBOX

Improvement science is not only a methodology but also a mindset and leadership approach. There are tools leaders develop and leverage when working with teams and communities. It is critical to focus not only on the methods and protocols, but on how improvers work with one another (Biag & Sherer, 2021; Zumpe &

DOI: 10.4324/9781003389279-11

Aramburo, in press). These mindsets and approaches are tools too; we frame them as such. We are first going to illustrate how tools of leadership skills and dispositions are critical in authentic improvement work. Discussing humility, trust, collaboration, reflection, and systems perspectives precedes the discussion of the technical tools (i.e., protocols) used in continuous improvement efforts.

Let's start with a discussion of one of the words in this chapter's title: toolbox. A toolbox can come in a variety of sizes, can be made from different materials, and is configured in several ways. When one of the authors, Katie, was preparing to go to college, she was gifted a very basic toolbox. It was plastic and about the size of a shoebox. Opening it revealed that the box was just an empty space – no compartments or dividers. This first toolbox held the essentials: a hammer, pliers, nails, screwdrivers, and a tape measure. Over 20 years later, she uses a toolbox three or four times the size of that first box and has collected additional tools and skills. However, her neighbor has an extensive collection of tools organized on shelves and hanging on the garage wall. In fact, there is not enough room for their car with all the tools and equipment in there! Katie can say, with confidence, that her neighbor has more experience, has stronger skills, and can converse eloquently in conversations about home improvement, tools, etc. Her neighbor would be much better positioned than Katie is to teach and mentor someone about using those tools.

There are a few points in relation to this leadership for improvement. First, our leadership toolboxes grow over time by collecting new information, developing our skills, evolving our professional habits and practices, and experiencing more novel scenarios. Although Katie has limited knowledge of home improvement, she as progressed and continues to grow. She will never have as many tools or as much expertise as her neighbor, and that is okay. She continues to improve and collect new tools along the way. Importantly, she also knows when to ask for help. Her neighbor clearly acquired more tools over time with more frequency than Katie has. This signals that the more we actively engage with and practice improvement approaches, the more extensive our own toolbox will grow.

The tools in the chapter include (a) leadership tools (e.g., communication, building capacity), (b) strategic connection and planning tools (e.g., aligning improvement with overall school mission, vision, and goals), and (c) improvement science tools or protocols (e.g., empathy interviews, driver diagrams, PDSA cycle protocols). In each section, we present the tools' purposes and ideas and examples for practical application, reflection, or capacity building. We hope that after you read this chapter, you will have a strong sense of the tools currently in your toolbox, the tools to polish or upgrade, and the tools to add (or maybe jettison if they are not effectively serving you and your team).

The authors have participated in numerous meetings and learning opportunities related to improvement science. An important point surfaces at these convenings: improvement science is not just the activity-centric/technical tools (e.g., templates, protocols) that help enact the process. Although using protocols to surface information makes them valuable, we encourage you to not get too hung up on the technical tools. Instead, focus on learning when and how to use tools as they align with your improvement purposes. Although we will connect leadership to the technical and instrumental methods of improvement science, this is not a step-by-step guide on how to use improvement science tools and protocols. Other notable scholars and improvers have already created and shared helpful improvement science tools and protocols (e.g., Carnegie Foundation for the Advancement of Teaching; Langley et al., 2009; Hinnant-Crawford, 2020; High Tech High Graduate School of Education, 2023), and we encourage you to seek those out.

TOOLS FOR IMPROVEMENT: LEADERSHIP SKILLS AND DISPOSITIONS FOR IMPROVEMENT

Many leadership skills and tools positively impact improvement work. In this section, eight tools are identified. *PSEL* Standard 10 states that "Effective educational leaders act as agents of continuous improvement" (NCPEA 2015, p. 18). Being an effective agent for continuous improvement requires attention to leaders' approaches to setting up their organizational conditions. Leadership tools of humility, honesty, transparency, patience, capacity building, collaboration, trust, and reflection help establish and nurture a learning organization for improvement. This is not an exhaustive list. Others (e.g., Biag & Sherer, 2021; Dixon & Palmer, 2020) have identified some similar and different leadership dispositions. Seek those out to continue to build up your toolbox. For now, we highlight eight tools and invite reflection on the status of each of these tools in your leadership toolbox.

Humility

An improver needs *humility*. Studies demonstrate successful leaders are confident but humble (Collins, 2001; Fullan, 2009; Grant, 2021; Oyer, 2015). Humility is demonstrated by a willingness to invite various stakeholder groups to the improvement table, for example, even when those groups reveal potentially hard-to-hear points (Khalifa, 2018; Militello et al., 2009). Confident leaders know that bringing various stakeholder groups into the improvement conversation is the right move. Remember when Ava's team realized they needed to talk to students in the GSA? They sought the stories of their students. They heard heartbreaking examples of some of the mistreatment students experienced. Ava's team listened. The team also humbled themselves by admitting that the adults in the building hadn't done enough.

Humble leaders listen in meaningful ways to how their leadership and their systems might be contributing to the negative experiences of stakeholders, and they value that perspective. Look at this definition that Dr. Brené Brown offers in her book, *Atlas of the Heart* (2021): humility is "openness to new learning combined with a balanced and accurate assessment of our contributions including our strengths, imperfections, and opportunity for growth." She goes on to pithily write, humility is saying, "I'm here to get it right. Not to be right." Oomph. Let's read that again, "I'm here to get it right. Not to be right." This approach aligns beautifully with improvement science; we focus on getting better at getting better. It does not actually matter who had the "right" idea, you (as the leader) or someone else. What does matter is that a leader supports an organizational culture for improvement that invites exploration and discovery of a promising direction – or a learning culture – described in Chapter 9. The leader is critical to setting up the organizational opportunities, space, and time to get it right.

It can feel personal when an idea "feels" like yours, and you think it's great. You might share it only to have people criticize it or suggest changes to it. It takes a purposeful mindset to welcome feedback. A helpful practice for leading with humility stemming from Baha'i faith emphasizes the collective. When a group is engaged in decision-making or action planning, the practice stipulates that once an idea is shared with the group, it no longer belongs to the individual who introduced it – it becomes collectively shared by the group. The group can adjust it, modify it, etc. (The Baha'i Faith, 2010). Because the individual who contributes the idea holds this group norm, they resist the temptation to be defensive or reject modifications of "their" idea. Practicing the transfer of idea ownership in a similar way may encourage group members to be more open to critiques of ideas in service of making improvements.

Don Berwick is the former president and chief executive officer of the Institute for Healthcare Improvement. In an hthUnboxed podcast episode, he shares with the host, Stacey Callier, that humility is a component of leadership that helps establish a learning environment for improvement. He says,

> Leaders who are best at nurturing environments for learning themselves are learners . . . So that means there's a certain level of humility; a high level of humility and empathy and relationship building, and curiosity. I don't think a good leader shows up with answers much. You're just not smarter than the people you're leading. You get paid more maybe, and you have a degree after your name, but you're not likely to be that much smarter. We are smarter together than separately. And so a leader who knows that and who's curious . . . [and asks] "What could I learn today? What do I not know that I could know?" that's a very important asset in improvement and it also signals to the workforce that that's a good question for them.
>
> (Berwick, February 24, 2021)

Humility invites opportunities to seek understanding and learn deeply about a system or phenomenon – a key component of continuous improvement (Militello et al., 2009). Morally, humility is required to ensure oppressive systems are being dismantled. Khalifa (2018) argues that if a leader like Ava is culturally responsive then, when practicing humility, she would "constantly [look] for signs that [she] is reproducing oppression in the school; will take that information head on and institutionalize the appropriate anti-oppression reforms" (p. 191). Grant, in his book, *Think Again* (2021), suggests that we harness a scientist-like mindset, which aligns with a humble improvement approach because, as Grant states,

> When we're in scientist mode, we refuse to let our ideas become ideologies. We don't start with answers or solutions; we lead with questions and puzzles . . . It means being *actively* open-minded. It requires searching for reasons why we might be wrong – not for reasons why we must be right – and revising our views based on what we learn.
>
> (p. 25)

Later he writes, "Scientific thinking favors humility over pride, doubt over certainty, curiosity over closure" (p. 28). Prioritizing getting it right and using humility to get out of our own way is central to improvement.

We can show that prior scholars and improvers espouse the importance of humility, but how does someone act humble? Researchers and improvers (e.g., Owens & Hekman, 2016; Berwick, 2021) offer samples of ways one might act with humility.

- *Admitting you do not know everything.* Saying, "I don't know" or "More information would be helpful for me to understand," are two direct sentences to demonstrate humility.
- *Making your learning journey explicit.* As a leader, since you hold power, you set the tone for meetings and other interactions. Acknowledging out loud in a meeting when new information helps change your thinking or places where you are working to learn more can signal to others that you are a continuous learner, and you recognize you do not think you know everything. You do not need to have all the answers, but you should be dedicated to figuring out where to go and/or to whom for answers. Think about when Ava and her inquiry group realized their deficit thinking and narrow view of what defines a family. It took humility to name it and to change how they talked about root causes of improvement.
- *Being quiet.* Sometimes, even as the leader, it is not helpful for you to be the one talking all the time. Remember what Berwick said? "I don't think a good leader shows up with answers much. You're just not smarter than the people you're leading. You get paid more maybe and you have a degree after your name, but you're not likely to be that much smarter." Listening to those around you empowers others and contributes to your understanding. This will be particularly important when valuing the voices of stakeholders who are close to the problem you are aiming to improve.

Honesty

We are going to assume that you, as an educational leader, do not lie – that you are honest in what you say or don't say. Now, When we refer to honesty for improvement, we mean an exercise in reflection. Are we being honest or forthcoming with ourselves in what is happening in our system? Are we willing to name areas in the system that need improvement and name what it will *actually* require to get there, even if that includes recognizing and admitting our own role in perpetuating the current situation and system? This can be challenging, scary even. Looking closely at data, we may see evidence or variation that requires a raw, not sugar coated interpretation that will be accompanied with discomfort, especially when changes to the system need to take place. One can demonstrate honesty by

- *Admitting mistakes, errors, or blunders.* Apologize when an apology is warranted and then open a dialogue to determine next steps. Again, Ava and her MHMS improvement team tried a change idea that did not work at all. Instead of hiding their mistake, they took the opportunity to mark it ceremoniously and publicly.
- *Communicating.* Even if it is tough, embarrassing, or ugly, as a leader, you will need to share hard-to-face information in a delicate, thoughtful, non-demeaning way that also helps people see what next steps will be needed.
- *Leading with integrity.* Being a leader with integrity requires acting principally, ethically, and respectfully (Oxford Languages, 2023). Are you someone that people would be willing to share something private with you or are you someone that people might say is effective at the job of principal, but there is something there they don't fully trust? Dig in there. Assess to what degree integrity serves as a pillar of your leadership.

Honesty goes beyond avoiding the easy-to-spot half-truths, omissions, or outright lies. We have already agreed that leaders should adhere to that basic definition. Honesty is a willingness to listen and to learn and to accept evidence related to improvement and the system. Based on improvement goals, leaders with an honest acceptance of the improvement areas will need to be compelled to engage in difficult work, productive conflict, and being okay knowing some people will sometimes be mad at you.

Transparency

An honest approach to the work does not stop with recognizing data, systems of oppression, and self-reconciliation. What follows is transparency with others about the discoveries, processes, progress, and steps. Leadership transparency also captures "the degree in which the leader reinforces a level of openness with others that provides them opportunity to be forthcoming with their ideas, challenges, and opinions" (Stansberry-Beard, 2013, p. 1032). *Transparency* in verbal or written communication requires attention to striking a delicate balance as a leader. Think of this type of scenario that Ava encountered. She left a meeting with all the middle school principals in the district; the superintendent shared information with the group about the district's direction and what moving in that direction involves. Ava needs to figure out what the teachers need to know to not to be left in the dark and to respect their professionalism. She is left needing to determine what should be shared and what doesn't need to be added to the already full plates of teachers. This tough determination requires careful consideration. This type of transparency is focused on task-related information sharing.

Transparency is a communicative element of continuous improvement; sharing efforts of the improvers, what is being learned, evidence of improvement, and the improvement processes with different stakeholder groups will help illustrate progress, generate momentum, and dispel rumors. When applying the tool of transparency to improvement work, considerations need to be made surrounding questions like

- What do those outside of the improvement team need to know about the improvement work?
- How does sharing elements like successful and failed testing cycles (e.g., PDSAs) forward the work and contribute to a learning culture?
- What and how frequently should information or updates be shared with teachers, students, families, the district, other schools, university partnerships, other districts?
- How do you work in partnership with parent and student representatives while also adhering to FERPA or other policies related to privacy and confidentiality?

You can demonstrate transparency through

- *Sharing learning.* Share improvement stories. Share learnings from the improvement work (i.e., successful, and failed PDSA cycles). Share bright spots that acknowledge win your improvement team accomplished (large or small) can engender enthusiasm in those external to the improvement team around the improvement work.
- *Engaging in clear messaging.* Make explicit why the improvement work is a priority and what the work will mean with individual, school, and district considerations to quell fears and inspire change.
- *Providing a clear picture of decision processes.* When you make a decision, offer the why and the how to your stakeholders. It is not unusual to hear from aspiring leadership students that it is only after they have started to shift from a teacher lens to a leader lens that they understand why their leader is doing what they are doing. Helping those you lead gain a clearer understanding of the process could help shift a reaction of "I don't know why the heck they did that!" to "Okay, I don't really like the decision, but I get why they made that decision."

(Hollingworth et al., 2017)

Patience

School leaders need to be patient; meaningful change takes time (Wasonga & Murphy, 2007). Improvement can be a roller coaster with bright spots and failed tests of improvement. When improvement teams experience failure, it does not necessarily signal that improvement efforts should be abandoned, and we should return to familliar routines or brand new, untested routines (e.g., the next shiny initiative). To strike the balance between hybrid, bottom-up decision-making and top-down direction, leaders need patience during each phase of improvement, from allowing teams to articulate their problem (even if it is not how you would have framed it) and supporting the team's evolution to redefining their problem of practice (Militello et al., 2009). They need to be patient when an improvement team does not find success in their first testing cycles. Instead of giving up or stepping in to wield decision-making authority, a patient leader serves as a facilitator and focuser promoting perseverance for improvement (Militello et al., 2009).

Impatient leaders may stymie improvement efforts or erode the trust of teachers (Wasonga & Murphy, 2007). A patient attitude is helpful to encourage persistence and fortitude when continuing down the road of continuous improvement. Demonstrating patience by commitment to the pace of actual improvement of a system will have lasting effects by

- *Not quitting too early.* Trust the process. Iterate change ideas, learn from failure, revise your theory of improvement, but stay the course.
- *Developing a realistic expectation of pace of work.* Improvement work can feel like it is going slowly. This is because educators have typically been socialized to identify a problem and then come up with solutions to fix it. However, improvement requires a deep understanding of the problem so your team is addressing the actual problem and not a symptom of a more adaptive, complex, underlying problem. The challenge of accepting the pacing will be especially true when you are in the "understanding the problem phase" since this phase requires your team to take the time to dig into the problem, gathering data from multiple sources. The team will likely be wanting to move on quicker than the process requires. As a leader, help the team spend adequate time in the understanding the problem phase and then later in the PDSA cycle phases to ensure the change idea is ready to be spread and scaled to a broader context/audience.
- *Communicating your confidence in the pacing to those inside the work.* Be ready for people to want to move quicker than is appropriate for a true continuous improvement approach. As the leader, you will want to model for your improvement team and teachers the patience necessary to slow down. The pace may seem slow, but the improvement outcomes will be more aligned and impactful in the long run.
- *Communicating your confidence in the pacing to those outside the work.* Districts emphasize urgency. Invite them into the process. Share what

you are learning. Celebrate early wins and bright spots. Your stories of improvement will help increase confidence in how you are approaching improvement.

Capacity Building

Capacity building is a leadership tool for improvement. Empowering others builds the capacity of your team. Militello and colleagues (2009) found "principals are facilitators and focusers who create the conditions that support the important work of the teachers and other staff" (p. 108); they are not dictating every move of the staff. Being a school leader who directly and/or indirectly embodies improvement mindsets and practices helps the educational professionals in the sphere of influence learn more about improvement, building professional capacity for engaging in improvement. Capacity building efforts focused on improvement science include coaching, teaching, and facilitating the improvement science process; guiding fishbone diagram development; empathy interview plans; and PDSA data collection and analysis techniques. Capacity building focused on the organization assures and encourages the improvers to engage in the processes authentically even when it is uncomfortable. Chapter 9 discusses this organizational capacity building in much more detail.

Collaboration

The executive chef in a restaurant will sacrifice the quality of the dishes if they try to prepare the ingredients, take the orders, cook every item, serve the meals, bus the tables, seat patrons, answer the phones, et cetera all by themselves. The same is true for school leaders. Leaders do not need to be the sole hero working in isolation; "Leaders should not walk the road of improvement alone" (Militello et al., 2009, p. 86). Approach the improvement journey as a solo endeavor, and you will be left stalled on the side of that road. When applying the tool of collaboration to improvement work, considerations need to be made surrounding questions like

- Who can help me here?
- Where are my limits? What don't I know yet? What skills don't I have yet? Who can help complement and supplement my skillset and understanding?
- Who will offer an alternative (and necessary) perspective to the work?

Leaders can demonstrate collaboration by

- *Committing to a team orientation*: Adjust work structures (e.g., time, resources) to ensure a group of people can make progress and engage in collective sensemaking (e.g., Dixon & Palmer, 2020; et al., 2017).

- *Flatten hierarchical structures*: Like Dr. Berwick said earlier, "you're just not smarter than the other people in the room," so when you are working with the team, you as the leader will need to model how to invite and then value others' ideas, insights, and voices. One way to visualize this is to imagine if someone who had no familiarity with the people in the team or the project came and observed a team meeting. After the meeting someone asked them who they thought was in charge. What would a team meeting look like, and sound like to result in that visitor being unable to identify who held the most positional authority.
- *Engaging thought partners*: Sometimes we need trusted critical friends who can be thought partners for us.

Trust

Brené Brown captured that "Trust is not built in big, sweeping moments. It's built in tiny moments every day." Trust and effective leadership are linked through "professional structures – such as opportunities for collective inquiry, scrutiny, reflection, and decision making" (Tschannen-Moran, 2009, p. 218). You can gain trust by trusting. Trusting your teachers, staff members, families, and communities signals respect, active listening, humility, and an open mind (Khalifa, 2018; Tschannen-Moran & Gareis, 2015). In equitable improvement work, school leaders will need to relinquish a solid amount of control (Militello et al., 2009). Trusting relationships makes relinquishing control not quite so difficult.

One can demonstrate trust by

- *Following through on requests and needs.* There is a scene in the show *Ted Lasso*. As the new coach to the Richmond Greyhounds Football Club, trust had not yet been established between Coach Lasso and his players. Players were very skeptical. In an early episode, Coach Lasso learned from a player that there was terrible water pressure in the locker room showers. It seemed like a minor, forgettable plot point. Later in the episode, however, players discovered that the water pressure had been wildly improved. Coach Lasso heard his players and did something about it. That small move caused a shift in how the players began to view their new coach. The players noticed he was listening and took care of their concerns. Now, we will note that that leadership decision did not result in 100% trust among 100% of his players, but it was one positive step toward building trust. That is how it goes. The pathway to a trusting relationship is laid one action at a time.
- *Sharing information appropriately.* Sometimes reflecting on the opposite of the positive characteristic can help make sense of what the characteristic, when demonstrated effectively, looks like and sounds like. We will use that approach here. How might someone in the workplace break trust? One way may be that someone shares information that was not theirs to

share, or they did not have permission to share or that they should not be sharing.

Reflection

Reflection is a hallmark of effective leadership practice (Senge, 2006). Reflection invites opportunities for transformative learning (Mezirow, 1990). We determine where our thinking led to appropriate or inappropriate interpretations and how our thinking aligned with or diverged from our values. Critical reflection calls on "leaders and educators to consistently look for how they are positioned within organizations that have marginalized students; they then find ways to personally and organizationally resist this oppression" (Khalifa, 2018, p. 59). Khalifa encourages professional educators to reflect on areas of the school operations where oppressive systems lie. Be a critical reflector in spaces of "resource allocation, employment decisions, school climate, relationship with district administration and policies, and community engagement" since each deserves attention; and critical reflection may unearth where improvement work is needed.

Recognizing that reflection is an important professional habit and prioritizing reflection as a worthy commitment means it is built into professional routines. Individual reflection can be done in independent and in group settings. You can reflect when you're commuting to work, at your kitchen counter enjoying the first cup of coffee or tea each morning, or walking the dog. Each day, Ava finds herself reflecting on how her workday went on her drive home or to her graduate classes. She uses that quiet time after class to think and synthesize what she has heard and learned in class to how she sees it playing out in her own context.

Improvement teams should carve out opportunities for more formal individual reflection as well. During these moments, a team can "reflect on professional practice, including leading continuous improvement efforts {which} invites opportunities to {consider} future actions that might modify or alter current practice" (Militello et al., 2009, p. 63). It is a collaborative practice for an improvement team to reflect on the work they are doing and the improvements they are making. Improvers use reflection when studying what happened in an iterative testing cycle. Reflecting, or studying the results of the "do" portion of a PDSA cycle, shapes the steps in the next testing cycle.

When applying the tool of reflection to improvement work, Ava considers group reflection practices and processes. The group reflection opportunities surface interpretations of how they think the work is going and how the group is meeting their espoused norms and expectations. Ava used group reflection as a means for the team to evaluate the extent to which their predictions and hypotheses aligned with or diverged from what happened during different improvement phases (Dixon & Palmer, 2020). Action Inventory 8.1 poses some reflection questions for improvement team members.

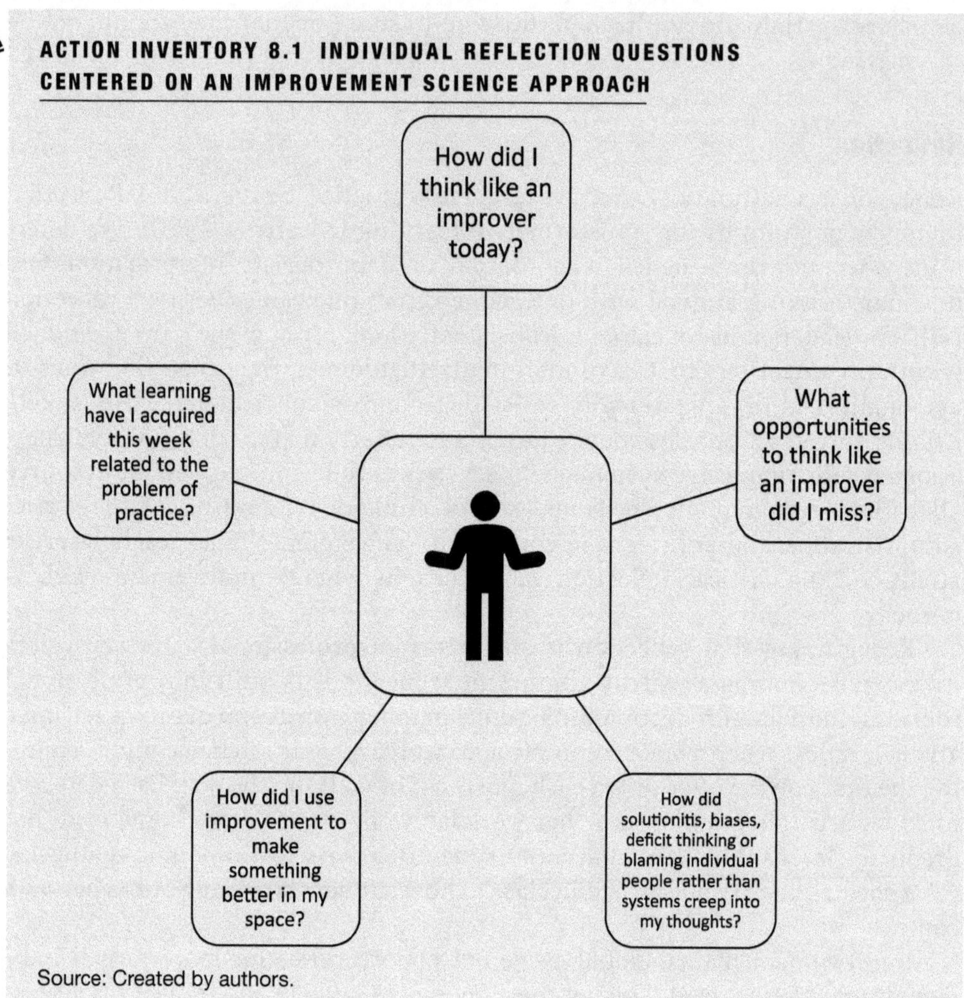

SUPPORT MATERIAL
ACTION INVENTORY 8.1 INDIVIDUAL REFLECTION QUESTIONS CENTERED ON AN IMPROVEMENT SCIENCE APPROACH
How did I think like an improver today?
What learning have I acquired this week related to the problem of practice?
What opportunities to think like an improver did I miss?
How did I use improvement to make something better in my space?
How did solutionitis, biases, deficit thinking or blaming individual people rather than systems creep into my thoughts?

Source: Created by authors.

Group discussions can build off people's individual reflections. However, the condition of psychological safety needs to be present. Psychological safety is achieved when people feel safe to be transparent, take risks, hold themselves and others in the group accountable, and have challenging conversations with one another (Brown, 2018; Dixon & Palmer, 2020; Grant, 2021; Sinek, 2019).

One can demonstrate reflection for improvement through

- *Dedicating regular time*. The improvement team needs regularly scheduled time to engage in guided group and individual reflection.
- *Questioning purposefully*. Asking poignant questions related to how people are thinking about, feeling about, and making sense of the improvement work and their role in it. Further, posing questions can require teams to

deeply interrogate the improvement work and their individual roles in the work in service of continuous improvement.

- *Establishing a running record*: Having a physical place (e.g., running document, notebook) to capture reflections. Zumpe and Aramburo (forthcoming) talk about how records of practice "make it possible for colleagues to 'see' the same thing and develop shared professional knowledge" (np).
- *Inviting opportunities to identify the team's edges of growth*: Identifying the edges of growth helps answer the post-reflection question of "now what?" Purposefully talking about edges of growth invites a calibration of progress toward goals, purposes, and values and how the team might engage in continuous improvement themselves/for the team.

TOOLBOX INVENTORY

So far, leadership tools have been the focus of the chapter. In the spirit of continuous improvement and embodying the leadership tools, we pause for you to take inventory of your own practice (Action Inventory 8.2). In the checklist, we invite you to engage in a self-assessment of the leadership tools currently in your

ACTION INVENTORY 8.2 SELF-REFLECTION OF LEADERSHIP TOOLS

Leadership Tools: Skill or Disposition	I own this tool and am so good at using this tool that I could mentor others on what using this tool could successfully look and sound like.	I own this tool and have some confidence in using this tool, but I am not ready to mentor others in using this tool.	I know what this tool is, but it is not a tool I own; or I own this tool, but I do not readily use this tool. A mentor would be helpful for me to learn to better use this tool.
Humility			
Honesty			
Transparency			
Patience			
Capacity Building			
Collaboration			
Trust			
Reflection			

toolbox. As you answer, we encourage you to really practice each of those eight leadership tools (e.g., honesty, humility) when determining your comfort with and helping others use these tools.

TOOLS FOR IMPROVEMENT: STRATEGIC CONNECTION AND PLANNING TOOLS

Leaders developing the tools, skills, and dispositions to lead continuous improvement in the absence of a plan for connecting improvement work to existing or emerging goals, initiatives, practices, missions, or visions will not be as effective as they could be. The toolbox also needs tools for (a) seeing the big picture, (b) aligning initiatives, (c) communicating the interconnected nature, and (d) communicating when changes are afoot. We will refer to such strategies as strategic connection and planning tools.

When principals take a systems-level view of their school, it places them on a "balcony" to view the "big picture" of their environment (Heifetz & Linsky, 2009). This balcony metaphor was introduced in Chapter 5. From the balcony, the principal sees the system's components, what everyone is doing, and what efforts or priorities align. Leaders identify not only the different areas in the system but also articulate to others how areas connect; they provide a big picture map of how improvement work connects or relates to different areas of the system.

If you have ever watched a professional American football game, some coaches are seated in an area high above the field away from the head coach and other coaches. The coaches quickly and effectively communicate with their colleagues who are on the field about what they are seeing from their vantage points: plays unfolding, weaknesses in the opposing team's offensive drives, holes in their own defensive formation, etc. They see the game from a different perspective, which allows them to observe things differently than standing on the field. These coaches have a responsibility to communicate their observations and recommendations. Like the football coach watching above, principals who take opportunities to zoom out to see their whole school will identify pieces of the system that those closest to the action might not be able to see from their vantage point. Principals observe and communicate what they notice about the school to their staff. The principal needs to be comfortable in being both "on the field" and shifting to take a broader landscape view.

Effective leaders make connections across work practices and goals see the interplay of the work practices and goals themselves (Hollingworth et al., 2017). Central to successful continuous improvement is purposefully and clearly articulating those intersections for their staff through effective communication about alignment and interconnectedness. Clearly communicating alignment of improvement efforts is about sharing what improvement teams are working on and how it connects to all stakeholders' work. If introducing change is part of this conversation, it is helpful for many people to get clarity on what will remain the same (Grant, 2021).

Since school leaders have more frequent opportunities than those teachers to zoom out and take a systems view of their school, they should not assume connections in practices, initiatives, and so on are obvious to everyone. Instead, leaders should be direct and transparent about the connections they are seeing and check-in with others to understand the degree to which they are seeing connections and if those connections are authentically resonating with them. For instance, Randy may hear Ava verbalize where she sees connections between US history's instructional goals and the school's overall vision statement, but due to the policies the district's school board is considering, this connection is not resonating with Randy. Another one of Ava's teachers does not fully see the connection between the school's continuous improvement work and his subject of teaching Mandarin since the conversations about continuous improvement have primarily been centered on mathematics. Upon realizing these disconnections, Ava planned to make explicit connections between improvement work to specific instructional areas across her school.

Finding appropriate and effective times to communicate the interconnectedness and alignment of the various efforts in the school is a consideration for leaders. Staff meetings or small team meetings might be examples of collective opportunities for sharing to take place. This could be particularly important when introducing something new.

SUPPORT MATERIAL

ACTION INVENTORY 8.3 STRATEGIES FOR COMMUNICATING ALIGNMENT

Strategy	Description
Concept Map	• Develop a concept that shows the interconnected of different initiatives or work practices as it relates to continuous improvement processes. Share this visual tool with staff. • Include specifics on what connects
Disseminating Ideas in Talking Points	• Use sentence starters like, • "I am making connections between X and Y. Here is what I am seeing and what that could mean for our future work" • "We are talking about Y. See how this part of Y includes ABC? Now look at X, which we have been focused on for a long time now. We are not jumping to a new thing. Look at how DEF in X are similar to ABC. This is well-connected to the successful structures already in place. We will build off of what we have. We are not going to re-invent the wheel here..."
Cross-Role Discussion Facilitation	• Facilitate a conversation with teachers, staff members, or teams to surface what connections exist from their perspectives. • Use the team-generated ideas to then move into more detailed planning and implementation opportunities to incorporate improvement. • Make the connections available for ongoing reference by the team and others

Source: Created by author.

Leadership tools can help support connection tools. Like earlier, in the spirit of continuous improvement and living the leadership tools, we pause to take inventory of our own practice. In the checklist in Action Inventory 8.4, we invite you to engage in a self-assessment of the connection tools currently in your toolbox. As you answer we encourage you to really practice the other leadership tools when determining your comfort with and helping others use connection tools.

ACTION INVENTORY 8.4 SELF-ASSESSMENT OF CONNECTION TOOLS

In the checklist, engage in a self-assessment of the Connection tools currently in your toolbox.

Leadership Tool: Making Connections to Existing Goals	I own this tool and am so good at using this tool that I could mentor others on what using this tool could successfully look and sound like.	I own this tool and have some confidence in using this tool, but I am not ready to mentor others in using this tool.	I know what this tool is, but it is not a tool I own, or I own but I do not readily use this tool. A mentor would be helpful for me to learn to better use this tool.
I purposefully zoom out to take a "balcony" view or zoom in to get a closer view of what is happening in my school.			
I see the alignment between and among initiatives.			
I have used any of the suggestions in Action Inventory 8.3 to communicate the alignment and interconnected nature of different initiatives in place at my school to my staff and stakeholders.			

TOOLS FOR IMPROVEMENT: PROTOCOLS, GUIDES, RESOURCES

The final set of tools carry out the methods of improvement science through technical, step-by-step protocols. These protocols help improvement teams organize their priorities, data, thinking, progress, and next steps. To effectively use these protocols, the leadership and connection tools we've already covered will be necessary.

We acknowledge that several other improvement scientists and improvement scholars have already developed excellent resources. Thus, in this section, we will provide an overview of different improvement science protocols that effective improvers often use, and we provide suggestions on where you can get more details on how to facilitate the use and completion of each.

An improvement science approach can be organized into phases (you read about these phases in both Ava's story and across Part II). We are now moving into a description of the tools that can be leveraged during improvement processes. The first phase is problem identification and understanding the problem. In this phase improvers may use fishbone diagrams, organize existing available data, talk to people close to and impacted by the improvement area, map out the steps that result in a problematic outcome, and seek out external resources and information. The second phase is developing a driver diagram that illustrates a team's theory of improvement. The third phase is selecting and iteratively testing change ideas using an approach like a PDSA cycle that then leads to scaling evidence-based improvement.

PHASE 1: PROBLEM IDENTIFICATION AND UNDERSTANDING THE PROBLEM

During this phase, improvers are dedicated to both naming a problem in their system and then taking steps to learn more about the problem. Educators are skilled at identifying when something isn't going well. Educators are astute observers of their classrooms and schools. Educators can access a plethora of data from their own assessments or from state or national tests, et cetera. Chapter 5 really targeted how to identify a problem including how to determine if you and your team have identified the "right" problem. Now, let's get into how we can deeply understand the problem.

Root Cause Analysis: Fishbone Diagram

Teams can complete different types of root cause analyses. Hinnant-Crawford (2020) offers several options for new improvers to determine root causes. One of the most well-known root cause analysis tools is the Ishikawa or fishbone diagram. The fishbone serves as a visual landing place for you and your team to capture potential root causes. A fishbone diagram can be created during a brainstorming team meeting and then revisited as your team learns more information related to your problem of practice (Carnegie Foundation for the Advancement of Teaching, 2018). If you don't have multiple versions of a fishbone to capture your ongoing learning, you're doing it wrong.

Refer to Action Inventory 8.5 and Chapter 1 to see what a fishbone diagram looks like. Begin building this diagram by writing the exact problem you are trying to solve in the "head" of the fish. Root cause themes/categories and specific contributing factors become the bones of the fish.

In her improvement work, Ava's team developed their fishbone after doing some other data collection. They had lots of data, and they organized their findings on large chart paper with post-it notes to brainstorm then arrange the elements or components in their system contributing to the problem. This is an effective approach when working in person. Virtual tools like Google's Jamboard can simulate the chart paper and post-it experience. You can see an example of a fishbone created in Jamboard in Chapter 1.

SUPPORT MATERIAL

ACTION INVENTORY 8.5 FISHBONE TEMPLATE

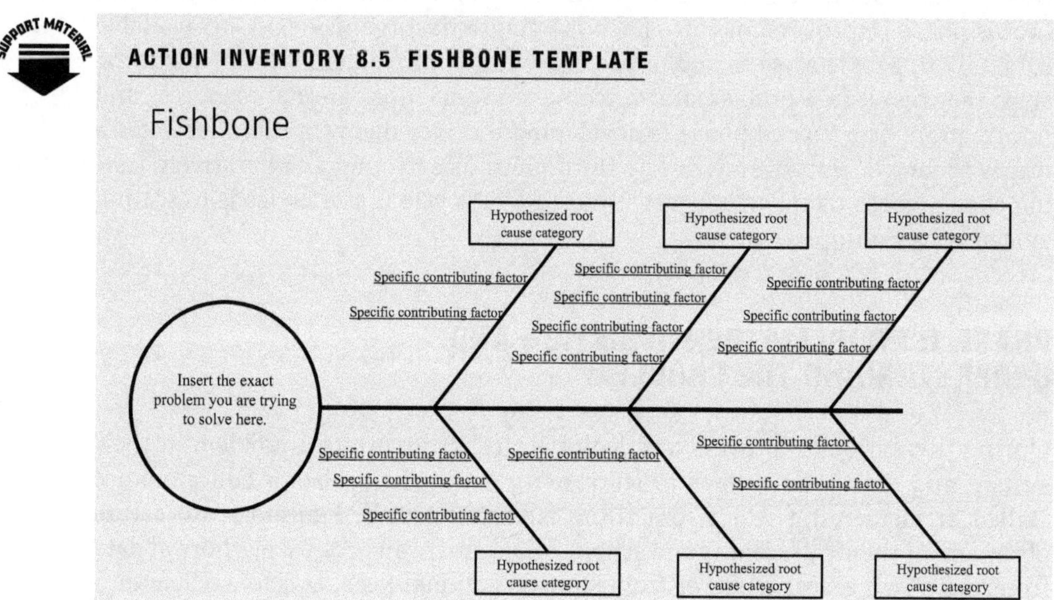

Capturing Local Data

Organizing existing data is important; making explicit what additional data contributes to your team's understanding of the problem is also important. You likely have piles of helpful data at your fingertips: assessment data, school climate data, attendance data, discipline data, enrollment data, teacher observation data, and so on. Find and synthesize local data (quantitative and qualitative) related to your problem of practice. The protocol in Action Inventory 8.6 can help your team know what data you have and reveal what data you still need. Like the fishbone, populating this type of protocol is not a one-time event. You will likely come back to this time and time again as you draw on additional data.

Notice Action Inventory 8.6 asks for the type of data. This can help your team visually assess if there is a balance of the data types you're leaning on and may signal if additional qualitative or quantitative data are needed.

ACTION INVENTORY 8.6 DATA INVENTORY

Evidence/ Data	Type of Data (quant or qual)	Source	Included in your fishbone/existing understanding or new understanding?

Empathy Interviews

To understand how the problem impacts people, talk with them. Empathy interviews are conversations with those connected to the problem to better understand how the problem impacts them or how they experience the problem (Hinnant-Crawford, 2020). How do you make sure you are speaking to the right people? First, we recommend developing a user map like the one shown below in Action Inventory 8.7. To do this, write the problem in the center circle, then connect the different user groups to that circle. Remember in Chapter 6 when Ms. Chris Butler was trying to figure out why a group of her students were late on Mondays,

SUPPORT MATERIAL

ACTION INVENTORY 8.7 USER MAP

User group impacted by problem

User group impacted by problem

Insert the the specific problem you are trying to solve in this circle.

User group impacted by problem

User group impacted by problem

User group impacted by problem

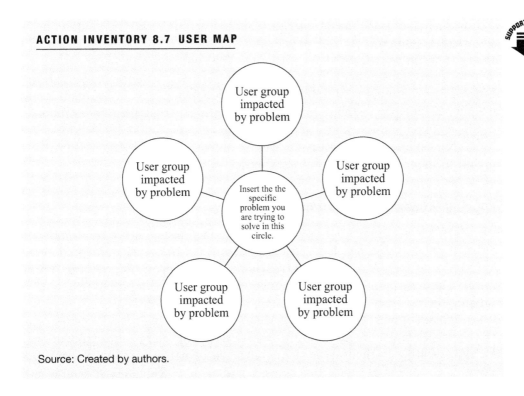

Source: Created by authors.

Wednesdays, and Fridays, and she talked to them and their second period teacher to try and learn more? Those were empathy interviews. Ava's professor had them conduct empathy interviews with students, teachers, and families. Then, the MHMS improvement team decided to do additional interviews with those closest to their problem. Ava recognized that students, teachers, parents, and school counselors were directly connected to their problem of focus.

After you map who is impacted, make plans to talk to representatives from these groups. Keep the following in mind:

- Be sure to resist defaulting to speaking only to those to whom it would be easy to listen. As an improver we must intentionally seek out and listen to and believe the experiences of those who are acutely impacted by the problem.
- The number of interviews will be dependent on an improvement focus. We cannot tell you how many interviews to do; you'll have to figure that out with your team based on what you are learning. Sometimes after some empathy interviews are completed, it becomes evident that other interviews are needed. Be open to being flexible on the number of people from whom you learn.

Sometimes the "interview" part of empathy interviews can make them seem like they are very formal, structured, time consuming endeavors. They are none of those things. Empathy interviews are short, focused, and person-centered. Think about asking someone just a handful of questions to learn how they are impacted by the problem. These conversations can happen before or after school, waiting in the car rider line, during the lunch hour, walking down the hall, etc. Your improvement team will need to decide what to ask. High Tech High offers helpful question stems such as "Tell me about a time when . . ." or "If you had a magic wand . . .". With your team, determine what you could ask to help you hear people's stories and experiences. When you ask people to share their stories, there are some things you must be mindful of. If your problem of practice centers issues of equity, asking people their stories could be painful. Trust, gentleness, an open mind, and psychological safety are paramount.

After each interview, capture and reflect on your learning. Add new learning to your fishbone and mapping information.

Mapping Processes and Journey Tools

It is advantageous to map out how the problem manifests. The point of mapping is that it can identify the places in the system (i.e., the steps) that could be an entry point to intervene and improve. Sometimes mapping the process can be confused with mapping your improvement processes. For our purposes in understanding the problem phase, we are mapping the user's experience. For instance, if the problem of practice is related to students' access to high-level courses (e.g., AP classes), then you might map the process capturing every step a student goes through resulting in them either being enrolled or not enrolled in a high-level course. Your map might look a bit like a board game playing surface where each step in the process looks like a landing place on a gameboard. There are different ways to approach the design. On some maps, different shapes can signal different system considerations. For example, a circle can represent a point in the process/system where a decision is made. You can make your maps as intricate in the shape coding as you would like. You can find different types of mapping approaches on improvement websites, and some were described in Chapter 5. Check out the different kinds and select which design makes the most sense for your team's focus.

Scanning Outside the Organization Tools

Think about a challenge you had at work or in your personal life where you wanted to talk with and get advice from someone outside of the situation. You needed to speak to someone not close to what you were dealing with. This was a time that demonstrated how helpful it can be to step out of your own orbit to see what others have to say about the situation with which you're grappling. Unfortunately, many of the problems we need to tackle in our schools are problems other schools are also experiencing. While obviously no two contexts are the same, improvers can look to others who have experienced a similar problem and seek out their experience as a starting point and a place you may not have previously noticed. Looking externally also may help get ideas to try in our own context. You might want to look in analogous settings or schools like yours that have faced similar problems with some success. Your district supervisor or your informal and formal leadership networks might be able to connect you to other schools. You might look to research, practitioner articles, podcasts, presentations, discussions with experts, keynote addresses, etc. Think broadly about where you could seek information to help deepen your understanding. In Action Inventory 8.8, we provide an example of a space to organize your learning

ACTION INVENTORY 8.8 SUMMARIZING RESEARCH AND PRACTICAL SOURCES

Source type (person/expert, literature/research article, other article (e.g., EdWeek), report, podcast, etc.)	Name of source	Link/location of source	Why this source could be helpful	What you learned from this source
1.				
2.				
3.				
4.				

from outside your own circle. A tool like this helps facilitate your team's organization of the helpful external information your team finds.

Approaches to understanding the problem from multiple perspectives move your team toward determining a direction for focused efforts. To prepare your team for the next phase, make sure your fishbone is up-to-date and includes the understanding gleaned from local data, mapping insights, empathy interview evidence, and ideas from outside sources. Here we introduced root cause analysis first. Some improvement teams will want to start with a fishbone, and then gather data. Others, like the MHMS team in Chapter 1, will gather data and then complete the fishbone exercise. There are different ways to approach the process. What is most important is that you revisit your thinking throughout the process as new learning emerges from data.

PHASE 2: DEVELOPING YOUR THEORY OF IMPROVEMENT

A driver diagram is another concept-map-looking tool that captures what the team wants to achieve. It answers the improvement question, "How will we know when a change is an improvement?" In the driver diagram, instead of again starting with naming "What is the exact problem I'm trying to solve?" start with an aim that articulates the specific vision of improvement. The aim is like a SMART goal. The driver diagram includes not just the aim, but structures, systems, processes, and so on that are connected to the aim. For example, if you want to increase the amount of sleep you get each night by 30 minutes, you will need to address elements or drivers such as schedules, routines, eating, caffeine intake, exercise, stress, and materials (e.g., bed, pillows). You saw several examples of Ava's driver diagrams in Chapter 1.

There are at least two paths you may take when moving into this phase. One approach is to build out a driver diagram centered on the whole problem. Another approach that could be friendlier to addressing multifaceted, complex problems may be to build a driver diagram based on improving one part of the problem. This aligns with making incremental changes to the system to lead to systemic, lasting changes (Bryk et al., 2015). First, look at your fishbone. Then, select *one* bone of the fish to tackle first. Take that bone and expand it out into a driver diagram.

Look at Action Inventory 8.9 and follow the prompts to complete this protocol. Now that you and your team can see the direction of where you might target changes, it's time to pick a change idea to test. Look at the change ideas. Which would be the easiest to test? Which of those easy-to-test changes holds the biggest promise of impact? Is there an easy-to-test change idea that is connected to multiple drivers? Those are some questions to consider when moving toward Phase 3, the testing phase.

ACTION INVENTORY 8.9 MOVING FROM A FISHBONE TO DRIVER DIAGRAM

Driver Diagram

1. What bone of the fish are you addressing: ____________________
2. What will it look like when that bone improves? Fill in the blanks.

   By [insert month, year], [insert fishbone cause category], will [insert improvement goal] as evidenced by [insert what you want to see from qualitative or quantitative data].

   Congratulations, you've drafted an aim statement!
3. Put the aim statement in the driver diagram.

Insert aim here

4. Now that you have your aim. What are 3-5 areas in the organization that connect to your aim (e.g., hiring, assessment/evaluation, relationships): ____________, ____________, ____________, ____________.

   Congratulations, you just identified some primary drivers that are connected to your aim!
   List each of those in the boxes to the right of the aim statement in the diagram. Add or remove boxes as necessary for your specific focus.

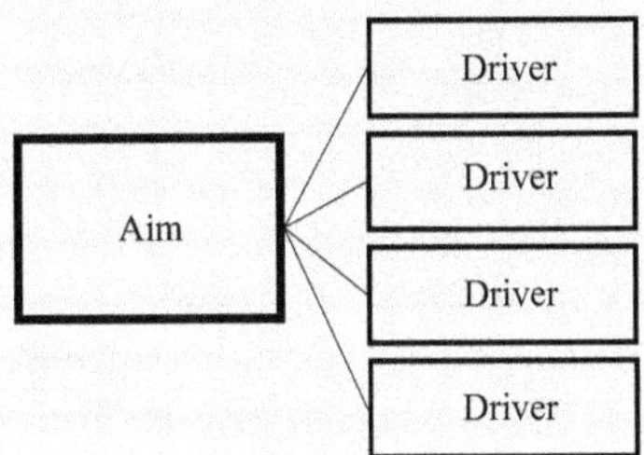

5. What are the processes or steps that are involved in each of the areas in the organization you named above? (e.g., interviews, recruitment fairs, feedback sessions)

Area 1 processes: ____

Area 2 processes: ____

Area 3 processes: ____

Area 4 processes: ____

Congratulations! You just identified some secondary drivers that connect to the organizational areas that connect to your aim.

List each of those in boxes to the right of the drivers. Draw lines that connect the processes to the corresponding primary driver(s). Add or remove boxes as necessary for your specific focus.

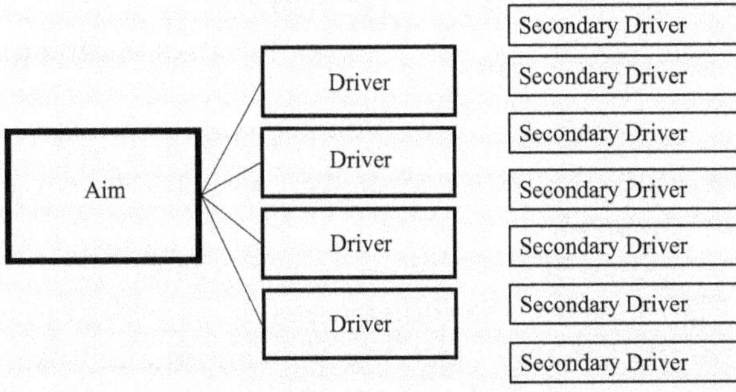

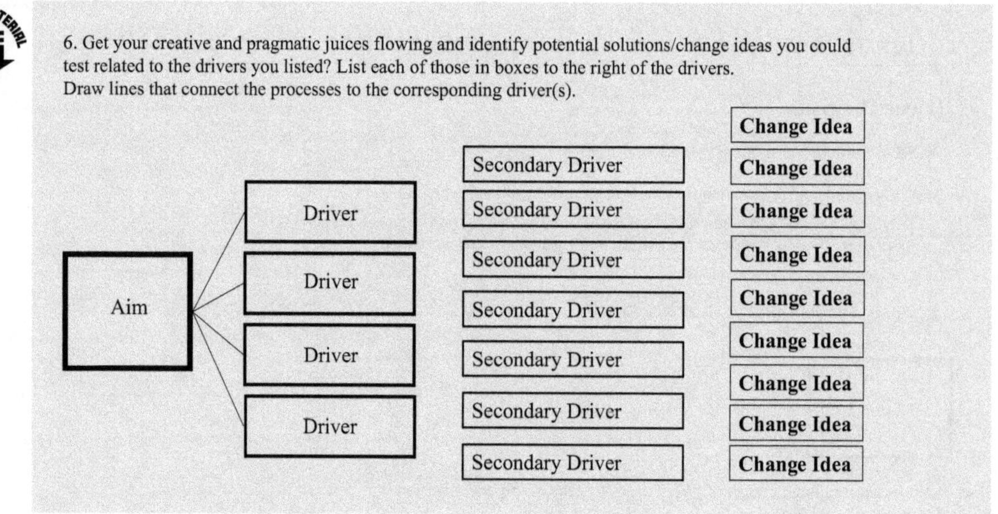

PHASE 3: TESTING YOUR CHANGE IDEA AND NETWORKING WITH OTHERS

Recall the iterative testing theme from Chapter 6 and the examples of iterative testing in Chapter 1. Iterative tests of change can use protocols to guide and organize the process. There are several iterative testing frameworks: PDSA cycles, plan-do-check-act (PDCA) cycles, strategize-implement-analyze-reflect (SIAR) cycles (Perry et al., 2020), etc. The PDSA cycle is most identifiable by improvement scientists. There are several protocols available for you to use. Appendix B in Langley's and colleagues' (2009) book, *The Improvement Guide*, provides protocols. High Tech High's protocol library offers key questions to be answered at each stage of the PDSA cycle. In addition to tracking these iterations, the tracker should also include information about

- What change idea is being tested
- The overall goal of the test
- What driver (and/or cause) is the change idea meant to improve
- How did the change idea demonstrate an equity orientation

(Wilhelm et al., in press)

Action Inventory 8.10 includes elements from multiple existing protocols. You can use something like this to track your progress as well as mark a clear line between one trial's learning and the next.

In actual improvement work, you will probably have more than three cycles to try. When Ava engaged in PDSA cycles, she sometimes found she had to add several more columns to her improvement project. So, add columns or trials as needed.

ACTION INVENTORY 8.10 PDSA TRACKER

Trial 1	**Trial 2 – Are you abandoning, adopting, or adapting the change idea from Trial 1?** ______	**Trial 3 – Are you abandoning, adopting, or adapting the change idea from Trial 2?** ______
Plan: What is the change idea you want to try? And when? What are the steps to implement the change idea? Who is responsible for the test? List 3–5 predictions related to time, format, feelings, execution, details that your team predicts will happen during the test. 1. ______ 2. ______ 3. ______ 4. ______ 5. ______	***Plan***: What is the change idea you want to try? And when? What are the steps to implement the change idea? Who is responsible for the test? List 3–5 predictions related to time, format, feelings, execution, details that your team predicts will happen during the test. 1. ______ 2. ______ 3. ______ 4. ______ 5. ______	***Plan***: What is the change idea you want to try? And when? What are the steps to implement the change idea? Who is responsible for the test? List 3–5 predictions related to time, format, feelings, execution, details that your team predicts will happen during the test. 1. ______ 2. ______ 3. ______ 4. ______ 5. ______
Do: Carry out implementing the change idea. Collect qualitative and quantitative data related to implementing the change idea and the results of implementation.	***Do***: Carry out implementing the change idea. Collect qualitative and quantitative data related to implementing the change idea and the results of implementation.	***Do***: Carry out implementing the change idea. Collect qualitative and quantitative data related to implementing the change idea and the results of implementation.
Study: What do you notice from your data? How did the results align with what you thought was going to happen during the test?	***Study***: What do you notice from your data? How did the results align with what you thought was going to happen during the test?	***Study***: What do you notice from your data? How did the results align with what you thought was going to happen during the test?

<table>
<tr>
<td>Act: Now that you studied this implementation trial . . . Decide.
1. Do you want to abandon the change idea because the trial was a disaster?
2. Do you want to adopt the change because the data from the implementation suggest it was a successful change idea that made improvements in service of meeting your aim?
3. Do you want to adapt the change idea by making a tweak to the change idea and test the change idea again?</td>
<td>Act: Now that you studied this implementation trial . . . Decide.
1. Do you want to abandon the change idea because the trial was a disaster?
2. Do you want to adopt the change because the data from the implementation suggest it was a successful change idea that made improvements in service of meeting your aim?
3. Do you want to adapt the change idea by making a tweak to the change idea and test the change idea again?</td>
<td>Act: Now that you studied this implementation trial . . . Decide.
1. Do you want to abandon the change idea because the trial was a disaster?
2. Do you want to adopt the change because the data from the implementation suggest it was a successful change idea that made improvements in service of meeting your aim?
3. Do you want to adapt the change idea by making a tweak to the change idea and test the change idea again?</td>
</tr>
</table>

As principal, be thoughtful about how these improvement science protocols and tools are used in your specific context and be aware of which members of your improvement team may need to help. Awareness of our own capacity can help us be aware of our own needs as well as others' needs. Look at Action Inventory 8.11 and decide where you are today on your comfort and experience with the different improvement science tools.

Action Inventory 8.11: In the checklist, engage in a self-assessment of the improvement science tools currently in your toolbox.

ACTION INVENTORY 8.11 SELF-ASSESSMENT OF TOOLS

Improvement Tool	I own this tool and am so good at using this tool that I could mentor others on what using this tool could successfully look and sound like.	I own this tool and have some confidence in using this tool, but I am not ready to mentor others in using this tool.	I know what this tool is, but it is not a tool I own, or I own it, but I do not readily use this tool. A mentor would be helpful for me to learn to better use this tool.
Gathering and analyzing local data			
Scanning outside the organization: Collecting practical expertise, seeking research/literature, podcasts, talks, resources, etc.			
Mapping			
Empathy interviews			
Root cause analysis (e.g., fishbone)			
Driver diagram			
Iterative cycles (e.g., PDSA)			

The tools or protocols introduced in this chapter are leveraged effectively when those leading this work use the connection tools meaningfully during the processes. In the checklist, engage in a self-assessment of the improvement science tools currently in your toolbox.

Earlier you named where you felt leadership and connection tools are needed when engaged with the improvement science tools. In Action Inventory 8.12, we offer a matrix that illustrates how certain leadership and connection tools could be utilized when using improvement tools.

ACTION INVENTORY 8.12 TOOL CROSSWALK

Improvement Tool	Leadership Tool	Connection Tool
Gathering and Analyzing Local Data	Capacity Building Honesty Humility Reflection Transparency	Seeing alignment
Collecting Practical Expertise	Humility Reflection Trust	Zooming out
Literature	Capacity Building Humility Reflection	Zooming out
Mapping	Collaboration Honesty Patience Trust	Taking a systems view: Zooming both in and out; Seeing alignment
Empathy Interviews	Capacity Building Honesty Humility Patience Transparency	Zooming in
Theory of Improvement (e.g., driver diagram)	Collaboration Patience Transparency	Seeing alignment
Iterative Cycles	Reflection Patience Transparency	Zooming in

When coupled with effective leaders and trusting teams, facilitating the work of improvement, and building out understanding of systems, problems, and strategies to address the problems for systemic change will be forwarded.

CONCLUSION

We introduced that idea of improvement tools with Ava's story in Chapter 1. As you may have noticed, the title of this chapter includes the word "tools," but we expand upon the technical or protocol-based conceptualization of what a tool is to encompass leadership and connection tools.

Moral Values

By including leadership and connection tools into this conversation, we center values that continuous improvers use as foundational to their improvement work. Thus, when making improvement decisions, using leadership tools such as humility, honesty, transparency, patience, capacity building, collaboration, trust, and reflection, among others can keep central the group's why, improvement goals, and support the shift in power and social dynamics to something less hierarchical and more appreciative. From there, the technical tools (e.g., PDSA cycles) can help guide each phase of your team's improvement.

Social Relations

Humble educational leaders, for example, will bring important stakeholder voices into the improvement work because they accept that to work toward equity, they need to be intentionally collaborative and invite others (often those who are not employed by the school or school district) who have expertise and experiences different from those of the school leader and leadership team. Humble leaders will be willing to honestly and transparently self-assess where they truly are in their leadership and continuous improvement skills and dispositions. Understanding that it is through this exercise in humility, honesty, transparency, patience, capacity building collaboration, trust, and reflection, leaders will be able to build their own capacity, build the capacity of others, and improve.

Instrumental Methods

There are tried and true improvement science tools discussed in the last section of this chapter. Those tools are invaluable to enact the improvement science process. We encourage you to expand your definition of tools to move past the technical skills, protocols, exercises, and activities to acknowledge and develop the tools of leadership and tools of connection into your toolbox. We think you will probably need an upgraded toolbox to fit your newly acquired and further developed tools. Who knows, you may even need a garage like that of the neighbor to organize all your tools! But remember, stay focused and humble.

Additional Protocol Resources

Books

- Langley, G. J., Moen, R. D., Nolan, K. M., Nolan, T. W., Norman, C. L., & Provost, L. P. (2009). *The Improvement Guide* (2nd ed.). Jossey-Bass.
- Hinnant-Crawford, B. N. (2020). *Improvement Science in Education: A Primer.* Meyers Education Press.

Other Resources

- Carnegie Foundation for the Advancement of Teaching: www.carnegiefoundation.org/resources/
- HTH Protocol Library: https://hthgse.edu/research-center/protocol-library/
- Institute for Healthcare Improvement (IHI): www.ihi.org/resources/Pages/HowtoImprove/default.aspx
- New York City Department of Education Design Improvement Handbook: www.weteachnyc.org/resources/resource/nycdoe-improvement-science-handbook/

NELP and PSEL Connection Box for Educational Leadership Faculty

Leadership and improvement tools can be helpful instruments for leaders to lean on when guiding continuous improvement in their schools. PSEL Standard Ten includes a focus on leadings demonstrating "strategies" and "adaptive approaches," while NELP standards One, Two, and Seven capture leadership tools such as collaboration and reflection or using data, which will contribute to how improvement tools can leverage improvement (NPBEA, 2018).

BIBLIOGRAPHY

The Baha'i Faith. (2010). *Transforming collective deliberation: Valuing unity and justice*. www.bahai.org/documents/bic/transforming-collective-deliberation-valuing-unity-justice

Berwick, D. (2021, February 24). Don Berwick on improvement as learning. *High Tech High*. https://hthunboxed.org/podcasts/s02e13-don-berwick-on-improvement-as-learning/

Biag, M., & Sherer, D. (2021). Getting better at getting better: Improvement dispositions in education. *Teachers College Record, 123*(4), 1–42. https://doi.org/10.1177/016146812112300402

Brown, B. (2018). *Dare to lead*. Penguin Random House.

Brown, B. (2021). *Atlas of the heart*. Penguin Random House.
Bryk, A. S., Gomez, L. M., Grunow, A., & Lemahieu, P. G. (2015). *Learning to improve: How America's schools can get better at getting better.* Harvard Education Press.
Carnegie Foundation for the Advancement of Teaching. (2018). *Causal systems analysis & fishbone diagrams*. Teaching Commons.
Collins, J. (2001). *Good to great: Why some companies make the leap and others don't.* William Collins.
Dixon, C. J., & Palmer, S. N. (2020, April). *Transforming educational systems toward continuous improvement: A reflection guide for K-12 executive leaders.* www.carnegiefoundation.org/resources/publications/transforming-educational-systems-toward-continuous-improvement/
Fullan, M. (Ed.). (2009). *The challenge of change: Start school improvement now!*. Corwin Press. https://doi.org/10.4135/9781452218991
Grant, A. (2021). *Think again*. Viking.
Heifetz, R. A., Linsky, M., & Grashow, A. (2009). *The practice of adaptive leadership: Tools and tactics for changing your organization and the world*. Harvard Business Press.
High Tech High Graduate School of Education. (2023). *HTH protocol library.* https://hthgse.edu/research-center/protocol-library/
Hinnant-Crawford, B. N. (2020). *Improvement science in education: A primer.* Meyers Education Press.
Hollingworth, L., Olsen, D., Asikin-Garmager, A., & Winn, K. M. (2017). Initiating conversations and opening doors. *Educational Management Administration & Leadership,* 174114321772046. https://doi.org/10.1177/1741143217720461
Institute for Healthcare Improvement (IHI). (2023). *Free resources.* www.ihi.org/resources/Pages/HowtoImprove/default.aspx
Khalifa, M. A. (2018). *Culturally responsive school leadership*. Harvard Education Press.
Langley, G. J., Moen, R. D., Nolan, K. M., Nolan, T. W., Norman, C. L., & Provost, L. P. (2009). *The improvement guide* (2nd ed.). Jossey-Bass.
Mezirow, J. (1990). *Fostering critical reflection in adulthood* (by J. Mezirow and Associates). Jossey Bass.
Milder, S., & Lorr, B. (2018). New York City public schools improvement science handbook. *WeTeachNYC.* www.weteachnyc.org/resources/resource/nycdoe-improvement-science-handbook/
Militello, M., Rallis, S. F., & Goldring, E. B. (2009). *Leading with inquiry and action: How principals improve teaching and learning.* Corwin Press.
National Policy Board for Educational Administration (NPBEA). (2018). *National Educational Leadership Preparation (NELP) program recognition standards building level,* 142. www.npbea.org
National Policy Board for Educational Administration (NPBEA). (2015). Professional standards for educational leaders national policy board for educational administration. www.npbea.org
Owens, B. P., & Hekman, D. R. (2016). How does leader humility influence team performance? Exploring the mechanisms of contagion and collective promotion focus. *Academy of Management Journal, 59*(3), 1088–1111. https://doi.org/10.5465/amj.2013.0660
Oxford Languages. (2023). *Honesty.* Oxford English Dictionary. www.oed.com/
Oyer, B. J. (2015). Teacher perceptions of principals' confidence, humility, and effectiveness implications for educational leadership. *Journal of School Leadership, 25,* 684–719.

Perry, J. A., Zambo, D., & Crow, R. (2020). *The improvement science dissertation in practice: A guide for faculty, committee members, and their students*. Meyers Press.

Senge, P. M. (2006). *The fifth discipline: The art and practice of the learning organization*. Broadway Business.

Sinek, S. (2019). *The infinite game*. Portfolio.

Stansberry-Beard, K. (2013). Character in action: A case of authentic educational leadership that advanced equity and excellence. *Journal of School Leadership, 23*.

Tschannen-Moran, M. (2009). Fostering teacher professionalism in schools. *Journal of Educational Administration, 45*(2), 217–247. https://doi.org/10.1177/0013161X08330501

Tschannen-Moran, M., & Gareis, C. R. (2015). Faculty trust in the principal: An essential ingredient in high-performing schools. *Journal of Educational Administration, 53*(1). https://doi.org/10.1108/JEA-02-2014-0024

Wasonga, T. A., & Murphy, J. F. (2007). Co-creating leadership dispositions. *International Studies in Educational Administration (Commonwealth Council for Educational Administration & Management (CCEAM)), 35*(2). http://cceam.net/wp-content/uploads/2019/01/ISEA_2017_45_1.pdf

Wilhelm, A. G., Gray, D. S., & Crosby, E. O. (In press). Building capacity for continuous improvement: Iterating to center racial equity in a PK-8 community school. In E. Anderson & S. Hayes (Eds.), *Continuous improvement: A leadership process for school improvement*. Information Age Publishing.

Zumpe, E., & Aramburo, C. (In press). Developing enabling conditions for continuous improvement: Building foundational team "habits of mind." In E. Anderson & S. Hayes (Eds.), *Continuous improvement: A leadership process for school improvement*. Information Age Publishing.

CHAPTER 9

Building Organizational Capacity for Continuous Improvement

Chapter Highlights

1) The improvement team may not have the capacity ...and/or each member may not have... the same level of readiness to focus on continuous improvement.
2) Attention to building the capacity of improvers to take a learner stance is critical.
3) School leaders are positioned to identify and support capacity building for their team(s) through adaptive practices.
4) Articulating what an improvement culture looks like will help improvement teams lead change.
5) Attention to trust within the improvement team and larger organization is key and can be developed through improvement routines.
6) A robust data infrastructure is essential to developing the organizational capacity of the school(s).

CHAPTER OVERVIEW

Part I of this book identifies skills and practices for equity-oriented improvement science, enacting the leadership practices described in the standards. Part II describes the deceptively simple and undeniably complex improvement science process. This chapter describes how you and your leadership team create the organizational conditions that support the learning process. Professional and organizational capacity are interrelated. The professional

DOI: 10.4324/9781003389279-12

capacity of the individual educator contributes to the collaborative capacity of the team, increasing the overall organizational capacity of the school(s). Building upon the toolbox chapter about highlighting leadership capacity, this chapter presents educational leaders with guidance on capacity building in others (e.g., the improvement team and school organization). To practice meaningful continuous improvement work and to make improvement science an operational norm, identifying the level of professional and organizational capacity is key.

INTRODUCTION: A MULTITUDE OF LEADERSHIP PRACTICES

You might feel overwhelmed by all that is expected of an improvement science leader. That is normal. School leadership requires a wide range of skills, knowledge, and capabilities. It is typical to need support learning to lead improvement and not everyone can enroll in an EdD program like Ava. Biag and Sherer (2021) suggest two ways for a leader to develop the dispositions and skills necessary for improvement: an improver can seek guidance from a coach and/or develop a learning community of trusted colleagues. A district that facilitates such supports throughout schools in the district helps leaders build capacity to improve. One of the most successful schools with which one of the members of the author team worked, has engaged in this work for 4 years with an improvement coach and a community of colleagues. The school is still growing and learning every day; improvement does not end, it is ongoing. Remember at the end of Ava's story how her professors pushed her to think more about how she set up the conditions to support continuous improvement. Even after years of learning with her classmates and school team, she was still developing new skills and tools for improvement.

The work is complex, and you are not expected to build all the organizational capacity before starting to "learn by doing." A reciprocal relationship exists between improvement, organizational capacity, and leadership. In one school we work with, the improvement team emerged from an existing leadership team structure and included instructional coaches, the assistant principal, and the principal. As the team engaged in the improvement science process, they came to understand that they could not improve student learning until they improved their collective understanding of learning and norms and habits of collaboration. The team identified a new improvement focus: *Staff culture and instructional leadership team culture are healthy and productive so we can model it and student achievement can soar and be equitable.* With the guidance of an improvement coach, this team designed their first change idea, creating a shared vision of success for the school with a focus on equity. The improvement team created this vision and iterated it; they aligned their future change ideas to the

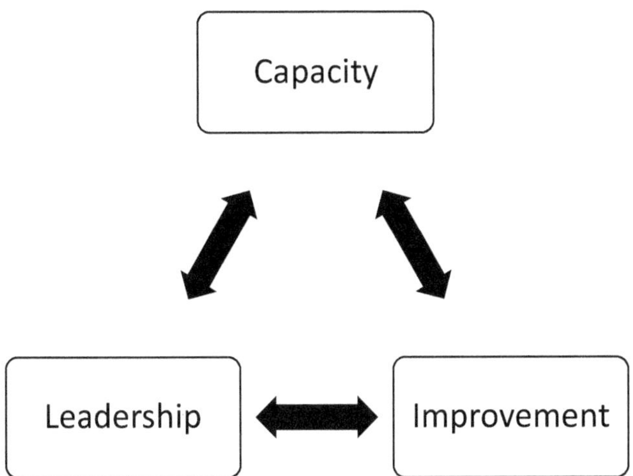

Figure 9.1 Reciprocity Between Leadership, Improvement, and Capacity Building.

vision, including a template created for teacher coaches to discuss how equity was or wasn't part of the instructional planning process and lesson delivery.

The team developed greater trust and agreement around their collective responsibility and a common definition of good equitable instruction and how to improve it. Their coach commented that if a teacher asked any member of that team to define their instruction vision for all students and how to achieve it, they would provide the same answer. The team explained that working together led to (a) being intentional about the work and taking the time to make sure it was the right work, (b) leaning into difficult conversations and being explicit in what drives them as individuals and as a team, and (c) building consensus and hearing everyone's perspective. The team's ability to lead, improve, and build capacity was developing simultaneously through their improvement science work increasing the collective responsibility of the team for improvement. We will unpack these ideas throughout the chapter. Capacity building is necessary for improvement, and the changes resulting from improvement build more capacity (Anderson, under review). See Figure 9.1.

Engaging in improvement science grows capacity over time. Depending on the structures and practices with which you are starting, your school or team may require five to ten years of development. Continuous improvement is so named because there is always the opportunity to iterate and learn through ongoing inquiry. The great news is you can still identify and solve problems as you develop capacity! You will just keep "getting better at getting better" the longer and more deeply you engage with continuous improvement (Bryk et al., 2015). Action Inventory 9.1 invites you and your team to reflect on the structures that are currently in place in your context.

ACTION INVENTORY 9.1 STATUS ON CURRENT STRUCTURES FOR COLLABORATION AND BUILDING CAPACITY

Structure	Circle where your current structures are.		
Time	Everyone involved in the improvement team's regular work dedicates time to meet consistently.	There is a consistent time to meet, but not everyone can make it consistently.	It is a struggle to find a common time for the improvement team to meet consistently.
Space: meeting	There is always a private, physical, or virtual place for the improvement team to gather.	The team has a consistent private space to meet, but it is not unusual for the space to be used for a different purpose and a new location needs to be found on meeting day.	It is hard to find a place for the team to meet, or it is hard to find a place for the team to meet that is not too public.
Space: organizing improvement work data/ artifacts (e.g., fishbone diagram, empathy interview data, school-based local data)	The team has a dedicated place to store/ organize their improvement data.	There are multiple places where the improvement data are stored/organized (e.g., multiple places on google drive, box, physical copies in file folders).	There is not a dedicated place for the team to store/organize their improvement data.
Meeting norms	The team has co-constructed and/or agreed upon norms for meetings. These norms are respected and adhered to at each meeting.	The team has co-constructed and/ or agreed upon norms for the meetings. These norms are often, but not always, respected and adhered to at each meeting. – or –	The team has not yet developed and/or agreed upon meeting norms.

Structure	Circle where your current structures are.		
		The team has norms that are not written down nor explicitly agreed upon, but there is a consistent understanding of how the group operates.	
Trust	The team consistently demonstrates (a) willingness to take the time needed to improve systems, (b) collaboration, (c) respect for one another and the work, (d) engage in sensitive conversations, and (e) hold one another accountable.	The team demonstrates an inconsistent demonstration of (a) willingness to take the time needed to improve systems, (b) collaboration, (c) respect for one another and the work, (d) engage in sensitive conversations, and (e) hold one another accountable.	It is evident the team lacks trust in one another. – or – It is evident the team lacks trust in the process.
Shared vision of the improvement work	The team has co-constructed and/or agreed to the purpose of the improvement work, and the team has a confident understanding and commitment to the focus.	The team has a purpose, but it is not fully understood or committed to by every member of the group.	There is no explicit purpose or focus for the improvement work. – or – There are multiple purposes of the improvement work which cause confusion.

Now, review the results. As you continue reading the chapter, jot down some ideas on how you might build the capacity in the areas you deem needing attention.

Area (circle one)	**Ideas for building capacity**
Time | Space Norms | Trust Shared Vision	
Time | Space Norms | Trust Shared Vision	
Time | Space Norms | Trust Shared Vision	

Organizational Learning

To engage improvement science requires the capacity of organizations to learn as a collective. Organizational learning is "the deliberate use of individual, group, and systems learning to embed new thinking and practices that continuously renew and transform the organization in ways that support shared aims" (Collinson & Cook, 2007, p. 8). Improvement leaders who seek organizational learning need to develop coherent learning structures and understand their role in individual and collective learning. As Kezimi and Resnick (2019) point out, "Learning processes are inextricably linked with power and ideology and their manifestations in schooling practices" (p. 394). It is not as simple as presenting new ideas; the uptake of ideas is dependent on the ways improvers work together to learn and change practice and how individual educators make sense of their role in improvement. Educators want to do the best job for students, but schools and districts do not always organize around building the capacity to learn and improve. Kezimi and Resnick (2019) share, "How schools are organized to nurture {the premise that educators want to do well} creates the organization's ability to flourish. We see school leadership as integral to how schools are organized to support teachers' collective learning" (p. 395). Organizing to flourish, improve, and collectively learn requires building capacity.

What Is Capacity Building?

Capacity building for improvement science develops systems for organizational learning. King and Bouchard (2011) found that many traditional approaches to school improvement – such as reforms to increase accountability, expand school choice and promote turnaround and closure – fail to create lasting change in the education system in part because they do not change the capacity of the school, as an organization, to learn. This relationship between what an educator knows and does and how they can improve is captured in the United Nation's definition of capacity building "as the process of developing and strengthening the skills, instincts, abilities, processes, and resources that organizations and communities need to survive, adapt, and thrive in a fast-changing world" (United Nations, 2023). The United States Department of Education adds, "Capacity building . . . strengthens an organization's ability to fulfill its mission by promoting sound management, strong governance, and persistent rededication to achieving results" (2015). Capacity building is constituted at the individual, organizational, and systems levels.

The need for leaders to build their individual professional capacity is highlighted in the professional standards for building leaders (Elmore et al., 2014). Each NELP standard has the stem: "Candidates who successfully complete building-level educational leadership preparation programs understand and demonstrate the ***capacity*** to promote the current and future success and well-being of each student and adult by applying the knowledge, skills, and commitments necessary to." This stem implies there is a relationship between how a leader is prepared; the knowledge, skills, and commitments a leader practices; and the capacity, not only for change but for cultivating skills in others to collaborate in these efforts. A leader and improver develop professional mindsets, dispositions, skills, and behaviors that allow continuous improvement to flourish (Biag & Sherer, 2021; Dixon & Palmer, 2020; United Nations, 2023). In schools, this may include leaders with positional power like principals, assistant principals, deans, team leaders, or any educator engaging in improvement.

The "organizational level" means those structures, processes, and practices within the institution that influence "the ability of an organization to adapt to change" (United Nations, 2023, np). In schools as organizations, collaborative capacity may include the professional community structures or "practices for supporting and developing school staff, practices for cultivating and distributing leadership among staff, and providing professional learning that promotes reflection, cultural responsiveness, digital literacy, school improvement, and student success" (NELP Component 7.2 Content).

Systems-level capacity building is how the organization relates to other organizations in the same system or to external practices and policies that influence the success of an organization. In schools, the system would include district-level policies and practices, as well as the families and communities the school serves. Within each of these three levels, capacity consists of (a) information or knowledge, (b) skills or practices, (c) structures, and (d) processes (United States Department of Education, 2013). See Figure 9.2.

Leaders of improvement can help others learn about the process and those new to the work engage the process – building and sustaining momentum

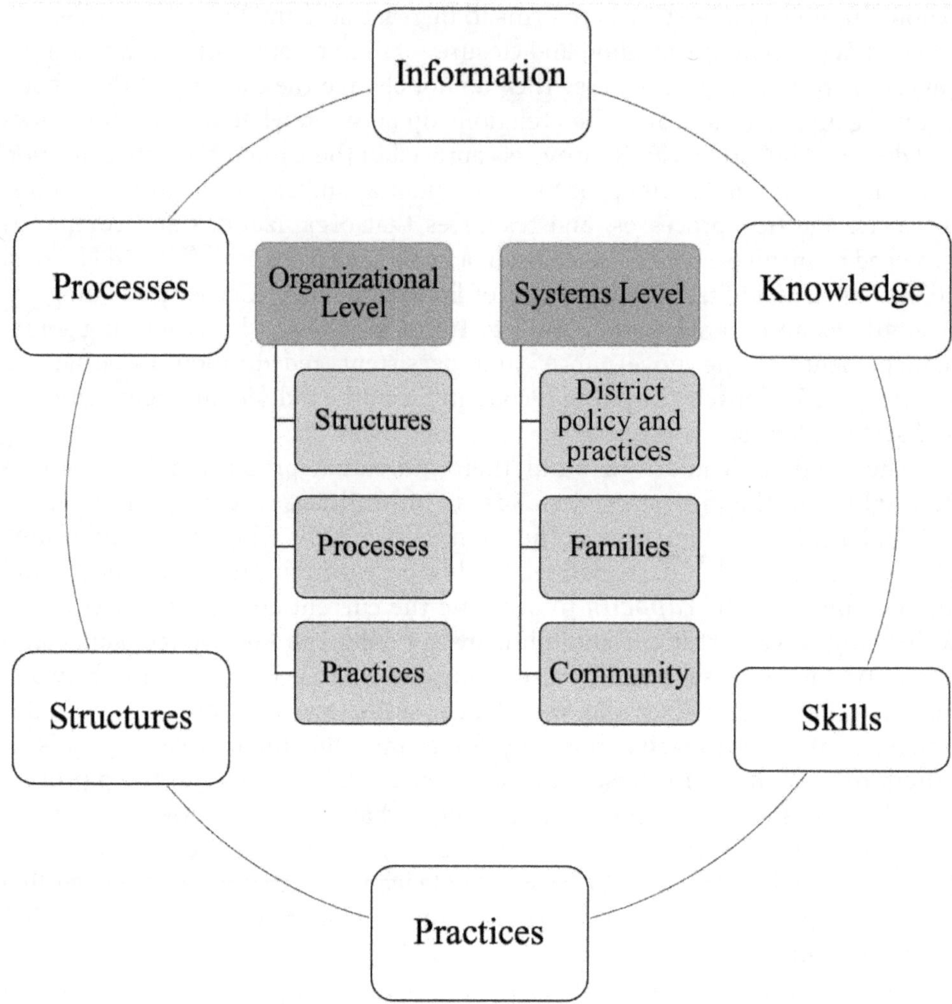

Figure 9.2 Elements of Capacity Building.

Source: Created by author.

for continuous improvement. Galloway and Ishimaru (2020) define organizational leadership "as constructed through collective activity (Engestrom & Sannino, 2010; Spillane, 2005), entailing participatory and shared learning to address persistent, unsolved problems (like racial disparities), where old or ineffective practices are replaced with radically different ones" (Engeström & Sannino, 2010, p. 110). Framing leadership to be collective, participatory, shared, and radical aligns with ways in which we will discuss leadership for building organizational capacity for improvement science. The tools in the previous toolbox chapter create a foundational approach to being an organizational leader.

Key Areas of Organizational Capacity Building for Improvement Science

We define building organizational capacity for improvement science as the ability to "ensure a sustainable improvement culture, environment, and infrastructure in which people take a learner stance, utilize data, and develop organizational routines to improve equity and student learning and achieve *adaptive, transformational change*." (Anderson et al., forthcoming, np). We discuss building the organizational capacity for continuous improvement with the school as the unit of change; however, these areas apply to districts or institutes of higher education. The areas of capacity building, guided by leaders, are (a) learner stance, (b) improvement culture, (c) adaptive practices, (d) data infrastructure, and (e) improvement routines. Each consists of knowledge or information needed to develop group capacity in those areas. That knowledge manifests itself as skills or practices individuals and groups must develop, structures for capacity or the aspects of the organization that must be developed to build capacity, and the processes or ways in which you build that capacity. Leaders are responsible, at least in part, for creating the conditions to develop the knowledge, skills, structures, and processes of the organization, and there are certain practices that support those conditions to build capacity for improvement. A summary of the information presented in this next section is included in Table 9.1.

The next sections explain each of the five areas of organizational capacity and describe leadership practices that help develop and support organizational capacity. We also discuss interrelated organizational readiness factors that can bolster or hinder the development of this organizational capacity followed by barriers to developing capacity. Figure 9.3 shows the relationship among these concepts.

Leadership for a Learner Stance

Each improvers' learner stance is a key capacity for continuous improvement in schools (Anderson et al., forthcoming; Biag & Sherer, 2021). A learner stance includes dispositions and mindsets that create conditions for learning and, therefore, for continuous improvement. The learner stance primes the pump for improvement. Leaders support the development of a learner stance for themselves and others by (a) developing beliefs and mindsets about improvement, (b) collecting and learning from input from teachers and families, (c) focusing on engaging in critical self-reflection and exploring values, and (d) offering meaningful, equity-focused professional learning related to improvement (Elmore et al., 2014; Forman et al., 2017). Ava modeled a learner stance for her MHMS improvement team. She created space for them to make sense of the improvement process. In her school, her team already approached improvement with curiosity, but she helped them develop the ability to critically reflect by embedding opportunities for exploring their personal beliefs and experiences with race and gender into their meetings. Her team was diverse, and

Table 9.1 Organizational Capacity by Knowledge, Skills, Structure, Processes, and Leadership Practices.

	Information or Knowledge for Capacity	*Skills or Practices for Capacity*	*Structures for Capacity*	*Processes for Capacity*	*Leadership Practices*
Learner Stance	• Consider the content and conditions that surround the focus of improvement • Ability to discuss DEIAJ and use a DEIAJ lens to explore root causes, drivers, and strategies	• Develop improvement dispositions and mindsets • Make DEIAJ central to the work • Ask probing questions, listening, seeking multiple points of view	• Job-embedded professional learning	• Use the model of improvement with a focus on who is involved and who is impacted	• Offer meaningful, equity-focused professional learning • Make it normal to get input from teachers, families, and students and act on that input • Create individual efficacy for improvement
Improvement Culture	• Consider the importance of collaboration and collective responsibility	• Productive culture that meets changing needs, challenges status quo, and focused in success • Normalize race-focused conversations both and invite dialogue about DEIAJ within and beyond equity team meetings • Promote a culture of risk-taking and experimentation • Norms of open communication and transparent decision-making that allow for empowerment	• Collaborative professional learning structures • Decentralized, shared governance, democracy, and teacher voice	• Social interactions that promote psychological safety • Empowerment through inclusion in the improvement process	• Practice human-centered leadership • Share leadership and empower people • Encourage a willingness to try new things and learn from them and model learning in public • Believe in collaboration and collectivism • Promote transparency, openness, and trust

Adaptive Practices	• Understand systems and systems of oppression • Understand that variation in outcomes are a result of systems of oppression and change requires shifts in power	• Develop values and dispositions that use systems thinking to explore norms, practices, and routines that are the cause of inequities, ensure school-wide DEIAJ policies and practices, and sustain change in systems	• Integrative structures and process that allow for whole-school and team levels to possess orient toward action	• Integration of structures and practices, alignment of beliefs and values with those structures and practices, and the coherence of the organization are all necessary for adaptive change	• Create opportunities for improvers to grapple with oppression, power, and race • Create a whole school- improvement strategy, teacher involvement in decisions, and shared understanding of effective practice • Provide resources to support improvement work
Improvement Routines	• Prepare teams with an understanding of what constitutes teamwork and effective teaming • Team's understanding of effective practice • Leadership support for teams • Use of strategic team practices	• Develop routines that sustain engagement with equity	• Create systems for improvement routines • Foster enabling conditions to help build routines • Focus on group structures and protocols for collective work that are aligned with goals and draw on faculty knowledge and skills	• Create individual team processes that foster a learning environment	• Establish working agreement and norms that support improvement routines • Calendar regular meeting time and space
Improvement Data	• Understand types of data that inform improvement • Approach data with a race and equity lens	• Ability to collect and analyze the types of data that inform improvement	• Infrastructure for collecting, organizing, and analyzing data to inform knowledge • Tight learning loop that allows for improvers to engage with data to understand what works, for whom, and under what conditions	• Engage in disciplined inquiry • Situate improvement work in data • Consider the types of data that create deeper understanding and guide improvement	• Facilitate the gathering and organizing of improvement data to help guide the understanding of what needs to change and the strategies for change • Establish practices that support qualitative data and stories

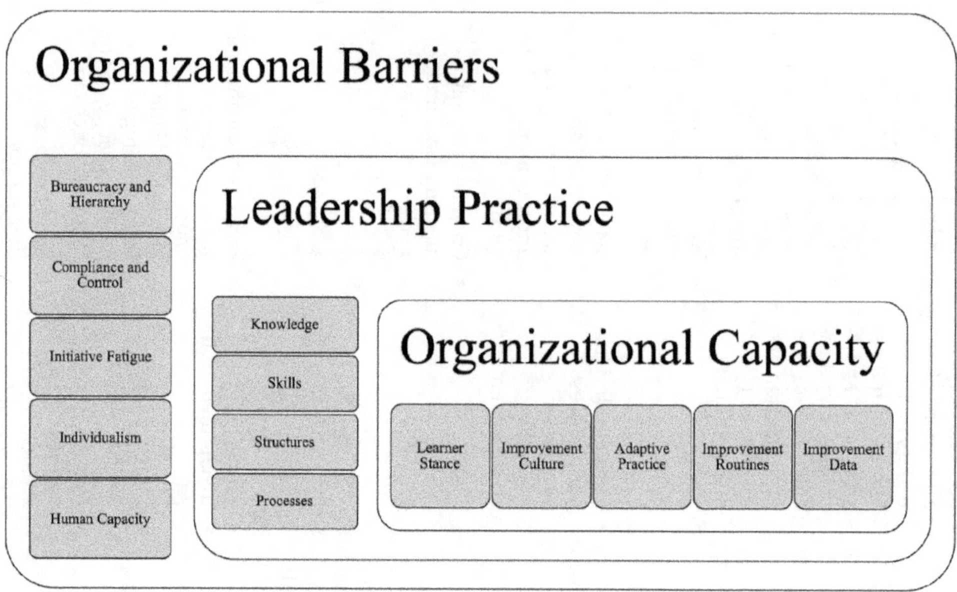

Figure 9.3 The Nested Layers of Organizational Capacity for Improvement.

it was important that they explored their understanding of cultural responsiveness and inclusion individually and together, so they could operationalize these concepts in shared ways. They shared their assumptions about the problems within the school and then interrogated those throughout the improvement science process.

Beliefs and Mindsets About Improvement

Building from Wenger's (1999) work on situated learning, Biag and Sherer (2021) argue "Learning entails more than the acquisition of cognitive skills; it also involves the development of identities, habits, and approaches to professional work" (p. 7). Improvers need to be open to and prepared for the discomforts that come from learning. They should be aware of their own learning tendencies and be willing to explore and develop their improvement mindset, a set of dispositions, knowledge, and beliefs that facilitate improvement. As the improvement science tenet reminds us, our understanding of a problem is "possibly wrong and definitely incomplete." These improvement mindsets undergird learning.

- **Asset-based mindsets:** "Everyone in the organization is capable of developing the knowledge, skills, and capabilities to improve their work in support of the organization's improvement efforts" (Dixon & Palmer, 2020, p. 6).
- **Curiosity, humility, and vulnerability:** "Genuinely interested in how and why things work and are willing to think deeply about a problem before considering

solutions," "recognize that all improvement knowledge is provisional," and "willing to take risks and learn in public" (Dixon & Palmer, 2020, p. 6).

- **Welcoming uncertainty and ambiguity:** "Coping productively with not having the answers and embracing the need to collectively learn how to improve enables executive leaders to adjust to changing circumstances to advance improvement" (Dixon & Palmer, 2020, p. 6).
- **Scientific reasoning:** "Habitually and rigorously question their assumptions, asking themselves and others, 'How do we know?'" (Dixon & Palmer, 2020, p. 7).
- **Systems thinking:** "Understanding the big picture while also seeing interactions and interdependencies among the structures and processes" (Dixon & Palmer, 2019, p. 7).
- **Willingness to rethink assumptions:** "The flexibility to update [your] practices in light of new evidence" (Grant, 2022, p. 64).
- **Commit to and be receptive to change (as educators):** Encourage questioning the status quo and be open to new ideas.

Leaders must develop improvement mindsets in others through professional learning and social interactions. The more willing leaders are to present themselves as a learner and genuinely model these mindsets in their work with teachers, students, and families, the more progress they can make.

Input From Teachers and Families

An improver should engage in the model of improvement with a focus on empathy and equity (e.g., who's involved? who's impacted?) learning from teachers, families, and whomever is connected to or impacted by the problem (Hinnant-Crawford, 2020). Understanding the experience of others (empathy) and enduring commitment to keeping students at the center of improvement informs the learner stance. Improvers in a learner stance ask questions while seeking multiple perspectives and listen to and act upon what they learn and encourage user-centered practices throughout the organization (Elmore et al., 2014). The needs of students and communities are central to the improvement process and should be a focus of learning.

Critical Self-Reflection and Values

A learner considers the content and conditions of improvement and develops system-wide capabilities that address those conditions by making DEIAJ central to the work. Improvement work is value laden. Grant (2022) writes, "Who you are should be a question of what you value, not what you believe. Values are your core principles in life . . . Basing your identity on . . . principles enable you to remain open-minded about the best ways to advance them (p. 64)." To develop a learner stance for improvers, organizations must focus on conditions that help individuals in the organization explore their values through critical self-reflection (e.g., Khalifa et al., 2016).

Equity-Focused Professional Learning for Improvement

Leaders create a learner stance within their teachers and staff by building individual skills through training and developing people, supporting team building, promoting organizational learning, and encouraging ongoing learning (Elmore et al., 2014; Garvin et al., 2008; Murphy & Meyers, 2008). Professional learning must be sustained, job-embedded, and connected to a coherent strategy (Blank & De las Alas, 2009; Darling-Hammond et al, 2009; Elmore et al., 2014). Professional learning develops DEIAJ values and uses a DEIAJ lens to explore root causes, drivers, and strategies to explore power dynamics that are essential to equity-oriented improvement science (Galloway & Ishimaru, 2020). Ava did not just assume her teachers and community had improvement mindsets or liberatory design mindsets; she offered professional learning opportunities that reflect and develop these mindsets in teachers and support staff.

One of this book's authors develops school-based teams for improvement. She and her team created space both within and across the schools to explore the liberatory design mindsets mentioned in Chapter 4. At each step in the improvement process is a set of DEIAJ prompts teams to stop and discuss. When the improvement team is conducting root causes analysis – based on empathy interview data, disaggregated data, research and practical knowledge, and systems and process mapping – the schools discuss the prompts in Action Inventory 9.2 (based on the work of the NEP). They are all applying improvement science to problems of equity and opportunity.

ACTION INVENTORY 9.2 PROMPTS TO DEVELOP A LIBERATORY DESIGN APPROACH

1. How can we ensure we are reaching a point of view that is authentic and not distorted by biases?
2. What is the larger ecosystem in which our improvement focus lives? What influences it?
3. Are our identified root causes based on deficit understandings of the populations we serve?
4. Have we looked at the root causes with a diversity, equity, inclusion, antiracist, and just (DEIAJ) lens?

When they come together as a network, the individual improvers explore liberatory mindsets in role-alike groups (e.g., principals, teacher leaders, teachers, and support staff). The groups have prompts to explore DEIAJ practices, critically reflecting on current and past work and demonstrating vulnerability by sharing openly. Over time, the facilitation team deepened the prompts, with the educators recently being asked to reflect on when they have had to bracket their own feelings to uphold DEIAJ values – demonstrating humility. When the author and her team of coaches recognize a school or individual needs more development of the DEIAJ lens, capability, or process, their improvement coach incorporates that into professional learning within their coaching sessions. These activities are intended to develop the learner stance and prepare mindsets to engage in improvement.

Application of learner stance by Ava and MHMS: MHMS developed improvement mindsets through working together. They focused on who was impacted and created professional learning for the improvement team and the whole school to understand LGBTQ+ students' needs and experiences. The school prioritized the needs of the LGBTQ+ students and families, even though they were a small percentage of the students, making inclusion central to their work, gathered input from LGBTQ+ students through empathy interviews, collected their stories throughout the process, and humbled themselves as they heard stories of negative experiences and bullying that were allowed to happen. Ava made sure they approached the work with an asset-based mindset and called it out when deficit thinking creeped in while encouraging people to be vulnerable and curious about the needs of LGTBQ+ students.

Leading for an Improvement Culture

Leaders create and sustain a stable and supportive improvement culture (Anderson et al., forthcoming). As Nasir (2011, p. 29) explains,

> Schools and classrooms are culturally lived and experienced; in that, they are culturally organized, guided by norms, conventions, artifacts, and involve social interaction. They are also potential spaces of empowerment, marginalization, and identity building (i.e., spaces where cultural and identity trajectories are offered and taken up).

An improvement culture is dependent on how leadership practices and structures (a) share leadership and empower people by allowing for teacher involvement in decisions and believing in collaboration, collectivism, and public learning; (b) model and promote a culture of risk-taking and experimentation by encouraging a willingness to try new things and learn from them by promoting transparency and trust (See Chapter 8); and (c) push against the status quo (Elmore et al., 2014; Garvin et al., 2008; Murphy & Meyers, 2008; Spillane et al., 2001).

Teacher Involvement in Decisions: Collaboration, Collectivism, and Public Learning

To ensure collaboration and collective learning, norms of open communication and transparent decision-making are required (discussed in Chapter 8); these create the trust and morale that allow for empowerment (Murphy & Meyers, 2008). The more each member of the school has input into and understanding of leadership decisions and processes, the more likely they are to engage in improvement in meaningful ways.

Sharing leadership can be done through structures for shared decision-making such as consensus-building protocols (See Seeds for Change, for examples). Consensus-building protocols include working as a group to determine possible decisions, listing proposed responses, and having each team member add a mark next to the decisions she/he/they support. Another consensus-building activity is to have the group respond to a proposed decision with a thumbs up, thumbs down, or thumbs to the side – not moving forward with that decision until everyone has moved to a thumbs up.

Throughout the improvement science process, there are opportunities to cultivate teacher and staff empowerment through inclusion in the improvement process and fostering sense of belonging in the organization through collective responsibility. In most of the schools we have observed problem-solve using improvement science, the principal has seen increased faith in their leadership ability, as evidenced in both their formal and informal evaluations by teachers.

In addition to shared leadership and decision-making, leaders must consider the learning structures that value collegiality, peer learning, and relationship building. Schools that employ collaborative team structures, using distributed or shared leadership, are better positioned for continuous improvement. Working in collaboration is a cornerstone of continuous improvement. Militello and colleagues (2009) explain, "Leaders play a crucial role in establishing a culture with mutual respect and participatory governance" (p. 112). Learning together and from one another helps to learn more and learn faster (Bryk et al., 2015). Collaboration marks a marquee element of improvement science; principals should "invite; they include; they create opportunities for engagement" (Militello et al., 2009, p. 125).

For instance, schools with professional learning communities, communities of practice, and other structures for cross-cutting team time, including school leadership teams with teacher leaders, use existing time and space for collaborative problem-solving (see Action Inventory 9.1). Schools that already approach problem-solving through a lens of equity and are comfortable using data to explore problems are set up for success. Schools that don't use equity-oriented data will need to develop professional learning structures and norms that expect and support equity-oriented improvement.

Risk-Taking and Experimentation

Improvement science requires improvers to trust the process while navigating the discomfort of ambiguity. We wrote about trust in the leader in Chapters 1, 3 and 8. There is the need for trust throughout the organization. Cosner (2009) and Bryk et al. (2010) found that the social resources that lead to collegial trust influence teacher development and the ability to talk about improvement. The levels of trust within the organization have a large influence on readiness for continuous improvement, but the improvement science process can also build trust because attention is paid to the social processes.

Trust is developed over time through the "regular interaction, cooperation, and coordination" of social processes (Cosner, 2009, p. 251). Trust is established when people work together in highly interdependent teams, perform tasks, commit to their shared agreements, and celebrate the outcomes of their work together. Bryk and colleagues (2010) explain that trust makes people more willing to engage in improvement, work together to solve problems, and strive toward a school's vision and mission. Trust begets commitment to continuous improvement. Leaders build capacity for trust through repeated and structured social exchanges by shaping a cooperative culture, establishing norms for interaction, intervening to resolve conflicts, removing barriers, and increasing opportunity for interaction (Cosner, 2009).

Trust sets the stage for risk-taking. Improvers need to be willing to test bite-sized ideas and make small mistakes rather than go too far down a committed pathway without evidence of the pathway's promise. This is similar to how a scientist thinks. As Grant (2022) writes, to "reach the correct answer in the long run . . . that means they have to be open to stumbling, backtracking, and rerouting in the short run" (p. 72). An improvement culture emphasizes the need to anticipate and embrace failures, for failure reveals new learnings. It is hard to achieve success without trying different changes along the way – some of which may not work. Improvers must be able to see that failure is an opportunity to learn.

In education, we are not always open to the idea of failure. Failure is penalized. Due to traditional system of beliefs about failure and success, many people are not comfortable sharing the ways in which they have failed, learned, and grown because they fear it will be used for external accountability or evaluation instead of as a way to get better. Don Berwick 2021b, in a podcast about improvement in healthcare, shared,

> When you try to do something better, you can fail, and it's often helpful to have somebody with you that says, "Oh, I know what that's like." I mean just the social support system of being in a network of trying to do things together, it's more fun and it's more sustaining. Someone can help you get up when you fall down. You can celebrate together. You can grieve together.

Learning is social, which requires the need to feel safe (Elmore et al., 2014; Higgins et al., 2012; Honig, 2008). Psychological safety, developed through community support for trying new things, must be a priority for leaders. Psychological safety creates social conditions that support the ability to be open about challenges and areas for growth and the willingness to seek help from peers or mentors

(Edmondson 2019; Edmondson et al., 2016; Garvin et al., 2008; Higgins et al., 2012). In Ava's story, she ceremoniously celebrated her improvement teams' failure to model an improver's approach to failure.

One way to foster safety is to celebrate improvement work and highlight wins and successes of the process to communicate value and spread the learning from failed tests of change. For instance, in a network of schools with which one of the authors works, she encourages the improvement teams to share successes and areas of growth side-by-side to encourage the recognition of both. In a mid-year meeting, one of the schools shared their progress with the group and glossed over the failure to pick an appropriate problem. The other schools brought this lack of transparency forward – not to critique but to explain that having one school hide its failures limited what the other schools could learn from that group.

Disruption of the Status Quo

Improvement culture pushes against the status quo and focuses on successful improvement. Murphy and Meyers (2009) found that for an organization to improve, the culture must be supportive and adaptable to the changing needs. The culture must be open to probing, seeking multiple points of view, validating those points of view, and then acting on what has been learned (Elmore et al., 2014). The organization must have norms that invite dialogue about DEIAJ and include the values of the community and all marginalized groups (Zumpe & Aramburo, in press).

The leader must design interactions with colleagues to discuss data about racial equity and other inequities to facilitate data conversations that are safe but honest. Dialogue about DEIAJ should prompt improvers to explore systems of power, privilege, and oppression. Singleton's (2014) set of four agreements for courageous conversations about inequities specifically race. These include

- **Stay engaged** – Engagement in the moment and sustained over time is core to the conversation. If people appear disengaged, it is important to stop and name the disengagement, reflect upon it, and discuss why that might be happening.
- **Expect to experience discomfort** – Disengagement and discomfort go hand in hand. Conversations about race and equity require self-awareness and self-reflection. Individuals must admit where beliefs come from and be open to changing beliefs through learning. It may be emotional, and sitting in those emotions is necessary for growth.
- **Speak your truth** – Fear of saying the wrong thing leads to dishonesty. Prompts to gain the truth might include the following,
    - Can you tell me what you mean when you say. . .? Is it possible for you to say more about . . .?
    - Have the thoughts you shared been shaped by others or is this your own personal perspective?

- Why do you think others might want to challenge your perspective? (Singleton & Hayes, 2008, p. 21)

- **Expect and accept a lack of closure** – We are always learning. Race and equity are ongoing topics that require a sustained commitment to discussion and dialogue.

Upholding these agreements will require a facilitator, whether that person is the school leader, another member of the leadership team, a district leader, or an external provider. You may want to work on developing a culture that supports "calling in," not "calling out," a concept explored by Loretta Ross in several TED talks (TED, 2022). "Calling in" is done when people use questions and prompts to explore beliefs and ideas. The types of prompts that would call someone into a courageous conversation include

- "I'm curious. What was your intention when you said that?"
- "How might the impact of your words or actions differ from your intent?"
- "How might someone else see this differently? Is it possible that someone else might misinterpret your words or actions?"
- "Why do you think that is the case? Why do you believe that to be true?" "What is making you the most fearful, nervous, uncomfortable, or worried?"

(Harvard Diversity, Inclusion, and Belonging, 2023, np)

There are times for calling out, especially when the comment is harmful or makes people feel unsafe, but, when engaging in dialogue, calling in – through one-on-one or small group conversations may be more productive.

An improvement culture must support community input. Community input is central to an improvement culture since students and families are the ultimate "user" in our schools. Their input must be sought, and attention must be paid to seeking diverse perspectives with a range of experiences. From a DEIAJ lens, Singleton and Hays (2008, p. 20) shared,

> Through normalizing the presence of multiple perspectives, we can avoid a situation in which one dominant way of understanding race invalidates all other experiences and different points of view. We discover just how racialized our own identities and viewpoints have been.

There are ways leaders can facilitate and coach their team to gather such input that can be part of a school's norms and practices. Two protocols for dialogue that are inclusive of the community are fishbowl conversations or kiva circles, referenced in Ava's story and Chapter 6 as equity-focused practical measures. Both methods include a structure where small groups hold conversation while other small groups are listening. Such protocols give everyone present the opportunity to share their perspective equally and encourage others to listen to those perspectives.

Application of Improvement Culture by Ava and MHMS: MHMS saw solving the problem of inclusion and culturally responsive as a collective task. They had to resist the way they had always done things, which required dialogue about why pronouns and deadnaming were important and how bullying impacted students' mental health; MHMS tried things that were risky in some schools and communities, like drag reading hour. Ava and her team focused on the needs of their school community and supported teachers who needed deeper support to understand why inclusion for LGBTQ+ students was an improvement focus. They also celebrated learning from failed change ideas like the pronoun campaign MHMS set up and equity team and created spaces for teachers to have courageous conversations and explore their own equity journey. The school systems for authentic collaboration and decision-making using consensus making to include more than just formal leaders.

Leading for Adaptive Practices

Improvement organizations address adaptive elements crucial to producing transformational, sustainable change (Anderson et al., forthcoming). Leaders build capacity for adaptive change by (a) practicing systems change; (b) understanding the role of oppression, power, and race and creating opportunities for improvers to grapple with these ideas; (c) creating coherence and integration; and (d) providing resources to support improvement work (Biag & Sherer, 2021).

Systems Change

Adaptive improvement practices focus on systems. The leader and improvement team begin with an honest, authentic assessment of the landscape of the system. They should demonstrate familiarity with using root cause analysis and systems analysis tools (See Chapter 6). Improvers use systems thinking to explore norms, practices, and routines that are the cause of inequities; ensure schoolwide DEIAJ policies and practices; and sustain change in systems. In taking a systems perspective, organizational leadership for equity only exists if educators understand that disparate outcomes are a result of structural and institutional conditions, therefore, power must be shifted (Biag & Sherer, 2021; Galloway & Ishimaru, 2020). To explore inequity, the school needs to confront complicity in an oppressive educational system and as reflected in current organizations (Khalifa et al., 2016).

Oppression, Power, and Race

Leaders need to support teachers and the community in examining policies that place a heavier burden on BIPOC students, teachers, or staff to focus improvement work and then facilitate the exploration and redesign of policies and procedures as well as change institutional and classroom-level dynamics (e.g., Khalifa et al., 2016). One way to highlight inequities is to conduct an equity audit or equity visit to understand the landscape of the school through data collection and analysis (Green, 2017; Roegman et al., 2019; Skrla et al., 2009). The improvement team needs to pay attention to factors that cause variation in experiences and outcomes (rather than ignoring them or being unaware). Leaders who hold space for the community to reflect, express, and process experiences, sharing thoughts and emotions (Irby, 2021)

The team needs to examine power relationships with a willingness to transfer or give up some of their power or control. Understanding inequity must lead to action by cultivating school-wide DEIAJ curriculum, pedagogy, and assessment practices, and developing a system of support and accountability around equity. To accomplish transformative change, leadership at the school may need to encourage and bolster relationships with other organizations and external providers that have an equity focus.

Integrated and Coherent Structures and Processes and Shared Beliefs

Improvement requires integrated and coherent structures and processes (Elmore et al., 2014; Honig & Hatch, 2004; Childress et al., 2007) that allow for schools and teams to possess an orientation toward equity, action, and persistence (Biag & Sherer, 2021). It is necessary to align beliefs and values with those structures and practices. To make sure teachers are more prepared to engage in improvement work (Forman et al., 2017), improvers must establish shared beliefs about teaching and learning and about how to work together by establishing and maintaining a coherent vision, strategy, and improvement agenda (Forman et al., 2017). For instance, when designing change ideas and iterating and spreading them through the school, there are complementary systems of adult learning that build the content knowledge and required skills to take up that change. Adult learning should be responsive to the data collected about the success and failure of the change ideas and the user perspective.

Resources to Support Improvement Work

Districts and schools build capacity for sustaining change by providing resources to support improvement work (Biag & Sherer, 2021). Resources come in many forms including human resources, such as coaches or other professionals who are committed to leading improvement work, and fiscal resources, such as a financial commitment to supporting improvement efforts through professional learning resources or stipends for teacher leaders to engage in the work. Leaders may want to assign the facilitation of this improvement work as a school-level role, especially if they don't have the ability to lead the work. A leader needs to explore new and creative ways to leverage resources and assets to support improvement work.

Application of Adaptative Practices by Ava and MHMS: Ava learned about oppression and created book groups to explore the topic more deeply. The improvement team used systems analysis and casual analysis to understand the problems as a newly established practice for all adaptative challenges. Ava looked at all the school's structures and processes and aligned them to be coherent; their school improvement goals in their SIP plan aligned with their theories of improvement and their collaborative structures and professional development. She worked with her community to create shared beliefs about learning that were codified in the expectations of students and teachers, in teacher professional learning and evaluations, in student assessment, and a shared strategy for improvement.

Leading for Improvement Routines

Organizational routines foster innovation, equity, and improvement through the system by creating both time and space for improvement work, ideally within existing structures and processes (Anderson et al., forthcoming). Leaders build capacity for improvement routines by (a) actively working to establish organizational processes, (b) calendaring regular meeting times and spaces (Anderson et al, forthcoming), and (c) developing working agreements that reflect those shared understandings (Elmore et al., 2014; Garvin et al., 2008). These routines increase understanding, develop intentional practices, and lead to more action (Murphy & Meyers, 2008) by creating individual team processes that foster a learning environment, creating systems for improvement routines, and fostering enabling conditions to help build routines. To sustain adaptive, transformational change, leaders must establish and maintain systems for sustained collaboration and build structures for professional communities.

ACTION INVENTORY 9.3 REFLECTION QUESTIONS: IMPROVEMENT ROUTINES

1. What organizational routines currently exist (e.g., PLCs, common planning times, staff meetings, professional learning time)?
2. Where are their places of potential to modify or establish routines to forward improvement work?
3. What needs to be deprioritized or moved off the list of responsibilities in order to make the necessary room for improvement work?

Organizational Processes

Improvement routines should reflect group structures and protocols, faculty knowledge, and aligned goals for collective work (Childress et al., 2007, Elmore et al., 2014; Honig & Hatch, 2004; Galloway & Ishimaru, 2020; Newmann et al., 2001). The leader should build collective routines for a learning culture; create the structures and processes for building teams, including cross-level or vertical teaming; and prepare teams with an understanding of what constitutes teamwork, effective teaming, strategic team practices, and leadership support for teams (Elmore et al., 2014; Murphy & Meyers, 2008). Teams should focus on developing routines that sustain engagement with equity, such as purposeful equity check-ins built into the improvement process (Galloway & Ishimaru, 2020). Improvers must also implement routines that normalize race-focused conversations within and beyond equity team meetings (Galloway & Ishimaru, 2020).

Regular Meeting Times

Scheduling regular meetings is an essential routine. Successful improvement teams create regular, even weekly, time to engage in improvement science, embedding it in existing practices, such as leadership team meetings, department meetings, professional communities or communities of practice, or professional learning and coaching cycles. We have worked with many schools over the last several years, and the most successful schools meet weekly, for about an hour, with their external coach for root cause analysis and data exploration, discussing the theory of improvement, and planning as well as studying a change idea. Successful schools develop processes for keeping notes on their progress and for reinforcing steps between meetings. These routines keep the momentum of the work and allow improvement science to become part of the fabric of the school.

Working Agreements and Norms

Improvers should develop working community agreements and working norms for meetings and interactions. Such norms allow improvers to engage in the type of vulnerability, open sharing, and group discussions about problems and strategies necessary for adaptive change. Norms should be based on improvement mindsets and should demonstrate humane approaches to working with people (e.g., compassion, humility, respect, and vulnerability), commitment to democratic values should support and develop psychological safety and should encourage curiosity and scientific reasoning.

Haskell and colleagues (2007) define working agreements as "guidelines that define how groups want to work together, and what they want in the working environment and from each other to feel safe and free to learn, explore and discover" (np). Working agreements are easier to create and uphold when there is trust in the leader and in each other. For example, a professional organization in which we participate created the following working agreements that guide our work together:

- Be fully present.
- Share the air.
- Seek to understand.
- Be mindful of your impact on others.
- Defer judgment.
- Maintain confidentiality.
- Be generous with each other.

Creating agreements as a group helps ensure the agreements meet your specific group's needs. At one point in our work, we became mindful of the fact that while we had working agreements, we could benefit from conversational values that would help ensure equity of voice in our community. Those were adapted from Wheatley's (2009) *Turning to one another: Simple conversations to restore hope to the future*:

- We acknowledge one another as equals.
- We try to stay curious about each other.
- We slow down so we have time to think and reflect.
- We practice self-awareness and are mindful of our impact on others.
- We ensure equity of voice.
- We expect conversations to be messy at times.

Such norms and agreements can help facilitate adaptive change.

Application of Improvement Routines by Ava and MHMS: MHMS had structures for collaboration including meetings scheduled for the improvement team, equity teams, and routines for testing change ideas. MHMS had working agreements that each team created collectively, and MHMS developed shared norms for collaboration for all meetings, professional learning, and professional communities.

ACTION INVENTORY 9.4 SURFACING SHARED BELIEFS, NORMS, AND IMPROVEMENT AGENDA

Directions: This 3-step process can be used by your team to articulate (a) shared beliefs, (b) shared working norms, and (c) improvement agenda.

Step 1

Who: Improvement team
When: Early in the process (if possible)

1. Each team member gets nine post-it notes (i.e., three post-it notes for each of three areas).
2. Individually, team members will list three priorities for shared beliefs about teaching and learning, working norms, and developing an improvement agenda; writing one per post-it note.
3. Facilitators could pose the following to invite responses:

    a. Shared beliefs: To help us in our improvement work, we need to articulate specific core beliefs about teaching and learning that we hold that will help ground our efforts. On three of your post-it notes, write three priorities you would like to lift up as something we might agree to as a group related to teaching and learning.
    b. Working Norms: To help us in our improvement work, we need to articulate specific core beliefs that capture what it looks like and sounds like for us to work together as an improvement team effectively and respectfully. On three of your post-it notes, write three priorities you would like to lift up as something we might agree to as a group related to our working norms.
    c. To help us in our improvement work, we need to articulate specific core beliefs about our improvement agenda that will help ground our efforts. On three of your post-it notes, write three priorities you would like to lift up as something we might agree to as a group related to our improvement agenda.

4. Set up three distinct spaces in the room (e.g., chart paper); one space is dedicated to each of the three areas.
5. Have team members place their nine post-in note answers in the appropriate areas around the room.
6. Select which topic you would like to talk about as a group. Give the group time to review everyone's contributions.
7. Move post-its around to group them if similar answers exist.

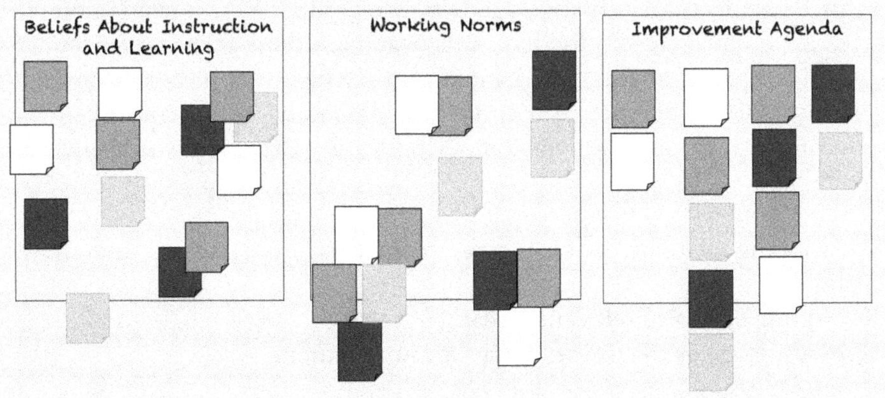

8. Give every group member a marker or a sticker and invite them to select their top two priority points by placing a sticker next to it or starring it using the marker.
9. Then, discuss as a group the top three to five areas the group indicated as top priorities to develop the team's agreed upon (a) shared beliefs, (b) shared working norms, or (c) improvement agenda elements.
10. Capture these three to five points and ensure that consensus is reached. In this case, consensus means, every member agrees, can live with, or will not impede efforts connected to the list of items.
11. Record the final list and make it available for reference at all future meetings.
12. Repeat steps 6–11 with the remaining topics.

Leading for Data for Improvement

A school needs the capacity for responding to improvement data through data infrastructure and data practices that engage in disciplined inquiry (Biag & Sherer, 2021; Boudett et al., 2013; Bryk et al., 2015; Hinnant-Crawford, 2020). We defined improvement data in Chapter 6. Here we focus on the structures and systems that support the collection and exploration of data or capacity to measure if growth is sustained. Leaders build capacity for data for improvement through (a) facilitating gathering and organizing of improvement data to guide understanding what needs to change and the strategies for those changes and (b) establishing practices that support gathering and analyzing qualitative data and "street data."

Data Infrastructure

A robust data infrastructure is essential to developing the organizational capacity of the school(s) and should include structures for collecting, organizing, and analyzing data to inform knowledge (Elmore et al., 2014; Garvin et al., 2008). The leader must create individual and organizational capacity to collect and analyze the types of qualitative and quantitative data that inform improvement. The school should operate in a culture of data (qualitative and quantitative) targeted toward improving learning. A data infrastructure would include the following:

- Developing systems for capturing, evaluating, distributing, and effectively using knowledge
- Providing access to relevant research
- Providing access to relevant data for improvement

- Establishing analytic structures with a system of measures
- Ensuring quality of social interaction (matters of trust, power, and professional identity) during data use
- Facilitating data conversations that are safe but honest and designing interactions with colleagues to provide and discuss data pertaining to racial and other equity gaps.

Consensus on how each of these will be operationalized is necessary, including who (e.g., individual person or role) will be the point person for that element: Who is the point person for gaining access? Facilitating conversations, etc.?

Support for Gathering and Analyzing Data

Building the capacity to use data fruitfully must consider the types of data that create a deeper understanding and guide improvement (Galloway & Ishimaru, 2020). These data are not aggregated accountability data, but are instead, practical measures tied to specific actions that tell stories of individuals' skills and opportunities for learning and are reflective of equity values (Hinnant-Crawford, 2020). Data should be used in real-time to improve student learning based on knowledge of existing research on learning.

The organization must situate improvement in data, approach data with a race and equity lens, and create a tight learning loop (Anderson et al., forthcoming). To situate improvement within a data conversation, the leader must build capacity for data collection and analysis within the school, scan outside of the organization and draw on external knowledge from research, scholarship, and practice. The goal should be to develop collective knowledge building around complex problems and solutions, comprehend variation in the adaptations and performance of the intervention across contexts, and learn from those further along in the work.

To analyze data with a DEIAJ lens, educators should approach data with deconstructive and reconstructive knowledge frameworks and be open to multiple, unexpected, non-dominant ways of knowing (Khalifa et al., 2016). Teachers and improvement teams should explore racially disaggregated data authentically; the purpose is not simply to point out gaps but to gain an understanding of the opportunities present or not present. Taking a DEIAJ lens to data includes interrogating what data are missing and making a plan to gather those data. For instance, the team may discover they can identify outcomes but not experiences. One way to collect missing data is to collect stories of human-centered experiences (Safir & Dugan, 2021). Human stories can demonstrate success and provide nuance to the challenges the school faces, the success of a change idea, or the progress toward addressing a driver in the journey toward success. Attention must be paid to ensuring the quality of social interaction during data use (matters of trust, power, and professional identity).

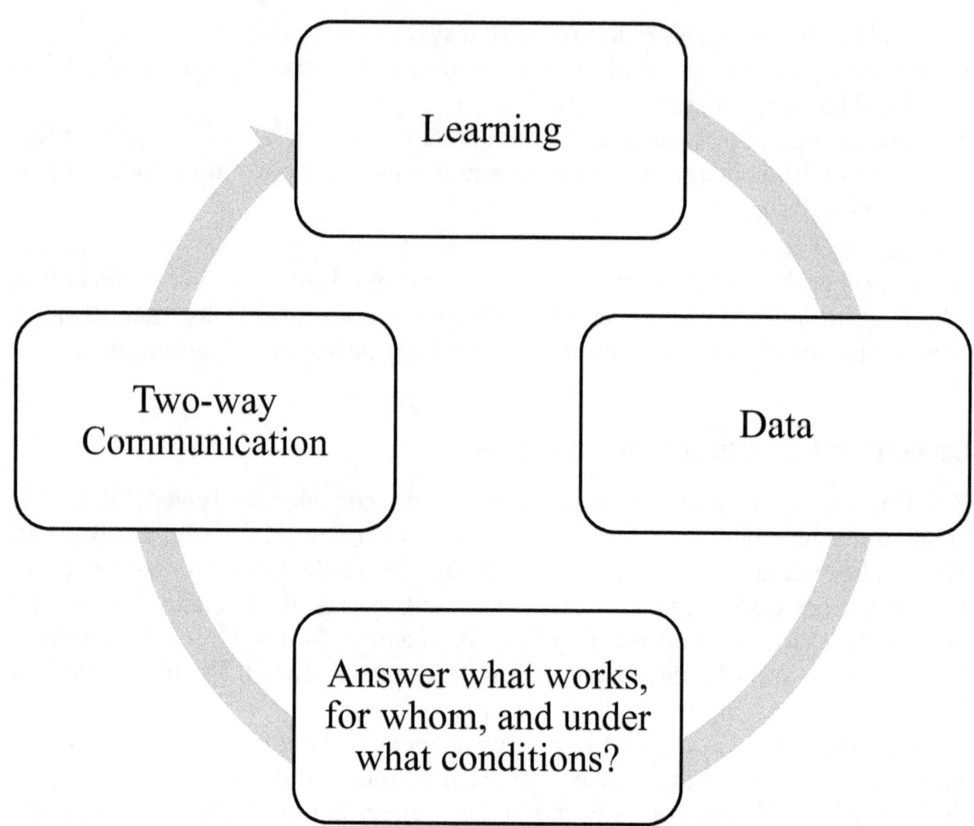

Figure 9.4 A Learning Loop.

Source: Created by the authors.

Learning Loop

The data should be used for learning and improving through a learning loop that allows improvers to engage the data to understand what works, for whom it works, and under what conditions (Langley et al., 2009). The learning loop is driven by feedback as a form of learning not as expert critique (Anderson & Davis, Under review). The organization must include a feedback loop that shares insight with leadership at multiple levels and between schools and the district and school and community (Figure 9.4). Improvers should elevate and share key insights that emerge from the work of individual members and smaller teams. The goal of the learning loop is to develop collective knowledge building around complex problems and solutions and also to coordinate developing, testing, and refining to accelerate learning. Leaders establish an environment where data are used as a tool for improvement, and not as a punishment.

Application of Data for Improvement by Ava and MHMS: Ava worked with all her teachers to expand their understanding of what constitutes data and how to use data for improvement instead of evaluation or accountability. She hired a data coordinator to organize the data and provide technically appropriate systems of data collection, management, and analysis. MHMS used collected short-cycle data through PDSA cycles as well as data to understand the process and progress toward school-wide improvement.

Challenges and Barriers to the Organizational Structures of Schools and Districts

The five areas for capacity mentioned earlier (learner stance, improvement culture, adaptive elements, improvement routines, and data to inform improvement) are essential. The more well-developed these areas are, the greater the readiness for organizational commitment. There are organizational factors that impact the ability to develop organizational capacity for continuous improvement and improvement science. In some cases, these structures are within the control of a building-level leader, and in others, they are the status quo the leader will need to disrupt to be able to engage improvement science in the most impactful way.

Hierarchy and Bureaucracy

Throughout this chapter and book, we suggest sharing leadership, encouraging collective responsibility, and including the community in decision-making. Working in this way requires overcoming a common barrier to improvement – a top-down leadership approach. The idea of one leader who decrees what will happen and monitors the staff and students for compliance is a bureaucratic approach that limits the innovation and collaboration that is necessary for change in complex adaptive systems. In Chapter 7 we described the bottom-up, top-down (hybrid approach) to leadership (Anderson et al., under review; Greenhalgh & Papoutsi, 2019; King & Bouchard, 2011). This model puts the onus of developing structures to support decision-making and improvement processes on the district or state leaders and then allows the strategies and decisions to happen in a local context at the school level. This model promotes and relies on a collective, coherent set of intentions including the vision for teaching and learning, the norms and working agreements mentioned before, and the structures and processes for working vertically.

Compliance and Control

Another barrier emergeing from hierarchical, bureaucratic systems is that schools and school systems operate within an accountability structure that doesn't account for variation and the potential to learn from that variation – focusing instead on percentages instead of people. Throughout this chapter, there are some implicit leadership implications around fear. Fear is a critical part of the conversation because improvement will not take place if there is fear in the organization (Berwick, 2021a). Leadership sets the tone, culture, and climate of the school. The leader creates conditions to invite productive improvement work. Not every school will be able to do this work. Leaders cannot create an authoritative organization and effectively implement improvement science in that organization. Principals and superintendents are the formal authority, but leaders must be aware of how that authority is wielded "because in an environment of fear and surveillance, measurement is the tool of abuse. In an environment of learning, measurement is the tool of growth" (Berwick, 2021a). Educators want to do well and impact student learning and well-being. Educators need to be supported instead of sanctioned. It is important to avoid making improvement science work focused on compliance and control – failing into accountability patterns – and, instead, learning and improving as a collective unit.

Initiative Fatigue

The overwhelming commitment of people's time and a lack of coherent initiatives can create a barrier. Frustration and a learning curve may arise for people in a system that operates on urgency seemingly without a true purpose (see Chapter 7). Improvers may feel they are at the mercy of others' turbulent agenda and uncertain funding streams. Leaders who avoid the new-school-year-new-initiative tendency will find more authentic opportunities for systemic changes and staff commitment because they know the work will not be jettisoned after a single school year.

Individualism

The focus on individualism, commonly associated with schools and teachers, can be detrimental to building the capacity for continuous improvement. Continuous improvement work needs individuals to see the problems for improvement as collective responsibility toward which each member of the community has unique perspectives and assets. For example, in a district one of the authors supports with improvement, many educators at the schools remarked that one of the biggest benefits of working on improvement science in a network was that they were able to share ideas. The political and economic realities of the district created competition between schools, which motivated them to keep good ideas to themselves instead of sharing them widely. This mentality is at odds with systemic improvement and building organizational capacity; it is common in many districts and schools.

Human Capacity

The last challenge is the human capacity present in the school. Human capacity includes the number of staff, the number of open positions and attrition trends, the length of time the leader has been with the organization, and how well the leader knows the staff. In schools where the staff turns over, it is hard to gain momentum, especially when the people leaving are part of the improvement team. One author of this book worked with one skilled leader and improvement scientist who changed schools and districts with a plan to lead her new school through a similar problem of practice in a similar manner with a bundle of change ideas that had worked in her last school. Essentially, she was spreading her learning to a new school. She quickly came to realize that different circumstances in her new building were not yet conducive to continuous improvement and that she had to shift her focus to building professional and organizational capacity to lead change. This points to the importance of knowing your staff, including their strengths and tolerances for trying new things. The staff must know and trust the leader. Turnover and the churn of leaders and teachers in the education system complicates building the necessary capacity for improvement – often slowing down the improvement process.

In our work with schools and districts, we have found that a first-year principal, even one with experience leading in other settings, may not be able to lead continuous improvement work toward change. The leader needs time to understand the organization and to get to know the people. However, she can begin to lay the groundwork for the collection of data to understand schools' challenges and engage in problem formation that helps define the problem. This process will develop the norms, shared beliefs, trust, and culture discussed in this chapter.

CONCLUSION

This chapter describes how leaders of improvement help others learn about the improvement science process and meaningfully engage with the work, building and sustaining momentum for continuous improvement. Fundamentally, the leader must have an improvement mindset (Biag & Sherer, 2021). Effective change results from building the capacity to engage an improvement mindset and promoting an organization-wide culture of improvement. That culture should be based on adaptive change and should have established routines that support the development of a learner stance.

Social Relations

Trust and psychological safety are central capacities for improvement that is highly relational, collaborative, and collective. We emphasized the need to anticipate and embrace failures since failures reveal new learnings about a problem of practice and the need to explore DEIAJ. The culture must support social structures and routines that have healthy ways of dealing with change.

Improvement science is focused on inclusivity by gaining multiple perspectives, allowing people to share stories, and emphasizing change to inequitable systems and power dynamics. Galloway and Ishimaru (2020, p. 111) sum it up well.

> We argue that developing organizational leadership capacity for equity includes facilitating the collective capacity of not only teachers and staff, but also students, families, and community members, to lead for equity, with the aim of providing high-quality education for each student. It entails critical consciousness-raising and action, where the entire school community is engaged in inquiry, dialogue, and collaboration grounded in systemic and historical understandings of disparities. Such leadership creates a culture where teachers and staff regularly examine their own and others' practices and collaborate around equitable teaching and learning.

A leader needs to anticipate discomfort in engaging user-centered design work that may disrupt power structures and plan for supporting teachers and support staff through that discomfort. Leaders can do this by emphasizing the importance of non-judgmental thinking, showing their own willingness to interrogate existing beliefs and practices, developing implementers' will (enthusiasm, motivation, and commitment) to carry out innovation, and promoting aligning behavior and decision-making to a collectively-owned vision and strategy.

Moral Values

Capacity building emphasizes improvement mindsets, community norms and agreements, and working structures that prioritize teacher voice for teachers closest to the problem. Leaders and teams must show a willingness to interrogate existing beliefs and practices and develop implementers' will (enthusiasm, motivation, and commitment) to carry out innovation. Leaders need to promote aligning behavior and decision-making to a collectively-owned vision and strategy.

Instrumental Methods

A robust data infrastructure is essential to developing organizational capacity. Building capacity for improvement is about generating opportunities to create, learn, and adjust, independently and collectively. There must be an emphasis on improvement data – what it is, how to use it, and how to share it more broadly to learn. Structures (e.g., norms, space) need to be in place for exploring data in teams and for generating knowledge to be shared widely. This data culture and infrastructure is translated to change through adaptive practices that focus on systems change and improvement routines that provide space for improvement work. These data should help understand the system and help the improvement team connect the root causes of the problem to the solutions (e.g., change ideas) and to understand how to change the system to disrupt current oppressive systems through a recognition we are all implicated in the system, and we all have the agency to change it.

NELP and PSEL Connection Box for Educational Leadership Faculty

In addition to PSEL Standard 10, this chapter aligns closely with NELP Standards One and Seven. NELP Standard One, which focuses on the mission, vision, and core values, includes two components that state that "program completers understand and demonstrate the capacity to" (1.1) "collaboratively evaluate, develop, and communicate a school mission and vision designed to reflect a core set of values and priorities that include data use, technology, equity, diversity, digital citizenship, and community" and (1.2) "lead improvement processes that include data use, design, implementation, and evaluation."

NELP Standard Seven, which focuses on professional capacity, includes "the capacity to improve and engage staff in a collaborative professional culture, engage staff in professional learning, and improve systems of supervision, support, and evaluation that promote school improvement and student success." The components state that program completers understand and demonstrate the capacity to (7.2) "develop and engage staff in a collaborative professional culture designed to promote school improvement, teacher retention, and the success and well-being of each student and adult in the school" and (7.3) "personally engage in, as well as collaboratively engage school staff in, professional learning designed to promote reflection cultural responsiveness, distributed leadership, digital literacy, school improvement, and student success."

PSEL Six focused on professional capacity. Professional capacity is also mentioned in standard element 7e, where similar to NELP Standard Seven, the standard suggests that leaders, "develop and support open, productive, caring, and trusting working relationships among leaders, faculty, and staff to promote professional capacity and the improvement of practice," standard elements 9b and 9c which mentions "resources for professional capacity" as part of operations and management, and standard element 10f that discussed the leaders' ability to "assess and develop the capacity of staff to assess the value and applicability of emerging educational trends and the findings of research for the school and its improvement."

Finally, this chapter addresses NELP Standard Six and PSEL Standard Nine: "Operations and Management." NELP Standard Six states, "to improve management, communication, technology, school-level governance, and operation systems; to develop and improve data-informed and equitable school resource plans; and to apply laws, policies, and regulations." PSEL

Standard emphasizes that the leaders must: institute, manage, and monitor operations and administrative systems that promote the mission and vision of the school (9a); strategically manage staff resources, assigning and scheduling teachers and staff to roles and responsibilities that optimize their professional capacity to address each student's learning needs (9b); seek, acquire, and manage fiscal, physical, and other resources to support curriculum, instruction, and assessment; student learning community; professional capacity and community; and family and community engagement (9c); develop and maintain data and communication systems to deliver actionable information for classroom and school improvement (9g); and manage governance processes and internal and external politics toward achieving the school's mission and vision (9l).

BIBLIOGRAPHY

Anderson, E. (under review). Designing for equity: Adaptive change through continuous improvement. Submitted to *AERA Open*.

Anderson, E., Cunningham, K. W., & Richardson, J. W. (under review). Framework for implementing improvement science in a school district to support sustainable growth.

Anderson, E., & Davis, S. (under review). *Coaching for equity-focused continuous improvement: Facilitating lasting change*. Submitted to *Journal of Educational Change*.

Berwick, D. (2021a, February 12). Don Berwick on improvement as learning. *hthUnboxed*. High Tech High Graduate School of Education. https://hthunboxed.org/podcasts/213-don-berwick-on-improvement-as-learning/

Berwick, D. (2021b, June 17). Don Berwick on building courageous networks. *hthUnboxed*. High Tech High Graduate School of Education. https://hthunboxed.org/podcasts/s2e21-don-berwick-on-building-courageous-networks/

Biag, M., & Sherer, D. (2021). Getting better at getting better: Improvement dispositions in education. *Teachers College Record, 123*(4), 1–42. https://doi.org/10.1177/016146812112300402

Blank, R. K., & De las Alas, N. (2009). *The effects of teacher professional development on gains in student achievement: How meta analysis provides scientific evidence useful to education leaders*. Council of Chief State School Officers. www.ccsso.org/Documents/2009/Effects_of_Teacher_Professional_2009.pdf

Boudett, K. P., City, E. A., & Murnane, R. J. (2013). *Data wise: A step-by-step guide to using assessment results to improve teaching and learning*. Harvard Education Press.

Bryk, A. S., Gomez, L. M., Grunow, A., & Lemahieu, P. G. (2015). *Learning to improve: How America's schools can get better at getting better*. Harvard Education Press.

Bryk, A. S., Sebring, P. B., Allensworth, E., Luppescu, S., & Easton, J. Q. (2010). *Organizing schools for improvement: Lessons from Chicago*. University of Chicago Press.

Childress, S., Elmore, R. F., Grossman, A., & Johnson, S. M. (2007). *Managing school districts for high performance: Cases in public education leadership*. Harvard Education Press.

Collinson, V., & Cook, T. F. (2007). *Organizational learning: Improving learning, teaching, and leading in school systems*. SAGE Publications, Inc.

Darling-Hammond, L., Wei, R. C., Andree, A., Richardson, N., & Orphanos, S. (2009). *Professional learning in the learning profession*. National Staff Development Council. https://eric.ed.gov/?redir=http%3a%2f%2fwww.learningforward.org%2fdocs%2fpdf%2fnsdcstudy2009.pdf

Dixon, C. J., & Palmer, S. N. (2020). *Transforming educational systems toward continuous improvement: A reflection guide for K-12 leaders*. The Carnegie Foundation for the Advancement of Teaching. www.carnegiefoundation.org/wp-content/uploads/2020/04/Carnegie_Transform_EdSystems.pdf

Edmondson, A. C. (2019). The fearless organization: Creating psychological safety in the workplace for learning, innovation, and growth . John Wiley & Sons.

Edmondson, A. C., Higgins, M., Singer, S., & Weiner, J. (2016). Understanding psychological safety in health care and education organizations: A comparative perspective. *Research in Human Development, 13*(1), 65–83. https://doi.org/10.1080/15427609.2016.1141280

Elmore, R. F., Forman, M. L., Stosich, E. L., & Bocala, C. (2014). *The internal coherence assessment protocol & developmental framework: Building the organizational capacity for instructional improvement in schools*. Research Paper. Strategic Education Research Partnership. https://files.eric.ed.gov/fulltext/ED564482.pdf

Engeström, Y., & Sannino, A. (2010). Studies of expansive learning: Foundations, findings and future challenges. *Educational Research Review, 5*(1), 1–24. https://doi.org/10.1016/j.edurev.2009.12.002

Forman, M., Stosich, E. L., & Bocala, C. (2017). *The internal coherence framework: Creating the conditions for continuous improvement in schools*. Harvard Education Press.

Galloway, M. K., & Ishimaru, A. M. (2020). Leading equity teams: The role of formal leaders in building organizational capacity for equity. *Journal of Education for Students Placed at Risk (JESPAR), 25*(2), 107–125. https://doi.org/10.1080/10824669.2019.1699413

Garvin, D. A., Edmondson, A. C., & Gino, F. (2008). Is yours a learning organization?. *Harvard Business Review, 86*(3), 109. https://hbr.org/2008/03/is-yours-a-learning-organization

Grant, A. (2022). *Think again: The power of knowing what you don't know*. Viking.

Green, T. L. (2017). Community-based equity audits: A practical approach for educational leaders to support equitable community-school improvements. *Educational Administration Quarterly, 53*(1), 3–39. https://doi.org/10.1177/0013161x16672513

Greenhalgh, T., & Papoutsi, C. (2019). Spreading and scaling up innovation and improvement. *BMJ*, l2068. https://doi.org/10.1136/bmj.l2068

Harvard Diversity, Inclusion, and Belonging. (2023). *Calling in and calling out guide*. https://edib.harvard.edu/files/dib/files/calling_in_and_calling_out_guide_v4.pdf?m=1625683246

Haskell, J. E., Franck Cyr, L., & McPhail, G. (2007). Strengthening your facilitation skills: Level 1 curriculum. *Faculty and Staff Monograph Publications*, 89. https://digitalcommons.library.umaine.edu/fac_monographs/89

Higgins, M., Ishimaru, A., Holcombe, R., & Fowler, A. (2012). Examining organizational learning in schools: The role of psychological safety, experimentation, and leadership that reinforces learning. *Journal of Educational Change, 13*, 67–94. https://doi.org/10.1086/589317

Hinnant-Crawford, B. (2020). *Improvement science in education: A primer*. Spaulding.

Honig, M. I. (2008). District central offices as learning organizations: How sociocultural and organizational learning theories elaborate district central office administrators' participation in teaching and learning improvement efforts. *American Journal of Education, 114*(4), 627–664. https://doi.org/10.1086/589317

Honig, M. I., & Hatch, T. C. (2004). Crafting coherence: How schools strategically manage multiple, external demands. *Educational Researcher, 33*(8), 16–30. https://doi.org/10.3102/0013189x033008016

Irby, D. (2021). *Stuck improving: Racial equity and school leadership.* Harvard Education Press.

Kazemi, E., & Resnick, A. F. (2019). Organising schools for teacher and leader learning. In *International handbook of mathematics teacher education* (Vol. 3, pp. 393–420). Brill.

Khalifa, M. A., Gooden, M. A., & Davis, J. E. (2016). Culturally responsive school leadership: A synthesis of the literature. *Review of Educational Research, 86*(4), 1272–1311. https://doi.org/10.3102/0034654316630383

King, M. B., & Bouchard, K. (2011). The capacity to build organizational capacity in schools. *Journal of Educational Administration, 49*(6), 653–669. https://doi.org/10.1108/09578231111174802

Langley, G. L., Moen, R. D., Nolan, K. M., Nolan, T. W., Norman, C. L., Provost, L. P. (2009). *The improvement guide: A practical approach to enhancing organizational performance* (2nd ed.). Josey-Bass.

Militello, M., Rallis, S. F., & Goldring, E. B. (2009). *Leading with inquiry and action: How principals improve teaching and learning.* Corwin Press.

Murphy, J., & Meyers, C. V. (2008). *Turning around failing schools.* Corwin Press.

Nasir, N. (2011). *Racialized identities: Race and achievement among African American youth.* Stanford University Press.

National Policy Board for Educational Administration. (2015). *Professional standards for educational leaders 2015.* Author. www.npbea.org/psel/

National Policy Board for Educational Administration. (2018). *National Educational Leadership Preparation (NELP) program standards: Building level.* www.npbea.org

Newmann, F. M., Smith, B., Allensworth, E., & Bryk, A. S. (2001). Instructional program coherence: What it is and why it should guide school improvement policy. *Educational Evaluation and Policy Analysis, 23*(4), 297–321. https://doi.org/10.3102/01623737023004297

Roegman, R., Allen, D., Leverett, L., Thompson, S., & Hatch, T. (2019). *Equity visits: A new approach to supporting equity-focused school and district leadership.* Corwin.

Safir, S., & Dugan, J. (2021). *Street data a next-generation model for equity pedagogy and school transformation.* SAGE Publications.

Seeds for Change. *Consensus decision-making.* www.seedsforchange.org.uk/consensus

Singleton, G. E. (2014). *Courageous conversations about race: A field guide for achieving equity in schools.* Corwin Press.

Singleton, G. E., & Hays, C. (2008). Beginning courageous conversations about race. In M. Pollock (Ed.), *Everyday antiracism: Getting real about race in school.* The New Press.

Skrla, L., McKenzie, K. B., & Scheurich, J. J. (Eds.). (2009). *Using equity audits to create equitable and excellent schools.* Corwin Press.

Spillane, J. P. (2005). Distributed leadership. *The Educational Forum, 69*(2), 143–150. http://doi.org/10.1080/00131720508984678

Spillane, J. P., Halverson, R., & Diamond, J. B. (2001). Investigating school leadership practice: A distributed perspective. *Educational Researcher, 30*(3), 23–28. https://doi.org/10.3102/0013189x030003023

TED. (2022). Don't call people out: Call them in| Loretta Ross [video]. *YouTube.* www.youtube.com/watch?v=xw_720iQDss

United Nations. (2023). *Capacity-building*. www.un.org/en/academic-impact/capacity-building

United States Department of Education. (2015, January). *Conceptualizing capacity building*. www2.ed.gov/about/offices/list/osers/osep/rda/cipp2-conceptualizing-capacity-building-2-10-15.pdf

Wenger, E. (1999). *Communities of practice: Learning, meaning, and identity*. Cambridge University Press.

Wheatley, M. (2009). *Turning to one another: Simple conversations to restore hope to the Zumpe, E., & Aramburo, C. (In press). Developing enabling conditions for continuous improvement: Building foundational team "habits of mind." In E. Anderson & S. Hayes (Eds.), Continuous improvement: A leadership process for school improvement. Information Age Publishing. future*. Berrett-Koehler.

CHAPTER 10

Policy Considerations for Continuous Improvement

with David Osworth

Chapter Highlights

1) Leaders bridge standards, policies, improvement science, and organizational practices.
2) Continuous improvement is outlined in the PSEL and NELP standards as a leadership practice and in some states those standards are required directly or indirectly.
3) Federal, state, and local policies, specifically the Every Student Succeeds Act (ESSA), create opportunities for equity-oriented continuous improvement.

CHAPTER DESCRIPTION

This chapter offers a policy context and rationale for a continuous improvement approach in leadership. Federal policy, state policies, and alignment with the PSEL and NELP standards can be a complement to both integrating change ideas as well as overcoming barriers related to both existing policy and political context challenges. This chapter will offer suggestions on how the leadership can lean on policy to help mitigate, reduce, or remove improvement barriers.

INTRODUCTION: DEFINING CONTINUOUS IMPROVEMENT THROUGH POLICY OPPORTUNITIES

Every improvement requires change, but change is challenging. Deviating from the status quo is difficult. As a leader, you interact with people daily and make decisions with or on the behalf of people with whom you work. With a solid

DOI: 10.4324/9781003389279-13

amount of confidence, we predict you could tell stories illustrating how efforts to facilitate changes in your school or district are met with resistance. Think about one time you had a great idea, your enthusiasm grew, and you wanted to share it with others so the idea could begin to become a reality. Then you tried to get a group of people on board: What happened? What were the successful ways you were able to cultivate enthusiasm in others to come along with you toward this idea? What were the not so successful ways?

You are familiar with PSEL's Standard 10, which includes finding "coherence among improvement efforts and all aspects of school organization, programs, and services." Opportunity to cohere changes and improvements with formalized policy exists because policy informs practice and identifies areas of prioritization. As an educational leader or someone who helps support and develop educational leaders, you are an active stakeholder or policy actor in implementing policy (Fowler, 2013; Mitra, 2018). Policy can support a continuous improvement mindset and approach. Three key areas to explore the nexus of policy, standards, and improvement include

1) Continuous improvement at different policy levels.
2) Continuous improvement in policy and in NELP/PSEL.
3) Educational leaders' bridge of leadership standards with continuous improvement and their professional practices and goals.

Leaders can facilitate change and ease the accompanying angst by explicitly situating the need for change as connected to a larger schema or system. This connection strengthens the rationale for change in others. A connective tissue for shepherding change is linking change to your organization's values, mission, and vision (See Chapter 3) and then articulating how those also align with policy language.

Let's start with surfacing connections between the common values and goals for your organization (e.g., mission, vision) and the improvement focus of your school. If an improvement focus doesn't connect to your school's mission, vision, goals, and values, it is probably not advantageous to focus on that change; you need to abandon that idea and direct your efforts elsewhere. Making a logical connection that demonstrates the *why* behind the change and connects *how* it aligns with *what* the school community holds as important, reveals the worthiness of the change, engages authentically with the goals, mission, vision, and values and conducts a litmus test for if the change reflects those goals, mission, vision, and values. You should be able to craft a sentence that reads something like the statement in Figure 10.1.

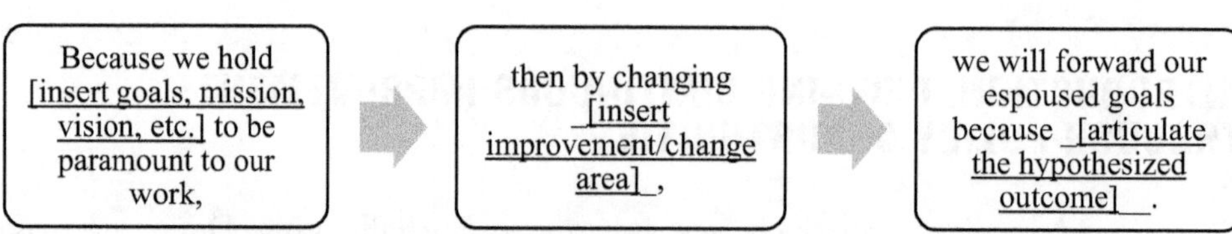

Figure 10.1 Connecting Change to Organizational Goals, Mission, and/or Vision.

Source: Created by author.

A leader determines how policy catalyzes improvement efforts by connecting an improvement focus to your organization's values and goals. Policies are important to consider since they can provide one or more of the following:

- Legitimacy to the improvement focus
- An argument for continuing to work on your improvement focus if external stakeholder voices challenge the efforts
- Guidance
- Technical assistance
- Resources (e.g., funding).

Federal policy language explicitly calls for continuous improvement approaches to addressing problems of practice in state ESSA plans. To meet federal requirements, individual states, to varying degrees, have crafted formal policy language prioritizing continuous improvement (Cunningham & Osworth, 2023). A determination of the degree to which there are implicit or other opportunities to engage in continuous improvement while connecting to the standards and policies can provide you the policy connection to supporting your improvement work.

Defining Policy

We are going to use McGuinn's and Mannas's (2013) broad definition of policy. Policy is "the array of initiatives, programs, laws, regulations, and rules that the governance system chooses to produce" (p. 9). Sometimes policies are formal. Codified laws, regulations, and rules can be considered capital "P" policies. They are written and approved and distributed in some way (e.g., laws, handbooks). Policies might be codified by the federal Department of Education (e.g., ESSA), state legislatures (e.g., South Carolina Read to Succeed Act), or local jurisdictions (e.g., city ordinance). Many states' policies require alignment to a set of leadership standards that impact the decision-making and practice of both administrators as well as those who prepare them for this role (i.e., educational leadership preparation faculty) (Anderson & Reynolds, 2015). Standards such as PSEL and NELP are often included in formal policy language.

Other times, policies refer to a norm or routine. These policies are not laws; they are initiatives, programs, or accepted practices. The policies may not be written down or formalized. We can call those lower case "p" policies. Sometimes norms or organizational habits or practices are misidentified as a formal policy but in actuality, it is a norm.

Both capital "P" policies and lower case "p" policies are important to identify as you navigate policy spaces.

Ensure that the policy is "real" before making decisions. Individuals or groups (e.g., committees) are sometimes convinced something is a policy, but when trying to locate the policy, there is nothing corroborating the claim. People simply heard something was policy. That lower "p" policy is entrenched in the

ACTION INVENTORY 10.1 IS IT REALLY BIG "P" POLICY?

Off the top of your head, select two to five policies that impact your continuous improvement work as an educational leader. Then, for each one, analyze whether it is an official, codified policy (P). Identify where it is in documentation. Then, star those that connect (directly or indirectly) to your improvement work.

Policy	Policy (capital P) or policy (lower case p)	Where is the policy written (i.e., source)?
1. Example: Teachers are expected to respond to emails within 36 hours.	policy	Cannot find it anywhere. Verbally communicated in staff meetings by an AP
2. Example: Any student who is identified as multilingual is automatically enrolled in a pull-out class for 60 min a week.	Policy	District handbook and board notes from 4/1/2007
3. Example: Teachers turn their work computer and charger into the technology interventionist before they leave for summer.	policy	Not written anywhere. Verbally communicated via email by technology interventionist
4. Example: Students turn their school computer and charger into the technology interventionist during the last two days of the school year.	Policy	District handbook School handbook Contract families sign when picking up their computer and charger
5.		
6.		
7.		

organizational practices without anyone checking to see if that policy actually existed. (Sometimes it didn't!). We bring this distinction up to highlight the level of flexibility in policy that potentially exists in different spaces and on different issues. It behooves educational leaders to investigate their policy environment in order to guide their school community on accurate information.

Policy and Preparation Program Accreditation: Considering the PSEL and NELP Standards

NELP standards and PSEL are corresponding standards. The NELP standards regulate programs that prepare educational leaders. These standards articulate the content to include in a high-quality, impactful leadership development experience for aspiring educational leaders. NELP standards can be adopted by a preparation program independently or in conjunction with program accreditation expectations. PSEL informs what a school leader should know and be able to do. These standards are used for determining if individual leaders have the skills to obtain licensure or are prepared to lead in schools and districts.

Standards, whether or not offi cially codifi ed, are policy. NELP or PSEL standards may or may not be categorized as formal policy documents. Anderson's and Reynold's 50 state analysis (2015) reveal that many states require alignment to leadership standards. Adherence to a particular set of standards is directly or indirectly included in formal policy. The explicit naming of NELP or PSEL standards in state rules and regulations is direct inclusion.

Institutions of higher education, such as the university Ava is enrolled in, go through a process to get accredited by an external accrediting body. Broadly, accreditation means that an "institution maintains a certain level of educational standards" as officially determined by a recognized accreditation agency (Department of Homeland Security, n.d.). This accrediting body stipulates expectations and awards accreditation worthiness accordingly. The accreditation body, Council for the Accreditation of Educator Preparation (CAEP) oversees accreditation. CAEP accredits over 400 educator preparation programs (i.e., teacher and administrator) in 45 states (CAEP, 2021) CAEP uses the NELP standards in their accreditation process, which can therefore, make NELP an indirect or implicit policy requirement for those states who require CAEP accreditation. Although a state's formal education policy may not "officially" include NELP in its directive, the standards are still applicable since an oversight body relies on them.

Although some states may codify the use of certain standards, others may not, but programs may still choose to use NELP. In some locales, the standards are guidance documents for program development. Other states create these standards. Notably, states like Iowa, for example, use the Iowa Standards for School Leaders which are adapted from NELP (see Iowa Department of Education, n.d.). It can be a little fuzzy, as you have perhaps gathered, on what may constitute "official" and direct policy requirements and what is "indirect" policy.

ACTION INVENTORY 10.2 CROSS WALK ACROSS EDUCATIONAL LEADERSHIP AND CONTINUOUS IMPROVEMENT. WHAT DOES YOUR STATE REQUIRE?

State Name	Require PSEL or State Standards Aligned to PSEL	Require NELP	CI as Process (not only outcome)	State Name	Require PSEL	Require NELP	CI as Process (not only outcome)
Alabama		CAEP	o	Montana		CAEP	✓
Alaska	x	CAEP	o	Nebraska	x	CAEP	o
Arizona	x	CAEP	o	Nevada	State Dept. of Ed.	UNLV uses in program	o
Arkansas	x	CAEP	x	New Hampshire	x	CAEP	o
California		CAEP	o	New Jersey	x	CAEP	o
Colorado		CAEP	o	New Mexico		CAEP	o
Connecticut		CAEP	o	New York	x	CAEP	x
Delaware	x	CAEP	x	North Carolina		CAEP	o
Florida		CAEP	o	North Dakota		CAEP	x
Georgia	x	CAEP	✓	Ohio		CAEP	o
Hawaii		CAEP	✓	Oklahoma		CAEP	✓
Idaho	x	CAEP	o	Oregon	x	CAEP	o
Illinois	x	CAEP	x	Pennsylvania		CAEP	x

Indiana	x	CAEP	o	Rhode Island	Yes		o
Iowa	x	Iowa Dept. of Ed. (their accrediting body) uses NELP	o	South Carolina		CAEP	o
Kansas	x	CAEP	o	South Dakota		CAEP	o
Kentucky	x	CAEP	o	Tennessee		CAEP	✓
Louisiana	x	CAEP	o	Texas		CAEP	o
Maine	x	CAEP	o	Utah	x	CAEP	o
Maryland	x	CAEP	o	Vermont	x	CAEP	x
Massachusetts		CAEP	o	Virginia		CAEP	o
Michigan	x	CAEP	x	Washington	x		✓
Minnesota	x	CAEP	x	West Virginia	x	CAEP	x
Mississippi	x*	CAEP	o	Wisconsin			✓
Missouri	x	CAEP	o	Wyoming	x	CAEP	o

Notes: Washington, DC and Puerto Rico have CAEP institutions.
CAEP Accreditation label determined b https://caepnet.org/~/media/Files/caep/governance/caep-annualreport2021.pdf?la=en
PSEL Standard Alignment determined by https://principalstandards.gtlcenter.org/compare-state-results?
www.ksde.org/Agency/Division-of-Learning-Services/Teacher-Licensure-TL/Educator-Evaluations/Non-KEEP-Districts
www.schools.utah.gov/file/dad2122c-490f-4987-b9d3-799ce3771e44?TSPD_101_R0=08a7ed7a88ab20004d05962dbd1570056 88277cd07e4966f695a5c768c58a95306058b4e8e9698d608418448b214300087ddc76c6dd2502c08d7d5fea124afabd1d6ee28c2 a0e591c3c0c46166469daac3ffc2d25683147023b56ba37b822181
www.npbea.org/?da_image=official-adoption-map

CI in State ESSA Plan determined using Cunningham and Osworth (2023). (✓ = commitment; x = emerging commitment; o = not committed)

Review Action Inventory 10.2. Does your state directly or indirectly require alignment to NELP or PSEL standards? What implications does your state's leadership standards and accreditation requirements have on your leadership within a continuous improvement space? If your state is directly or indirectly requiring alignment to standards as part of policy, how might that support your improvement efforts?

Federal Policy and Continuous Improvement and Improvement Science

ESSA replaced NCLB in 2015; it is the most recent iteration of the ESEA, a federal education policy originally signed into law during the Lyndon B. Johnson administration in 1965. ESEA goes through periods of revision and renewal. ESSA seeks to redistribute control back to individual state education agencies (SEAs) and aims to remedy some of NCLB's more unattainable aspects (Mathis & Trujillo, 2016). ESSA provides greater flexibility in how states meet federal requirements.

As we move from the macro level of education policy (federal) down to the micro levels (school districts and individual schools), we see how the layers of education policy are operationalized and particularized for specific school contexts. Under ESSA we can think of the various layers of policy as an inverted pyramid. At the top, the federal level provides larger and perhaps more broad expectations for what schools in the United States need to achieve. This is further refined at the state levels with the creation of ESSA state plans that articulate the SEA's specific areas of focus. At the local level (including both school districts and individual schools) these policies are embedded within the specific local contexts of the district. Administrators, both at the district and school level, have the challenging task of creating and implementing policies that serve their school districts while also meeting the expectations of both the state and federal policy (Honig, 2006a, 2006b; Honig & Hatch, 2004). In Figure 10.2, we show how the policy levels are linked. You'll notice that the federal level connects to both K–12 and higher education contexts.

State Policy and Continuous Improvement and Improvement Science

ESSA requires SEAs to submit ESSA-based plans to the U.S. Department of Education; states ensure adherence with federal guidelines to secure the funding tied to policy expectations. The Department of Education provides templates and guidelines for these plans. The process is standardized, and plans undergo a peer review process (Osworth & Cunningham, 2023). State ESSA plans are publicly available and guide school districts (local policy makers) on compliance with the federal policy. Since school leaders need to be aware of and deliver on ESSA requirements, you may already be familiar with multiple components of the Act.

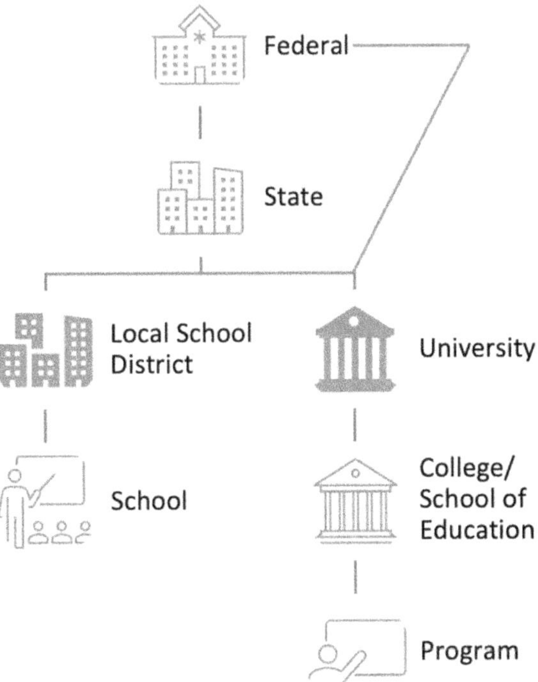

Figure 10.2 Levels of Education Policy.
Source: Created by authors.

State plans approved by the US Department of Education act as a roadmap for how each state addresses ESSA requirements, including implications for professional educators and decision makers defining improvement. An analysis of ESSA policy documents – the *Revised State Template for the Consolidated State Plan* (i.e., *State Template)* and the *State Plan Peer Review Criteria* (i.e., *Review Criteria*) – provided by the US Department of Education by all 50 states, Washington, DC and Puerto Rico revealed these documents did not explicitly include continuous improvement as a federal expectation for practice but the term "continuous improvement" was prevalent across all state plans (Cunningham & Osworth, under review). States typically did not emphasize continuous improvement as a process, like we have framed it in this book (i.e., improving systems). Instead, states focused on overemphasis improvement outcomes rather than improving systems through improvement science. This trend is likely left over from the previous expectations of NCLB (Mathis & Trujillo, 2016).

Much like NCLB, the focus solely on outcomes assumes that by simply collecting measures of all students, all students will improve (Darling-Hammond, 2007). To our readers serving in states such as California, Montana, and South Carolina, you are beholden to a state plan focused on reporting accountability as quantitative evidence to state and federal levels. So, in order for you to meet your stated improvement goals that value user voice, community input, and improving systems, you may find yourself seeking support outside of state-provided resources. The responsibility for using methods and mindsets that treat continuous improvement as process, will land on the shoulders of school level educators, namely educational leaders. Conversely, when specific improvement science tools are included in state plans, it signals the importance of creating knowledge focused on the *why* specific areas of improving the system are effective rather than solely focusing on outcomes (e.g., test scores and graduation rates).

Although federal or state policymakers may not ask you to use improvement science, there is likely room to connect improvement goals and efforts to required policy. That's encouraging and exciting, right? Variation exists in how SEAs articulated the use of improvement science to meet the need for continuous improvement. A handful of state plans contain notable improvement science-specific language (see Cunningham & Osworth, 2023). These states not only emphasize continuous improvement but incorporate the methods or instruments of improvement science into their ESSA plans. Hawaii, Tennessee, and Washington reference improvement science explicitly and include marquee improvement approaches such as NICs and iterative cycles (e.g., PDSA). Hawaii, Pennsylvania, and Delaware each include the PDSA process in their plan. Similarly, language in Michigan's plan states, "We plan to integrate a focus on process data, and implementation data, so that districts can engage in the gather, study, plan, do cycle more frequently" (p. 86). Some ESSA state plans note the use of NICs at the state level. NICs allow for collaboration across different contexts as they approach the same problem of practice. In Georgia's ESSA plan, NICs were specifically identified as a tool to increase literacy across the state, and many states regardless of the density of improvement science language in their state plans showed the potential for networked learning (Cunningham & Osworth, under review). For your reference, you can use state plans from Arkansas, Georgia, Hawaii, Oklahoma, Montana, Tennessee, Washington, and Wisconsin for direction on explicitly including improvement science centric elements into their ESSA plan.

Local Level: Adhering to State Level and Context-Specific Requirements

Local K–12 education leaders should be well versed in their SEA's ESSA plan and understand how their policies can support school leaders in complying with state expectations while improving systems for students in their schools. There is an opportunity to create policies that bridge context-specific continuous improvement needs while meeting the state and federal expectations. In states where improvement science is present in the state plan, it may come more naturally for LEA policies to leverage these same instruments to meet the state and federal requirements.

Policy Barriers to Adopting an Improvement Science Mindset

School leaders have a challenging job. A leader needs to be nimble and savvy to navigate the multiple layers of policies (i.e., federal, state, and district) while attuning to the implementation of policy to meet the specific needs of their students and school communities. The following are two barriers (and potential strategies to address them) that you have or will face related to improvement science and policy. It may be advantageous to understand your state-specific ESSA plan so you can bridge policy requirements and student needs. For school leaders adopting an improvement science approach this may be more easily aligned if they are in a state where there is explicit alignment to NELP and PSEL and/or improvement science language directly in their ESSA plan (e.g., Arkansas, Georgia, Hawaii). Do not worry, hope is not lost if you find yourself in a state that has little to no improvement science instrumentation or language articulated in the state plan. There are absolutely opportunities for school leaders to use improvement science as a vehicle for continuous improvement efforts.

Barrier 1: Existing Policy Language

Federal policy invites each state to articulate priorities and directions and how they plan to meet the requirements ESSA mandates. Because states craft plans that can look different from one another, some administrators might, at first glance, find their state plan's language to be a barrier to the work. For example, state plans focused on accountability measures may place the emphasis of improvement on outcomes rather than inviting a perspective that sees improvement as a process or approach (Cunningham & Osworth, under review). The perception is there is less latitude to engage in the improvement process of *disciplined inquiry*. SEAs emphasize fast paced responses. Bryk and colleagues (2015) note that improvement in public education is characterized by, "implement fast, learn slow, and burn goodwill as you go" (p. 113). Changes to how to improve may be destined to fail as they are not fully fleshed out, leading to an adopt, attack, abandon cycle becoming the norm in school improvement (Rohanna, 2017).

Suggestions to Address Barrier 1

School leaders can use the tools of improvement science as the vehicle to achieve outcomes within the expectations and goals of the SEA's plan. Recall that California's ESSA plan does not prioritize improvement science. However, Bryk (2020) noted that the school district in Fresno, California, used improvement science, to identify the leaky pipeline from their schools to college enrollment. They implemented change ideas that ultimately helped to increase the conversion of high school graduates to college students.

Every ESSA state plan requires measures of interim progress toward a specific goal. Jamie was an EdD student in Ava's inquiry group. Recently, she shared with Ava how her district aligns their goals with their state's ESSA state plan requirements when determining their school-based school improvement plan goals. Her school district is concerned about a traditional accountability measure, the high school graduation rate. An expectation included in the state's ESSA plan is to make measurable interim progress of a 5% increase in the graduation rate each year. A team of district administrators convened a group of high school principals, assistant principals, school counselors, and social workers and tasked this group with figuring out how attain this 5% increase.

The school leaders wanted to understand how the current systems result in each school's current graduation rate. The group decided at each of their respective high schools, they would assemble a team of leaders and teachers to tackle this problem of practice. At Jamie's school, their team prioritized being user-centered in their understanding of the current problem (Langley et al., 2009). Therefore, with changes to increase graduation rate impacting students and classroom teachers, they recruited representatives from each of these groups to be involved in their improvement process. After assembling this group, they gathered data on the problem and completed a fishbone diagram. This process surfaced root causes of the graduation rate from different perspectives. They created a driver diagram to capture their theory of improvement around low graduation rates. Jamie shared with Ava that despite the state not explicitly suggesting improvement science be used, the leaders took it upon themselves to harness the effectiveness of improvement science methods to adhere to the ESSA state plan.

Several weeks later, Ava checked in with Jamie. Jamie described how after her team drafted a driver diagram, they were able to land on what part of the system to begin improving. A process of disciplined inquiry cycles revealed promising directions in changes to make (Bryk et al., 2015). Using tools like the PDSA cycle Jamie's team began to measure the effectiveness of strategies. What her team noticed was that in her school, a significant sized group of students who were not graduating on time were also not meeting the English and Language Arts (ELA) requirements. They also noticed the trend was evident as early as ninth grade. This led to a change idea, additional push-in instruction in certain classes in ninth grade to help support ELA teachers as they address the needs of all their students. The PDSA cycles allowed Jamie's team to be mindful and deliberate and allowed for course corrections and additional testing to maximize the improvement to the systems. Their change idea started small. It helped improvers learn fast and will give them valuable information as they work to scale it to the rest of the school while also adhering to their policy requirements.

Jamie also mentioned to Ava that because other high schools in their district were working on meeting the same district ESSA goal, she was able to share and learn from the other schools' work and improvement discoveries (Bryk et al., 2015; Langley et al., 2009). Bryk and colleagues (2015) noted, "when many more individuals, operating across diverse contexts, are drawn together in a shared learning enterprise, the capacity grows exponentially" (p. 143). The ability to form an NIC within a district or even across a state provides an opportunity to utilize improvement science when working toward the expectations set forth in the state's ESSA plan. You can work with your school district's leaders like Jamie did. You could also expand to connect with others in your state who are tackling similar problems of practice that are linked to state policy goals. Working across a variety of contexts with more people increases the ability to learn.

Barrier 2: Sociopolitical Climates

Across the United States, school leaders are navigating contentious sociopolitical climates. In some states, equitable schooling is under attack by parents and political groups. The use of improvement science backed by policy provides school leaders a way to navigate difficult environments.

Suggestions to Address Barrier 2

ESSA focuses on increasing equitable outcomes for specific student groups; ESSA plans are required to provide plans for increasing achievement for emergent bilingual students, migratory students, and students with disabilities, among others. Federal and state policies (such as ESSA) require attention to various outcomes for student groups, allowing for school leaders to engage in equity work backed by policy. This policy creates the imperative for the work and can be cited when leaders receive pushback from community or political groups. Federal policy may be a point of persuasion to help leaders be confident. The state created and received federal approval of their ESSA plan that addresses goals related to the improvement of outcomes for students, especially marginalized reporting groups. Therefore, one strategy can include making this connection, as well as the intersection with other policies (e.g., IDEA, Title IX) obvious for those in your school community.

Connecting policy to improving systems intersects with ways in which improvement science can help public schools address persistent equity issues so every student receives a high-quality education (Biag, 2019; Bryk, 2020). When using improvement science school leaders must ask themselves, "what works? for whom? and under what conditions?" (Bryk et al., 2015, pp. 13–14). These questions allow us to not only determine specific underserved populations but also to interrogate the systems and structures creating these inequities. Engaging in improvement science shifts the focus away from individual students and to the system. Deficit framing of students and myths of meritocracy are mitigated, and systems change can occur.

Improvement science, when used correctly, becomes a powerful tool for equity. It may be clear for you to see the connection between your improvement goals and state policy, but it may not be clear for everyone. Figure 10.3 is a visual tool you can use to help illustrate the connections. Completing this tool will

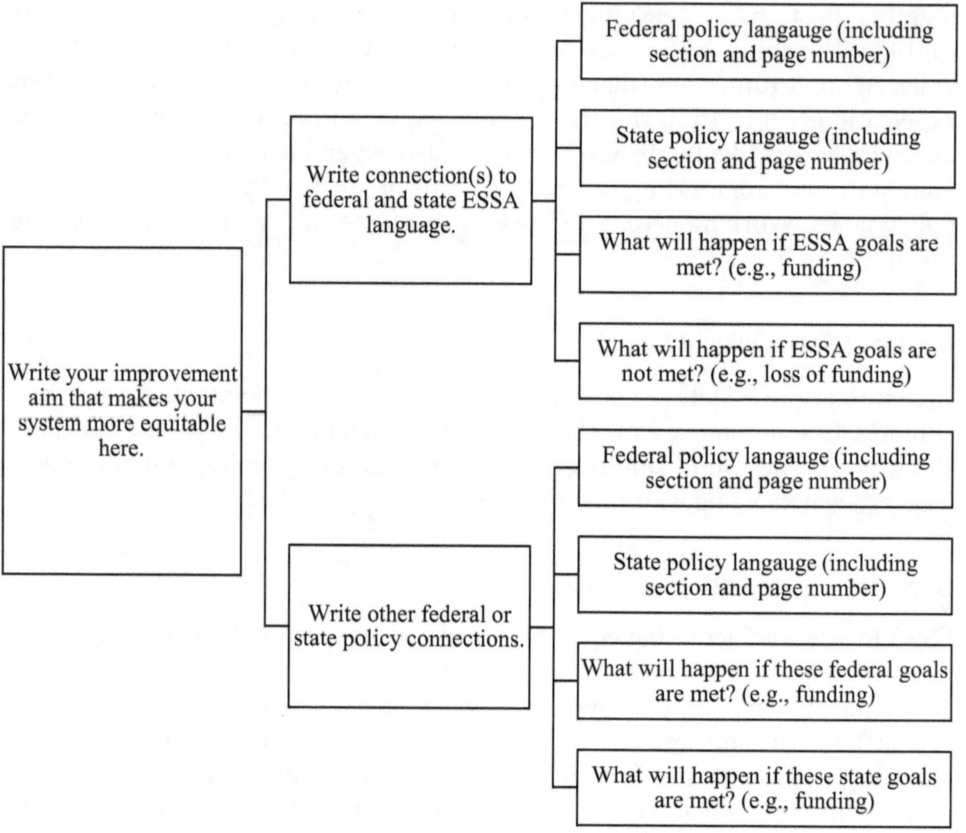

Figure 10.3 Aligning Policy with Improvement Aims.

Source: Created by authors.

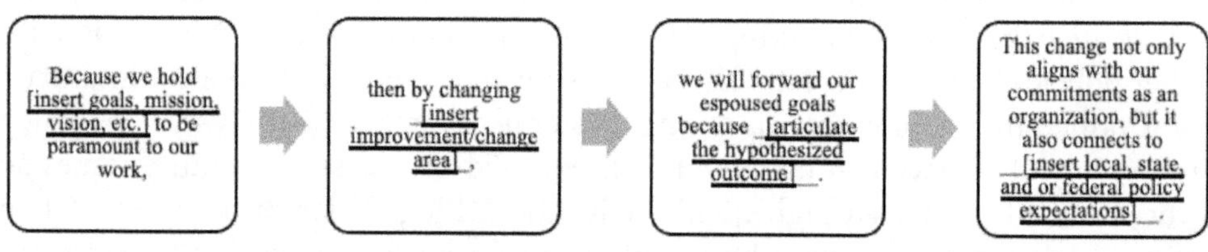

Figure 10.4 Connecting Change to Organizational Goals, Mission, and/or Vision With Policy.

Source: Created by authors.

require you to dig into your school or district and your State ESSA plan, so you may need to dedicate time to populating this protocol.

Now, you can add to the sentence you crafted earlier. You can extend your change idea's alignment to your goals, mission, and vision with a federal, state, or local policy alignment connection. Figure 10.4 shows how this extension might read.

Ava facilitated a proactive approach to connecting her team's improvement efforts to policy. She asked Marcus and Randy to operate as connectors. Connectors lift up those places where improvement work and policy exist. They answered the questions in the third column in Action Inventory 10.3. While Marcus and Randy were working on the answers to the connector questions,

Ava, Isabella, and Chris started work as communicators. Although they needed some of Marcus's and Randy's answers before finalizing their communication artifacts, they spent time identifying their audiences and building out drafts of messages to include in newsletters, board meetings, or handouts to families/caregivers and community members. Ava wanted to ensure she and her team were crafting the message and cohesively finding the connection to policies rather than waiting for a potentially inaccurate message to be crafted by someone outside of her school or district.

ACTION INVENTORY 10.3 CONNECTORS AND COMMUNICATORS

Role	Action	Questions to Answer
Connector	Find direct and indirect connections to existing policy that supports the direction of your improvement team. Develop a visual representation of this connection (e.g., one-page handout, figure).	1. How does our state ESSA plan connect to our improvement work? a. What benefits exist from adhering to the ESSA plan? b. What risks are we taking by not adhering to the ESSA plan? 2. How do other federal policies and laws connect to our improvement work? a. What benefits exist from adhering to the federal policies? b. What risks are we taking by not adhering to the federal policies?
Communicator	Develop a simple but effective way(s) to describe what, why, and how your improvement work relates to policy. Share the deliverables from the "Connector" section of this table to relevant people linked to your improvement work.	1. What is the improvement work you are doing? 2. What is the why behind the improvement work? 3. In what ways does your work connect to other goals (e.g., policy, mission, vision, goals)? 4. How will you make progress on the improvement work connected to policy?

How do you see your role as a leader, connector, and communicator of policy and improvement in your context?

CONCLUSION

For some of you, the way ESSA state policy is written, engaging in improvement science will have a more direct and straightforward approach. For instance, our colleagues in Georgia and Arkansas can lean on the language in state policy as a direct rationale for addressing problems of practice in incremental ways and using improvement science to do so. It would behoove practicing administrators to be familiar with what is included in their state's ESSA Consolidated Plan. When changes are posed, and administrators are receiving pushback, being able to connect the changes to the mission and vision of the school as well as alignment to federal and state policy strengthens arguments to support your goals and improvement processes.

Moral Values

Federal and state policy, including the standards threaded throughout this book, and the implementation of ESSA as the paramount education policy, support equity and justice centered missions, visions, values, and goals. The PSEL and NELP standards empathize being moral, ethical, and culturally responsive. There is explicit language that requires equity, social justice, and a cultural responsiveness to be foremost in how leaders are prepared and licensed. Educational leaders are required to provide opportunities for historically marginalized groups to achieve better outcomes. An improvement science process focused on changing the system to better educate all students.

Social Relations

Policy implementation is the job of all educators. Improvement science is a way to work together across schools, districts, and states to implement improvement within the parameters of both capital "P" policy and lower case "p" policy. The networked learning discussed in this chapter and throughout the book is a way to effectively and equitably enact the policies that regulate school systems.

Instrumental Methods

Continuous improvement is used to fulfill the standards and current federal policy. ESSA provides overarching requirements for public schools in the United States, and each SEA is responsible for a plan that outlines how to meet the requirements of the policy. School leaders are required to engage with the various levels of policy by complying with district, state, and federal requirements. Implementing policy impacts practice (Mitra, 2018). This top-down-bottom-up enterprise of policymaking can position educators as both policy creation influencers and policy enactors. Which direction your role is taking at any given time is not necessarily a critical distinction when engaged in the work of improvement. What is important, however, is the awareness you, as educational leaders, have the power to be a policy actor.

NELP and PSEL Connection Box for Educational Leadership Faculty

This chapter bridges state and federal policies with leaders' continuous improvement efforts. PSEL Ten asks leaders to use a systems perspective to help with "coherence among improvement efforts." Policy is one driving element of a system. Systems and policy considerations are also directly or indirectly included in NELP standards One, Three, Four, Five, Six. Standard Five specifically asks for leaders to develop abilities to "*collaboratively engage the larger organizational and policy context to advocate for the needs of their school and community.*"

BIBIOGRAPHY

Anderson, E., & Reynolds, A. L. (2015). *Research-based policy for principal preparation program approval and licensure* (U.C.E.A., Ed.). University of Virginia. www.ucea.org/resource/policy-reports/

Biag, M. (2019). Navigating the improvement journey with an equity compass. In R. Crow, B. N. Hinnant-Crawford, & D. T. Spaulding (Eds.), *The educational leader's guide to improvement science* (pp. 91–124). Meyers Press.

Bryk, A. S. (2020). *Improvement in action: Advancing quality in America's schools.* Harvard Education Press.

Bryk, A. S., Gomez, L. M., Grunow, A., & LeMahieu, P. G. (2015). *Learning to improve: How America's schools get better at getting better.* Harvard Education Press.

CAEP. (2020). *Vision, mission, and goals.* https://caepnet.org/about/vision-mission-goals

CAEP. (2021). *2021 annual report.* https://caepnet.org/~/media/Files/caep/governance/caep-annualreport2021.pdf?la=en

Cunningham, K. M. W. & Osworth, D.* (Under Review). Improvement Science and the Every Student Succeeds Act: An Analysis of the Consolidated State Plans.

Cunningham, K. M. W., & Osworth, D. (2023). A proposed typology of states' improvement science focus in their state ESSA plans. *Educational Policy Analysis Archives.*

Darling-Hammond, L. (2007). Race, inequality, and educational accountability: The irony of "no child left behind." *Race Ethnicity and Education, 10*(3), 245–260. https://doi.org/10.1080/13613320701503207

Department of Homeland Security. (n.d.). *The basics of school accreditation.* https://studyinthestates.dhs.gov/the-basics-of-school-accreditation

Fowler, F. (2013). *Policy studies for educational leaders: An introduction.* Pearson

Honig, M. I. (2006a). Street-level bureaucracy revisited: Frontline district central-office administrators as boundary spanners in education policy implementation. *Educational Evaluation and Policy Analysis, 28*(4), 357–383. https://doi.org/10.3102/01623737028004357

Honig, M. I. (Ed.). (2006b). *New directions in education policy implementation: Confronting complexity.* State University of New York Press.

Honig, M. I., & Hatch, T. C. (2004). Crafting coherence: How schools strategically manage multiple, external demands. *Educational Researcher, 33*(8), 16–30. https://doi.org/10.3102/0013189X033008016

Iowa Department of Education. (n.d.). *Iowa standards for school leaders.* https://educateiowa.gov/pk-12/educator-quality/administrator-quality#Iowa_Standards_for_School_Leaders

Langley, G. J., Moen, R. D., Nolan, K. M., Nolan, T. W., Norman, C. L., & Provost, L. P. (2009). *The improvement guide* (2nd ed.). Jossey-Bass.

Mathis, W. J., & Trujillo, T. M. (2016). *Lessons from NCLB for the every student succeeds act* [White Paper]. National Education Policy Center. Retrieved January 3, 2021 from http://nepc.colorado.edu/publication/lessons-from-NCLB

McGuinn, P., & Manna, P. (2013). Education governance in America: Who leads when everyone is in charge. In P. Manna & P. McGuinn (Eds.), *Education governance for the twenty-first century: Overcoming the structural barriers to school reform* (pp. 1–20). Brookings Institution Press.

Mitra, D. (2018). *Educational change and the political process.* Routledge.

National Policy Board for Educational Administration. (2015). *Professional standards for educational leaders 2015.* Author. www.npbea.org/psel/

National Policy Board for Educational Administration. (2018). *National Educational Leadership Preparation (NELP) program standards: Building level.* www.npbea.org

Nevada Department of Education. (2021). *NEPF/PSEL crosswalk: The nevada educator performance framework for school administrators and the professional standards for educational leaders.* https://doe.nv.gov/uploadedFiles/ndedoenvgov/content/Educator_Effectiveness/Educator_Develop_Support/NEPF/NEPF_PSEL%20Administrator%20Crosswalk%20(2).pdf

Osworth, D., & Cunningham, K. M. W. (Forthcoming). Improvement science and the every student succeeds act: An analysis of state guidance documents. *Planning and Changing, 51*(1/2).

Rohanna, K. (2017). Breaking the "adopt, attack, abandon" cycle: A case for improvement: Science in K-12 education. *New Directions for Evaluation, 2017*(153), 65–77. https://doi.org/10.1002/ev.20233

Whiston, B. J. (2017, November 15). *Michigan's consolidated state plan under the every student succeeds act.* Michigan Department of Education. www.michigan.gov/mde/-/media/Project/Websites/mde/Year/2017/12/08/MichiganESSAPlan_111517.pdf?rev=55ba01754e78412dbc38c05dc24f85ac&hash=B5B098E4B92ED42DB124C894C9C636D1

Conclusion

We see this book as an invitation to act. Throughout the book, we provide examples of what leaders and improvers should do. While none of us is on Ava's team, nor have we learned about and engaged in equitable improvement alongside her, it is through Ava's experience that we can begin to see the process, with its challenges and merits, come to life. The contemporary public education system is rife with misconceptions but also ripe with opportunity. Implicit and sometimes explicit in our discussion of leading continuous improvement was a critique of current practices that we hope to disrupt. Sinek (2019) writes that leaders in organizations need to reframe their work to recognize that "money is a result and not a purpose." Similarly, within a neoliberal education policy space, educational leaders and policy makers need to reframe the definition of education to recognize that test scores are a result, not a purpose and develop a culture where "work has value beyond the money they make for themselves, their companies or their shareholders" (p. 87). We need to reframe the work of leaders to develop improvement mindsets and cultures that see learning as the purpose of schools not only for students in classrooms, but across the organization. To do this, disruption of the status quo will be necessary. As the saying goes, *nothing changes if nothing changes*. While we referenced the status quo in Chapter 9, we didn't necessarily define what it meant for the reader. When we think of the status quo in education we think of the following six areas for change. As you read these, reflect on how continuous improvement approaches could intersect with each.

MYTHS OF MERITOCRACY MINDSETS

- Ignoring the systemic impact of racism
- Addressing gaps in achievement not gaps in opportunity
- Focusing on closing gaps instead of ideal states of liberation

DOI: 10.4324/9781003389279-14

The myth of meritocracy underlies our discussion of equity and justice throughout this volume. This myth is predicated on the belief that each person has the same opportunity for success and that success in school is based solely on effort. Throughout the last ten chapters, we have emphasized the systemic impact of racism or other forms of oppression on our schools and children. The goal of improvement – as expounded upon in Chapter 4 – should be to liberate marginalized groups from the expectations based on dominant cultural ideologies and social constructs such as white supremacy culture, Anglo-prioritized curriculum, Christian-centric values, and gender-conforming structures to invite other races, backgrounds, abilities, religions, and gender identities to diagnose gaps in opportunity, rather than a limiting focus on "closing the achievement gap." Implementing thoughtful change ideas is one way to work to reify the status quo.

MISSED OPPORTUNITIES TO LEARN

- Emphasizing competitiveness over collective learning
- Hiding failure and avoiding learning
- Conducting evaluation without feedback and learning
- Ignoring assets in communities

It was hard for Ava and her team to admit when a change idea did not go as planned. Marcus shared he was embarrassed. Chris felt inadequate and the whole team felt that failing was hard to accept. Competition has driven an obsession with evaluation as an end goal instead of using evaluation to determine areas for improvement. The belief in educational competition compels people to want to hide failures instead of collectively learning from them. Missed opportunities to learn are the result of focusing on competition, accountability, evaluation, and deficit thinking instead of organizing learning. Just as there is a reason or a system behind the current results we see, there is a reason and a system that has led to educators being uncomfortable with using failure as an opportunity to learn and not to judge; since the release of *A Nation at Risk* in the 1980s, our school systems have responded to the report's concerns by focusing on sanctioning schools and teachers for not meeting a narrow and externally defined metric for effectiveness or success (i.e., a test score). Educators have been cornered by those policy metrics into a focus on closing gaps (as referenced earlier and in Chapter 10), which results in striving for compliance instead of harnessing learning from our experiences in trying to improve systems in order to create the conditions for positive outcomes for students. In the process, assets of numerous communities have been lost or undervalued as we strive for test scores at the expense of learning. This is an important leadership opportunity. Reflect on the enactment of leadership from Chapters 3, 8, and 9 and connect what Ava did to help her team still learn from failure even when it was hard and uncomfortable. How might you, an educational leader, help push against the overemphasis on test scores to foster a learning culture in your school? How might you help teachers who are nervous to share where things might not have gone as successfully as hoped so that learning and improvement can be encouraged and supported.

MISPLACED BLAME

- Focusing on what individuals (teachers, student, leaders) are doing wrong
- Failing to emphasize human-centered approaches to developing and supporting educators
- Blaming marginalized communities for schools' problems

Misplaced blame is pointing fingers at what individuals are doing wrong instead of how we can change our schools. In improvement, there is the adage, "every system is perfectly designed to get the results it gets." Therefore, it is the system that needs attention, not individuals. As we referenced in the preceding chapters, locating problems within people instead of within the system leads to failed improvement. In other words, how can the system support or set up the conditions for the individuals who are navigating said system? Too often proposed solutions to educational problems often fail to consider the interrelated system, nor the human element of change. By blaming teachers for problems that are embedded in an unjust, unsupportive system, we do not encourage professional growth. By blaming marginalized communities for schools' problems, educators fail those communities every day. Ava's team did not develop a new code of conduct first, but instead explored what was going on in their system related to the problem. Remember when Chris's third period students were late to class on Mondays, Wednesdays, and Fridays? Chris approached improvement in a systems way. Chris did not tell the students who were late, "Well, you just need to be faster getting to my class;" she investigated what was going on in the system and with a colleague, addressed the conditions surrounding the students so that those conditions could be improved to lead to higher likelihood of success.

MISREPRESENTATION OF THE SYSTEM

- Oversimplifying a complex system
- Reducing the complexity of the human experience to data and numbers
- Lacking Indigenous voice

Misplaced blame is in part due to misrepresentation of the reasons for improvement. We are misrepresenting the work of school when we oversimplify a complex system (e.g., If only we had more professional development . . . or more time). We are misrepresenting the human experiences when we reduce humans to numbers. We are misrepresenting marginalized communities when we exclude Indigenous voices from the dialogue on schools and school improvement. The leadership and connector tools from Chapter 8 will need to be thoughtfully and intentionally applied to teams to interrogate and dissect complex problems and systems.

Partnering and collaborating on improvement work can foster opportunities to build relationships, grow trust, and encourage a learning organization to address the entrenched, wicked problems schools face.

MISIDENTIFIED PROBLEMS

- Failing to identify root causes
- Lacking a systems perspective
- Over focusing on aggregated data instead of people's stories

Misidentified problems grow out of lost opportunities for learning. Often, there is a failure to understand how some problems may be creating other problems in that system. We keep trying to solve a problem without identifying root causes in authentic, thoughtful, culturally relevant ways, which results in spending time, resources, and energy on symptoms of problems rather than the problem source. Chapter 5 offered strategies for teams to find the right problem to address. One way is to avoid efforts centered on the wrong problem. Talk to people! Across the chapters, ideas for connecting, inviting, and believing people were presented (e.g., empathy interviews, kiva circles, community walks). Ava and her team invited voices of those for whom the system was not working. They learned areas to focus on so they could dedicate efforts to addressing the right problem. Chapter 6 encouraged you to expand your definition of what data counts for improvement. Remember, by limiting our acceptance of data to quantitative data and/or quantitative data in the aggregate, we fail to hear from the people who are closest to the problem who are also the ones who can help identify promising change ideas to lead to systematic and lasting change.

MISMATCHED SOLUTIONS

- Prioritizing solutions that need a problem
- Suffering from solutionitis
- Reinforcing the -isms and solidifying a normative approach through solutions

Part and parcel to these misidentified problems are mismatched solutions. When we fail to properly identify a problem, we don't put forth solutions that change systems. This can lead to prioritizing solutions (often backed by powerful or well-financed educational entrepreneurs, interest groups, and advocacy coalitions) as the focus on improvement and then seeking the problem to match to those solutions. It can also usurp the contextual, local needs and voices of the school and the educational professionals working in them. Further, because there is often not time dedicated to developing alignment between solutions and problems, educators end up jumping to solutions without a full understanding of the problem. A lack of understanding of the problem, the system, and the human experience leads to solutions that reinforce the status quo, the -isms, and solidifies a normative approach to problems instead of the types of responses that would disrupt inequities, injustices, and oppression.

LEADERSHIP FOR CHANGE

Leadership is key to overcoming those long-standing pitfalls. Leaders who enact continuous improvement will develop valuable leadership skills (e.g., working with data, humility, communication, fostering a psychologically safe learning organization) that are central to addressing the aforementioned six myths and mistakes of our educational system. This leadership response situates the ideas covered throughout the chapters in this book. Similar to each chapter's conclusion, we have captured these major ideas within the categories of moral values, instrumental methods, and social relations.

MORAL VALUES

- **Core values** – Improvement science with an equity orientation is fundamentally about identifying and enacting core values of equity, justice, humility, transparency, honesty, inquiry, and more. These values come to life through the theory of improvement and small tests of change.
- **Critical Consciousness** – Critical consciousness is the ability to unearth those core values and put in the work to shift mindsets toward being equitable, systems oriented, and community-centered.
- **Cultural Responsiveness** – Putting that critical consciousness into action is demonstrating cultural responsiveness by creating schools that uphold an emphasis on the assets of all children and families.
- **Citizenship** – Improvers are part of a broader community whose interests and values should be central to continuous improvement.

INSTRUMENTAL METHODS

- **Complexity** – Schools and school systems and complex. Improvers need to unpack and name those complexities in order to address them.
- **Coherence** – Improvement, without a guiding vision or theory of improvement, is disjointed and adds complexity. Coherence is necessary for spreading change.
- **Change** – Positive change is the ultimate goal of improvement.

SOCIAL RELATIONS

- **Collegiality** – Improvers should work together in productive, authentic ways that do not avoid difficult conversations but create the culture to learn and grow from them.
- **Collaborative Culture** – Improvement is done with people, by people, for people.
- **Communication** – Improvers need to be transparent and communicate regularly with all users and stakeholders within the school and in the community at large.
- **Collective Understanding** – Inquiry must be based on a collective understanding of both the current and ideal state, the intended goals of improvement, and a shared knowledge of what is improvement.
- **Community** – Continuous improvement should be co-owned by community members and facilitated by leaders instead of the sole responsibility of a formal leader.

The NELP and PSEL standards invite leaders to prioritize continuous improvement with an equity lens and to be attuned to creating the conditions for improvement in their organizations. Continuous improvement guided by what works (or is not working), for whom, and under what conditions leverages human-centered efforts critical for the equitable improvement of the pressing challenges schools face. The PSEL were "designed to ensure that educational leaders are ready to effectively meet the challenges and opportunities of the job today and in the future of education, schools and society continue to transform" (National Policy Board for Educational Administration, 2015, p. 1). The NELP standards help guide those responsible for the preparation of leaders to meet the PSEL by offering a framework for faculty in preparation programs to design program experiences to "address the most critical knowledge and skill areas for beginning building-level educational leaders" (NPBEA, 2018, p. 3). Both sets of standards attend to a values-based approach to continuous improvement. And while the term continuous improvement suggests that the work is never done and therefore leaders will be embarking on a long journey, there will be moments, pivotal moments along the way when, because of you and your team's dedication to improvement work, you will be able to (a) articulate the exact problem you helped solve, (b) identify change ideas that helped address the problem, and (c) communicate the qualitative and quantitative evidence your team used to know when a change was an improvement including how and when that change could be spread and scaled. Improvement work is iterative. Improvement work is hard. Improvement work requires collaboration and reflection and dedication. Improvement work requires not only you but also your trusted team. Improvement work must dismantle systems of oppression through community-informed practice.

BIBLIOGRAPHY

National Policy Board for Educational Administration. (2015). *Professional standards for educational leaders*. Author. www.npbea.org/wp-content/uploads/2017/06/Professional-Standards-for-Educational-Leaders_2015.pdf

NPBEA. (2018). *National Educational Leadership Preparation (NELP) program recognition standards building level*. www.npbea.org

Sinek, S. (2019). *The infinite game*. Penguin Books.

Appendices

Appendix A

Crosswalk of Chapters and Standards

Chapters	*NELP Standard Components*	*PSEL Standard Elements*
2: Continuous Improvement	**Component 1.2:** Program completers understand and demonstrate the capacity to lead improvement processes that include data use, design, implementation, and evaluation. **Component 6.2:** Program completers understand and demonstrate the capacity to evaluate, develop, and advocate for a data-informed and equitable resourcing plan that supports school improvement and student development. **Component 4.4:** Program completers understand and demonstrate the capacity to collaboratively evaluate, develop, and implement the school's curriculum, instruction, technology, data systems, and assessment practices in a coherent, equitable, and systematic manner.	**6d.** Foster continuous improvement of individual and collective instructional capacity to achieve outcomes envisioned for each student. **7c.** Establish and sustain a professional culture of engagement and commitment to shared vision, goals, and objectives pertaining to the education of the whole child; high expectations for professional work; ethical and equitable practice; trust and open communication; collaboration, collective efficacy, and continuous individual and organizational learning and improvement. **10a.** Seek to make the school more effective for each student, teachers and staff, families, and the community. **10b.** Use methods of continuous improvement to achieve the vision, fulfill the mission, and promote the core values of the school. **10c.** Prepare the school and the community for improvement, promoting readiness, an imperative for improvement, instilling mutual commitment and accountability, and developing the knowledge, skills, and motivation to succeed in improvement. **10d.** Engage others in an ongoing process of evidence-based inquiry, learning, strategic goal setting, planning, implementation, and evaluation for continuous school and classroom improvement.

(Continued)

(Continued)

Chapters	*NELP Standard Components*	*PSEL Standard Elements*
	Component 5.2: Program completers understand and demonstrate the capacity to collaboratively engage and cultivate relationships with diverse community members, partners, and other constituencies for the benefit of school improvement and student development.	**10e.** Employ situationally-appropriate strategies for improvement, including transformational and incremental, adaptive approaches and attention to different phases of implementation. **10f.** Assess and develop the capacity of staff to assess the value and applicability of emerging educational trends and the findings of research for the school and its improvement. **10g.** Develop technically appropriate systems of data collection, management, analysis, and use, connecting as needed to the district office and external partners for support in planning, implementation, monitoring, feedback, and evaluation. **10h.** Adopt a systems perspective and promote coherence among improvement efforts and all aspects of school organization, programs, and services. **10i.** Manage uncertainty, risk, competing initiatives, and politics of change with courage and perseverance, providing support and encouragement, and openly communicating the need for, process for, and outcomes of improvement efforts. **10j.** Develop and promote leadership among teachers and staff for inquiry, experimentation and innovation, and initiating and implementing improvement.
3: Leadership	**Component 1.1:** Program completers understand and demonstrate the capacity to collaboratively evaluate, develop, and communicate a school mission and vision designed to reflect a core set of values and priorities that include data use, technology, equity, diversity, digital citizenship, and community.	**1a.** Develop an educational mission for the school to promote the academic success and well-being of each student. **1e.** Review the school's mission and vision and adjust them to changing expectations and opportunities for the school and changing needs and situations of students. **1f.** Develop shared understanding of and commitment to mission, vision, and core values within the school and the community.

Component 6.1: Program completers understand and demonstrate the capacity to evaluate, develop, and implement management, communication, technology, school-level governance, and operation systems that support each student's learning needs and promote the mission and vision of the school.	**3g.** Act with cultural competence and responsiveness in their interactions, decision making, and practice. **3h.** Address matters of equity and cultural responsiveness in all aspects of leadership. **3d.** Develop student policies and address student misconduct in a positive, fair, and unbiased manner.
Component 7.4: Program completers understand and have the capacity to evaluate, develop, and implement systems of supervision, support, and evaluation designed to promote school improvement and student success.	**4a.** Implement coherent systems of curriculum, instruction, and assessment that promote the mission, vision, and core values of the school, embody high expectations for student learning, align with academic standards, and are culturally responsive. **4b.** Align and focus systems of curriculum, instruction, and assessment within and across grade levels to promote student academic success, love of learning, the identities and habits of learners, and healthy sense of self. **6a.** Recruit, hire, support, develop, and retain effective and caring teachers and other professional staff and form them into an educationally effective faculty. **6e.** Deliver actionable feedback about instruction and other professional practice through valid, research-anchored systems of supervision and evaluation to support the development of teachers' and staff members' knowledge, skills, and practice. **6f.** Empower and motivate teachers and staff to the highest levels of professional practice and to continuous learning and improvement. **6g.** Develop the capacity, opportunities, and support for teacher leadership and leadership from other members of the school community.

(Continued)

(Continued)

Chapters	*NELP Standard Components*	*PSEL Standard Elements*
		7c. Establish and sustain a professional culture of engagement and commitment to shared vision, goals, and objectives pertaining to the education of the whole child; high expectations for professional work; ethical and equitable practice; trust and open communication; collaboration, collective efficacy, and continuous individual and organizational learning and improvement. **8b.** Create and sustain positive, collaborative, and productive relationships with families and the community for the benefit of students. **9a.** Institute, manage, and monitor operations and administrative systems that promote the mission and vision of the school. **10j.** Develop and promote leadership among teachers and staff for inquiry, experimentation, and innovation and for initiating and implementing improvement.
4: Equity	**Component 3.1:** Program completers understand and demonstrate the capacity to use data to evaluate, design, cultivate, and advocate for a supportive and inclusive school culture. **Component 3.1:** Program completers understand and demonstrate the capacity to use data to evaluate, design, cultivate, and advocate for a supportive and inclusive school culture. **Component 3.3:** Program completers understand and demonstrate the capacity to evaluate, cultivate, and advocate for equitable, inclusive, and culturally responsive instruction and behavior support practices among teachers and staff.	**1c.** Articulate, advocate, and cultivate core values that define the school's culture and stress the imperative of child-centered education; high expectations and student support; equity, inclusiveness, and social justice; openness, caring, and trust; and continuous improvement. **2c.** Place children at the center of education and accept responsibility for each student's academic success and well-being. (Implicit in all standards.) **2d.** Safeguard and promote the values of democracy, individual freedom and responsibility, equity, social justice, community, and diversity.

Component 4.4: Program completers understand and demonstrate the capacity to collaboratively evaluate, develop, and implement the school's curriculum, instruction, technology, data systems, and assessment practices in a coherent, equitable, and systematic manner.	**3a.** Ensure that each student is treated fairly, respectfully, and with an understanding of each student's culture and context. **3b.** Recognize, respect, and employ each student's strengths, diversity, and culture as assets for teaching and learning. **3c.** Ensure that each student has equitable access to effective teachers, learning opportunities, academic and social support, and other resources necessary for success. **3e.** Confront and alter institutional biases of student marginalization, deficit-based schooling, and low expectations associated with race, class, culture and language, gender and sexual orientation, disability or special status. **3h.** Address matters of equity and cultural responsiveness in all aspects of leadership.
Component 5.2: Program completers understand and demonstrate the capacity to collaboratively engage and cultivate relationships with diverse community members, partners, and other constituencies for the benefit of school improvement and student development.	
Component 5.1: Program completers understand and demonstrate the capacity to collaboratively engage diverse families in strengthening student learning in and out of school.	**5a.** Build and maintain a safe, caring, and healthy school environment that meets the academic, social, emotional, and physical needs of each student. **5b.** Create and sustain a school environment in which each student is known, accepted and valued, trusted and respected, cared for, and encouraged to be an active and responsible member of the school community. **5d.** Promote adult-student, student-peer, and school-community relationships that value and support academic learning and positive social and emotional development. **5f.** Infuse the school's learning environment with the cultures and languages of the school's community. **7c.** Establish and sustain a professional culture of engagement and commitment to shared vision, goals, and objectives pertaining to the education of the whole child; high expectations for professional work; ethical and equitable practice; trust and open communication; collaboration, collective efficacy, and continuous individual and organizational learning and improvement.

(Continued)

(Continued)

Chapters	*NELP Standard Components*	*PSEL Standard Elements*
		8a. Are approachable, accessible, and welcoming to families and members of the community. **8b.** Create and sustain positive, collaborative, and productive relationships with families and the community for the benefit of students. **8c.** Engage in regular and open two-way communication with families and the community about the school, students, needs, problems, and accomplishments. **8h.** Advocate for the school and district and for the importance of education and student needs and priorities to families and the community. **8i.** Advocate publicly for the needs and priorities of students, families, and the community.
5: Problem	**Component 5.1:** Program completers understand and demonstrate the capacity to collaboratively engage diverse families in strengthening student learning in and out of school. **Component 4.1:** Program completers understand and can demonstrate the capacity to evaluate, develop, and implement high-quality, technology rich curricula, programs, and other supports for academic and non-academic student programs. **Component 4.2:** Program completers understand and can demonstrate the capacity to evaluate, develop, and implement high-quality and equitable academic and non-academic instructional practices, resources, technologies, and services that support equity, digital literacy, and the school's academic and non-academic systems.	**3b.** Recognize, respect, and employ each student's strengths, diversity, and culture as assets for teaching and learning. **3c.** Ensure that each student has equitable access to effective teachers, learning opportunities, academic and social support, and other resources necessary for success. **3e.** Confront and alter institutional biases of student marginalization, deficit-based schooling, and low expectations associated with race, class, culture and language, gender and sexual orientation, disability or special status. **4a.** Implement coherent systems of curriculum, instruction, and assessment that promote the mission, vision, and core values of the school, embody high expectations for student learning, align with academic standards, and are culturally responsive. **4b.** Align and focus systems of curriculum, instruction, and assessment within and across grade levels to promote student academic success, love of learning, the identities and habits of learners, and healthy sense of self.

	Component 4.3: Program completers understand and can demonstrate the capacity to evaluate, develop, and implement formal and informal culturally responsive and accessible assessments that support data-informed instructional improvement and student learning and well-being. **Component 4.4:** Program completers understand and demonstrate the capacity to collaboratively evaluate, develop, and implement the school's curriculum, instruction, technology, data systems, and assessment practices in a coherent, equitable, and systematic manner.	**4c.** Promote instructional practice that is consistent with knowledge of child learning and development, effective pedagogy, and the needs of each student. **4d.** Ensure instructional practice that is intellectually challenging, authentic to student experiences, recognizes student strengths, and is differentiated and personalized. **5e.** Cultivate and reinforce student engagement in school and positive student conduct. **6g.** Develop the capacity, opportunities, and support for teacher leadership and leadership from other members of the school community. **6d.** Foster continuous improvement of individual and collective instructional capacity to achieve outcomes envisioned for each student. **8c.** Engage in regular and open two-way communication with families and the community about the school, students, needs, problems, and accomplishments. **10f.** Assess and develop the capacity of staff to assess the value and applicability of emerging educational trends and the findings of research for the school and its improvement.
6: Data	**Component 1.2:** Program completers understand and demonstrate the capacity to lead improvement processes that include data use, design, implementation, and evaluation. **Component 3.1:** Program completers understand and demonstrate the capacity to use data to evaluate, design, cultivate, and advocate for a supportive and inclusive school culture.	**1b.** In collaboration with members of the school and the community and using relevant data, develop and promote a vision for the school on the successful learning and development of each child and on instructional and organizational practices that promote such success. **4g.** Use assessment data appropriately and within technical limitations to monitor student progress and improve instruction. **9g.** Develop and maintain data and communication systems to deliver actionable information for classroom and school improvement.

(*Continued*)

(Continued)

Chapters	*NELP Standard Components*	*PSEL Standard Elements*
	Component 4.4: Program completers understand and demonstrate the capacity to collaboratively evaluate, develop, and implement the school's curriculum, instruction, technology, data systems, and assessment practices in a coherent, equitable, and systematic manner. **Component 6.2:** Program completers understand and demonstrate the capacity to evaluate, develop, and advocate for a data-informed and equitable resourcing plan that supports school improvement and student development.	**10g.** Develop technically appropriate systems of data collection, management, analysis, and use, connecting as needed to the district office, and external partners for support in planning, implementation, monitoring, feedback, and evaluation.
7: Networks and Systems	**Component 4.1:** Program completers understand and can demonstrate the capacity to evaluate, develop, and implement high-quality, technology-rich curricula, programs, and other supports for academic and non-academic student programs. **Component 4.2:** Program completers understand and can demonstrate the capacity to evaluate, develop, and implement high-quality and equitable academic and non-academic instructional practices, resources, technologies, and services that support equity, digital literacy, and the school's academic and non-academic systems. **Component 4.3:** Program completers understand and can demonstrate the capacity to evaluate, develop, and implement formal and informal culturally responsive and accessible assessments that support data-informed instructional improvement and student learning and well-being.	**1d.** Strategically develop, implement, and evaluate actions to achieve the vision for the school. **4c.** Promote instructional practice that is consistent with knowledge of child learning and development, effective pedagogy, and the needs of each student. **4d.** Ensure instructional practice that is intellectually challenging, authentic to student experiences, recognizes student strengths, and is differentiated and personalized. **6g.** Develop the capacity, opportunities, and support for teacher leadership and leadership from other members of the school community. **6d.** Foster continuous improvement of individual and collective instructional capacity to achieve outcomes envisioned for each student.

	Component 4.4: Program completers understand and demonstrate the capacity to collaboratively evaluate, develop, and implement the school's curriculum, instruction, technology, data systems, and assessment practices in a coherent, equitable, and systematic manner. **Component 5.2:** Program completers understand and demonstrate the capacity to collaboratively engage and cultivate relationships with diverse community members, partners, and other constituencies for the benefit of school improvement and student development.	**8e.** Create means for the school community to partner with families to support student learning in and out of school. **8j.** Build and sustain productive partnerships with the public and private sectors to promote school improvement and student learning. **10h.** Adopt a systems perspective and promote coherence among improvement efforts and all aspects of school organization, programs, and services.
8: Leadership Toolbox	**Component 2.1:** Program completers understand and demonstrate the capacity to reflect on, communicate about, cultivate, and model dispositions and professional norms (e.g., equity, fairness, integrity, transparency, trust, digital citizenship, collaboration, perseverance, reflection. lifelong learning, digital citizenship) that support the educational success and well-being of each student and adult. **Component 2.3:** Program completers understand and demonstrate the capacity to model ethical behavior in their personal conduct and relationships and to cultivate ethical behavior in others. **Component 6.1:** Program completers understand and demonstrate the capacity to evaluate, develop, and implement management, communication, technology, school-level governance, and operation systems that support each student's learning needs and promote the mission and vision of the school.	**2a.** Act ethically and professionally in personal conduct, relationships with others, decision making, stewardship of the school's resources, and all aspects of school leadership. **2b.** Act according to and promote the professional norms of integrity, fairness, transparency, trust, collaboration, perseverance, learning, and continuous improvement. **2e.** Lead with interpersonal and communication skill, social-emotional insight, and understanding of all students' and staff members' backgrounds and cultures. **3g.** Act with cultural competence and responsiveness in their interactions, decision making, and practice. **7c.** Establish and sustain a professional culture of engagement and commitment to shared vision, goals, and objectives pertaining to the education of the whole child; high expectations for professional work; ethical and equitable practice; trust and open communication; collaboration, collective efficacy, and continuous individual and organizational learning and improvement.

(Continued)

(Continued)

Chapters	*NELP Standard Components*	*PSEL Standard Elements*
		8d. Maintain a presence in the community to understand its strengths and needs, develop productive relationships, and engage its resources for the school. **8h.** Advocate for the school and district and for the importance of education and student needs and priorities to families and the community. **8i.** Advocate publicly for the needs and priorities of students, families, and the community. **10i.** Manage uncertainty, risk, competing initiatives, and politics of change with courage and perseverance, providing support and encouragement, and openly communicating the need for, process for, and outcomes of improvement efforts.
9: Organizational Capacity	**Component 3.1:** Program completers understand and demonstrate the capacity to use data to evaluate, design, cultivate, and advocate for a supportive and inclusive school culture. **Component 3.3:** Program completers understand and demonstrate the capacity to evaluate, cultivate, and advocate for equitable, inclusive, and culturally responsive instruction and behavior support practices among teachers and staff. **Component 4.1:** Program completers understand and can demonstrate the capacity to evaluate, develop, and implement high-quality, technology-rich curricula, programs, and other supports for academic and non-academic student programs.	**1g.** Model and pursue the school's mission, vision, and core values in all aspects of leadership. **2f.** Provide moral direction for the school, and promote ethical and professional behavior among faculty and staff. **4a.** Implement coherent systems of curriculum, instruction, and assessment that promote the mission, vision, and core values of the school, embody high expectations for student learning, align with academic standards, and are culturally responsive. **4b.** Align and focus systems of curriculum, instruction, and assessment within and across grade levels to promote student academic success, love of learning, the identities and habits of learners, and healthy sense of self.

Component 6.1: Program completers understand and demonstrate the capacity to evaluate, develop, and implement management, communication, technology, school-level governance, and operation systems that support each student's learning needs and promote the mission and vision of the school.	**5c.** Provide coherent systems of academic and social supports, services, extracurricular activities, and accommodations to meet the range of learning needs of each student. **6a.** Recruit, hire, support, develop, and retain effective and caring teachers and other professional staff and form them into an educationally effective faculty.
Component 7.2: Program completers understand and have the capacity to develop and engage staff in a collaborative professional culture designed to promote school improvement, teacher retention, and the success and well-being of each student and adult in the school.	**6c.** Develop teachers' and staff members' professional knowledge, skills, and practice through differentiated opportunities for learning and growth, guided by understanding of professional and adult learning and development. **6f.** Empower and motivate teachers and staff to the highest levels of professional practice and to continuous learning and improvement.
Component 7.3: Program completers understand and have the capacity to personally engage in, as well as collaboratively engage staff in, professional learning designed to promote reflection, cultural responsiveness, distributed leadership, digital literacy, school improvement, and student success.	**6g.** Develop the capacity, opportunities, and support for teacher leadership and leadership from other members of the school community. **7a.** Develop workplace conditions for teachers and other professional staff that promote effective professional development, practice, and student learning. **7b.** Empower and entrust teachers and staff with collective responsibility for meeting the academic, social, emotional, and physical needs of each student, pursuant to the mission, vision, and core values of the school. **7c.** Establish and sustain a professional culture of engagement and commitment to shared vision, goals, and objectives pertaining to the education of the whole child; high expectations for professional work; ethical and equitable practice; trust and open communication; collaboration, collective efficacy, and continuous individual and organizational learning and improvement. **7f.** Design and implement job-embedded and other opportunities for collaborative professional learning with faculty and staff.

(*Continued*)

(Continued)

Chapters	*NELP Standard Components*	*PSEL Standard Elements*
		9b. Strategically manage staff resources, assigning and scheduling teachers and staff to roles and responsibilities that optimize their professional capacity to address each student's learning needs.
		9c. Seek, acquire, and manage fiscal, physical, and other resources to support curriculum, instruction, and assessment; the student learning community; professional capacity and community; and family and community engagement.
		9g. Develop and maintain data and communication systems to deliver actionable information for classroom and school improvement.
		10c. Prepare the school and the community for improvement, promoting readiness, an imperative for improvement, instilling mutual commitment and accountability, and developing the knowledge, skills, and motivation to succeed in improvement.
		10d. Engage others in an ongoing process of evidence-based inquiry, learning, strategic goal-setting, planning, implementation, and evaluation for continuous school and classroom improvement.
		10g. Develop technically appropriate systems of data collection, management, analysis, and use, connecting as needed to the district office and external partners for support in planning, implementation, monitoring, feedback, and evaluation.
		10h. Adopt a systems perspective and promote coherence among improvement efforts and all aspects of school organization, programs, and services.
		10j. Develop and promote leadership among teachers and staff for inquiry, experimentation, and innovation and for initiating and implementing improvement.
10: Policy	**Component 2.2:** Program completers understand and demonstrate the capacity to evaluate, communicate about, and advocate for ethical and legal decisions.	**9h.** Know, comply with, and help the school community understand local, state, and federal laws, rights, policies, and regulations in order to promote student success.

Appendix B

List of NELP Standards

NELP Building-Level Standard 1: Mission, Vision, and Improvement: to collaboratively lead, design, and implement a school mission, vision, and process for continuous improvement that reflect a core set of values and priorities that include data, technology, equity, diversity, digital citizenship, and community.

NELP Building-Level Standard 2: Ethics and Professional Norms: to understand and demonstrate the capacity to advocate for ethical decisions and cultivate and enact professional norms.

NELP Building-Level Standard 3: Equity, Inclusiveness, and Cultural Responsiveness: to develop and maintain a supportive, equitable, culturally responsive, and inclusive school culture.

NELP Building-Level Standard 4: Learning and Instruction: to evaluate, develop, and implement coherent systems of curriculum, instruction, data systems, supports, and assessment.

NELP Building-Level Standard 5: Community and External Leadership: to engage families, community, and school personnel in order to strengthen student learning, support school improvement, and advocate for the needs of their school and community.

NELP Building-Level Standard 6: Operations and Management: to improve management, communication, technology, school-level governance, and operation systems; to develop and improve data-informed and equitable school resource plans; and to apply laws, policies, and regulations.

NELP Building-Level Standard 7: Building Professional Capacity: to build the school's professional capacity, engage staff in the development of a collaborative professional culture, and improve systems of staff supervision, evaluation, support, and professional learning.

List of PSEL Standards

1. Effective educational leaders develop, advocate, and enact a shared mission, vision, and core values of high-quality education and academic success and well-being of each student.
2. Effective educational leaders act ethically and according to professional norms to promote each student's academic success and well-being.
3. Effective educational leaders strive for equity of educational opportunity and culturally responsive practices to promote each student's academic success and well-being.
4. Effective educational leaders develop and support intellectually rigorous and coherent systems of curriculum, instruction, and assessment to promote each student's academic success and well-being.
5. Effective educational leaders cultivate an inclusive, caring, and supportive school community that promotes the academic success and well-being of each student.
6. Effective educational leaders develop the professional capacity and practice of school personnel to promote each student's academic success and well-being.
7. Effective educational leaders foster a professional community of teachers and other professional staff to promote each student's academic success and well-being.
8. Effective educational leaders engage families and the community in meaningful, reciprocal, and mutually beneficial ways to promote each student's academic success and well-being.
9. Effective educational leaders manage school operations and resources to promote each student's academic success and well-being.
10. Effective educational leaders act as agents of continuous improvement to promote each student's academic success and well-being.

Appendix C

Professional Standards for Educational Leaders

Standard 10: Effective educational leaders act as agents of continuous improvement to promote each student's academic success and well-being.

Effective Leaders

10 a) Seek to make school more effective for each student, teachers and staff, families, and the community.
10 b) Use methods of continuous improvement to achieve the vision, fulfill the mission, and promote the core values of the school.
10 c) Prepare the school and the community for improvement, promoting readiness, an imperative for improvement, instilling mutual commitment and accountability, and developing the knowledge, skills, and motivation to succeed in improvement.
10 d) Engage others in an ongoing process of evidence-based inquiry, learning, strategic goal setting, planning, implementation, and evaluation for continuous school and classroom improvement.
10 e) Employ situationally-appropriate strategies for improvement, including transformational and incremental, adaptive approaches and attention to different phases of implementation.
10 f) Assess and develop the capacity of staff to assess the value and applicability of emerging educational trends and the findings of research for the school and its improvement.
10 g) Develop technically appropriate systems of data collection, management, analysis, and use, connecting as needed to the district office and external partners for support in planning, implementation, monitoring, feedback, and evaluation.
10 h) Adopt a systems perspective and promote coherence among improvement efforts and all aspects of school organization, programs, and services.

10 i) Manage uncertainty, risk, competing initiatives, and politics of change with courage and perseverance, providing support and encouragement, and openly communicating the need for, process for, and outcomes of improvement efforts.

10 j) Develop and promote leadership among teachers and staff for inquiry, experimentation and innovation, and initiating and implementing improvement.

Index

For Product Safety Concerns and Information please contact our EU representative GPSR@taylorandfrancis.com
Taylor & Francis Verlag GmbH, Kaufingerstraße 24, 80331 München, Germany

www.ingramcontent.com/pod-product-compliance
Lightning Source LLC
LaVergne TN
LVHW081314040625
813008LV00008B/729

* 9 7 8 1 0 3 2 4 6 1 8 5 4 *